D1713484

Philippe Lacoue-Labarthe

John D. Caputo, *series editor*

PERSPECTIVES IN
CONTINENTAL
PHILOSOPHY

JOHN MARTIS

Philippe Lacoue-Labarthe
Representation and the Loss of the Subject

Representation and the Loss*
of the Subject

Perspectives in Continental Philosophy Series, No. 50
ISSN 1089-3938

Library of Congress Cataloging-in-Publication Data

Martis, John.
    Philippe Lacoue-Labarthe : representation and the loss of the subject / John
Martis. — 1st ed.
        p.   cm. — (Perspectives in continental philosophy ; no. 50)
    Includes bibliographical references and index.
    ISBN 0-8232-2534-8 (hardcover) — ISBN 0-8232-2535-6 (pbk.)
    1. Lacoue-Labarthe, Philippe.   2. Representation (Philosophy)   3. Subject
(Philosophy)   4. Subjectivity.   I. Title.   II. Series.
    B2430.L14664M37   2005
    194—dc22

                                                                    2005018165

Printed in the United States of America
07 06 05   5 4 3 2 1
First edition

*To my parents, John and Coral,
and my companions in
the Society of Jesus*

Contents

Preface and Acknowledgments

A study of Philippe Lacoue-Labarthe confronts peculiar difficulties. For some nearly thirty years now, his writing on literature and philosophy has been as highly praised for its distinctiveness and precision as it has been critically unplumbed. To read *Typography*, for instance, is to discover an original voice on questions ranging from mimesis to music, from autobiography to dramatic catharsis. And it is the same with other work he has produced—not prolifically, but penetratingly, with an at once refreshing and rigorous approach to questions central to Western philosophy in the wake of Heidegger. Particularly as these questions touch the *subject* of philosophy—that is, the subject stubbornly lodged between philosophy and literature, and resistant alike to identification and dismissal within either—Lacoue-Labarthe's is clearly a promising angle of access and address.

Yet there has been to date no book on Lacoue-Labarthe, and barely an extended scholarly article dealing with his thought on its own terms. This paucity contrasts with the abundance of material illuminating others with whom he shares a "family atmosphere," as the late Jacques Derrida called it: the hundreds of texts on Derrida himself and the growing profusion of writings on Jean-Luc Nancy, Lacoue-Labarthe's colleague and coauthor.

In redressing, to a small extent, this imbalance, I have been mindful of the probable reasons for it. Lacoue-Labarthe's journeys in reflection and criticism are as complex as they are satisfying. Typically, their intricate construction means they resist attempts at analysis that do not match them "twist for twist." The longer essays are centered on the reading of single texts, with detailed attention to one or two others providing foil or fuel. The author's engagement with these others exhibits a pattern that is, to my knowledge, unique. Each of the subsidiary texts is given attention in a separate sweep, which is used to bring the overall argument to a certain point. There the argument is temporarily abandoned, its fruit awaiting regathering later within a new sweep, begun from another angle and using another text. The overall impression is of a movement that is cumulative and satisfying in its reach, and comprehensive in attaining its conclusion.

From the point of view of analysis, this style of argument presents specific challenges. Irresistible and thorough, it is also curious and tantalizing, neither linear nor nonlinear, gathering force cumulatively, like a river swelled by successive tributaries to its end. This structure is echoed by the design of a typical Lacoue-Labarthian sentence: rarely satisfied with promoting a single point, its main clause diverts itself through a succession of supporting clauses and sub-clauses, each gathering further material, before the weight of the sentence eventually returns to its center. Thus, within each thought, qualifications are made, notions refined, parallels and exceptions noted, or even entire subsidiary branches of the argument chased to their destination.

A point is made by this style, as part of its distinctiveness and appeal: form must exhibit itself but must do so elusively, and with sufficient hint as to the limitations of form. For this very reason, any "linear" exposition of Lacoue-Labarthe's readings runs the risk of vitiating them. Nevertheless, given my own constraints here, I have worked by way of a thematic focus and a certain linearity of argument. The focus is made possible by the evident preoccupation of his work with the link between representation and subjectivity. In turn, the linearity is sustained by the possibility that, among the several motifs by which he depicts this link, one especially stands out as orienting and connecting the others: hyperbology. I have organized my argument around evoking the reach and power of this motif in the texts.

Organization is always, to some extent, imposition. For this I offer apologies in advance to Lacoue-Labarthe. But I have tried to organize patiently, by situating the points he makes in their own contexts whenever I have used or debated them. This means that my approach in most places still takes the shape of a close reading. It also means that I have followed the author in at least this regard: by reading relatively few texts, but attempting to read them well. To my mind, this was and is the only means of genuinely productive access to Lacoue-Labarthe.

That said, I have not eschewed critical distance from his texts or avoided the task of contextualizing him among his contemporaries. But I have left that distance and contextualization to evolve, as it were, organically, to take formal shape only in later chapters. By contrast, and quite deliberately, the first chapter, introducing the history of subjectivity, finds some impetus in Lacoue-Labarthe's own comments on that history. Those thoughts come from two lengthy conversations that he generously afforded me in Strasbourg, and to which my text also refers at other points.Given this approach, and bearing in mind the expectation that some readers may have of a framing analytical "placement" of Lacoue-Labarthe, I offer some brief contextualization now, to serve until later.

Two authorial personae of Lacoue-Labarthe bid for this contextualization. The first, shared with Jean-Luc Nancy, emerges from their commonly authored works. To many, the philosophizing Lacoue-Labarthe is not thought of separately from the philosophizing Nancy. Within their jointly authored productions, their individual contributions are never demarcated; instead, the reader is invited to associate all that is said with both authors or, more, with a single hybridized pen, a kind of "Philippe-Jean-Luc." Considered thus in tandem, Nancy and Lacoue-Labarthe are standard bearers for a school that has continued Derrida's critical stance toward the classical philosophical tradition culminating in Husserlian phenomenology and Heideggerian existential phenomenology. Nancy and Lacoue-Labarthe share 1940 as their year of birth, and they were exact contemporaries at the Ecole Normale Supérieure, the nurturing ground, since Jean Hyppolite, for successive generations of postwar continentalists and attendant movements. Ten years junior to Derrida, they were never formally his students. Nevertheless, they have clearly been influenced by him, to the point of emulation if not imitation, and dedication if not outright discipleship. The affiliation became most prominently attested in a conference organized by them at Cerisy La Salle in 1980, thematized in English as "The Ends of Man: Starting from the Work of Jacques Derrida." By and large, they have preferred the same types of analyses as he: patient readings of texts, from the philosophical to the literary and psychoanalytical, with the aim of deconstructively reopening experience to the ambiguity, and absence of essence, to which it has been closed by "theory" of one kind or another. This means that they are, like Derrida—and if the term can be employed without paradox—*resolutely* poststructuralist, or "dedicatedly deconstructive." In this they are distinguishable from others who have employed ostensibly deconstructive readings in the service of, as it were, reconstructions of their own: Girard, reading Deleuze and Guattari; Lacan, reading Freud and Saussure; the romanticists reading Kant, and attempting to relocate his lost subject in and as literature. Derrida made a point of deconstructing cryptoreconstructions. So too do Lacoue-Labarthe and Nancy, beginning with *The Title of the Letter* (on Lacan), continuing through *The Literary Absolute* (on the Schlegels, Schelling, and the German romanticists), and concluding with *Retreating the Political* (deconstructing the philosophical-political presumption of ideal "figures" of the human and the state).

Thus, then, the authorial identity shared by Lacoue-Labarthe and Nancy; less well known is the Lacoue-Labarthe of the individual works, which made their appearance in English translation only in 1989, with *Typography*. Here, the above-mentioned influences and allegiances are still operative, but now Lacoue-Labarthe "himself," as it were, emerges, distinguishable in his choices of subject, style, and "voice" from the joint authorial personality. Left to himself, Lacoue-Labarthe gravitates almost inevitably toward a consideration of the philosophical *cum* literary *subject* in its loss. "Subject," here, refers beyond an Aristotelian presumed "underlying" of existent beings to the post-Cartesian identification of that substratum with an ego, a unified thinking or writing self. Lacoue-Labarthe's authorial style and voice conspire to track the fruitless persistence of this subject's bid to establish itself as substantial, by escaping figurality. This self he sometimes considers in its generality. At other times it attracts his scrutiny in and as the specific thinker or writer synonymous with an ostensibly unified "body of work": Plato, Hegel, Heidegger, Nietzsche, Freud. Regardless, it is this focus on the lost subject as, as it were, dramatis persona, caught *in the moment and event of its loss*, that distinguishes Lacoue-Labarthe from philosophical like-minds (Deleuze, Foucault, Derrida, Blanchot, Nancy) as well as from those in relation to which his works establish more or less formal opposition (Girard, Lacan, Adorno). Thus presented, the two authorial personae are clearly not mutually exclusive, the Lacoue-Labarthe of the individual works taking particular shape—a silhouette—against the backdrop of the shared authorial identity. In the present text, I will be dealing with him as that single figure.

Acknowledgment and thanks are due several persons and groups, without whom this work could not have been brought to completion. Philippe Lacoue-Labarthe himself welcomed me in Strasbourg and afforded me time and extended conversation; my thanks are due Melissa McMahon, in Melbourne, for kindly helping with the initial transliteration and translation of the recordings. Kevin Hart, also in Melbourne, assisted with a blend of erudition, technical expertise, and encouragement that could not have been bettered. The project from which this work developed was based at Monash University, in Melbourne, and assisted by an Australian Postgraduate Award; my thanks go, again, to Kevin, and to Chris Worth, Andrew Milner, Gail Ward, Louise Mills, and the Postgraduate Centre staff for the support that helped make the period of the award so fruitful, and to Simon Critchley and Wayne Hudson for invaluable comments on the text that it produced.

I thank the ever-professional staff at Fordham University Press for their skills: diverse, focused, and always generously offered. Helen Tartar was challenging, patient, and encouraging at just the right times, Chris Mohney meticulous in reading the early copy, and Loomis Mayer understanding with the final revisions.

Likewise, I am grateful to my companions in the Society of Jesus: to successive Jesuit provincial superiors Bill Uren, Daven Day, and Mark Raper; to the Jesuit communities at Power Street, Hawthorn, and the Jesuit Theological College, Parkville; and to others too numerous to mention. One and all, they offered the familial warmth, good humor, care, and sometimes sheer room to move that are indispensable to endeavors such as this. Finally, I am indebted to the Chisholm family for bringing their long-standing support and friendship for me to bear on the weeks of writing. To Trish particularly, my deepest thanks for totally generous help. Within her thoroughgoing care, concern, and encouragement, the meticulous proofreading of endless drafts was only one component, but by no means the least valued.

Representation and Subjectivity
The Kantian Bequest Onward

Introduction: Reiterations Set around Kant

In approaching Lacoue-Labarthe's work, it is perhaps best to begin broadly, if simply, since deeper waters will present themselves soon enough. I have mentioned that to talk about his texts is to talk about both representation and subjectivity, and this is where I commence. As bequeathed to modern philosophy, the problem of the relationship between representation and subjectivity begins with Kant, and with the problem, highlighted by Kant, of the *presentation* of the subject—"subject," here, in the sense of both "self" and "object of experience."

For Western philosophy in Kant's wake, *presentation* of a subject—as such, and to sense perception—is an elusive grail. By contrast, *representation* becomes the way in which any encounter with reality is to be described, since everything always already presents itself as something else. Presentation, it might be said, itself bears the character of representation, and in so doing bids both to depict and to distort the "presented."

This is how the question about "presentation and subjectivity" becomes a question about *representation* and subjectivity. I focus in this work on these latter notions taken together, their entwinement manifested particularly starkly whenever Lacoue-Labarthe calls attention to the loss of the subject. He returns time and again to the question of this loss *within* mimesis, or *between* literature and philosophy. Therefore, my own introduction here begins by examining representation and subjectivity, both separately and in their historical connection, so as to contextualize my exploration of Lacoue-Labarthe. It continues by outlining the specific shape that the representation / subjectivity problematic assumes in his writings, and finally it goes on to outline the way in which subsequent chapters contribute to my main argument: that the notion of hyperbology, suitably developed, becomes a motif around which Lacoue-Labarthe's diverse explorations of the problematic can be gathered.

My introductory historical treatments of representation and subjectivity will not canvas them as they occur *ab initio* in philosophy. Space considerations preclude this, particularly in the case of representation, which has itself been presented and represented regularly from the first, as Walter Benjamin has famously observed.[1] Likewise, as will become clear in what follows, the subject becomes re-(re)presented at every turn of philosophy, so that a thoroughgoing survey of this development is also impossible here.

Instead, I take Immanuel Kant as my point of departure for both notions. This does not mean that the ambit of the problematic, or my treatment of it, is thereby restricted to its Kantian manifestation. Rather, as will rapidly become evident, this manifestation is pivotal for discussions in Lacoue-Labarthe that reach backward to the Greeks and beyond (since the Greeks are always susceptible to the demand for the pre-Greek), and forward to Nietszche and beyond (insofar as Nietzsche is interpreted and reinterpreted by Heidegger and Derrida, Lacoue-Labarthe and Nancy). Those discussions in turn constantly revise the terms of the received Kantian problematic of representation. They do the same with the question of the "subject" in Kant, and particularly, as I will show, with the question of the "split" in this subject.

In fact, my treatment of subjectivity here does initially encompass the philosophical beginning of the notion, but only insofar as this looks toward Kant, and the Kantian subject, the representability of which is an issue from the first. Representation, then, also figures when subsequent sections look at how the subject fares post-Kant: first, immediately beyond Kant, then up to the (Derridean) present, and, finally, within Lacoue-Labarthe's own method of approach to the intersection of the two notions. In taking up this last question, I make particular use of some provisional thoughts that Lacoue-Labarthe himself has recently offered.[2] The way will then be ready for me to outline the course my own argument will take in subsequent chapters, generalizing Lacoue-Labarthe's treatment of the representation / subjectivity link and then extrapolating from that treatment to a new description of subjectivity, one that, in my opinion, Lacoue-Labarthe's readings do not ultimately refuse.

Presentation and Representation in Kant

For Kant, we might say—to begin with a distinction that will be eroded later—presentation (*Darstellung*) relates to objects that are sensibly present and, in this sense, "objectively real." Conversely, representation (*Vorstellung*) pertains to objects that exist (or to objects as they exist) in thought, separately from any correlative sensible presentation. This distinction is the basis of Kant's description of cognition in the *Critique of Reason*. Martha Helfer calls attention to what amounts in Kant to a notion of "givenness" informing this description. Kant says:

> If cognition is to have objective reality, that is, a connection to an object, . . . then the object must be capable of being given in some manner.[3]

From what follows, it can be inferred that Kant identifies this "being given" with sensible presentation:

> That an object be given (if this expression be taken, not as referring to some merely mediate process, but as signifying immediate presentation [*Darstellung*] in intuition), means simply that the representation [*Vorstellung*] through which the object is thought relates to actual or possible experience.[4]

Here, the "immediate presentation in intuition" is related to "actual or possible experience." Kant is evidently thinking of *Darstellung* as presentation involving the immediacy of direct (rather than schematic or symbolic) availability to sensible experience. *Darstellung*, then, is, as Helfer says, "the making sensible of a concept." The concept "itself," as it involves thought, is a representation, not a presentation. Strictly speaking, it is *a representation that is presented*, as becomes clear when Helfer recalls the German here: *unmittelbar in der Anschauung darstellen*.[5]

This brings me to "representation" [*Vorstellung*]. Here already, its logical priority in respect to presentation is curiously undecided. "*Re*presentation" suggests a repetition of a prior presentation, that is, of a "presented" or "presentable" object of actual experience. But representation can also be approached in another, ultimately distinct sense, in which it retains a temporal if not also a logical priority over presentation. This may happen if, for instance, all "presentation," rather than being regarded as preceding its corresponding "representation," is treated as a *presenting* of what is *first* a representation.

The contrast and contest between these two approaches is very important. Thus Taylor, himself re-presenting Derrida, can say:

> Since representation invariably opens the gap it seeks to close, it is always "tied to the work of spacing." Spacing, however, "'is' the index of an irreducible outside, and at the same time the index of a *movement*, of a displacement which indicates an irreducible alterity." Inasmuch as all presentation is representation, the subject's struggle to secure identity and establish a proper name *inevitably* fails.[6]

Echoes of the (post)modern discontent that inspires the reconfiguration of representation will be found when Lacoue-Labarthe, in the company of Derrida, Nancy, and Blanchot, offers readings of Kant, Nietzsche, Freud, Heidegger, Lacan, and others. Paul Celan, as poet, is also in this latter group, but perhaps as a special case.[7]

Also, there already arises here the question of the *subject*, which presentation and representation are presumed to "give" to more or less immediate experience. I shall presently explain in more detail why the Kantian subject cannot present itself immediately, in that all its self-*representations* mark themselves as inadequate. But first it is pertinent briefly to mention two further aspects of the *Darstellung / Vorstellung* interface that have specific interest in relation to the overall argument I wish to pursue.

The first of these is the romantic reconfiguration of the notion of *Darstellung*, a move that bids to allow literature and poetry the possibilities of presentation formally denied to these by Kant. It will be seen as I proceed that romantic *Darstellung* is representation accorded the priority and experiential efficacy attending presentation — the presentation that "appears" in Kant only as a lacuna. Azade Seyhan, for example, says that

> in Romantic usage only *Darstellung* [as opposed to the other designators of representation — *Vorstellung* and *Repräsentation*] attains to a materiality of figural representation. [A study by Fritz Heuer maintains that] *Darstellung* distinguishes itself from exist-

ing notions of representation in its emphatic focus on poetic presence.[8]

A dual movement can be seen to be afoot in this passage, the second phase of which follows upon the first. In the first place, *Darstellung* is seen to be formally treated by the romantics as *representation* rather than presentation. Here, the romantics show awareness of the effectively "derivative" nature of what is "presented" in Kantian *Darstellung* and obviously choose to focus on this result of the event, that is, representation, rather than on the rather superficial Kantian designation of the "mode" of its occurrence, that is, presentation.

Then, however, *Darstellung* is redescribed so that, within this formal designation as representation, its function returns to that previously designated by Kant—presentation. This return, though, occurs by a path that Kant himself seemingly avoids, namely, "an emphatic focus on *poetic presence.*"[9] The possibility of a poetic or literary presentation of the subject, whether in the early romantic sense or under a more recent understanding attributable to Blanchot, will become an important backdrop to my generalization of Lacoue-Labarthe's account of subjectal loss.

The second aspect of the *Darstellung / Vorstellung* interface that has interest for the argument to be presented here is that Lacoue-Labarthe himself can be heard reflecting on the ways in which representation may relate to presentation. He remarks that

the entire dream (as Husserl said) of an auto-presentation, or even presentation of the subject, is a dream, because all presentation is a representation. . . . Now, if one attacks representation, in the philosophical sense of the term, in the determination of the truth as representation, or as adequation to a subject, or to an object, well and good. But there is another thing, it seems to me, in representation. In particular—now, I don't know how this works in other languages, but in any case in Latin and French, it is the same word: "representation"—the "re" of representation is an intensive. It is not an indicative, if you like—it signifies "to render present." . . . Thus . . . I would rather be close to, myself, a thought of . . . a "necessary representation." So, if you ask me whether it would be true (to say) that the subject can present itself: I don't think so. Rather, I think that there is a protocol, doubtless very very difficult to analyse, of representation in the sense of "to render present."[10]

What is of great interest here is that Lacoue-Labarthe is willing to accede to the thought of representation as a "rendering present" but discounts the possibility of pure presentation. I will return presently to this most intriguing of issues. Now, though, having demarcated the territory upon which the notion of representation will offer itself to scrutiny in Lacoue-Labarthe's work, I turn to a corresponding mapping of the regions in which the subject and subjectivity are to be found in Western philosophy. Kant will once more be treated as pivotal in this mapping.

The Subject and Subjectivity: Pre-Kant

Of the many basic concepts of traditional Western philosophy that contemporary continental philosophy has tended to unsettle—such as those of reason, being, logic. and essence—none is more basic, perhaps, than that of the subject itself. The term originates with Aristotle, in the *Logic,* where it designates that of which something might be predicated. "Subject" is characterized in essentially grammatical contradistinction to "predicate." This is so particularly in the sense of Aristotle's ultimate subject, a concept implied in his designation of *substance* as a subject that cannot be a predicate. He says that some beings "are called substance because they are not predicated of a subject but everything else is predicated of them."[11] But here Aristotle uses a single word for subject and substance—*hupokeimenon,* "that which lies under"; it is subsequent Latin translation of the word as *subiectum* and *substantia* that more clearly makes the point of this sentence.[12] This marks Aristotle's connection between the grammatical subject as an "underlying" and the notion of an "ultimate underlying."

The ultimate subject then, as an ultimate underlying, implicitly designates Being itself—that which is "at the bottom of things," that which purely "is," without further qualification. Lacoue-Labarthe himself recalls that, though the word "subject" joins the philosophical "vocabulary" only in modern times, it recoups from that point its identification with Being.[13] After Descartes, "subject" becomes

> a word that Kant installs definitively, in particular in the form of the transcendental subject. It's a word which, from a Latin origin, spreads into different European languages, all the while continuing to belong (for example—to take a reference that I know a little—in Rousseau) to the vocabulary of political philosophy, for example.[14]

But these uses have all respected the original association of the word with substance or Being; therefore,

> that the word has asserted itself as designating, from a certain period, Being, *Dasein,* is not at all an accident, occurs not at all by chance. It is because, in fact, this is the term which [it] had been designating for a very long time, that is to say, since Greek philosophy. [Being] is a quasi-synonym for what one calls substance—*sub-stantia,* or *sub-iectum*—it is practically the same thing, it means practically the same thing.[15]

From this declaration it can be deduced that the presumption of this subject predated Aristotle, since what purely *is*—grounding all appearances and relativizing them—also has a name in Plato, namely, the "idea." In any case, in both Plato and Aristotle, in different ways, subjectivity is sought in terms of substantiality. But this does not mean that the subjectivity implicit in Plato is that of a human subject. Or, to be more precise, it is not that of a *hupokeimenon* identified with the human events of thought, speech, willing, and so on. It is with Descartes that the possibility of this identification begins. Here is Lacoue-Labarthe explaining this concept, providing a bridge to the modern terrain from which his own investigation of the problem of subjectivity takes its departure:

> [For the Greeks] substance is objective. They would not have had the distinction between subject and object, in the modern sense of the term: substance, *hupokeimenon,* what is under things, at the bottom of things. Which one interprets, and which takes form later: as Reason, as logos, as God (the God of Philosophy). . . . And it is simply in the modern age that this substance becomes "substance" as we understand it, that is to say, in connection with man—and, from the first, to the man who is the philosopher, to the man who thinks. Which means that all thought since Descartes is defined as essentially subjective. Whether this subject be the individual who is philosopher (the single man who is philosopher, he who is in the "act of philosophizing," as the later Heidegger will say), or the whole of humanity (that is to say, Mind, as Hegel says), is not important—but the subject of modern philosophy is connected each time to man, which is not at all the case in ancient philosophy.[16]

All this is not new. What Lacoue-Labarthe recounts here is a history—of the notion of the post-Aristotelian subject—that is as familiar to philosophy as it has itself been subject to rewriting by seminal thinkers, each of whom adds a chapter that retrains the whole. Thomas Aquinas shapes the medieval identification of this substance / subject with the Christian God, as self-subsistent Being, whose very essence is to exist, so that *that* it is, is identical to *what* it is.[17] Descartes reidentifies this subject with the thinking self, via the cogito.[18] Kant, in response to Hume's skepticism, salvages this thought-based subjectivity.[19] But he does so only at the expense of admitting of the thinking subject as a transcendental ego, unified as regards apperception; he concedes to Hume the subject's lack of an originary intuition of itself.[20]

Subjectivity Since Kant: Its Entwining with the Question of Representation

It might be said that it is from this point forward in the history of subjectivity that its entwining with representation becomes an issue. All that I have said so far indicates the subject as a central preoccupation of Western philosophy from its inception. It also marks the key pre-Cartesian theoretical impossibility—that of *presenting* the subject to sensible intuition—as having become, since Kant, different and more provocative. This development may be seen as being due to Descartes. Once he had broached the conviction that sensible encounter with the newly characterized thought / subject was possible, Kant's retraction of this presentational possibility could not but take on the aspect of a deprivation. The absence of subjectal self-presentation was itself now bound to be represented *as* a loss, blamable upon the self-distancing undergone in the event of conceptualization.

As I have mentioned, Kant's use of the term *Vorstellung* identified all mental images as representations; he reserved the use of *Darstellung* to describe the occasion of actual or sensible presentation of these representations. In these terms, the subject, as I shall explain further below, becomes the culminating example of a *Vorstellung* that does not itself amount to a *Darstellung*. Or, alternatively, in the third *Critique*, the subject is a *Darstellung* that, rather than offering a *Vorstellung*, proffers *Vorstellungen* in illimitable excess.

Thus the subject after Descartes—the subject as ego—becomes ripe to be undermined *as* subject. In Kant, the "I" that is represented during thought is *only* a representation. It is a short step from this notion to an enumeration of the ways in which this representation is, anyway, a *false* representation of the subject.

Nietzsche, as Sarah Kofman points out, does just this, going back to Descartes. Kofman expounds a fragment in which Nietzsche "entraps" Descartes. She points out that if Cartesian indubitability is meant to correspond to immediacy of experience, and thus to link this immediacy with thinking, then something is awry:

> In fact, the *cogito* could not be a rational truth, an immediate certainty, for it implies a series of mediations that separate me always already from myself and that are so many beliefs, opinions, prejudices, "articles of faith," imaginative fictions.[21]

Here, the "beliefs, opinions," and so on are those that Nietzsche discovers hidden within the cogito, a complex word that Descartes has "seized brutally." Thus Nietzsche:

> In this famous cogito there is: (1) it thinks; (2) I believe that it is I who thinks; (3) . . . that "thinking" is an activity for which one must imagine a subject, if only "it"; and the *ergo sum* signifies nothing more. But this is a belief in grammar: one supposes "things" and their "activities," and this puts us far from immediate certainty.[22]

For Nietzsche, this does more than prove that the cogito is not immediately certain. It also raises the question of whether immediate certainty itself is not impossible of being had, as a *contradictio in adjecto*. The subject, once it has been equated with the unverifiable self-perception proffered by theoretical consciousness, has been reduced to something it is not or, worse still, to something nonexistent.

Whether Nietzsche's criticism of Descartes might have applied, mutatis mutandis, to Kant is a more involved question. On the one hand, Kant, in the first two *Critiques*, seems to be very clear that we cannot "know" the "I" in a more than transcendental way, that is, as an object of knowledge, in the Cartesian sense. For him, the syllogism that seems to deliver the "I" turns out to be a *paralogism*, whose logical error turns on an undistributed middle term. Thus it is true that

> I, as a thinking being, am the absolute subject of all my possible judgements, and this representation of myself cannot be employed as predicate of any other being.[23]

But this "absolute subject" is, he implies in the argument of the first edition (he uses a separate argument in the second edition), not "substance" in any useful or persistent way.[24] What was mooted in the premise was an "I" that was nonpredicable of any other being, as well as given with the permanence habitually attributed to objects in experience. But this latter attribute is absent. So, even though the syllogism formally works, this term "absolute subject" is, he implies, undistributable. So the minor premise "I as a thinking being . . ." cannot be used with its major premise:

> That, the representation of which is the *absolute subject* of all my possible judgements and cannot therefore be employed as determination of another thing, is *substance*.
>
> Given this, the desired conclusion, "Therefore I, as thinking being (soul), am *substance*," does not follow.[25]

All this is in line with Kant's previous observation:

> Since the proposition "I think" (taken problematically) contains the form of each and every judgement of the understanding and accompanies all categories as their vehicle, it is evident that the inferences from it admit only of a transcendental employment of the understanding.[26]

As I will show below, for Lacoue-Labarthe and Nancy this determinedly transcendental employment of the understanding in Kant translates into an "emptiness" in the Kantian cogito.[27] Nevertheless, Kant's third *Critique* arguably canvases, somewhere short of delivering, the possibility of a representation of the subject in connection with judgments of taste and the sublime. The relationship of this representation to Kantian *Darstellung* (as external or sensible *presentation*) becomes a crucial question.

To move on: Hegel and Heidegger also find fault, each in his own way, with the representation of the subject as cogito. Each explicitly or implicitly critiques his predecessors' attempts to repair and resurrect subjectal representation. Hegel points out, ultimately against Kant, that the event of naming already effaces the absolute singularity of the thing named.[28] This fate, of course, befalls the "I" as surely as it befalls any other named thing.[29] For Heidegger, the ego presents as a distraction from the truth about the unavailability of the subject—Being—to representational thought. Being itself is concealed, even as it reveals itself in the being of (particular) beings. The locus of this revelation is (the) human being as *Dasein*, but here *Dasein* signifies a mode of Being-in-the-world that is phenomenally prior to the "I" of self-consciousness. One of Heidegger's "first tasks" in *Being and Time* is "to show that the point of departure from an initially given *ego* and subject totally fails to see the phenomenal content of *Dasein*."[30]

Deconstruction, Representation, and Subjectivity

Thus, it might be said, Heidegger intends to suggest Being as an absent, and thus unrepresentable, subject. His own account of the *presencing* of Being is nevertheless marked with traces of the *origin* of the sendings by which Being is unconcealed in beings. Equally, *Dasein*, as a place where the difference between Being and beings unfolds, becomes a clandestine or potential "subject" or "underlying." This possibility is seemingly realized through the well-documented *Kehre* or "turning" in Heidegger's thought. Thereafter, he looks forward to a specific and future sending of Being—implicitly, an unconcealing of Being "itself"—that will repeat the original sending to the pre-Socratics.[31]

I am aware that some caution is needed here, since, in treating of the "subjectal" aspect of *Dasein*, I am reading a presumption of "subjectivity" into places where Heidegger formally discounts it. To avoid vastly oversimplifying Heidegger, such an interpretation must be carefully explained, and it must be supported with qualification and nuance, all of which we shall see Lacoue-Labarthe supply later on, in ample quantities.[32] That said, however, Heidegger's developed ontology remains arguably at odds with itself, mooting a representation of theoretically absent Being, as if such Being were "original" and, in this sense, at one time "present." Being thus depicted is a subject once again, as the origin of the *event* of thought, if not as the cogito.

What Heidegger does might be seen as the surrender to a temptation that, in broadly similar terms, Kant also exhibits in his third *Critique*. This is a temptation to go back "behind" a subject (which Kant formerly declared to be *only* a representation) retrospectively, to presume for it a presentability antecedent to the structure of thought. Implicit in this accession to the past and theoretical presentability of the subject is the more or less explicit hope of the *future* presentability of the subject. Kant's third *Critique*, as I will show, gives birth to this hope for the romantics and idealists who succeed him; Heidegger, after the *Kehre*, speaks of *Gelassenheit*, of the age when Being will be let be, as it was for the pre-Socratics.

My brief parade of seminal thinking on the (re)presentability of the subject is nearing its end. Enter now Jacques Derrida, seeking to re-explore the thought, implicit in the earlier Heidegger, of the radical absence of Being. Where Heidegger's notion of *Destruktion*—a return to thinking the being in its Being—has failed to attest this radical absence, Derrida works by complexly replacing *Destruktion* by its "other": *deconstruction*. I say "complexly" because the operation Derrida effects on Heidegger's notion hovers between reinterpretation and simple replacement.[33] As Hugh Silverman says,

> in Heideggerian terms, [deconstruction] does not operate at the ontic level of beings, nor does it attempt to give an account of Being. Rather it is performed or enacted at the very place of difference, in what Heidegger would call the Being of beings, the place of truth, of unconcealment, of disclosure. For Derrida, the place of difference is a line, a line between, a pairing and a separating.[34]

Heideggerian difference, then, is not discarded but is questioned as to its own interior division. Deconstruction invokes the play of *différance*, which sees the presumptions of both essence and self-presence as undone by previous and irreducible differences within language, and between speech and language, when the latter are invoked to signify presence.[35]

There is also writing, the favored playground of *différance*. Derrida turns to the subversion of presence that writing effects, and to the way in which this subversion is itself cloaked where philosophy marginalizes writing, not excluding those places where we find Heidegger's notion of "thinking." Alan Bass puts it succinctly:

> From Plato to Heidegger himself, Derrida demonstrates, there is a persistent exclusion of the notion of writing from the philosophical definition of the sign. Since this exclusion can always be shown to be made in the name of *presence*—the sign being most present in spoken discourse—Derrida uses it as a "symptom" which reveals the working of the "repressive" logic of presence, which determines Western Philosophy as such.[36]

Thus Derrida ultimately takes Heidegger beyond himself, for Heidegger had already argued that language precedes thought and "houses" Being. Furthering a trajectory launched by Saussure, Derrida notices the way in which Being might itself be regarded as an *absent* product of the language, signs, or texts that report it as presence.[37]

For Derrida, then, *absence* is radical and thoroughgoing. Representation manifests *original* difference in the sense of doubling a single that was always already past, that is, always already different from itself. The point of *différance* is that it renders difference "itself" as different from "itself"; this prevents difference from providing a "trail" to a subject presumed as originally identical with itself, and rendered as split only by the event of self-representation. But, in any case, self-representation, as a sine qua non of self-experience, mediates self-loss. For, as Bernet says, "Derrida's positive contribution to the analysis of self-experience is above all the indication of the necessity of self-*representation* and its *differential* structure."[38] In other words, for Derrida there is no self-experience without self-representation, but no self-representation without self-difference and hence loss of the self.

The foregoing becomes germane to the consideration of Derrida's discussion of Lacoue-Labarthian subjectal loss. When Derrida comments on Lacoue-Labarthe's treatments of representational self-loss, especially in its hyperbological overtones, he focuses on those aspects that mark this self-loss as *original*. There is little attempt to extrapolate from this original self-loss to a prospective "other" self *gained* through the movement of self-loss.

Derrida's thought, especially as it deals with the deconstructive loss of the subject who speaks or writes, must be taken as the backdrop to all that I say below in regard to Lacoue-Labarthe. Derrida is foregrounded only in the final chapter, devoted to a comparison and contrast of his own and Lacoue-Labarthe's approaches and conclusions. To the reader disappointed by this treatment, I must point out that I have deliberately treated Jean-Luc Nancy and Maurice Blanchot similarly because studies of these others are many, and attention to Lacoue-Labarthe is rare. My primary focus here remains a direct treatment of the connection between representation and subjectivity in Lacoue-Labarthe's writings.

Suffice it, at this juncture, to anticipate the result of this treatment by saying that Lacoue-Labarthe might be contextualized among his contemporaries as follows. Those who succeed Derrida are wont to identify the subject as a representation without prior presentation, or as, in Lacoue-Labarthe's words, representation as a *rendering* present rather than a re-presenting. If this is so, then Lacoue-Labarthe's particular métier, *within* this oeuvre, is the investigation of the subject as a *necessary* representation occurring in speech, writing, and mimesis generally.

Philippe Lacoue-Labarthe: A Loss of the Subject amidst the Necessity Attending Its Representation

This point about a necessary subjectal representation becomes useful, in fact, for outlining the pattern and content of the argument that the remainder of this book develops through a series of close readings of Lacoue-Labarthe's texts. The "necessary representation" of the subject is broached by Lacoue-Labarthe in two related senses. He is concerned, first, with the recurrence, the *necessity* of the (re)appearance of subject *as* a representation. Second, and within this event of subjectal representation, he is concerned with exploring the seemingly necessary recurrence of certain *elements* of subjectal return, elements that in fact attest to the *loss* of the subject, or to its disidentification from "itself."

Particularly in the early texts. which will be my main field of investigation in what follows, Lacoue-Labarthe's question broadly repeats itself as the following: How is it that the subject of philosophy, represented in literature as the subject of writing—both writer and written—is never a single representation and thus never a representation of a unified subject? Or, as Lacoue-Labarthe has put it, "When one writes, something is produced that breaches [*entame*], attacks, threatens always to destroy the subject who writes."[39]

In what follows, it will become evident how in text after text, but each time with a freshness of subject matter and a new angle of approach, Lacoue-Labarthe pursues, in its very irresistibility, this representation of the subject as lost to itself in writing and mimesis. I will give bibliographical details of the texts as I proceed. Several of these texts come from two collections of essays, *Le Sujet de la philosophie (Typographies I)* (1979) and *L'Imitation des modernes (Typographies II)* (1986). Others are included in books that Lacoue-Labarthe has authored individually and in collaboration with Nancy. The latter, relatively few, are always argued intricately, retaining also the rigor characteristic of Lacoue-Labarthe. I will not read the texts in chronological order but will employ them as they fit my purpose: first of all to develop a generalized account of Lacoue-Labarthian subjectal loss, and then to place this representation of a (lost) subject amidst corresponding representations offered by Lacoue-Labarthe's contemporaries.

This second phase will extend the investigation begun in the first by taking it toward an intriguing, multifaceted question: Might there be, after all, the depiction of a subject—a "deconstructive" subject, but a subject nevertheless—associated with the very consistency that imbues Lacoue-Labarthian subjectal loss? And what would it mean to name such a subject, and a subjectivity as such, once deconstructive subjectal loss has been conceded? How would the return of a "postdeconstructive" subject be anything other than the reinscription of a subject that is, *anyway,* part of the account of deconstructed subjectivity?

The question is a complex one, but a path to its answer is indicated in the tensions internal to my earlier extended quotation from Lacoue-Labarthe (see the excerpt associated with n. 10, above). There, his choice of the term "necessary representation" to explain his description of the subject is offered as denial of an alternative possibility: that he might be describing *presentation* of the subject. An intriguing space is opened here between the concepts of "presentation" and "necessary representation," a space that may be, however, no space at all. One might ask what, finally, the difference is between, on the one hand, a representation that is *necessary* and, on the other, *presentation,* given that the indispensability of the former matches the vividness and experiential immediacy that we associate with the latter. Granted, in order for this question not to be asked naïvely, presentation itself must first be redescribed, in freedom from its classical totalization by the notion of presence. Presentation must come to connote something akin to the sensible apprehension of a subject in "its" very dissolution. But once this redescription has been accomplished, might not subjectal presentation be found in and as the very *movement* by which the subject flees itself? "The sublime," as we shall hear Nancy say, "is presentation in its movement."[40]

I shall also note the affinity that Lacoue-Labarthe's explorations share with those of Maurice Blanchot, who himself typically pursued subjects at the point of the *experience* of self-loss, or, as he has called it, "the experience of non-experience."[41] In any case, my own exploration of the possibility of a "presentational deconstructive subjectivity" in Lacoue-Labarthe will serve, effectively, to distinguish Lacoue-Labarthe's approach to subjectal loss from that of Jacques Derrida.

All this, however, will be predicated upon my establishing in the early chapters a generalized description, in the various readings that I examine, of the movement of subjectal loss *à la* Lacoue-Labarthe. I shall move toward describing this movement and this loss in terms of *hyperbologic,* a term by which Lacoue-Labarthe extends and shapes the romantic notion of the hyperbolic so that it outlines a particular mechanism of subjectal loss through simultaneous juxtaposition and interaction of opposing representations of the subject.

My task will be to show that hyperbological subjectal loss — sometimes evident, sometimes clandestine — is a motif common to the typical Lacoue-Labarthian exploration of the terrain linking literature and philosophy. It is subjectal loss in this particular experiential mode that opens the way to the thought of a particular "presentational" subjectivity in Lacoue-Labarthe. Such (re)presentation, in its very "necessity," bids to accommodate, though nonreductively, the deconstructive play attending all subjectal representation.

The Structure of My Argument

My argument, then, is structured as follows. I begin in Chapter 2 by reading Lacoue-Labarthe's essay "Typography"[42] in apposition to elements of René Girard's *"To double business bound."* My purpose will be to identify the trappings of subjectal *return* in what is formally an exploration by Lacoue-Labarthe of subjectal loss. I hope thus to anticipate my later claim for a "structure of subjectivity" that, "despite all," is reiterated within a typical Lacoue-Labarthian account of subjectal loss.

Chapter 3 continues this course, taking up Lacoue-Labarthe's readings in two further essays, "Diderot: Paradox and Mimesis" and "The Echo of the Subject."[43] Canvasing the notion of Lacoue-Labarthian *désistance,* or the inevitable delay of the subject with regard to itself, I seek to explore the significance of a parallel representation: that of the thespian subject who deliberately or consciously withdraws from his or her acting persona and thus formally figures *désistance.* Here again, I suggest, we find a subject as such — that is, we have subjectal return. This return becomes "half" of the story of subjectal loss — the half that contributes to the undecidability of *désistance,* and hence to a representation of subjectal loss as the movement between these opposite representations of the loss itself.

The theme of subjectal return thus shows itself to be significant, but not in its own right. Bracketing this thought for later reconsideration, I next take up, in the three following chapters, the task of generalizing Lacoue-Labarthian subjectal loss as hyperbological. In Chapter 4, I pursue Lacoue-Labarthe and Nancy at work in *The Literary Absolute*[44] and argue that the exposition in that work attests to the *hyperbolical* in Kant and, incipiently, to what Lacoue-Labarthe will later name as the *hyperbological.* For an ambiguity may be detected in Kant's account of the impossibility of *presentation* (*Darstellung*) of the subject: Kant's third *Critique* hesitates between opposing *representations* of what this presentational inadequacy (and hence presentation itself) means.

Chapter 5 takes up several further texts in which the hyperbological is named and developed by Lacoue-Labarthe. Here, I seek to expound the "mechanism" that is hyperbological subjectal loss, in its general dynamic of an oscillatory loss of the subject between simultaneous and contradictory representations. Each representation is generated when a previous representation, taken to its extreme, "tips over," as it were, into its opposite. We have a clearer view here of hyperbological loss as itself a "necessary representation" of the subject. What is represented is an escape of something in the subject from "itself" even as it thinks, speaks, or writes in an attempt to fix itself.

That this hyperbology is to be found elsewhere in Lacoue-Labarthe, beyond the texts affording it explicit mention, I demonstrate in Chapter 6. In that chapter, I venture with Lacoue-Labarthe into the question of the essence of the political, and of the political subject. In "Transcendence Ends in Politics,"[45] Lacoue-Labarthe argues that the "new German subject" anticipated in Heidegger's Rectoral Address (1933) is overdetermined as a Nietzschean subject of the will to power. Lacoue-Labarthe does not mention a hyperbological counterpart to this representation. However, I argue that such a counterpart—a Heideggerian overdetermination of the Nietzschean subject—might be found. I draw here from Lacoue-Labarthe's *Heidegger, Art and Politics: The Fiction of the Political*[46] as well as from Heidegger's "The Word of Nietzsche: God Is Dead." I contend that the hyperbological is here on view at its most definitive, with its "oscillating" counterrepresentations refusing assimilation or sublation.

The development of my claim for hyperbology in Lacoue-Labarthe will be by this point essentially complete. In the final two chapters, I turn to placing this hyperbology, and its originator, in the context of his nearest intellectual neighbors: Jean-Luc Nancy, Jacques Derrida, and Maurice Blanchot. In these chapters, I also move toward considering the nexus between "necessary representation(s)" of a lost subject and a possible presentation of a "deconstructed subject." Might this latter subject be identified, after suitable provisos, with the *experience* of "its" own loss through doubling, that is, in the *movement* that is this loss?

Something of this is broached at the conclusion of Chapter 7, which is given over to a relevant comparison and contrast between Lacoue-Labarthe and Nancy, using as focus their relative essays on the sublime. Here, hyberbology in Lacoue-Labarthe comes to the fore as an exchange in the sublime between representations of the subject as *technē* (art) and *phusis* (nature), respectively. But I argue that Nancy's sublime has within it its own "hyperbology," matching and complementing that evoked by Lacoue-Labarthe. The Nancian hyperbological bids to offer a "presentation" of the subject as *sensed movement.* Under this description, the sublime is the subject sensed in and through "its" self-loss. It is the subject manifest in art, rendered sensible in and as its offering to another destiny.

The marks of "structural subjectivity" in Lacoue-Labarthe that the earliest chapters discovered will by this stage be seen to have been reactivated, even though they perhaps no longer attest to *structural* subjectivity as such. The chief component among these marks, subjectal return, was earlier seen as absorbed into a hyperbolical mechanism, which "in the end" attests to subjectal loss. Now, however, the return of the subject *as presented movement* potentially signifies the other of "structural subjectivity," inscribed in its terms but subverting it, namely, a *deconstructive* subjectivity.

The two words of this term take on equal weight in Chapter 8 as I place Lacoue-Labarthe in relation to Derrida and Blanchot, readily acknowledged influences on his work. Whereas Derrida's reading evokes the always already absent subject, and Blanchot's the subject "whose" absence is marked in a subjectal presence elsewhere, Lacoue-Labarthe engages the subject of writing, speaking, or acting in the very occasion and moment of its self-loss. This subject, it will have been amply seen by now, loses itself in finding that its every self-representation flows into an "other" and opposed representation.

My reasoning in these final chapters will tend toward a hypothesis of presentational subjectivity, developed along the following lines. Blanchot and Lacoue-Labarthe are arguably alike in addressing the possibility of a deconstructive subject "distributed between" a self and a "clandestine companion" (Blanchot's term). If so, there is nevertheless the following difference between them. The Lacoue-Labarthian subject is demarcated as an experiencing of this clandestine companion had *by* (or in) the ego. Blanchot's subject, by contrast, becomes (de)constituted as an experiencing of the *ego* had by, or through, its clandestine companion. In both cases, experience de-constitutes the experiencing self and the experienced self alike, thus becoming the "experience of non-experience" (Blanchot).

But this does not mean that the experiencing subject in Lacoue-Labarthe has experience predominantly *from* a point outside itself, as happens in Blanchot.[47] In approaching non-experience from the nearer side, Lacoue-Labarthe is not merely less frequently intractable than Blanchot. He is also able to begin with "ordinary" and concrete representations of the self and its companion, and to offer, as *hyberbology*, the "necessary representation" of the self as always in transit toward nonexperience. In the end, the necessity of representation becomes expressed also as the necessity of the *splitting* of this representation, peculiar to hyperbology. The subject in loss is "subject" of an experience that Lacoue-Labarthe tracks simultaneously as its own and that of a mimetic other. Hyperbology, necessary representation, and (possible) subjectal presentation might all be located, though initially deceptively, in the tension that holds this dipolarity of experience together. At its culmination, this train of thought suggests the possibility of a subject "located" in relation to this tension. Might this subject be found in and as the very "transport" between representations, "itself" "amounting to" a subject of *presentation*?

I now begin to unfold my main argument, which also provides the path to that additional hypothesis. Argument and hypothesis alike will draw fuel from the representational tension typically associated with Lacoue-Labarthian subjectal loss. But it will be useful to begin by considering a level at which that tension is signified as *salvaging* subjectivity. Such a signification ultimately proves unsustainable, if not naïve. But a demonstration of its limitations will yield valuable insights into Lacoue-Labarthian subjectal loss. These insights flower into more telling characterizations of the particular "mechanism" attending that loss. The most significant of those (re)present the subject as "one" that fails to coincide with itself. In one sense, that loss is the end of its subjectivity. In another and intriguing sense, which fuels both argument and hypothesis, the mode of the loss indicates a renewed beginning for that subjectivity.

2

Plato Pursued
Mimesis, Decision, and the Subject

Introduction: The Interplay between Subjectal
Loss and Gain

Two recurrent themes form the backdrop to my exploration of Lacoue-Labarthe here. The first is subjectal loss—the loss of the subject *of* philosophy, *in* literature and mimesis. The second, intertwined with the first, is in fact instrumental in stimulating the rigor with which the first develops. Broadly speaking, it can be named as the *refusal* of the subject to be lost or dismissed, that is, the *return* of the subject. This second theme, while continually reasserting itself, finally remains in fee to the first. Lacoue-Labarthe is concerned to explore how the return of the subject—or, more precisely, the *mode* of this return—also marks subjectal loss. My exposition here will propose a generalized account of the "mechanism" by which this loss occurs. However, as my argument develops, the second theme will bid to resurface in its own right, intriguingly denoting the possibility of an "other" return of the subject, in those very texts in which the formal return is dissipated into loss. I will ask if this possibility exposes a "structural subjectivity" that Lacoue-Labarthe's texts do not ultimately refuse. In any case, this second theme will finally emerge as equal in significance to the first in the matter of generalizing Lacoue-Labarthe's treatment of the relationship between representation and subjectivity.

In this chapter, I introduce the two themes for inspection in their intricate and emblematic entwinement in Lacoue-Labarthe's long essay "Typography."[1] By highlighting the matter of the "decision for subjectivity" in Lacoue-Labarthe, my reading will aim at bringing the durability of the second theme into view. This durability is occasionally occluded in the three chapters that follow, where my reading surrenders, by and large, to Lacoue-Labarthe's own preoccupation with subjectal *loss*. However, the final three chapters broach the possibility, already mentioned, of the subjectal "survival" or "return." This result will in some degree already have been anticipated in Chapters 3, 4, and 5, beginning even here. In other words, I follow Lacoue-Labarthe sympathetically, but also deconstructively. Though reading substantially *with* him, I will not prevent my reading from developing momentum in a contrary direction. The reading in those places becomes simultaneously an exercise in reading Lacoue-Labarthe *against* himself.

"Typography" concerns itself with the relationship between mimesis and subjectal representation in Heidegger and Plato. Can one straightforwardly protect the identity of the subject of experience by invoking the possibility of a nonmimetic description by the subject of itself, by way of contrast with mimetic art, the latter seen as "dissimulating" that subject? Lacoue-Labarthe, in the end, thinks not. His analysis gravitates toward Plato's attempt in *The Republic* to exclude mimetic expressions—the "make-believe" performances of actors and poets—from the State. He concludes that Plato fails to establish that mimesis as such *can* be excluded from the State, and correspondingly that this method of preserving the subject fails.

I will reflect here on Lacoue-Labarthe's manner of characterizing the Platonic philosophy and its Heideggerian interpretation. He regards both as attempting to secure subjectivity by a decision that protects or produces the subject: a decision that, Lacoue-Labarthe then argues, never occurs. "Typography" thus accounts both for the establishment of the subject and for the dismissal—in terms of decision delayed, and thereby denied—of its mimetic "doubles." My point in reflecting on this analysis will be to open the following question: At what level can the "deferral of decision" here be said to manifest subjectal loss, and/or to be effective in deconstructing subjectivity? The answer implicitly provided in "Typography" is both highlighted and subverted in another text, which I discuss in the final section of this chapter. There, what is of interest is Lacoue-Labarthe's critique of a theory concerning mimetic desire offered by René Girard as part of an ongoing debate between the two authors.

"Typography": The Disappearance of *Darstellung*

"Typography" involves Lacoue-Labarthe's attention to two stages in Plato's attempt at dismissal of mimesis from the State. In probing this repetition, Lacoue-Labarthe finds impetus for the interpretation of mimesis as a failed "installation" of the subject. He discovers the following connection, in Plato's thinking, between mimesis and subjectivity: that the exclusion of mimesis is oriented toward the protection of the self-identity of the subject. However, Lacoue-Labarthe concludes that Plato fails to establish that mimesis as such *can* be excluded from the State. If Lacoue-Labarthe's thinking is sound, he is undoubtedly also implying something important about subjectivity.

What, however, *is* this implication? (And it is here that oversimplification must be resisted and Lacoue-Labarthian intricacy accorded full respect!) Is it, as one recent article assumes, that subjectivity is hollow, that "subjectivity . . . implies an absence that cannot be filled?"[2] Is it rather, or also, that the subject has (or is, or undergoes) *désistance* (the term is a neologism that Jacques Derrida employed as a title when he introduced *Typography,* and that one reviewer was understandably deceived into taking as Lacoue-Labarthe's own term)?[3] Or is it, as Lacoue-Labarthe himself implies at the end of the essay, that the subject is maintained *as* subject only by being "mirrored" in texts, and that one day this mirror will shatter, releasing madness or "the very terrorizing instability that the mirror was supposed to freeze"?[4]

Each of these interpretations seems to capture something of what Lacoue-Labarthe is saying. If one hesitates in allowing any of them final interpretative status, it is for seemingly small reasons. Lacoue-Labarthe does not speak explicitly of subjectivity as involving "absence," though he does appear to treat mimesis as endless withdrawal. Again, he never actually employs the word *désistance* in "Typography," though the *désistement* or "delay" of the subject is a prominent part of his argument. Yet again, his final prediction, about the return of mimesis as the madness that ends subjectivity, is made in a speculative disconnectedness: "But, in a certain sense, in any case, 'I,' 'here' decline all authority in the matter. I simply wanted to see, 'me' too."[5]

It is appropriate, then, to avoid jumping to too reductive a conclusion as to what Lacoue-Labarthe might be saying here about the impossibility of characterizing the subject. In spite of everything, it may just be possible that his final reticence allows us to sift his exposition of Plato in search of a characterization of subjectivity. Perhaps, even, this characterization may be achieved despite Lacoue-Labarthe's own (confessedly nonconclusive) conclusion yet draw upon all the patient brilliance he has used to track Heidegger and Plato. It may emerge, even, from our following his exposition of what Heidegger and Plato avoid, and then asking whether there may be something that he himself avoids.

Here is one such direction—an initial one—for such a characterization: I suggest that Lacoue-Labarthe perhaps does not sufficiently recognize the element of "decision," *as* decision, in Plato's attempt to install subjectivity by dismissing mimesis. For Lacoue-Labarthe, "decision" is a broad term for the *will* by which mimesis is expelled—from the State *and* from the individual's own psyche—to make way for the fiction, the fashioning, of the subject. Lacoue-Labarthe interprets this decision in terms of an eradication of equivocity, but need he go so far? He admits but then bypasses the fact that the subject is marked through a structure of, as it were, self-protective decidings. But perhaps more could be made of subjectal structure as such, nonnaïvely, in its apparent *necessity*, that is, as the indispensability of the decision through which subjectivity is inevitably constituted.

Lacoue-Labarthe *does* recognize the decision that determines subjectivity. But for him it bids to become a decision linked to a specific aim, namely, the eradication of the intrinsic equivocity found in speech and writing. *In* itself, and *as* itself, decision perhaps becomes what he "avoids without avoiding" in his exploration of the link between mimesis and subjectivity. In tracking his argument here, I intend to elicit its characteristic persistence and patience, but also to determine the course by which these yield a theorization of subjectivity as perpetually deferred decision making. This theorization is refuted, at a "simple" but important level, by demonstrating the way in which experience provides a recurrent decision *for* a subjectal framework. Initially, this demonstration returns us to the question of the persistence of subjectal experience, the most obvious answer to which is given in terms of the "real" (self-)representable subject.

The question becomes an occasion for my exploring, in the chapters immediately following this one, the intricate interplay—between subjectal loss and subjectal return—that haunts Lacoue-Labarthe's analyses. This exploration will in fact see re-established, in the more sophisticated register that Lacoue-Labarthe calls the *hyperbological,* the play that subverts self-representation and marks self-loss. That in turn calls forth my own more encompassing account of the persistence of subjectal return, going through, but also somewhat beyond, Lacoue-Labarthe. At issue will be the survival of the subject in a *presentational* dimension that, while inseparable from representation (and thus from subjectal loss), is also *other* to it. This is the analysis that the present reading of "Typography" is intended to set in train.

Heidegger: The Avoidance of Plato's "Avoidance" of the "Subject" Mimetician

In "Typography," Lacoue-Labarthe comes to Plato by way of the Heideggerian critique of Platonic mimesis. That critique itself can be treated here only in outline. Its crux for Lacoue-Labarthe is Heidegger's description of the particular modification, in the modern age, of truth as *aletheia,* the unconcealment of Being in beings: Lacoue-Labarthe tracks this argument as it is found in Heidegger's lecture "The Question Concerning Technology," with support from other Heideggerian texts.[6] The clue to the modification is the association of the German word *Ge-stell* (connoting a shelf or pedestal) with major concepts of metaphysics, such as *Vorstellung* (representation) and *Darstellung* (portrayal, presentation).[7] Something is understood to "stand up" when either representation or presentation occurs; equally, *stell* is found in cognates for technology, both in its essence of yore, involving cultivation (thus *bestellen*) or production (thus *herstellen*) and in its modern essence, captured by the word *stellen* itself (to provoke, to confront, to challenge verbally).[8]

For Heidegger, incipiently linked in the essence of technology are the essence of (re)presentation (artistic *poiesis,* or *mimesis*) and the unconcealment of truth as production.[9] In its modern modification, this unconcealment has moved from production as cultivation of nature to production as confrontation of nature and the attempt to "reserve" its energy. Production in the latter sense yields the modern essence of technology. Both modifications, however, presume *production* or *Her-stellen*—as *installation,* of truth—to be the most radical meaning of *stell.* What has occurred is the transformation of *Bestellen,* so that

> the essence of technology entails, by way of *Be-stellen,* a sense of Being as stance, stature, station—as in "Greek," *stasis* or *stele*—

24 Philippe Lacoue-Labarthe

which is and which has always been, in the West, the sense of Being itself.[10]

The key issue here is the disappearance from view of the separate connotation corresponding to *Dar-stellung*. Lacoue-Labarthe quotes a key passage from "The Question Concerning Technology," in which Heidegger moves from discussing *stellen* in terms of "*Her-stellen* and *Dar-stellen*" (producing and representing) to considering the relationship to the *stellen* of the "provoking order." However, this consideration is made in terms of *Herstellen* only, as if *Herstellen* now uniquely represents *stellen*. Lacoue-Labarthe says that here "the *Herstellen* / *Darstellung* couple immediately breaks apart to the benefit of *Herstellen* alone. In fact, *Darstellung* disappears in two lines."[11] With this disappearance, implies Lacoue-Labarthe, the opportunity is lost for representation to be seen other than in relation to the subject (or the truth) of which it is an imitation or distortion.

Lacoue-Labarthe then pursues the perpetuation of this omission in Heidegger's treatment of Plato's *Republic*.[12] He finds that several elements in the treatment conspire to assimilate Platonic mimesis to truth, that is, to truth as disinstalled. Downplaying the discussion of art in Book II, Heidegger addresses the question of art as it appears in Book III. There, subordinating this question to that of poetry, says Lacoue-Labarthe, Heidegger "demonstrates that the artistic product, the *poietic*, is always simply the '*Darstellung* of what is.' "[13] Moreover, Heidegger presents Book III as anticipatory of Book X, since, again, "it is only after the elucidation of truth, in Book VII, that the essence of mimesis, the 'truth' of mimesis, can be decided."[14] The effective separation of art from truth—truth as *aletheia* as *Unverstelltheit*—in terms of which it has been characterized, is thus deferred to this later book.

In Book X, Plato describes the painter as "belonging to this class of demiurge."[15] Plato has just spoken about pointing a mirror in all directions; Heidegger, understandably but too easily, presumes that the reference to "this class of demiurge" makes of Plato's painter a "mirrorer" (*Spiegeler*) who produces a flimsy version of what is, as "*Darstellungsstoff*."[16] Heidegger thereby only fills in a gap that Plato, of necessity, has left. Heidegger, on Plato's behalf, infers a reversion of *Darstellung* to *Herstellen* at the very point where the nature of what is mimetically produced fails to be convincingly explained by Plato, since the analogy between a mirror image and an artist's production raises more questions than it answers. These elements are not specifically allocated, quite possibly because Plato realizes that any allocation would be immediately problematic. If the painter is the mirror, the metaphor fails to convey the dimension of *self*-manifestation that accompanies artistic depiction (and that Plato otherwise associates with craftsmanship): "Where have we ever seen mirrors reflect themselves?"[17] Equally, the metaphor limps if the painter is meant to be the *holder* of the mirror, for this holding can hardly be a demiurgic act—it represents at best a previous "installation" of the *eidos* as *eidolon*.[18]

For Lacoue-Labarthe, what is covered over by Plato in this move, which presumes a "what" as the identity of the artist's *product,* is the gap in the identity of the *artist,* or mimetician. Plato reverts to a (*Herstellen*-based) version of *Darstellung* by asking, "What is?"—a "Greek ruse" to avoid the question of the subject, says Lacoue-Labarthe, the modern version of this question, equally threatened by *Herstellen,* being "*Who works / manufactures what?*"[19]

Plato's "Failed" Dismissal of the Mimetic Persona

Thus Heidegger's overall exposition of Plato's *Republic* yields an assimilation of *poiesis* itself—of making or fictioning, including producing mimetically—to truth. Mimetic poiesis is read as the disfigurement of the true; *Darstellung* having been assimilated to *aletheia* as *Unverstelltheit,* no alternative figure is available with which to describe mimetic fictioning or fashioning.

For Heidegger, then, what Plato says confirms his own determination of the modern essence of technology: the confrontation or provocation of nature in such a way as to prize the storage or stabilization that facilitates later use. The "truth" of objects corresponds to the *installation* of Being in the occurrence of their fashioning. In the modern (post-Socratic) dispensation, truth as *aletheia,* the unconcealment of Being in beings, becomes *Unverstelltheit,* the "remaining standing" of Being in beings.

Correspondingly, Platonic mimesis is determined as falsity by virtue of its not letting Being "stand up" in the beings it represents. Mimetic production has meaning, never on its own terms—say, as "autoproduction"—but always in relation to an "original" adequation that allows truth to stand erect and Being to be unconcealed. Equally, this adequation never occurs: mimesis presents as a copying in which the truth fails to assert itself. Lacoue-Labarthe uses a colorful metaphor:

So, in mimesis, *aletheia* declines, lies down, corresponding to a "stretching out" of the *stele*. Mimesis is the "easy lay" [*la Marie-couche-toi-là*] of truth.[20]

This type of interpretation, says Lacoue-Labarthe, misses the real point of Plato's complaint against mimesis in *The Republic*. It fails especially to recognize and account for the dynamic involving Plato's two dismissals of mimesis from the State. "Why the need for a *double* dismissal?" Heidegger ought to ask. Plato's description of mimesis as presenting an *eidolon* (image) in which Being does not present itself (or stand up), as opposed to the *eidos* (in which it emerges truly), should itself provide sufficient reason to dismiss mimeticians. Seemingly, however, it does not. Lacoue-Labarthe suggests that closer attention to this clue (which Heidegger avoids, perhaps deliberately) reveals that Plato's challenge is not primarily how to discount *what* the mimetician produces. Rather, it is how to describe *who* the mimetician is.[21]

The challenge presents two difficulties, each of which threatens to dissolve the cozy distinction between originals and mimetic copies and to lead toward an abyss in which originals can no longer be sighted for endless mimesis. First, as Plato cannot really deny, those being dismissed as mimeticians in the first exclusion, in Book III, are themselves being dismissed *by* mimeticians. They are excluded in favor of what can at most be claimed as the "superior act" that is the polity of the city. Lacoue-Labarthe quotes the *Laws*:

> Respected visitors, we are ourselves authors of a tragedy, and that the finest and best we know how to make. In fact, our whole polity has been constructed as a dramatization of a noble and perfect life; that is what *we* hold to be in truth the most perfect of tragedies. Thus you are poets, and we are also poets in the same style, rival artists and rival actors [need one underscore this?], and that in the finest of all dramas, one which can indeed be produced only by a code of true law—or at least this is our faith.[22]

The obvious problem arises here: nothing except the faith of the citizens—we may say, here, their "decision"—in regard to one form of mimesis distinguishes this from the rival mimesis it would exclude. Exclusion here *is* decision, a gesture that founds the "officially approved act." Thus, as Lacoue-Labarthe says,

> if we are to believe Socrates (or "Socrates"), this expulsion would manifestly be the most decisive gesture as regards the

"foundation of the State," the gesture on which the uprightness of such a foundation would essentially depend.[23]

Filing, for later attention, this characterization of subjectivity as an effect of decision, I move to the second difficulty. The scare quotes ("Socrates," above) can be our beacon here, for if Socrates playing at citizen is not sufficiently mimetic to force us to qualify his expulsion of mimesis, our attention is called to a further mimetic level in the expulsion. Socrates himself is not himself but is "standing in" for Plato! Here, as throughout Plato's writings, Plato is quite happy in speaking through a persona, but here he does so precisely to condemn the activity of speaking through a persona. This is more than merely paradoxical: it presents as a reopening of subjectivity to the abyss of perpetual mimesis. The "founding act" that fixed Socrates as "himself," as a role in a defining drama—the finest drama of which he knew—is now shown to have failed to fix him as himself.

As already mentioned, though, Lacoue-Labarthe considers Plato as having been aware of this threat to his argument. He argues that Plato's attempt to contain the damage is (perhaps inadvertently, perhaps not) precisely demonstrated in the overall dynamic of mimetic expulsion that he offers. This dynamic is completed by the second expulsion, which occurs in Book X of *The Republic*. As Lacoue-Labarthe points out, this expulsion is specular, whereas the first was oral. It equates mimetic poetry with the work of a painter, and the painter's work, in turn, to the holding up of a mirror before nature. I have already pointed out the lacuna that Lacoue-Labarthe detects in regard to the elements of this metaphor: however its elements are allocated, it fails to render the artistic act as demiurgic.

Consequently, Lacoue-Labarthe proceeds with an exposition of Plato's duplication of the expulsion of mimesis. However, as I follow this exposition, I suggest consideration of the following hypothesis. Lacoue-Labarthe's tracing of Plato's rationale serves here to highlight the decision that constitutes the subject. Lacoue-Labarthe himself takes less than full notice of this, his attention being focused elsewhere, that is, on the *purpose* of the decision.

The exposition proceeds as follows. Lacoue-Labarthe first elicits, insightfully, the link for Plato between mimesis and subjectivity. He notices that Plato's initial expulsion of mimesis is oriented toward a decision distinguishing *haple diegesis* from mimesis. The term *haple diegesis* refers to the kind of "straight narrative" in which the narrator remains himself or herself rather than adopting another, mimetic, persona. Is the distinction sustainable? When is the enunciator her-self, or himself, *as opposed to* a "persona"? We all play a variety of roles—or, as we say, "wear different hats"—in the encounters of even a single afternoon and will answer the question "Who are you?" in different ways according to who is asking and why he or she wants to know. Is it reasonable to postulate an occasion of enunciation when the speaker has remained entirely herself or himself, without slipping into a "persona"? In any case, what would it mean to say that this had happened? Who would this persona, by implication more original than all personae, be, and why not just another per-sona?

Lacoue-Labarthe gives Plato credit for recognizing the difficulties here: if one puts Plato's requirement for *haple diegesis* beside his ad-mission from the *Laws* ("we are . . . rival artists and rival actors"), subjectivity becomes related less to an "original self" than to a "con-sistency as actor" in which the subject "decides" (in some sense of the word) "who" he or she will be and sticks to this persona, forsak-ing all temptation to adopt others.

How, then, are we to characterize the way in which this decision is meant to establish subjectivity, at least in Plato's thinking? Lacoue-Labarthe will work from here on to explore the decision in terms of its apparent *purpose*: the solving of the problematic of subjectivity in terms of what he calls "the problematic of the lie."[24] Plato is seeking to secure subjectivity by ensuring that when we speak, we speak as ourselves, in the sense of attaching ourselves to what we say rather than allowing our words to be heard as the words of others or, per-haps, of no one at all:

> This is why the *origin* of lying, of fiction, has to be sought actu-ally in the direction of what is properly called enunciation. It must be shown that the "mythic lie" proceeds essentially from poetic *irresponsibility*, that is, from a fundamental perversion of poietic practice, indeed—ultimately—*of linguistic practice in gen-eral*. It is because they put themselves out of reach and do not come to answer for their discourse, it is because they do not assist or attend their productions but instead do everything to give them the appearance of autonomy (of truth), it is because, finally, the author in them disappears and thus gives free rein to the circulation of language that poets "lie" and "show" them-selves to be incapable of decision before the natural *equivocity* of discourse.[25]

So Plato, for Lacoue-Labarthe, is aware of the *equivocity* of discourse—the possibility for words to conceal the identity of their utterer, to be unattributed quotations, as when actors speak. Plato's decision to expel mimesis has as its purpose the thwarting of this equivocity.

However, if this purpose is its raison d'être, the decision is already doomed to failure, for equivocity is ineradicably built into speech, and if reinforcement for the decision is sought in writing, we will find ineradicable equivocity in writing as well. Demonstrating this will be the task of an endgame: Derridean *différance* is not mentioned explicitly here, but it hovers confidently offstage. Plato can still make some good moves, but they will be met with broadly predictable replies, and the battle for a stable subject will inevitably be lost. Indeed, Lacoue-Labarthe, once he has linked the decision to this purpose (that is, the thwarting of equivocity), can equate the fulfillment *with* the decision and say that because the fulfillment never occurs, neither does the decision. We shall see this below as we play out the final moves.

First, though, it seems to me that Plato's "decision," here, occurs at (at least) two levels, which in Lacoue-Labarthe become conflated, but which under more scrutiny might be susceptible of different, separate treatment. At a first, simple level, the decision to exclude mimesis might be seen to be manifested, inevitably, wherever the mimetic event occurs. This might be called an *occurrent* level of the decision. The "occurrence," here, involves, minimally enough, a marking of the failure of the mimetic act to escape notice as such, and the raising of the question of the "copying" of the extant, and thus of the "real" and the "make-believe." But there is also a second level, one of *active decision,* shall we say, at which the further decision prompted by the occurrent decision is *made* (for example, when Socrates decides to exclude mimetic drama in favor of the "finest drama" that is the polity of the state).

At the second level, what has occurred at the first is developed as formalized exclusion. It may even be further formalized, as in *The Republic,* to serve a deeper purpose—say, that of ridding speech of its inherent equivocity. In this event, the decision would be considered effective if, at every deeper stratum of interrogation, it would be impossible for either speaker or listener to postulate more than one "who" behind a speaking voice. But the status of this further formalization could quite reasonably be practical rather than theoretical, for, given that the first-level decision cannot but occur whenever (re)presentation occurs, it is futile to expect a second-level decision to theorize it out of existence; it is better to choose one mimetic version over another (as Socrates' comment on the *Laws* appears to accept).

Does Plato recognize this? In terms of Lacoue-Labarthe's description, he does not. Consequently, there is need for the demonstration that he pursues to its conclusion. Of this we can now say the following, given the terms of the discussion set forth above: if it was ever Plato's intention, in the course of the second-level dismissal, to offer a further *theoretical decision* against mimesis (and in favor of subjectivity), I think that Lacoue-Labarthe demonstrates that Plato is unsuccessful. This does not mean, however, that Plato does not succeed in elaborating a "practical protection" of subjectivity, in terms of decisions at the first and second levels. I am suggesting that decision in itself—decision *for* a "who," as the one who attaches to his or her works, regardless of whether there is such a one—may be more significant than Lacoue-Labarthe credits in Plato's understanding of subjectivity.

Lacoue-Labarthe's Plato does in fact come to glimpse that the mimetic problem cannot be easily contained. Lacoue-Labarthe's exposition of this point is intricate, but I will attempt to do him justice. He suggests that, through Plato's writing of Socrates' script, his voice comes inevitably to underlie Socrates' pronouncements so that Socrates does ultimately become a mimetician. Thus

> in reality Plato—and this is the height of the paradox—does not speak one word of the *philosophical discourse itself*. . . . But in the *text* it is Socrates, "his" *mimos*, the mimetic part of "himself" who speaks philosophically.[26]

So the decision that would protect subjectivity is now referred to another decision. The philosopher "Socrates," *as* a figure—a speaking "figure"—now reflects an external will, a will behind its speaking. Because that external will is not represented directly in the dialogue but can be seen only (as it were) in reflection, the entire event of the oral expulsion of mimesis is confirmed as being itself mimetic. Mimesis is now—implicitly, incipiently—reflection, and the very decision to expel mimesis is itself mimetic, and therefore itself a reflection. The figure of the mirror, to be used in Book X of *The Republic*, is, Lacoue-Labarthe suggests, already embryonically here in Book III, in the failed attempt to dismiss mimesis orally:

This operation already has a mirror, a theoretical trap—a "thaumatic" machine in it. An extra one. And because of this everything is lost and swallowed in an abyss.[27]

What this swallowing means for Lacoue-Labarthe is the postponement of the antimimetic decision. I again suggest, however, as an alternative, that what happens here, and later, is that the decision becomes deprived of any *grounds* it might have been thought to have but remains a *decision,* capable of structurally engendering subjectivity.

Both views are supported, I think, by Lacoue-Labarthe's analysis of Book X of *The Republic.* Here, the second dismissal of mimesis frankly interprets mimesis as "mirroring"—a "specular" or visual interpretation this time. What could not establish itself orally (in the first dismissal), mimesis as accomplishing its own expulsion, has nevertheless been "trapped for view," in a special way, in the mirror that is writing—specifically, here, Plato's writing.

To explain how the mirror that is mimesis can trap its own reflection, Lacoue-Labarthe identifies the mimetic representation of mimesis as a *mise-en-abyme*—an artistic production the matter of which comprises infinite self-reference. The term derives from André Gide's popularization of a notion found in heraldry, where a shield may have inscribed upon it a figure representing itself. As Barbara Johnson explains, the term *en abyme* is

> now used whenever some part of a whole can be seen as a representation of that whole, often ad infinitum, as in the Quaker oats box on which a man holds up a Quaker Oats box on which a man, etc.[28]

So, by placing itself *en abyme,* writing *can* succeed in depicting itself as it is. That is, it evidences that what it *appears* to do is what it *genuinely* does: re-present a "real" subject. Specifically, "Plato"—the writing subject—is guaranteed *as* subject by his Socratic texts. The author of written texts is reflected in those texts, but reflected as one who is genuinely "outside" the text, who is real, himself or herself, and beyond the reach of the equivocity that bedevils oral speech.

Or so Plato—Lacoue-Labarthe's Plato—hopes. Here, however, as I have said, Lacoue-Labarthe has set Plato up for a fall. The fall comes through a demonstration of the delay, the distortion of what was never original, by which the identity of an "author" is created within a text. What the textual mirror "freezes" as reflection, yielding a subject, is always frozen, as it were, "as having already taken place." "A 'subject' never *coincides* with *itself,*" says Lacoue-Labarthe, referring to the way in which writing, as a general procedure, always "hollows out" what it appears to "install."[29] And this means, ultimately, that writing "does not infinitely reflect itself (place itself *en abyme*)."[30] Most important, in regard to my point here, it means, for Lacoue-Labarthe, that "*the decision* (regarding mimesis) never takes place."[31]

As I have suggested, however, if we distinguish between the mimetic decision and its ostensible theoretical purpose, an opposite conclusion can be entertained, namely, that the decision regarding mimesis, and its expulsion, must be said *always* to take place! In a minimal way, this has already become evident above, in the sense that the decision contrasting the subject with what is "external to the subject" is seen always to occur, as a sine qua non of experience.

I am plainly drawing here upon the formal intentionality of representational experience. Though this is not the final or most significant dimension of experience as such, it is one that always corresponds to a return of the subject, concurrent with every manifestation of its loss. This return is persistent: in later chapters, I shall show that even when the subject thus delivered is deconstructed, avatars of this return persist, if only to be subverted themselves. Where does the story end? The final and most interesting question raised by my argument is whether subjectivity itself finds identity guaranteed by its own subversion, as a "structure of loss."

That exploration, however, will come later. For the present, insofar as it is *decision* that is in question here, a subject of decision is always at hand. The actor slipping in and out of roles, the writer distinguishing herself from the "persona" of herself that her writing creates, any person having a conscious experience—all these find themselves within a representational structure that separates the "I" (or "me") that is "having" an experience from the experience that is being "had," including an experience of "performance" or "mimesis." It is simply necessary to point out that "subjectivity," in this sense, as a structural necessity of formally representational experience, survives the thrust of this final gesture of Lacoue-Labarthe's argument.

Observations such as this one admittedly pertain to representationally mediated "experience," or at least to experience as it becomes cast representationally, whatever its prior dimensions. Understood thus, experience can be expected *formally* to manifest the subject, if not as presence then as lack of presence. The experience that Lacoue-Labarthe will "interrogate" (to use a term of Heideg-ger's that Jean-Luc Nancy finds congenial) will be interrogated under this description.

This is far from ignoring the point of distinction that has informed Western philosophy since Heidegger: that experience is *Erfahrung* (that is, *prephenomenological,* corresponding to a preintentional mental state, unconscious to the self-object distinction) before it is *Erlebnis* (*phenomenological,* framed in intentionality, mental representation, and consciousness of the self-object distinction). The entire thought in *Being and Time* turns on this distinction, and on a concomitant charac-terization of human being as *Dasein. Dasein* is structured in and through a *preontological* understanding of Being, and only derivatively from this as subject of an *ontological* understanding of Being.[32] So *Er-fahrung* is certainly primary, and Hubert Dreyfus can say that

> Heidegger holds that *experience* (*Erfahrung*) discloses the world and discovers entities in it—and yet this does not entail the tra-ditional conclusion that human beings relate to objects by means of their *experiences* (*Erlebnisse*), that is, by way of mental states.[33]

Nevertheless, *Erlebnis* cannot be ignored and is to be had in any event of communication or conceptualization. Certainly, its constit-uent representational states are the means of *access* to naming, re-flecting, or writing about experience as *Erfahrung.* This is confirmed by, for example, every *textual-conceptual* presentation of Heidegger's own thoughts.[34] The subject returns here, but Heidegger seems un-concerned by this: we shall see Lacoue-Labarthe suggest that he re-frains from probing, *as event,* the place where subjectal loss is *effectively,* if paradoxically, mediated: writing. For example, in dealing with Nietzsche, Heidegger treats Nietzsche's *thought* as a metaphysi-cal subject; he avoids consideration of the *Nietzsche who writes,* and who is a subject-in-loss of this writing.[35]

For Lacoue-Labarthe, it is in such events that the subject can be seen to become lost in the very act of its multiple or oscillating return. And this, broadly speaking, is how experience engages Lacoue-Labarthe's interest: *as* Erfahrung, *which, when one comes to think, speak, or write of it, becomes inescapably cast as* Erlebnis, *and is thereby "undone," together with its "subject."*[36] This also raises the question of fictioning, that is, of what status might be accorded the passage to *Erlebnis,* or, obversely, of "what" *Erfahrung* might be before it is given name and form.[37] In any case, Lacoue-Labarthe tracks *Erfahrung,* "found" as its "other," within that which both forms and deforms it: writing, beset from within by a power of loss through which its subject deteriorates irremediably. The main portion of my argument follows Lacoue-Labarthe through a series of readings in which this loss is exhibited. For the present I simply recall, *against* Lacoue-Labarthe here, but ultimately in his favor, the structure of intentionality that can *formally* be invoked as "protecting" subjectivity within a mimetic event. The recognition of this structure will serve to promote a later and greater victory for subjectal loss, on Lacoue-Labarthe's own terms.

In sum, then, for the present: Lacoue-Labarthe's exposition of Plato can be taken as a demonstration of how a structure of subjectivity reiterates itself, at least "occurrently," even when the further theoretical moves that bid to establish it—say, those that credit it with the eradication of equivocity in speech and writing—remain unmet.

Later, I will have constant occasion to note various ramifications of the "occurrent decision" concerning mimesis. This will happen when Lacoue-Labarthe himself repeatedly treats of the *return* of the subject that accompanies what Derrida calls, speaking of Lacoue-Labarthe's emphasis,

> the stubborn permanence in the thoughts [of Heideggerian *Destruktion* and Nietzschean "demolition" alike] of a still Platonic *apprehension* of mimesis . . . an onto-mimetology.[38]

It is Lacoue-Labarthe's intention to demonstrate the subjectal loss that haunts this "onto-mimetology," which is also ontotypology—a logic by which Being, or the subject, is cast as a figure of "itself" and thus lost *as* itself.[39] Yet, as I have said, this loss *also* provides entry to the possibility of a subjectivity determined *otherwise* than as this loss because it has particular relation to the *mode* of the loss. It is that thought to which I will eventually return, after establishing that Lacoue-Labarthian mimetic return and subjectal loss are demonstrated through one particular, recurrent mode: hyperbology.

In the final part of this chapter, I wish, by turning to René Girard, to reinforce the question of a "mark of subjectivity" that might accompany the decision attending mimetic expulsion.

Mimetic Desire as Original Doubling: René Girard

Something of a description of a pretextual anthropological subjectivity is found in the thesis on mimetic desire that Girard has developed over several years and books—most relevantly to my purpose here, in the collection *"To double business bound."*[40] Basic to his argument is the empirical claim that desire has a mimetic structure: an individual desires an object, not for itself, but because another desires it. This competitive doubling of desire, with the corresponding character of the mimetic event as an attempt to *appropriate* the mimed object, is an element—is in fact *the* element—of mimesis that structures primitive worlds, and no less Plato's or ours. It lends societies a character—real and pretextual—of intrasocietal conflict, resolved only through a mechanism of unanimous victimhood that Girard finds written consistently, but necessarily clandestinely, into the myths of origin by which societies define themselves.

Thus, in the interview that concludes *"To double business bound,"* Girard says,

> At later stages in culture the function of ritual is taken over by literature, which reproduces the mystifications, but in certain instances—the great texts of Sophocles, Euripides, Shakespeare and the Bible—lifts the veil enough for you to glimpse the historical truth that lies at the origin.[41]

What interests me here is the impact that Girard's thesis of mimetic rivalry at the origin, producing what we might call a "pretextual substantiality" upon which texts are held subsequently to work, has on Lacoue-Labarthe's notion of the subject.[42] This interests Lacoue-Labarthe also: in "Typography," treating the arguments both in Girard's *Violence and the Sacred* and in his *"To double business bound,"* he takes issue with Girard's own account of Plato's failure to dismiss mimesis from the State.[43]

For Girard, the failure corresponds to Plato's unconscious representation, through his Socratic double, of his own mimetic rivalry with Homer—a rivalry for the myths of origin of the State. Plato's attempt at expulsion is itself a double of the tragedy that it accuses of being incapable of expelling desire as doubled; thus it itself (Lacoue-Labarthe here quotes Girard) "functions at a certain level, as an attempt at expulsion, perpetually renewed because it never reaches completion."[44] For Lacoue-Labarthe, however, this is not Plato's blind spot: Plato, aware of this rivalry, is also aware that there is no other course. Mimesis inevitably attempts to dismiss mimesis through a mimetic act infinitely repeated but perhaps, as we have already seen, finally demonstrating mimesis *as* mimesis by placing it *en abyme.*

Girard's reply is that his problem with Plato's method is more fundamental still than the question of Plato's realization or nonrealization of his doubling of Socrates. The problem lies with the undismissable nature of mimesis itself, which is a drive to doubling, occasioned by rivalry, that operates prior to and independently of its objects. In "Delirium as System," Girard had already said that

> desiring mimesis precedes the appearance of its object and survives, as we shall see, the disappearance of every object . . . [though the object] always comes to the foreground and mimesis is hidden behind it, even in the eyes of the desiring subjects. The convergence of desire defines the object.[45]

In short, mimesis is undismissable because it is itself structurally prerepresentational, and because it therefore makes no difference whether Plato's rivalry operates consciously or unconsciously. Girard counters Lacoue-Labarthe's quest for a decision, referring instead to a "mechanism" of mimetic return. I have preferred to retain Lacoue-Labarthe's terminology while distinguishing between the types of decision—"occurrent" and "theoretical"—that mimesis involves.

It is nevertheless important that Girard's mechanism is declaredly distinct from any philosophical act that would establish the meaning of mimesis (and hence of subjectivity). What can be taken from Girard is the insight that a mimetic "mechanism" occurs, one that in the end protects what I have been calling a "structure of subjectivity," in contradistinction to a self-identical philosophical subject. Again, denying Lacoue-Labarthe's contention that his "unanimous victim" hypothesis itself establishes an absolute through a philosophical *decision*, Girard says:

> All [my generative hypothesis] says is that, if mimesis is undecidable and worse than undecidable, there must be a mechanism of self-regulation somewhere and it must be mimetic, too. Through that mechanism, cultural forms can appear and stabilize to such an extent that philosophers can make mimesis safe for philosophy. The cultural stabilizations are not absolute but relative, of course, not universal but local; they are destined to last not forever, but for a time only, for the historical duration of specific institutions.[46]

Clearly, the question arises here of the nature of the "mechanism" that provides mimesis with self-regulation, and of how this mechanism escapes assimilation to philosophy. This is a question that Lacoue-Labarthe will continue to ask as he probes the totalization apparently marking other accounts of the mimetic event, such as those of Aristotle, Diderot, and Freud, among others.[47] Nevertheless, what Girard says here adds impetus to the point made earlier as we followed Lacoue-Labarthe's tracking of Plato: there appears to be a level at which Lacoue-Labarthe takes less than full account of the power of an always occurrent mimetic decision to deliver a subject.

Conclusion

It has not been my intent here to offer Girard's thesis unreservedly as a sustainable solution to the problematic aspects of Lacoue-Labarthe's perpetually delayed subject. That thesis takes its point of departure from claims for "real" extratextual truths that are regarded by Girard as directly confronting poststructuralist notions of textuality, truths regarding the generation of societies from an originary but now invisible conflictual mimesis. Lacoue-Labarthe will show, through various explorations of the link between philosophy and literature, that this subjectal return doubles and paralyzes itself. He will attest that, ultimately, the subject itself becomes not found but lost. I will argue that the variety of his demonstrations of the loss impute it to a mechanism that he sometimes names explicitly, and, at other times, allows only implicit scope: hyperbology. Hyperbological subjectal loss *is* marked in the realm of representation by the recurrent decision "for" the subject, but the subjectivity apparently engendered on this score might well—if both loss and return are to be taken seriously—be sought in another realm, that of *presentation*.

For the present, we can return to the closing thoughts in "Typography," with a sense of the persuasiveness, but also the incompleteness, attending Lacoue-Labarthe's prediction that mimesis, as pure production, will one day regain its power over subjectivity, producing personas at will, or that we shall see a release of "the very terrorizing instability that the mirror was supposed to freeze"; and, to reach Lacoue-Labarthe's terminus, "this would mean that mimesis leads to madness, and that madness is a matter of mimesis."[48]

I have suggested that such dire predictions go astray because they do not recognize what I have called, in a preliminary way, a distinction between "occurrent" and "theoretical" levels at which decisions may take place as "securers of subjectivity." More work remains to be done to unsettle "decision," at least as it appears at the occurrent level. In fact, such work *will* be done presently, and we shall see sub-jectal loss reassert itself more potently. But subjectal return, for the moment, matches subjectal loss in its appeal as an exploratory focus. Lacoue-Labarthe's exposition of Plato, penetrating though it is, leaves us wondering not so much when mimesis will come utterly to destabilize subjectivity as how subjectivity is to be characterized so as to account for its perpetual, and structural, regeneration in the teeth of endless mimetic movement.

3

Describing the Subject of Paradoxes and Echoes

Introduction: Subjectal Withdrawal as *Désistance*

I am now left with dual, and to some extent divergent, possibilities for advancing my exploration of Lacoue-Labarthe. On the one hand, it seems that "despite all," some account of "resurgent" structural subjectivity might be extracted from Lacoue-Labarthe's texts on subjectal loss, and perhaps it is worth exploring this theme of return. On the other hand, the qualifier "despite all" indicates that pursuit of this claim should perhaps take second place to my main task, which consists of eliciting, in Lacoue-Labarthe's own terms, the content, intricacy, and reach of his treatment of the interface between representation and subjectivity. And, in fact, I formally take this second course, saving confrontational engagement for later.

Nevertheless, as I have said, the opportunities for reading with and against Lacoue-Labarthe arise side by side. It soon emerges that an awareness of the possibility of "occurrent decision" for subjectivity in Lacoue-Labarthe can help open an interpretive context for conscious self-protective subjectal withdrawal within an overall account of subjectal *désistance*. This course, for some further distance, will thus keep generalized description and critique together, and the reader is therefore welcome to regard this chapter under either of those two rubrics.

I now take two further pieces from the collection *Typography*: "Diderot: Paradox and Mimesis,"[1] and "The Echo of the Subject."[2]

These essays offer themselves by dint of their comparable manner of searching for the subject, a similarity allied to an intriguing distance between them as regards the material that is probed. Their points of engagement prompt the particular questions I will be asking. Both continue the characterization, found in the essay "Typography," of the subject as a someone or something "in withdrawal"; both elaborate this loss in terms of a subjectal engulfing that is inevitable, and that is determinable as *désistance.*

The word *désistance,* of course, deserves explanatory attention. As already mentioned, it is not originally Lacoue-Labarthe's term. Jacques Derrida coined it to describe the Lacoue-Labarthian subject and chose it as the title for his introductory essay to Lacoue-Labarthe's collection titled *Typography.*[3] A neologism, *désistance* is designed to provide an English equivalent for Lacoue-Labarthe's *désistement,* itself meaning withdrawal or standing down.[4] Simply to use the English "desistance" would be problematic, Derrida argues: desistance involves the notion of ceasing or temporal interruption, which *désistement* does not connote.

How best to describe the way in which a Lacoue-Labarthian subject "desists" or "stands down" within an experience or its text? Derrida offers another somewhat intricate argument, which can be simplified as follows. To translate *désistement* as "desistance" would assimilate to *désistement* the *active* voice in which "desistance" is commonly employed, since to desist is to *withdraw oneself* from an action in which one is engaged. This active voice does accord, however, with the common French usage of *désistement,* which denotes the withdrawal or standing down of a person from a political position, a lawsuit, and so on, and which employs the reflexive construction *se désister.* But Lacoue-Labarthe's use of *désistement* differs from this usage, referring additionally to a withdrawal *of* the subject effected by something outside itself or even to a withdrawal of the subject *before* it has "come into" itself. His is not a *désistement* assimilable to either *désister* or "desistance"; Derrida says that it marks "a departure from the French idiom, so that the word can barely be translated in French."[5]

So Derrida suggests the word *désistance,* intended to incorporate the active voice of "desistance" while preserving the passivity of Lacoue-Labarthian *désistement.* Derrida is obviously implying, short of explicit declaration, that *désistance* would better suit Lacoue-Labarthe's purposes in French as well as in English. A final worry with regard to using *désistance* is that its "repatriation" into French might undermine its "active" dimension, since it loses as a reflexive counterpart *se désister,* that verbal form retaining its juridical association. But this connotation of passivity can and ought to be resisted. As Derrida says,

> if the "desistance" of the subject does not first signify a "*self-desistance,*" we should not come to some conclusion thereby about the passivity of this subject. Or about its activity. *Désistance* is better to mark the middle voice.[6]

In sum, then, a subject in *désistance* is one that is in withdrawal, in the sense either of withdrawing itself or of *being withdrawn*—or, better still, in the sense of remaining nicely balanced between these alternatives.

With due regard for this situation, Derrida refuses to allow the simple retranscription of *désistance* itself as "desistance." His refusal, however, does not prevent the English translators of Lacoue-Labarthe's text from using "desistance" to translate *désistement,* but with the sense of *désistance* kept in mind. Lacoue-Labarthe has given a broad indication that he accepts the point involved in transcribing *désistement* as *désistance.*[7] He makes no comment on the use of the English word "desistance." My own usage here, the point of which will become more evident below, respects Derrida's observations. I use *désistance,* untranslated, wherever Derrida uses it. I also use it to translate Lacoue-Labarthe's *désistement* wherever that word refers to the "balanced voice" withdrawal, neither clearly active nor passive, of which Derrida speaks. Here, as in the case of *différance,* I think there need be no hesitation in retaining the French word where no English equivalent will suffice.

On other occasions, however, I will wish to refer specifically, and virtually exclusively, to subjectal withdrawal in terms of an *active* voice. Sometimes this will be in connection with a connotation that I consider *désistement* to take in a particular Lacoue-Labarthian passage. At other times it will be in connection with a sense that *désistement* does not refuse, and that I wish to highlight. At still other times, I will want to refer independently to a version of the withdrawal that the subject undertakes of its "own volition." As can be seen, and as will become clearer below, it is natural to reserve the English word "desistance" for use on these occasions. Naturally, too, I am cognizant of Derrida's reservations regarding the limited referential capacity of English "desistance." Where I refer to "subjectal withdrawal," I mean to refuse neither the sense of withdrawal *by* the subject of itself nor the sense of withdrawal *of* the subject *from* itself. This latter is the withdrawing of the subject as if by an external agency, and especially before the subject has come into "self-possession." These distinctions will become clearer as we proceed.

As we shall also see, none of these formulations is entirely free of paradox. Subjectal withdrawal, even described as *désistement,* is figured as *passive,* that is, as something that "happens to the subject" within a text written by another. Equally, the countervailing representation of the subject as *actively* withdrawn—that is, as desistant— becomes important to a final rendering of subjectal withdrawal as undecidable between active and passive. Thus juxtaposed, the two representations render effective the *désistance* of the subject, in Derrida's terms.

One further distinction needs to be made here. Desistance, as the subjectal *self*-withholding that is "half" of subjectal *désistance,* need not be either voluntary or conscious; it merely signifies the subject regarded as *agent* in respect of what it does. For this circumstance, I will simply use the term "desistance." A further descriptor is needed to signify the voluntary or conscious (that is, "self-conscious") self-withdrawal of the subject, with which much of this chapter will be concerned. For this circumstance, I will use the terms "formalized" or "voluntary" desistance.

My main interest will be in showing that formalized desistance "mirrors"—and renders undecidable—subjectal *désistance,* itself *effectively* an involuntary subjectal withdrawal that otherwise bids to become a subject.[8] Later in this book, I will ask whether the terminology associated with *désistance* does not bid too completely to identify this notion with Derridean *différance*—a move which, in spite of everything, the Lacoue-Labarthian text might be held to resist.[9]

How, exactly, does *désistance* capture for Derrida the connotations attending the "standing down" to which *désistement* refers? For Derrida, *désistance* refers to the withdrawal of the subject before the ineluctable, something that "has to happen." The ineluctable presents itself as one of two types of experience: first as something that presents the experiencing "I" with what might be called, to paraphrase Derrida, a "future me"; and then, as a free subject, I am, in the very present, separated from this "me," which already comes toward me, as it were, from a future place. I am early in relation to this me. The experience Derrida has in mind here is evidently that of *enunciation*:

> I, the one who says it, precede and anticipate in this way the advent of what happens to *me,* which comes upon me or to which I come.[10]

Alternatively, this inevitable future event might for that reason be experienced as having already happened, a future that is already behind me. I am met in the present by a "me" who has already arrived: "I'm late."[11]

As Derrida describes it, *désistance* — in either mode, or in both together — names the undecidability peculiar to subjectal withdrawal as explored by Lacoue-Labarthe in his attentions to oral and written mimesis.[12] Certainly, as the analysis in "Typography" goes, mimesis only apparently offers a subject that it has doubled. Lacoue-Labarthe's point is that closer scrutiny reveals this prior subject as itself priorly *désistant*. The writing/written or enunciating/enunciated subject "never *coincides* with *itself*."[13]

Written into the places where mimesis is occurring, this withdrawal of the subject is inevitable and structural. But it finds interesting parallels in the differently described subjectal withdrawals in the texts I shall now consider. In "Diderot: Paradox and Mimesis," Lacoue-Labarthe broaches the deliberate withdrawal of an acting "subject" of theatrical mimesis from his or her stage character. Withdrawal, here, occurs by way of detachment, by a deliberate disidentification of actor from character. How might this apparently mimed version of *désistance* itself highlight the essence of Lacoue-Labarthe's thinking on subjectivity? If the subject of mimesis is always in *désistance* "anyway," what is added by a further representation of the subject as *consciously and deliberately* desisting from a role?

"The Echo of the Subject" affords a comparable view of this extra level of detached self-theorization. Lacoue-Labarthe studies an autoanalyzing autobiographer "split" between the figures of artist and scientist. Here, he proposes the figure of *rhythm* as the essence of the mimetic movement that "echoes" the subject to itself in prespecular fashion. Separated from this rhythm, the incipient subject finds "itself" trapped in a no-man's land of *Unheimlichkeit* (uncanniness), unable to find the reassuring echo that would double and so differentiate it. Loss of rhythm presents as loss of the subject, "in which case, rhythm would also be the condition of possibility for the subject."[14]

In "The Echo of the Subject," then, we might take Lacoue-Labarthe as determining that where rhythm fails to "occur," mimesis fails to occur, and this failure corresponds in turn to a failure of the subject to appear. By contrast with "Typography" and "Diderot: Paradox and Mimesis," in "The Echo of the Subject" there seems to be neither a "structural withdrawal" (*désistance*) of the subject nor any deliberated withdrawal that might mimic it. Paradoxically, this appears to confirm the propensity for mimesis to produce the subject "falsely," as a double without a single—as withdrawn, or as an "as if." But what, if anything, is added when the actor or agent, by a specific act of will, "mimics" this withdrawal? I turn first to "Diderot" to establish this and like questions relating to the "desisting subject." To note similarities and differences in the way *désistance* is depicted in the two texts is to recognize a "breadth" attending this notion. It is also to notice that the distance between the depictions paradoxically reinforces their closeness.

The investigations already share the broad context—of mimesis or the mimetic—seen in "Typography," which has discussed Plato's construal of mimesis as the doubling of an original.[15] This doubling yields evidence of a "subject" of mimesis in both senses: that of the creating artist, and that of the art that is produced. In both cases, there arises the question of the ontological status of the original. In all three texts, Lacoue-Labarthe's reflections are offered in the context of the debate, dating from rival interpretations by Plato and Aristotle, about just how mimetic art ought to relate to "nature." Does mimesis distort the original that it represents, or does it complete the original?[16] Lacoue-Labarthe uses the terms "restricted mimesis" and "generalized mimesis" to describe the way in which the Platonic model, presuming distortion, finds itself included and superseded in the Aristotelian model, which presumes completion. But an internal division in the resultant theorization remains, as reflected in a persistent ambiguity with regard to the criteria for successful artistic representation of a subject.

This is particularly evident in theatrical or autobiographical mimesis, where the mimetic "raw material" is the artist himself or herself. Here, because a miming self is presented simultaneously with a mimed other, the fragility of the distinction between the "faithful rendition" and the "creative production" of a subject is foregrounded. In turn, this leads Lacoue-Labarthe to a typically more urgent question: Does the subject "itself" survive close examination of the mimetic event, whether theatrical or literary? The alternative, in line with Derrida's critique of presence, is the possibility of representation without prior presentation, a doubling without a single.[17] In these terms, representation effects the mere, but eternally stubborn, illusion of re-presentation.

With these orienting issues and observations in mind, I shall take these two texts in turn.

Miming Subjectal *Désistance*: "Diderot: Paradox and Mimesis"

"Diderot: Paradox and Mimesis" sees Lacoue-Labarthe approach the relationship between subjectivity and mimesis directly, through the question of paradox. The specific paradox at issue emerges in a dialogue between two actors from Diderot's *Paradoxe sur le comédien* ("The Paradox of Acting"), and it relates to mimetic production, to a "theory on the art of the actor that offends common sense."[18] The question of the elusiveness of the actor's subjectivity is allowed to achieve gradual but eventually sharp focus.

Opening with a two-pronged question—"Who or what is the *subject* of a paradox?" but also "Who [in this text attributed to Diderot] takes, or can take, the responsibility for saying: 'I am the subject of this statement, this paradox'"?[19]—Lacoue-Labarthe considers the mode in which the paradox at hand is delivered. This delivery happens to be itself mimetic. It occurs during a stroll taken by two characters playing parts assigned them by Diderot, with ourselves as audience. Toward the end of their dialogue, the First Speaker has propounded a paradox on the theory of acting, to which the second has objected, initially merely with short interpolations. Lacoue-Labarthe says that the Second Speaker does hardly more than "cue his partner." Finally, however, he issues a challenge, which Lacoue-Labarthe paraphrases thus:

> You have just developed at length a *theory* on the art of the actor which offends common sense, and to which, as you see, I cannot subscribe; let us move to the *theater* and see if we can verify it.[20]

At this point, the narrator re-enters Diderot's account. He says:

> Our two interlocutors went to the playhouse, but as there were no places to be had they turned off to the Tuileries. They walked for some time in silence. They seemed to have forgotten that they were together, and each talked to himself as if he were alone, the one out loud, the other so low that he could not be heard, only at intervals letting out words, isolated but distinct, from which it was easy to guess that he did not hold himself defeated.
>
> The ideas of the man with the paradox are the only ones of which I can give an account, and here they are, disconnected as they must be when one omits in a soliloquy the intermediate parts which serve to hang it together. He said: . . . .[21]

Upon what basis does the narrator say, "The ideas of the man with the paradox are the only ones of which I can give an account"? Lacoue-Labarthe is interested in arguing the strict undecidability between two possible answers. The narrator knows *only* the First Speaker's thoughts either because he *is* the First Speaker, or, alternatively, because he as an external narrator *overhears* this speaker. "Nothing, absolutely nothing, allows us to decide," says Lacoue-Labarthe.[22] While the first theory supports itself self-evidently, the second possibility is not excluded simply by the First Speaker's declared inability to give the thoughts of the Second Speaker, given that the latter has retreated into a barely broken sotto voce.

This undecidability becomes Lacoue-Labarthe's entrée into the question of the dual place adopted by the narrating subject (call him Diderot), not only in this segment but previously in the text. Lacoue-Labarthe can notice the places where the narrator has already intimated that the First Speaker is Diderot, by identifying himself as the author of *Père de Famille*, or referring to the "speculative principles" of his aesthetic, or recounting his being greeted by Sedaine with "Ah! Monsieur Diderot, you are splendid!"[23] If the narrator is Diderot, then he has been, alternatively, or even perhaps at once, both an external overhearer of the dialogue and a participant internal to the dialogue. In two ways, this ambiguity regarding the identity of the enunciator of ("Diderot's") "The Paradox" carries over into and frames the very enunciation of the paradox itself.

First, clearly both "The Paradox" and the paradox are in fact successfully enunciated, even when their enunciators as such cannot be located. Diderot's description of the episode in the Tuileries merely highlights, by bringing it to crisis, a displacement (or dual placement) of the narrator that has been operative throughout his text.

Second, there is enunciation of the paradox by the First Speaker. This speaker has become, or has always been, undecidably, both *a* Diderot "within" the text and *"the"* Diderot "outside" it, "looking in." Lacoue-Labarthe marks this by pointing it out even before broaching the paradox:

> Who states the paradox? Who is its guarantor? At the same time excluded and included, inside and outside; at the same time himself and the other (or each time, one must suppose, himself as an other—hence the dialogic constraint, even in the monologue).[24]

"Who states the paradox?" At this point, one recalls Lacoue-Labarthe speaking about mimeticians, on Plato's behalf: "It is because they do not assist or attend their productions . . . that poets 'lie' and 'show' themselves to be incapable of decision before the natural *equivocity* of discourse."[25]

It can easily be shown that, mutatis mutandis, there is in any text or episode of reported speech this dual positioning of the author both inside and outside the event. There is thus already "no subject" or "a dual subject" whenever *anything* is enunciated. What, though, does the enunciation of a paradox—specifically, the paradox of acting— add to this situation? One might say that the key question is not "Who enunciates the (or a) paradox?" Rather, given that, in the terms considered here, no *one* ever enunciates anything, how is it that the notion of enunciation of a *paradox* relates to that phenomenon? More specifically, how does enunciation of the paradox of *acting*, with *its* particular content, relate to it? A related question might be this: Given that an eternally displaced subject "is" doomed always to be a doubled figure of itself, what interpretation is to be placed on the "conscious" recognition of this undecidability?[26] What is most interesting is that Lacoue-Labarthe does not actually ask these questions, though they are somewhat relevant to his investigation. I will try to keep them in mind as I follow Lacoue-Labarthe.

What is also of interest here is the representation of a subject who, in the theater *or* in "real life," consciously "figures itself" to match its inevitable *désistance*. The representation resurrects the figure of a subject "possessing" consciousness and will. The question of its significance yields an investigative interest to match and shadow Lacoue-Labarthe's own as he proceeds to find, in the content of the paradox, a theorization of mimesis that reinforces Diderot's artistic device.

First, though, let us follow his analysis. His point of departure in addressing the paradox is Diderot's apparent attempt to render, deliberately, two identities ambiguous: that of the author of his own text, and that of the enunciator of the paradox delivered within the text. How to approach this studied ambiguity? One expects first of all that Lacoue-Labarthe will notice the invidious position of the enunciator, who, if he is sincere, can be speaking as "himself" only if he speaks as another: the detached mimetician recommended by the paradox.

Lacoue-Labarthe indeed makes this move, but within a further frame—a description of what paradox in general means for Diderot:

> The paradox is thus not only a contradicting or surprising opinion. . . . It implies a passing to the extreme, a sort of "maximiza-

tion," as is said in logic nowadays. . . . Paradox is defined by the infinite exchange, or the hyperbolic identity, of contraries.[27]

This logic is "abyssal," is also "unceasing, endless," and thereby "without resolution," and, in this connection, *hyperbological*—a notion to which I shall of course return in this work.[28] In its abyssality, the logic engulfs, "endlessly and irremediably," the subject who enunciates it. Locating this abyssality in Diderot, Lacoue-Labarthe will then seek to draw it out into greater visibility, and in its general implications.

This visibility coincides, however, with a discovery. Diderot's model of theatrical mimesis is ostensibly that of Aristotle: a "restricted" imitative mimesis, allied irretrievably to a general, "supplementing" mimesis. Nevertheless, it harks back to Plato, reinforcing the economy organized around true and false imitation—how, we shall see presently. For Lacoue-Labarthe, this return of mimesis "itself," in place of the very subject it is figured as denying and displacing, betokens another false, or ghostly, return of the subject. I suggest, though, that this discovery can be interpreted differently, the better to signify the place of "representational mirroring" of a "structured subject" in relation to subjectal *désistance*.

First, though, I track Lacoue-Labarthe's approach to the paradox itself, formulated thus by Diderot:

> In my view he [the actor] must have a great deal of judgment. He must have in himself an unmoved and disinterested onlooker. He must have, consequently, penetration and no sensibility, the art of imitating everything, or, which comes to the same thing, the same aptitude for every sort of character and part.[29]

By "sensibility" Diderot means, as we still do in some contexts today, the quality of or capacity for "feeling things keenly." More pejoratively, and with the nuance probably intended by Diderot here, the word "sensibility" connotes the quality of emotional susceptibility, an *inability not* to feel things keenly.[30] This paradox is paradoxical indeed to anyone who expects that the more an actor feels the emotions attaching to a part, the better he or she will be able to perform. What does it say to Lacoue-Labarthe?

As he sees it, the requirement that the actor have "no sensibility" is in service of a more fundamental requirement: "the absence of any *proper* quality in one who intends to take up (or proves suited for) representation and production."[31] This marks the mimetician as a "man without qualities," and mimesis as a *law of impropriety* (that is, a law asserting the absence of the proper in mimesis itself).[32] Diderot is thus aligned with the Plato of *The Republic,* who, as Lacoue-Labarthe puts it, knows that

> the mimeticians are the worst possible breed, because they are no one, pure mask or pure hypocrisy, and as such unassignable, unidentifiable, impossible to place in a determined class or to fix in a function that would be proper to them and would find its place in a just distribution of tasks.[33]

Unlike Plato, however, Diderot was not opposed to mimesis per se. As I have said, Lacoue-Labarthe takes his argument as initially conveying a meaning for mimesis that is consonant with Aristotle's thought about art. Aristotelian mimesis is seen here as claiming a poietic essence, one that is distinct from nature, and by means of which it substitutes for and perfects nature.[34] As Diderot's argument develops, however, Lacoue-Labarthe observes its evolution into a directly anti-Platonic account that is, in the end, Platonic. Lacoue-Labarthe suggests that this regression is, at one level, an inevitable destiny for Aristotelian mimesis.[35]

This he explains in Diderot as follows. Implicitly, Diderot sees art as requiring protection in terms of its *purity* as a productive force. But the notion of protecting purity is the obverse side of a *presumption* in respect of nature, namely, the existence of "pure" nature as that which must be guarded against the possibility of its misrepresentation. There is reversion here to the Platonic account of art (that is, to mimesis), which upholds pure nature, albeit in terms of a specific interpretation. Mimesis itself is now pure nature, "nature itself"— nature's energy of production unencumbered by material channeling and available for "pure production."[36] The "Aristotelian" Diderot is not so far from Plato.

In these terms, says Lacoue-Labarthe, the mimetic gift is one of *impropriety.* The effect it produces is proportional to its freedom from attachment to a *proper* form, especially, here, the form of the acting subject. This subject best houses pure productive mimetic energy by itself becoming nothing. So here we have the connection to paradox in general, as "that hyperbolical exchange between nothing and everything," for "the more the artist (the actor) *is* nothing, the more he can be everything."[37] In this way he will have, says Lacoue-Labarthe (again recalling Diderot, this time in paraphrase), an "equal aptitude for all sorts of characters."[38]

"The more the artist (the actor) is nothing, the more he can be everything." I pause here to consider the point that I raised at the outset. Lacoue-Labarthe is interested in the way in which Plato's concept of acting reinforces that of Diderot. It is notable, though, that he does not mark here the differing intents of these two authors. Plato offers a *description* of the mimetician as, one might say ipso facto, a *no one*. Diderot offers a *prescription* for good mimesis, by way of a recommended disposition for the actor. Lacoue-Labarthe's reticence on this point corresponds to a reluctance to distinguish between the actor under two descriptions: first, as an already withdrawn subject, and, second, as one capable of shedding his or her identity by consciously "becoming" a desistant subject.[39]

There is here, if Lacoue-Labarthe will but engage it, a question of the splitting of *désistance* itself, its redistribution between subject as empty topos of process, on the one hand, and subject as agent, on the other. Equivalently, there is the suggestion of a point of suspension, of hesitation, perhaps of caesura, between the subject who has never been present at the scene of mimesis and the subject who withdraws from that scene, perhaps in mimicry of the other withdrawal. Diderot, for example, "practices what his paradox preaches" by deliberately dissociating himself from this text in which "he" is a speaker. What does "will," and what does the decision to withdraw, add here, where the "subject," willing and/or deciding, has always already withdrawn?

Again I mark this question as one to keep in view while moving on with Lacoue-Labarthe. By this point, he has assimilated mimesis in Diderot to Platonic nature as impropriety. He now reflects further on the way this assimilation is written into other elements, explicit or implicit, of Diderot's observations on acting. Mimetic art, which is obviously nothing like life, presents itself as offering the essence of whatever it depicts and, in this sense, as *more* real than life.[40] A good actor—Diderot mentions Clairon—works with great exertion to get as near as possible to a "model" of a part she is playing, but which is not "herself," and which she then withdraws from, to avoid becoming a "possessed" subject. If she does not withdraw, mimesis works through "her" as a subject. This is *passive* mimesis, says Lacoue-Labarthe. It is cathartic, in the best tradition of Aristotle, purgative of unwanted emotions. And this is also how it can take hold of the subjects in an audience. But mimesis, here, is not a pure productive force.

But there is also mimesis working at an empty and emptied place, through a nonsubject, a subject withdrawn from "itself." This is *active* mimesis:

> For inasmuch as it implies a subject absent from itself, without properties or qualities, a subjectless subject, a pure *no one*, mimesis is by definition (so long as one is not frightened by it in advance) *active*.[41]

Here, to conclude his argument, Lacoue-Labarthe returns to his original question, now unanswerable. He has anatomized the desirability, in Diderot's terms, of erasing the subject of mimesis. Meanwhile, he has discovered, in the mimetic delivery of Diderot's paradox, a Diderot "absent from himself." This discovery prompts a major question—about the possibility of being a self-alienated actor—but also a larger question about then having a vantage point from which to describe this situation coherently: "To have no character, to be no one—or everyone. Who can know this? And who, above all, can say it?"[42]

In the case of Diderot and the paradox ("The Paradox"), this latter question becomes specific and historical:

> Who, consequently, will have enunciated the paradox? . . . I do not believe, for example, that we can simply say: it is he, it is Diderot who states the paradox. . . . For something was compelling him too powerfully to renounce the subject.[43]

This leads to a more ambitious, general claim for the subjectal loss involved in mimetic production:

> But I would say that this subject that refuses or renounces itself—that risks, everything considered, this impossibility—has something to do with what we ourselves should give up calling the subject of thought, art, or literature.[44]

The subject, then, absents itself "from itself" during mimesis, thereby becoming unpossessable by the mimesis that transforms "it." It is this paradoxical hollowed figure that emerges from Lacoue-Labarthe's excursion into Diderot's paradox.

I now turn an inquiring eye toward this figure, in terms of the questions I raised earlier. Is self-absence possible of attainment, even by a good actor or mimetician? How might we further characterize the experience in which one becomes "nothing," or "no subject," while, say, performing an agonized Hamlet or writing a poem, letting mimesis as pure productive force work at the "site" that is the assemblage of one's faculties? Lacoue-Labarthe does not say. But let us dwell for a moment on this point, in the interest, again, of examining the subject, which in one light *suffers* withdrawal, as a producer of mimesis, but in another *deliberately* withdraws "into itself" to allow mimesis free play.

One possible version of the "self-absent" subject connoted here is an otherwise contentless idea or figure, a figure representing non-figurement. A mimetician would bear this detached figure in mind while acting, as a subject or self dissociated from himself or herself. The term "himself" or "herself," in this case, signifies the stage character with which the actor has totally identified.

In Diderot's terms, however, the self-absent subject is able to see and judge its own performance. So, inverting my previous suggestion, and keeping in mind Diderot's description of Clairon, we could interpret the stipulation for self-absence in the following way: the actor is to withdraw mentally from the "self" that is her character on stage, remaining as a detached or withdrawn subject. The "self" that is before the audience is then no subject but, as it were, a "hollow self," a site of pure mimetic action.

This of course raises a question—*the* question. *Who* delivers the words and actions of the stage character, if these come from a self that is not a subject? What is the philosophical status of that "hollowed out" self? In turn, this question always indicates a prior question concerning its own enunciator or author. We have seen that Lacoue-Labarthe proceeds from and returns to the way this "original" question becomes presented *en abyme* in Diderot's "The Paradox of Acting." "Who enunciates the paradox?" becomes a representation of "Who announces 'The Paradox'?"

All of this sharpens my original question concerning the distinction and/or interplay between the two types of desistant "subject" canvased here. The first now obtains as a "figure of will" who desists from his or her work but still becomes represented through it (examples: Diderot "himself"; Clairon). The second "subject" is a putative "prefigural" writing or performing subject, rendered as *anyway* in *désistement* (or *désistance*), or lost to itself within the mimetic event. This is the "I" that is, as Lacoue-Labarthe says, always "fleeing" during writing. It is equally fleeing during lived experience, which itself has the structure of writing.[45]

I continue to pursue here the first of these subjects. The figuring of subjectal withdrawal as deliberate or "volitional" becomes interesting when one observes, with Lacoue-Labarthe's help, the reach of the subjectal subversion corresponding to *désistement/désistance*. What collapses is the distinction between literature and philosophy and their respective subjects: the subject who, "on the one hand," writes or performs, and, "on the other," acts or thinks. To the extent that no act or thought can exist independently of the text that frames it, the refusal to appear of the subject of writing corresponds also to the nonarrival of the subject of philosophy.[46]

Literature (what is fictioned) and philosophy (what is "true") are bridged by this insight. The *désistance* of the subject who creates the "text" of his or her *stage* acts is related to the *désistance* of the subject who creates the "text" of his or her "real life" acts. The thrust of the deconstructive enterprise corresponding to *désistance* is the claim that the event of fictioning is the event of the withdrawal of the (presumed) "real" subject who is the agent of the fictioning. The subject present and detectable, but always as other to itself, always as figuring of something prior, is the subject of philosophy. This is the subject represented successively to and through philosophy as Cartesian cogito, Kantian transcendental Ego, Hegelian dialectical subject, and Freudian amalgam. The subject of literature can hardly be sought except as this subject, by way of the question "Who?" Likewise, the subject of philosophy cannot be presented except representationally—mimetically—and again it is literature as the medium of this representation that most interests Lacoue-Labarthe. Literature both makes and breaks philosophy, producing its subjects as writers and the written, but always as other than themselves.

Lacoue-Labarthe's early work repeatedly concerns itself with tracing in literature the places where the subject of philosophy—figure, type—works relentlessly to assert itself in the teeth of endless mimetic movement. There is figured and "approximated for view" a subject that, since it is "in *désistance*," is in fact unrepresentable. What the figuring and the approximation signify, and *how* they signify, is the question at hand. I have suggested that it is to this end that Lacoue-Labarthe's investigations can in some places be usefully shadowed in their own right and in other places taken beyond themselves. Thus "Diderot: Paradox and Mimesis" has offered the subject of mimesis as *no one*, but it has done this by way of discussing a subject that "productively" figures itself in detachment from its "producing self." For alternative and comparable versions of the subject, in both its figured and *désistant* aspects, I now turn to "The Echo of the Subject."

"The Echo of the Subject": (A)rhythm as *Désistance*

In "The Echo of the Subject," Lacoue-Labarthe offers a typically patient, single-minded, complex exploration, scrutinizing the return and loss of the subject in its incipient figuration as *rhythm*. "Rhythm," here, is not yet Hölderlinian rhythm, with an implicit capacity for exhibiting its own still heart, its caesura.[47] But it anticipates that later characterization; what attracts Lacoue-Labarthe in both cases is the possibility of the deconstruction of the subject of rhythm. His particular interest is in how this deconstruction proceeds from a recognition of mimesis as an irresistible figuring force, which nevertheless effects the withdrawal of the subject it figures. My own attention will be directed toward the figuration in the text of conscious or "voluntary" subjectal withdrawal, that is, toward voluntary subjectal desistance. I want to give this figuration a place in Lacoue-Labarthe's overall explication of subjectal withdrawal situated amidst subjectal return.

I first trace, as economically as possible, the course of Lacoue-Labarthe's reading, itself an absorbing example of his style. "The Echo of the Subject," about three times as long as the essay on Diderot, nevertheless also consists of several tantalizing surges by which Lacoue-Labarthe advances his quest, each wave receding to join forces with a new wave that swells more strongly to the shore. The quest originates in a question: "What connection is there between *autobiography* and *music*?" Or, more precisely and explicitly: "What is it that ties together autobiography, that is to say, the autobiographical compulsion [*Zwang*] (the need to tell, to confess, to write oneself), and music—the haunting by music or the musical obsession?"[48]

For an answer, Lacoue-Labarthe reads an autobiographical passage, "The Haunting Melody," the third and culminating part of a book of the same name by the psychoanalyst Theodor Reik.[49] Reik, upon hearing unexpectedly of the sudden death of a close senior colleague, Karl Abraham, finds himself humming a tune. He will later identify this recurrent music as the first bars of the chorale from the last movement of Gustav Mahler's Second Symphony. The haunting nature of the tune, the fact that it returns whenever Reik thinks of Abraham, moves Reik to commence a remarkable self-analysis, beginning on the day he heard the news, December 25, 1925, and continuing over the next twenty-seven years.

If Reik identifies some aspects of this musical compulsion, Lacoue-Labarthe identifies others, his motive being to frame Reik's own framing of his autobiographical discoveries. Lacoue-Labarthe observes wittily that "with a spontaneity . . . entirely induced by Freud" (to whose psychoanalytic school Abraham belongs), Reik's analysis is directed not at, say, discovering the link here between music and his own mourning, or mourning in general, but rather at "simply . . . seeking in the words of the chorale, in the text of Klopstock, the reason for the obsessional return of the melody."[50]

Lacoue-Labarthe tracks Reik's story as an autobiography of an autoanalysis. Reik's account gravitates toward an attempt to discover the connection between the music and his own unconscious. As Reik describes the autoanalysis, it goes through several failed attempts and missed clues. It finally succeeds when he makes the connection between Mahler's psychological state during his writing of the Second Symphony and his own psychological state upon hearing of Abraham's death. In each case, the death of a friend who is also a rival and critic has occurred, and the "unknown self" is celebrating its impending resurrection and freedom from a rival's adverse judgment.

At each point of Reik's story, the clues that he admits to missing, or that he is inhibited from investigating, become points to be gathered by Lacoue-Labarthe. They all relate to "style": Abraham's northern German accent, for instance, or Reik's self-conscious use of stylish "i" sounds at Abraham's funeral. In musical terms, what raises its head here is style as the musical: repetition as rhythm. Reik, says Lacoue-Labarthe, is unconsciously threatened by the notion of being influenced by music at this chaotic, presubjective level, and at each point where style or mood or musical rhythm becomes a plausible clue, he begins a new line of investigation. Lacoue-Labarthe moves carefully through what Freud and Reik both ignore, in terms of the possibility that music can resonate with the prefigured self.[51] Space precludes a recounting of that analysis here, but Lacoue-Labarthe's rationale in pursuing it is germane to my purposes.

Lacoue-Labarthe's interest in Reik's journey comes from his having noticed the way the story puts on joint display the phenomena of autobiographical compulsion and musical obsession. Lacoue-Labarthe gradually implicates autobiography in what eventuates as the most stubborn resistance to the deconstruction of the subject of philosophy. Despite the fact that the subject of writing is always un-decidable between the figures of the subject who is written and the subject who is writing, philosophy always tends to become autobiography and to install its authors as figures. Lacoue-Labarthe wryly remembers Nietzsche on this point, from *Beyond Good and Evil*: "Gradually it has become clear to me what every great philosophy so far has been: namely, the personal confession of its author."[52]

The link he discovers between the two compulsions or obsessions at issue is the following: all autobiography is the frustrated attempt of the writing subject to install itself. It is frustrated because autobiography always writes the myself who is not myself but a dead other, figured as "other" under mimesis. Unable to offer resolution of this frustration, the autobiographical act contains the interminable impetus toward renewal and repetition of itself. Turning Reik's account to his own purposes, Lacoue-Labarthe finds a correspondence between this repetition and the rhythm by which music figures the subject out of chaos."[53]

There are several points at which this argument canvases the subject's *désistance* in relation to autobiography. Here, I notice two such points that advance my discussion of Lacoue-Labarthe's treatment of Diderot. They touch on the relationship between the *désistant* subject and the figured subject, insofar as the latter exhibits various types of self-detachment.

Désistance *and "Desistance": A Description in Terms of Layers of Textuality*

First, Lacoue-Labarthe makes the following telling observation in discussing the proneness of Reik's autoanalytic approach to lose the subject it seeks. What is problematic is Reik's position, "*as subject of the theory of the subject* (or as *subject of psychoanalysis*)."[54] Clearly, "subject" here signifies undecidably. Reik, as subject, is inescapably caught between *producing* (as an artist) writing that can be theorized while also *theorizing* (as a scientist) from that which he writes. Correspondingly, the figures with which he identifies the patient (himself) in analysis come in pairs of opposites, and he is always at least two at once. Lacoue-Labarthe says:

> What Reik invites us to think, in other words, is that the subject "desists" ["*désiste*"] because it must always confront *at least* two figures (or one figure that is *at least* double), and that its only

chance of "grasping itself" lies in introducing itself and oscillating *between* figure and figure (between artist and scientist, between Mahler and Abraham, between Freud and Freud).[55]

Here, "between Freud and Freud" means "between Freud the scientist and Freud the artist." As Lacoue-Labarthe notes, Reik holds Freud to be

a "great writer," comparable to the greatest (Sophocles, Shakespeare, etc.), of whom Freud himself was jealous even as he recognized his debts.[56]

My interest lies in noting the two types of subjects, and in relating them to the splitting that occurs in Diderot's self-detached actor. Here again we have an artist, split between a mimetic producer and an onlooker coolly assessing the production. The reader will recall that, in our reading of Lacoue-Labarthe's account, Diderot's insensible actor volitionally withdraws from the site of the mimetic enactment, becoming at that site "a" *no one* and in this way replaceable there by the stage character she is portraying, a character effected through unfettered mimetic production.

However, there may be nothing, including volition, outside the text. Subjectal withdrawal can be traced through a number of overlapping "shells" here, each corresponding to a text and its author. The enumeration of these is an intricate but, I think, interesting and fruitful exercise.

To begin with, there is Diderot's text interpreting the mimetic event, which includes the voluntary self-withdrawal of the artist that is its desideratum. Within this text, an actor, Clairon, is described as *consciously* exemplary of such a withdrawal. That is, she figures—as writer *and* reader—in a second text, one that tells her of her self-devised withdrawal from her theatrical production. But as the theatrical production itself can be taken as a (third) "text" produced by Clairon, the second text is no less than the account of her voluntary abdication, her abdication as "Clairon" from the site of production of this third text, even while she is engaged in the writing of it. The account of voluntary abdication corresponds to the writing of the new (second) text, in which the abdication can be read, even by the abdicator (or the "abdicator").

Let us relate this to what I have already said regarding the relationship between the *désistant* subject and what we have called its "figured" counterpart. The question can be refined, once it is noticed that the subject of *désistance* is itself a figure (that is, a figure of "withdrawal"). So we are in fact discussing a distinction between this figuring and the different figuring—the formalized figuring of desistance—that attends the "deliberate" detachment of a subject from its productions. In terms of what I have said, any production is, in the first instance, the writing of a "third text," the writing subject of which "desists" as a structural matter of course, as never coinciding with itself. One element of this structural desistance is a split— between writer and theorizer of writing—corresponding to what might be called an "incipient second text" in which this split awaits theorization in a "second text proper." This second text either figures the split as such or expresses it in a "parallel" description that emphasizes, say, the "voluntary" or deliberate desistance of writer (as reader, as judge) from her "self" as author.

In this light, the comparison between the actor Clairon in "Diderot: Paradox and Mimesis" and the psychoanalyst Reik in "The Echo of the Subject" provides a display of alternative types of "second texts." Both of these identify the splitting or withdrawal of the writing (acting) subject. But there is between them at least one seemingly significant difference. Clairon ("Clairon") has, as it were, paralleled "her" own desistance, in a second text that is both written and read by her. By contrast, the splitting of the subject "Reik" as artist or scientist is evidenced or formally figured in a "second text" written not by himself but by another, and likewise read not by himself but by others. The psychoanalyst Reik is *"subject of the theory of the subject,"* as a subject simultaneously producing both itself *and* a theory of itself—and this is emphatically so in the case of *self-analysis.* But he remains without any self-awareness in this regard. Clairon, in one sense, is also in this position. Even as the "detached" subject that "reads" its own work from a critical distance, she cannot but have been working from a base of implicit self-theorization. And, of course, a further "detached self" that could notice this theorization would be unaware of its own prior self-theorization, and so on.

In this last sense, the *désistance* of the subject split between action and theorization is endless, and perhaps susceptible to representation only *en abyme,* as we have already seen Lacoue-Labarthe observe.[57] What is depicted *en abyme* is the infinite deferral of the identity of what is withdrawn. The subject is, in its very subjectivity, "revealed" as a withdrawn subject, itself in turn revealed as a withdrawn subject, and so on. The connection between this *désistance* and voluntary subjectal withdrawal (within the overall textual event in which both become manifest) might be drawn as follows: the narrated "voluntary" withdrawal of a subject from its mimetic performances mimics, by way of formal textual figuration, the *désistance* that is a structural part of *any* textual representation. In other words, what is represented here is a volitionally cast writing and subsequent reading, "by" the subject, of its own "nonvolitional" detachment from the mimetic site.

The two events of detachment mirror each other, as it were. But in terms of being determinative of subjectal withdrawal, they are in fact alternatives, and one must be allocated priority if the determination is to be made. As I have described things above, the nonvolitional "descriptive shell" is prior, but a little thought reveals that the opposite situation is also plausible. Inter alia, this opens the possibility of theorizing the withdrawal of the subject at a new level, that is, *in terms of the undecidability between volitional and nonvolitional withdrawal of the subject.* To concretize this observation in terms of the text at hand, which "Clairon" writes the text in which she is a detached spectator of her stage character? The "spectator-Clairon"? Or another "Clairon" that is fleeing this identity and writing as it flees? And, again, is not the authority of *this* representation itself relativized by the desistance of its author ("me"), and so on? Thoughts such as this are behind my previous suggestion that undecidable withdrawal may signal itself only *en abyme*.

This possibility yields an interesting conclusion with regard to the main question guiding my reading of Lacoue-Labarthe in this chapter: What is the specific value of voluntary and formalized subjectal withdrawal, where this "echoes" the involuntary and nonformalized withdrawal connoted by *désistance*? The answer allows me also to nuance, as follows, the conclusion from the previous chapter. It now appears that a formalized withdrawal that bids to protect the identity of the withdrawn subject "anyway," and that is analogous in this respect to the "occurrent decision" in the previous chapter, is no longer protected from undecidability. Abyssality reaches "backward" to engulf and undo the subject of this decision to withdraw, or to write the text in which he or she is a spectator. In this sense, Lacoue-Labarthe has been proved right—the decision never occurs.

What, then, has been achieved with regard to my overall task of characterizing both subjectal loss and subjectal return, and these both with and against Lacoue-Labarthe? The reader may be tempted to ask whether, given that Lacoue-Labarthe's conclusion in "Typography" has now been vindicated, the Hegelian-like *aufhebung* of the notion of subjectal return achieved here has rendered its previous stage (the analysis of the "occurrent decision" in the previous chapter) pointless. I think not, for the following simple reason. It is true, on one level, that "formalized *désistance*" or its analogue, the "occurrent decision," now becomes incorporated into a wider schema—*désistance* as undecidability, or as "the decision that never occurs." On another level, however, this defeat of the concept of the "occurrent decision" has contributed to success in regard to the quest of which it is a part: the search for a meaning, in relation to *désistance*, for undeniably persistent structural subjectivity.

I return now to "The Echo of the Subject," and to the second point at which the interaction between *désistance* and its voluntary version (formalized desistance) is elicited. Lacoue-Labarthe moves toward locating the autobiographical and the rhythmic compulsions together. Jointly, they evoke the undecidable, fatally hesitant subject of mimesis, caught between categories I have already broached: self-consciousness and unself-consciousness, volition and nonvolition, authorship and readership.

Subjectal Withdrawal as (A)rhythmic Unheimlichkeit

The scene is found toward the conclusion of "The Echo of the Subject."[58] Lacoue-Labarthe turns to Reik's reading of a text in which Mahler has interpreted a segment of his Second Symphony. The music is that which has haunted Reik since his hearing of his colleague's death and motivated his autoanalytic search. Mahler's text and music, as Reik reads them, signify Mahler's psychological identification with his colleague and competitor von Buhlow, whose death is the precondition for Mahler's own freedom and "resurrection." Reik then moves on to discerning an equivalent "meaning" of Mahler's music in his own case, its evocation of a resurrection for Reik himself, through substitution of Reik's own identity for that of his dead colleague, Abraham.

Reik's intriguing pathway to self-analytic resolution stands in contrast to the significance that Lacoue-Labarthe finds in Mahler's text, and in Reik's employment of it. What attracts Lacoue-Labarthe is the splitting, the wandering of the subjects in the text—Mahler, Reik, the autobiographical subject itself. His investigation moves toward the moment in the text when repetition is marked as the *failure* of rhythm. Here, there occurs that nonreturn of the subject that is, paradoxically, the essenceless essence of mimesis.

I want to consider the components of this paradoxicality along the lines marked out above. Curiously, an *uncanny* balance again comes to the fore as the elements of Mahler's text, and Lacoue-Labarthe's treatment of Reik's treatment of these, come to be explored. The balance is between formalized (self-conscious) subjectal withdrawal and the uncharacterizable subjectal *désistance* for which I have suggested this formalized desistance "stands."

The text in question is the second of two program texts intended by Mahler to interpret his Second Symphony narratively but nonreductively.[59] In the symphony there occur two interludes between the first movement, which recounts the funeral ceremony of the dead hero, and the final, resurrectional, scene. Lacoue-Labarthe's attention is drawn to the second interlude, with its textual interpretation by Mahler and then Reik.[60] This interlude, meant to evoke the memory of happy times, begins with a remembered "image of an hour of happiness, long passed."[61] Mourning of a friend's death has been temporarily displaced by a pleasant memory: the past is brought forward to the present, and the dead person is alive. But when the daydreamer awakes, it is to a disorientation from (or of) the present. There is an incomprehensible bustle of surrounding life, which appears

> as ghastly as the moving of dancing figures in an illuminated dance hall into which you look from the dark night, from so far away you cannot hear the music. The turning and moving of the couples appears then to be senseless, as the rhythm clue is missing.[62]

Lacoue-Labarthe seizes upon the phrase "the rhythm clue is missing" as identifying the key element in this *unheimlich* (uncanny, especially in the Freudian sense) scene. He is condensed and complex in the exposition of these lines, and care must be taken to ascertain the point he is making.[63] Paraphrase is called for, as follows. If the dead past is returned to cotemporality with the "real time" of the present, then the present itself fails to remain present except as dislocated, consigned to uncanniness. Mahler's scene of awakening, of returning to life, corresponds to "a forgetting."[64] That is, the attempt to move from the life of (or as) a "dead other" to "present life" encounters a withdrawal of the always already dead subject.

This withdrawal is covered over only with a forgetting of the "past," which is also a forgetting of the "pastness" of the present. In short, present life is here confronted with its own "essence" as past, and with its refusal of this essence. Lacoue-Labarthe here recalls a parallel Freudian thesis: the impossibility of believing in one's own death.[65] In Mahler's description, the subject *in uncanny withdrawal of itself* is presented by music *en abyme*. Music, so to speak, captures its "own" lack of essence by exhibiting itself "minus" this withdrawn essence—that is, without rhythm, in an enactment that becomes *unheimlich*.[66]

For Lacoue-Labarthe, it is also in this way that obsession by music—the haunting, recurring tune—resonates with the autobiographical compulsion. The latter, as the attempt of a "self" to write itself, becomes instead the presentation of a self withdrawn from the self it has written. His argument to this effect I have mentioned earlier; for example,

> autobiography, the biography of the *dead* other, is always inscribed in an agon—a struggle to the death. . . . Every autobiography is in its essence the narrative of an *agony*, literally. This is why (among other reasons) it is not incorrect to substitute "thanatographical" for "biographical": all autobiography, in its monumental form, is *allothanatography*, if not *heterothanatography* (if the figure is never just one).[67]

The thought here can be paraphrased as follows. "I" am always already dead because everything I say and do I cannot but do as an other. I cannot return to life by recounting my life story, because the autobiographical act itself produces me as other in the past. It becomes a record pertaining to a dead other—an *allothanatography*. And yet and for this very reason the autobiographical act repeats itself compulsively and futilely in trying to resurrect "me." It does succeed in marking me as a figure, but only as (at least) *two* figures simultaneously: as writer and as written. Neither of these is me, and between them "I," as subject, slips away into irretrievable loss.

What, then, accounts for the continued (re)erection of the subject? Incessant mimesis, as repetition, repeats the Same, but always as both the Same and an Other. However, there is *rhythm*. Rhythm is repetition. Not being random, it has form, but prespecular form—*rhuthmos*. This form, Lacoue-Labarthe argues, gives the subject to itself, prespecularly, as an echo rather than a reflection. In this way, the subject—or presubject—resurrects itself "prespecularly." The notion here is of what we might call a preobjective presence, the subject as a semiformed "it" or "there," preliminary to its resurrection as a figure:

Rhythm manifests and reveals, gives form and figure to, makes perceptible, the *ethos*. . . . To this extent, then, it should perhaps be recognized that rhythm is not only a musical category. Nor, simply, is it the figure. Rather, it would be something between beat and figure that never fails to designate mysteriously the "ethical."[68]

Yet, in Mahler's account, it is in the *withdrawal* of rhythm that the connection between rhythm and the subject is revealed. Or this occurs in the disconnection between mimetic repetition and rhythm, a *disconnection* that speaks to Lacoue-Labarthe of a prior *unconnection*.[69] The reminiscer, suddenly awaking to the surrounding life, finds it uncanny, presented through dancing movements without form, or rather with form that is devoid of recognizability. As Mahler says, "The turning and moving of the couples appears then to be senseless, as the rhythm clue is missing."[70] For Lacoue-Labarthe, the withdrawal of rhythm means a paradoxical manifestation of mimetic repetition as itself. One can say, paraphrasing him again, that mimesis here "purely" expresses itself as the production of nothing rather than the repetition of anything previous. Or one can sharpen the paradox, distinguishing between repetition and its "content," by saying that here we have repetition without the impetus to rhythm — without a doubling that ties repetition to that *of which* it is the repetition:

> The absence of rhythm, in other words, is equivalent to the infinitely paradoxical appearance of *the mimetic itself*, the indifferentiable as such, the imperceptible par excellence.[71]

In other words, the withdrawal of rhythm corresponds to an absence of mimesis as *rhythmic repetition*. Paradoxically (and, granted, this statement is itself self-negating) this withdrawal allows mimesis to make an appearance precisely because it does not appear as such. In this uncanniness, then, the mimetic finally makes its (non)appearance as "itself."

I can now relate the above to my previous framework involving first, second, and third texts. Here, we have further textual theorization of "both" the *désistant* and the formally desistant subjects of mimesis. Let us retrace in some detail the part of Lacoue-Labarthe's analysis that feeds this insight. He skillfully proceeds to connect the immediately aforementioned episode of *Unheimlichkeit*, in Mahler's program, with what we might call the anatomy of the autobiographical compulsion. This anatomy is exposed as the attempt, endlessly renewed, to write a present self rather than a dead other. Its obverse side is that of the loss of that self, amidst "its" striving for self-gain.

The very writing necessary to preserve the self of experience has always already killed that self and relegated it to otherness. *Unheimlichkeit,* uncanniness, marks the distance between life and its constant encounter with the subject as a dead other, the product of writing as *allography,* or *allothanatography.*[72] The disoriented "awakening to life" by which the survivor returns from his happy reminiscence signifies just this. It corresponds, Lacoue-Labarthe reminds us, to a scene of *forgetting* about death. The survivor ceases to mourn vicariously for death (his friend's, but also his own) by reliving former joyful moments spent in the company of the "other" (read, the self).[73]

Here, however, undecidability strikes again. In terms of all that Lacoue-Labarthe has said previously, this awakening or forgetting is a going to sleep, an awakening from, a forgetting of, the "truth" of the subject—that is, its *delay* in relation to the figure that is "itself."[74] As an awakening, it is unsuccessful, or only half-successful, consigning the "real" world to incomprehensibility. In the absence of (an experience of) the rhythmic repetition by which figuration yields location in the living world, the "subject" is delivered into a twilight realm. There we find the *désistance* (or is it voluntary desistance?) of this subject, figured as the *absence* of meaning. Indeed, what is figured is the withdrawal of the distinctions that make for subjectivity itself. Lacoue-Labarthe says:

> Missing is the repetition from which the division might be made between the mimetic and the non-mimetic: a division between the recognizable and the non-recognizable, the familiar and the strange, the real and the fantastic, the sensible and the mad— life and fiction.[75]

What we have here is a figuration of the *désistance* of a subject cut off from the "echo" of itself:

> Without the beneficial doubling . . . , the immediate certitude of "primary narcissism," its confused, blind, ante-specular recognition is shaken.[76]

"In which case," Lacoue-Labarthe adds, "rhythm would also be the condition of possibility for the subject."[77]

Unheimlichkeit, here, corresponds to the "infinitely paradoxical appearance" of pure mimesis, or *the mimetic itself,* in the very failure of mimetic doubling to appear.[78] The withdrawal of the subject through this final uncanniness is less a withdrawal than a nonappearance or, more exactly, a nonecho. The subject has been relegated to an always prior dissolution, in a region where repetition utterly fails to appear as such.

Even here, however, there is a witness to the power of mimesis endlessly to resurrect itself. The nonappearance itself appears, being figured as a doubling of the desisting subject. Mahler's watcher, observing incomprehensible figures at a dance, is himself another representation of the uncanniness and exclusion they represent. The *désistant* subject then, as both site and victim of mimetic activity, is doomed always to arrive too early or too late to experience itself as such. It cannot but continue seeing or hearing "itself" in a figure (or two), celebrating "its" own disidentification, "its" own dispossession.

Let me put what has emerged here, in relation to my hitherto developed description, in terms of texts and layers of textuality. I have suggested that for Lacoue-Labarthe, in "Diderot: Paradox and Mimesis," Diderot's account of the actor's deliberated detachment from his or her dramatic part comprises a "second" text that mirrors or parallels the structural desistance of the subject in the innermost ("third") text. This third text narrates the *involuntary* experience of subjectal desistance in theatrical acting or, for that matter, in agency in "ordinary life." *Voluntary* detachment corresponds to a description of the second text as *both written by and read by the desisting subject "himself"* (or, in the case of Clairon, "herself"). By contrast, the split subject that is the psychoanalyst "Reik" in "The Echo of the Subject" is noticed as *désistant* in a "second text" that he has *neither written nor read himself*, the theorization of *désistement* or *désistance* being accomplished here by Lacouc-Labarthe's analysis so that we have "structural" *désistance* without a volitional counterpart.

What might be said here of the most recent of the texts discussed above: Mahler's program, and particularly the part of it that Lacoue-Labarthe has so carefully plumbed? "Mahler" writes "himself" into the second person; and then he writes this "You" into an uncanny distance from itself, at a moment of *unheimlich* self-awakening. By comparison with the situation described in previous examples, here the subject is found in a *truly intermediate position* with regard to the mode of its desisting. As subject, its "identity" is bound up neither with self-theorization nor with nontheorizability but rather with an (itself appropriately hazy and indeterminate) theorization of nontheorizability. Thus, between "Diderot," *voluntarily withdrawn* within his (miming) self and *aware* of this detachment, and "Reik," *involun-*

tarily withðrawn within his (autoanalyzing) self and *unaware* of this detachment, there should be room to describe the subject of *Unheimlichkeit,* the subject *involuntarily withðrawn* within his (awakening, forgetting) self, but in some wise *aware* of this detachment.

Conclusion: *Unheimlichkeit* as *Déʃiʃtance* Undecidably Represented

Precisely this conscious but involuntary withdrawal is signified in Mahler's text: here, the desisting of the subject indeed occurs within a "second text" that, while not written by the subject of desistance, is nevertheless readable, and read, by this subject. The subject, "awakening" from pleasant reminiscence about his friend, does not "choose" to find the reality to which he returns disjointed and capable of delivering neither a world nor himself as a part of that world. Rather, this dislocation is what "happens" to him when *pure mimeʃiʃ* "happens," as pure process, without a causal agent. It happens precisely in the *failure* of rhythm, and therefore of mimesis, to occur.

Nevertheless, this same "happenstance" delivers him as a subject self-aware of its desistance or detachment from the site of "its" existence. This detachment is from the coherent worlds that were generated in its (former) place, with itself as, inter alia, author-reader. The new figuring of desistance has, strictly speaking, *no* author. The putative author of Mahler's text, enclosed within it, is a subject that writes itself as present and then discovers itself as absent. Here, then, once again, is Mahler's description of this experience:

> When then the daydreamer awakens from his fantasy and returns to life, it may be that the unceasingly moving, never understandable bustle of life becomes as ghastly as the moving of dancing figures in an illuminated dance hall into which you look from the dark night, from so far away that you cannot hear the music. The turning and moving of the couples appears then to be senseless, as the rhythm clue is missing.[79]

The "half-awakening" of Mahler's mourning subject constitutes a poised hesitation between two worlds, a caesura within an otherwise incessant interchange between the writing and reading that figures the subject. As such, it comes nearest to theorizing the untheorizable *déʃiʃtance* dividing the subject from itself—nearer than the self-conscious figuration in Diderot, nearer also than the unconsciously configured splitting in Reik.

Earlier, I pointed out that the figuring of deliberate or voluntary subjectal desistance might usefully be regarded as parallelling involuntary desistance. Here, their mutual tension becomes vital to signifying *désistance* itself undecidably so that it does not totalize texts in which it is an organizing concept. In Mahler's treatment of subjectal *Unheimlichkeit*, and in Lacoue-Labarthe's assimilation of that treatment to an explication of autobiographical compulsion, this tension becomes itself delicately, even "perfectly," represented.

My conclusion here—the construal of figured desistance as part and parcel of the undecidability of *désistance* itself—in one sense settles the question of its significance and even assimilates it to the overall theory of subjectal loss for which *désistance* stands. Later, however, subjectal return, *as* return, will be seen to have more robust life, bound up with the possibility that representation might be (re)presentable otherwise: as *presentation*.[80] Treatment of that particular thought, however, must await the further development of Lacoue-Labarthian subjectivity, on its own terms. That development I am now ready directly to resume, in Chapter 4.

Literature
Hints of the Hyperbological

Introduction: *Désistance, The Literary Absolute,* and the Kantian Aesthetic

My preliminaries now being over, the particular mode of access that I bring to Lacoue-Labarthe ought to have become clear. I hope, as it were, to "frame" Lacoue-Labarthe, but without framing him in the pejorative sense of the term. This is a delicate path to tread; interrogative frameworks, such as that provided by my question about persistent subjectal return, can easily extrapolate an author like Lacoue-Labarthe "beyond himself." The danger is usually forestalled if one returns, as I do now, to considering the author on his own terms. In this chapter, I forsake, for the present, the ghost of the regained subject and invoke once more the framework of Lacoue-Labarthian subjectal loss. I offer both a bridge to the full context in which Lacoue-Labarthe detects that loss and a preliminary glance at the notion that unifies his account of the loss—the *hyperbolical*. Chapter 5 then takes up in detail the development of the hyperbolical as hyperbo*logical*—the latter thought offering, in my opinion, the key to thematizing the Lacoue-Labarthian oeuvre.

I take my departure here from Lacoue-Labarthe's treatment of Kant, and particularly of Kant's third *Critique*.[1] Lacoue-Labarthe's engagement with this work is found in his best-known book, *The Literary Absolute: The Theory of Literature in German Romanticism*, his second extended authorial enterprise with Jean-Luc Nancy.[2] *The Literary Absolute* construes the early German romantic theory of literature as underpinned by a particular philosophical search for the subject, emergent in response to a particular problematic of subjectal loss, deriving from Kant. It is the *terms* of this perceived Kantian problematic, rather than its specific romantic solution, that I find informative as regards Lacoue-Labarthe's position on subjectal loss.

Here, I probe the problematic in more detail than is offered in *The Literary Absolute*.[3] I hope to locate in the third *Critique* the notion of presentational *excess* that is a general feature of Lacoue-Labarthe's description of subjectal loss. This I do by exploring the incipient romanticism in the third *Critique*, taking as my point of departure *The Literary Absolute*, itself indebted to Walter Benjamin's *Der Begriff der Kunstkritik in der deutschen Romantik*.[4] As Lacoue-Labarthe points out in introducing that work, Benjamin's Kant is "fundamentally Romantic."[5] Benjamin's work provides a backdrop for my own exploration here of a particular equivocation within Kantian *Darstellung*. As foreground, I engage further with Martha B. Helfer's *The Retreat of Representation: The Concept of Darstellung in German Critical Discourse*.[6] Helfer reflects and develops the contributions by Benjamin, Lacoue-Labarthe, and Nancy in a manner particularly relevant to my study.

Following Helfer for some distance, but deepening and then building upon her description, I hope to demonstrate that Kant hesitates between describing the presentation of the subject in terms of, alternately, *absence* of form and a *surfeit* of form(s). The subject, thus found in two ways at once, is lost within the Kantian aesthetic, within which presentation in fact does exceed the subject or idea it is intended to "define." Kant's attempts to cope with this excess give rise to his ambiguity in characterizing it; there is then detectable in the aesthetic a presentational hyperbolic (implicitly a hyperbo-*logic*), corresponding to a *désistant* (or desistant) subject. I begin by rehearsing in outline how that very subject is implied by the exposition in *The Literary Absolute*, with the authors' suggestion that the romantic thesis of an absolute and infinitized romantic subject is merely our own naïveté.[7]

Désistance *Renewed: The Subject of Literature as a Mimetic Subject*

The Literary Absolute examines the romantic understanding that gives literature responsibility for producing the idea or subject absolutely.

Under this reading, the philosophical subject—that which *is*, as the *idea*, or *being*—at once both produces literature (as theorizer) and is produced by it (as theorized). Literature produces philosophy, but not as a distinguishable other, that is, not as having an "ideal" fabric transcendent over its own. The subject that literature elaborates thereby escapes the Kantian split between an "originating" yet un-theorizable subject of moral action, on the one hand, and, on the other, the equally untheorizable, insubstantial, yet theorizing subject of pure reason, determinable only as the "transcendental unity" at-tending apperception.

Lacoue-Labarthe and Nancy's argument is as follows. In Kant, nontheorizability of the subject is connoted in the first two *Critiques* by the unpresentability to the mind of the *Ding-en-sich*, the thing in itself. The romantics seek to restore the possibility of this originary intuition. In doing so, they provide a new account of the truth of literature. Following a clue in the third *Critique*, they hit upon litera-ture as iteratively and infinitely *presenting* that which it seems to re-present, but which apart from the presentation never *is*. However, as Lacoue-Labarthe and Nancy suggest, this account becomes assimi-lated to a traditional account of subjectivity. Presuming a unitive or organic thrust within the *work* that is literature, the romantics finally tell us that literature moves toward an adequate presentation of what *is*. Literature thus understood as absolute, say the authors, frames our own present, mediating subjectivity as an ersatz substantiality.[8] Their demonstration here is of a piece with Lacoue-Labarthe's other explorations of the insistent return of the *figure* (the subject, as type).[9]

Subjectal Désistance *and the Kantian Provenance of* Romantic *Darstellung*

All this is evidenced in the provenance that our authors attach to the romantic project. The romantics inherited the problem of the Kantian subject unable to have an originary experience of itself. This inability corresponds to the split in the subject, between subjectivity experi-enced as freedom and subjectivity experienced as (determined) na-ture. The third *Critique* moves in two directions to solve this split and locate the possibility of subjectal self-experience.[10] It envisages the subject as given to itself as the *reflection* of its synthetic function, and/ or as its threefold presentation (*Darstellung*),

> by means of the Beautiful in works of art (the formation of *Bilder* able to present liberty and morality analogically), by means of

the "formative power" (*bildende Kraft*) of nature and life within nature (the formation of the organism), and finally by means of the *Bildung* of humanity (what we retain under the concepts of history and culture).[11]

Here, however, what *is* is not, finally, either presented or presentable. Kant's resolving mechanism does not become (Hegelian) sublation or dissolution. The subject is not directly reflected by life or history: there is in Kant no *analogon* for life itself, and history is referred to an *infinite* telos.[12]

Faced with this, the romantic-idealist dispensation adopts as its point of departure what Lacoue-Labarthe and Nancy call a *will to system*: the attempt to interconnect the opposing poles of Kantian subjectivity in an overarching system. The paradigmatic work here is *The Earliest System-Programme of German Idealism*, which our authors consider as having been most probably authored by Schelling.[13] The *System-Programme* delineates what they call a "system-subject": a subject who, being absolutely free, creates the world as an extension of this ideal freedom, within which the apparent determinism of nature is also subsumed. This idealist project contains the possibility of construing the system and the system-subject organically rather than categorically. Seen thus, what *is* evolves as *life* (system as living, as organic, rather than as "pigeonholing"), and specifically as *beautiful* life. Beauty becomes the overarching Idea in which truth and goodness are reconciled. The *Darstellung* of the subject as formative power, *bildende Kraft*, becomes the *Darstellung* of the subject as aesthetic power, *aesthetische Kraft*. The subject is produced by life, so long as it is understood that "the life implied here is *beautiful*, and the organism which it animates, or within which it occurs, . . . is essentially the *work of art*."[14]

Thus the manifestation of the subject occurs through the *Darstellung* of *Darstellung*—the presentation of presentation itself—in which literature consists. The resolution occasioned therein, intrinsic to the function of literature as art, is explored by Lacoue-Labarthe and Nancy in twelve texts from the *Athenaeum*, all produced in the "not quite two years and hundreds of pages" that this journal comprised.[15] I omit the details of these analyses but use the authors' general conclusions as context for my return to the Kantian problematic of aesthetic presentation.

To some extent, Lacoue-Labarthe and Nancy themselves make this return: they argue that the method of resolution in these early romantic texts inevitably involves replacing the free subject (of ideal-ism) with another subject, organic and infinitized. The resolution em-ploys a "spiral" between chaos and system, leading to a subject manifest as "Subject-Work and the Work-Subject."[16] This subject is, for example, on view in the case of a stage character, who is at once both "the produced" *and* "producer of the Subject." As part of an artistic mimetic event, this subject is

> capable (undoubtedly *for this very reason*) in its presentation or staging of re-producing or re-constructing the Subject, a Sub-ject that is auto-constituting, auto-mimetic, auto-ironic . . . and that auto-imagines, auto-*bildet,* auto-illuminates itself: the Subject-Work.[17]

Lost by Kant, then, the subject is found *as* the Work—or, more precisely, the Work in a spirally progressive dialectic with "its" own generating spirit. Lacoue-Labarthe and Nancy do not use the word "dialectic" here; historically speaking, Hegel is still to come, and they are anyway keen to distinguish the romantic "spiral of spirals" from the Hegelian "circle of circles."[18] But whatever the name for the mechanism of resolution, its effect is to reiterate the subject as the telos of literature, as that which literature strains toward producing. True, it "aggravates" and "infinitizes" the thinking of the subject as totality.[19] In the end, though, it must be regarded as having fallen short of Kant's hopes, if such they were, for a characterization of pre-sentation apart from the subject. Romanticism, in its birth as well as in its perpetuation in our own era, has not lost its classical subjectal assumptions:

> In short, we ourselves are implicated in all that determines both literature as auto-critique and criticism as literature. Our own image comes back to us from the mirror of the literary absolute. And the massive truth flung back at us is that we have not left the era of the Subject.[20]

Still, the work-subject of literature is generated in a spiraling that works by *exceeding* (itself). Enter here the notion of the *hyperbolic*, which keenly informs Lacoue-Labarthe's analyses of the nexus of literature and philosophy. Literature has an impetus toward re-marking and exceeding not only content but also *forms* (that is, phi-losophy) or genres. Lacoue-Labarthe and Nancy comment on *Athen-eaum* fragment 116, with its adjuration that romantic poetry should sometimes mix and sometimes fuse poetry and prose, geniality and criticism, the poetry of art [*Kunstpoesie*] and the poetry of nature [*Naturepoesie*]. . . . [In contrast to other types of poetry] . . . [i]t alone is free.[21]

They go on to explore the hyperbolization here, and in Friedrich Schlegel's *Dialogue* on poetry, as "nothing other than the literalization of the organic metaphor," that is, "the very effectuation of the idea of *organon*—or of the *organon* as idea."[22] Hyperbolization effects the unity and systematicity corresponding to presence of a subject, by way of a seamless traversal between forms, which amounts to a continual exceeding of (any) particular form.

It seems, then, that my analysis of Lacoue-Labarthian subjectal *loss* is still at the threshold of its commencement—*The Literary Absolute* finally emphasizes subjectal return rather than loss. And yet, at its end, we are at exactly the point where the notion of the "hyperbolic" might be coaxed toward its sister notion of the *hyperbologic*, which signifies for Lacoue-Labarthe the *failed* recuperation of aesthetic hyperbolization to the paradigms of systematicity, subjectal return, and the metaphysics of presence. Two questions demand to be posed. How, exactly, does the presentational *excess* that accompanies art, including literature, bid to be assimilated to a mechanism of subjectal gain? And, from another angle, what "play" might there be in this mechanism, capable of subverting this subjectal gain, returning aesthetic *Darstellung* instead to the realms of subjectal *désistance*?

The Aim of This Chapter

In this context, my task in the present chapter finds clearer definition. Taking my cue from *The Literary Absolute*, I examine Kant's treatment of the sublime in his third *Critique*, attempting to point out how he fails to notice the subjectal *gain* associated with the presentational excess of the sublime. I move toward attributing this gain to what Lacoue-Labarthe later develops as the hyperbologic. This point will doubly lead me into my proposed generalization of subjectal loss in Lacoue-Labarthe.

First, I hope to deepen the aspect of equivocity associated with the literary-aesthetic hyperbolic, since it is that aspect which is crucial to Lacoue-Labarthe's account of hyperbological subjectal suspension. I hope to show how this equivocity goes back to the third *Critique*. (Some of what I say will be reinforced later, when I follow Lacoue-

Labarthe's explicit discussion of the sublime, in his "Sublime Truth."[23]) To do this, I will use Helfer's *The Retreat of Representation*, a work that in some ways opens Kant to the Lacoue-Labarthian hyperbologic better than does Lacoue-Labarthe himself.[24] Helfer pays passing critical attention to *The Literary Absolute*, but I will be even more interested in her direct discussion of Kant, for which she is in turn indebted to Jean-Luc Nancy as well as to Hans Graubner.[25]

Second, going via Kant allows me to link Lacoue-Labarthe's argument in *The Literary Absolute* itself to elements of the Lacoue-Labarthian hyperbological. It turns out that this text "convicts" the aesthetic subject of the hesitation and *désistance* that the notion of the hyperbological marks in Lacoue-Labarthe's later work.

Romantic *Selbstdarstellung* as Infinitization of the Subject

Again, it helps briefly to anticipate the second point before embarking on the first. I have already noted that, in *The Literary Absolute*, the perspective of *désistance* is retained; this also means rejection of the alternative perspective, which takes Kant's *Critique of Judgement* as successfully resolving the impasse between the Kantian subjects of knowledge and freedom. As we have seen, *The Literary Absolute* also hints at the triumph of *désistance* over what Lacoue-Labarthe and Nancy identify as a restoration of the subject by Kant's romantic successors, with their particular extrapolation of the Kantian resolution. The romantic solution, the authors suggest, succeeds only in restoring an infinitized version of a subject immediately available to itself, through an *intuitus originarius*, as in the Cartesian dispensation overturned by Kant.

How does this extrapolation operate, and why is it inadequate? More or less faithfully, the romantics develop a hope found in Kant, by looking to art to provide the *Darstellung* of the subject: the appearance before the senses of the *idea* itself. Key to this notion is the associated claim that, in art, *Darstellung* becomes *Selbstdarstellung*, a word whose meaning is nicely undecidable between "self-presentation" and "auto-presentation." "Self-presentation" can be used to subsume all the meanings that would "return" Kantian apperception to the realm of Cartesian originary intuition. The subject of this intuition exists independently of the objects it perceives. Its representation of these objects in artistic productions is also self-(re)presentation, an ongoing "presenting of itself to itself." In other words, the subject here is an entity available to speculative determination in the self-(re)presentation that is *Selbstdarstellung*.

Nevertheless, *Selbstdarstellung* as "auto-presentation" bids to subsume an essentially different set of meanings, a set that seems to cross the former set and double it without, however, coinciding with it. "Auto-presentation" suggests the "automatic" presentation that occurs in the absence of a separate, producing self, and which generates what we might call the "effect of the subject." One interpretation of this is that through art, *presentation itself* finds sensible presentation as a subject. Presentation, here, corresponds to the harmonizing of understanding with imagination that for Kant occasioned the sensing of beauty, and the judgment of taste. Here, it is as if *Darstellung* "itself," in "its" very unpresentability, were producing itself, employing the processes of which the self-possessed Cartesian subject might (mistakenly) feel in some command. "Auto-presentation"—pure process—is here, then, the absolute subject. It is the object as an "event of presentation" that has produced itself and thereby also become its own (producing) subject.

It is in this sense that the notion of art as *Selbstdarstellung* intersects with the notion of the subject and "infinitizes" it. The subject is now no longer to be sought as that which is "behind" representation but rather as the event of *presentation* "itself," occurrent through the interminable series of (re)presentations by which art critiques itself.

Thus described, the subject has touchpoints with the subject sought as beauty in the second part of Lacoue-Labarthe and Nancy's *System-Programme*. It is also of a piece with the system-subject of the first part (a subject of absolutely free will, as a formative power that creates rather than reports the world). Its subjectivity corresponds to something intermediate between will and mechanism, perhaps the very "something" sought by post-Kantians in order to reconcile "system and freedom."[26]

But this description is arguably equivocal as regards the subjectivity—in the sense of substantiality—of its putative "infinitized subject." For might not art as autopresentation be taken as presentation *without a subject*? Alternatively, might it not be taken as presentation, the subject of which is an *als ob*, always already a "re-presentation"? This seed of equivocity connects the investigation carried out in *The Literary Absolute* with what Lacoue-Labarthe emphasizes in *Typography*: that, paradoxically, pure art (pure mimesis) appears only when it "presents" the absence of a subject. That is, art comes into its own, becomes "essentially" itself, when, as it were, it manifests the *loss* of the very subject that it apparently "doubles" or produces for visibility—when it absolutizes, not the subject, but the *désistance* of this subject.[27]

This proposition sets the terms for my investigation here of Kant. The question is whether the presumption of sensible presentational excess (the hyperbolic) *as such* might be read into the Kantian aesthetic. If so, the root of the Lacoue-Labarthian hyper*bologic* loss of the subject will be found in Kant himself. Also, we can conclude that the romantics have rerouted the Kantian text, transforming its intrinsic bent toward subjectal loss, or *désistance*, into infinitized subjectal *arrival*. The tempting, but ultimately insufficient, alternative is to take the romantic extrapolation of Kant on its own terms. In this case, the notion of aesthetic subjectal gain, which the romantics developed, is of a piece with the way in which the third *Critique* seeks to differentiate the beautiful from the sublime.

To decide between these alternatives, it is necessary to turn to the respective Kantian treatments of the beautiful and the sublime. These bid to sketch a coherent interrelationship between subjectal gain as *form* and subjectal loss as (re)presentational excess. The accounts engage each other in terms of alternative interpretations of *Selbstdarstellung*: as a "*Darstellung* of *Darstellung* itself,*"* or, in the third *Critique*, as what Kant terms *negative Darstellung*. My entrée for discussion of this engagement is Helfer's book.

Martha Helfer: The Romantic "Extrapolation" of Kant toward an Aesthetically Mediated "Pure Presentation"

The Retreat of Representation traces the thought of *Darstellung* through four case studies, traversing idealism, Jena romanticism, and work by Herman von Kleist that is "fundamentally opposed" to both of these. Helfer argues that "the Idealist and Romantic theories of representation that come into being around 1800 develop as a direct result of *aporiae* in Kant's notion of *Darstellung*."[28]

As I have said, Helfer's approach highlights the transition from Kant's attempt to find a *Darstellung*-related subjectivity to the romantic conclusion that the subject arises through representation as poesy. She agrees with Lacoue-Labarthe and Nancy that

the notion of *Darstellung* inevitably involves the question of the relationship between philosophy and literature, and . . . this question is first raised by the structure of critical discourse in Kant's critiques.[29]

For Helfer, as for the authors of *The Literary Absolute*, a focus on the subject accompanies the focus on representation. One of three reasons why Kant introduces the notion of *Darstellung* in his first *Critique* is

the fundamental question that will determine the direction of Idealism and Romanticism in the wake of Kant, how to guarantee that the sensible subject can define itself as a moral subject of reason.[30]

Helfer distinguishes between Kantian *Vorstellung* and *Darstellung*. *Vorstellung* is "representation" as an a priori perception in the mind, while *Darstellung* is representation as sense-perceptible and/or actual to the mind. This distinction between the notions is made on the basis of "inner" and "external" realization of form. With some qualifications, it survives in the romantic development of the terms, as is also pointed out in Seyhan's *Representation and Its Discontents*.[31] In *The Literary Absolute*, all that remains of the "I" of the transcendental aesthetic of the *Critique of Pure Reason*, and of the moral subject of the *Critique of Practical Reason*, is an "empty form"; in terms of the distinctions made by Helfer and Seyhan, this claim offers the earlier Kantian subject as a *Vorstellung* without a *Darstellung*.

According to *The Literary Absolute*, the "solution" to this problem is broached in the third *Critique* through an "analogical" *Darstellung*: a subject analogized in terms of the *Bildung* or formative power "it" enacts in history, culture, or art. Is a presentation of the subject effected by such a *Darstellung*, or is it not? Helfer attacks the inherent equivocity here from another angle, concentrating on tracing Kant's concept of the sublime *negative Darstellung* of the sublime, which "functions as a panacea for the various shortcomings in Kant's elaboration of the *Darstellung* problematic."[32]

Helfer examines the pure but, to her, insufficiently sensible version of self-sensibility that the third *Critique* offers in relation to human experience of the beautiful and the sublime.[33] The beautiful involves "an indirect presentation (*indirekte Darstellung*) of the moral good, as 'originally determining' for the subject."[34] The sublime involves "a negative presentation (*negative Darstellung*) of the 'idea of humanity in our subject.'"[35]

She describes how Kantian *negative Darstellung* is understood as presenting the subject:

Negative Darstellung forces the subject to think the supersensible —the idea—without actually producing an objective presenta-

tion of this idea. Thus it presents nothing except the process—
the striving or effort (*die Bestrebung*)—of *Darstellung* itself.

This "pure *Darstellung*," Helfer suggests, is self-presentation; it is
Selbstdarstellung

> in the Romantic sense of the word, and it is no coincidence that
> the notion of "negativity" becomes constitutive for Idealism and
> Romanticism.[36]

It is interesting to see how Helfer sees *negative Darstellung* as avail-
ing itself of romantic (re)interpretation. The Kantian notion of *negative Darstellung* eventually comes to include connotations of
(re)presentational fulfillment in linguistic rather than mathematical
terms. In part, this is due to Kant himself. Realizing that "language
prevents philosophical discourse from achieving the 'pure' representation of mathematics," Helfer says, "Kant unwillingly admitted the
poetic into the rhetorical exposition of his *Critiques*."[37] She is pointing
here to Kant's realization that language in general is capable of determining representation. Thus logical exposition or prose cannot
match, and in fact *thwarts*, the kind of purity of representation accorded to subjects by mathematics; Kant hoped that, obversely,
poetry might *mediate* such representation. The "unwillingness"
Helfer mentions relates to Kant's wish nevertheless to avoid the conclusion that poetics could deliver *negative Darstellung* as *Selbstdarstellung*, that is, as an empirical "objective" presentation of the subject
"itself" in the romantic sense.

In broad terms, Helfer's account allows the following distinction
to surface: faced with the empirically infinite aspects of presentation,
Kant chooses to identify the subject with reason's striving to order
this presentation; the "romantic" alternative is identification of the
subject with the content of imaginative presentational excess itself.
This subject is associated, not with the perceived absence of determi-
nacy in the presentational process, but with the event of the prolifer-
ation of presentation, although it is presumed as an infinitized
process.

However, as Helfer points out, and as we shall see below, the distinction between the experiences of *negative Darstellung* and *Darstellung* "itself" is not so easily sustained. Kant's account of sublime
negative Darstellung includes his acceptance of the notion that the presentation of the sublime might occur in, and might enhance, art.[38]
Putting this together with Kant's references in the first *Critique* to a

"purity" of presentation that could be achieved only in poetics, one might conclude that Kantian *negative Darstellung* amounts to an event of *Selbstdarstellung*, in the strong sense of "presentation itself" rather than the weak sense of "presentation of the unpresentability of the subject." This, at any rate,

> is clearly the conclusion that the Romantics draw from the *Critiques*, and it is a conclusion, Nancy has suggested, that Kant was aware of but avoided.[39] If this is the case, then the final limit that *negative Darstellung* demarcates is the border between critical discourse and poetry.[40]

Here, rather than saying, on Nancy's behalf, that Kant rejected the possibility of a poetic *negative Darstellung*, Helfer implies that Kant's "avoidance" of the romantic conclusion was merely formal.[41] Her thought, then, is this: Kant's account of the sublime is implicitly congenial to the possibility of a poetic *negative Darstellung* that, as *Selbstdarstellung*, provides the pure presentation that critical discourse (that is, philosophical presentation) cannot supply.

What follows, if Kantian sublime *negative Darstellung* is tied to Kant's account of the presentational excess attending art? Canvasing this connection, the arguments in *The Literary Absolute* and *The Retreat of Representation* imply, as one possibility, that the *aesthetic* sublime (as excess) becomes assimilated to the Kantian *natural* sublime. In both, then, we have the presumption of a self-present subject, albeit manifested "negatively," and the romantic inscription of the subject is in fact a repetition of the Kantian inscription. Conversely, though, the assimilation ought also to work in the reverse direction: there ought in Kant to be preliminary evidence of the *désistance* that accompanies the romantic inscription, the *désistance* of the subject within *literature*.

Désistance, in the latter context, is abundantly treated in Lacoue-Labarthe. *Désistance* in the Kantian context itself is less explored. Or rather, it is explored in relation to the Kantian *sublime*, but less in relation to the sublime dimension of the aesthetic. Still less is it treated in relation to the Kantian description of the aesthetic idea itself. Yet in Kant, the passage from *negative Darstellung* to the *aesthetic* idea perpetuates the assimilation of *sensibility* to the *striving for figuration*. Within this assimilation, however, sensibility is also marked as escaping its own telos by providing *too much* figuration. In terms we shall also find Lacoue-Labarthe explicitating later, presentational hyperbolic is here already manifest as hyperbologic, and "desistantly" so.

Deconstructive Interplay between *Negative Darstellung* and the Aesthetic Idea: An Introduction

To investigate this, I shall return to the place in the third *Critique* where the notion of *negative Darstellung* makes its appearance. It will then be possible to measure this notion against its aesthetic counterpart, the *aesthetic idea*. Kant, employing both notions, has approached the problem of "containing" presentational excess from a direction opposite to that which Helfer later takes in commenting on the *Critiques*. Juxtaposing these two approaches yields an interesting result: a hesitation occurs in the Kantian construal of the *Darstellung* of the subject. This hesitation corresponds incipiently to the very oscillation of the hyperbolic that I shall develop in Chapter 5 as the Lacoue-Labarthian hyperbo*logic*, which marks the *désistance* of the subject.

Sublime Presentation in Nature and Art through A Priori Purposiveness of Reflective Judgment

I begin by considering how, in Kant, the experience of the sublime, involving the feeling of a peculiar combination of pain and pleasure, bids to connote a presentation of the subject. Given that this subject is noumenal, and thus, by all Kantian criteria, unpresentable, "presentation" here might be expected to be analogical. Indeed, as we have seen, Kant formally describes this as "negative presentation (*negative Darstellung*) of the "idea of humanity in our subject."[42]

Kant might be allowed to elaborate here. He refers the feeling of the sublime to "respect for our own destination"; later in the same sentence this becomes "respect for the idea of humanity in our subject." He has, a few lines previously, defined "respect" as the "feeling of our incapacity to attain to an idea which is a law for us." To put it simply, he is identifying the feeling of the sublime with the "presentation without presentation" of this essence of the human: the demand (which reason makes of the imagination) for unified presentation of what impinges on the senses.

Thus "attainment" [*Erreichung*] of the "idea of humanity" would here involve the satisfaction of a demand made by reason, regarding "comprehension . . . of a given object in a whole of intuition."[43] This satisfaction is impossible, so what results as experience is a combination of pain at this impossibility and pleasure nevertheless in the demand as law. This experience of cognitive demand and failure is specifically mediated by the natural sublime; then, however, by a "subreption," or displacement, the respect attending the sublime experience is accorded to the "object" of nature itself, when in fact

> that [object of nature], as it were, makes intuitable for us the
> superiority of the rational vocation of our cognitive powers over
> the greatest power of sensibility.[44]

Kant's qualification ("as it were") is intriguing. It exemplifies a coyness that, Helfer notes, is characteristic whenever Kant describes the *Darstellung* of purposiveness attending the sublime.[45] To what extent does Kant mean to (dis)qualify the "intuition" of the vocation of reason that the sublime provides? To answer this question, we must consider the nature of the judgment that facilitates the *Darstellung* of the sublime "object," and likewise of its aesthetic counterpart, to reason.

Though the employment of the faculty of judgment is of key interest in the first two *Critiques*, it is the *Critique of Judgement*, as its name suggests, that canvases the nature of judgment itself. Kant's aim is to find, for judgment, "a principle of its own," one that would "not be derived from *a priori* concepts."[46] This suggests that judgment is to be investigated in a sphere where it is exhibited free from its prior determination within the contexts of employment by pure or practical reason. Kant turns to "those judgements called aesthetic, which concern the beautiful and the sublime in nature and art"; while these exhibit the "perplexity" attending a principle of judgment, they also, implicitly by this same token, allow "a critical enquiry [in search] of a principle of judgement [which is] the most important part of a critique of this power."[47] The enquiry finds that judgment proceeds in either of two modes. The first and obvious one is the determinant mode, corresponding to the shaping by the imagination of sensible particulars to fit preexisting universals.

It is the second mode, however, that generated the key insight for the third *Critique*. For Kant, the discovery of this mode corresponds to revelation of the "pure essence" of judgment itself: the search by the imagination for the universalizing of sensible products even in the absence of concepts. The mode is that of *reflective* judgment, which applies when "only the particular is given and judgement has to find the universal for it."[48] The principle informing this mode is that of *purposiveness*. It is found expressed in the purposiveness ascribed by the mind to nature, as "a special *a priori* concept that has its origin solely in reflective judgement."[49]

Reflective judgment is itself a distinctive and intrinsically subjective activity. This becomes clear as Kant explains how reflective judgment employs an a priori principle of purposiveness in our cognition of nature, seeking to subsume the particular under the unknown general, that is, in the absence of a concept of the understanding, or the idea of reason, that can represent the unity it seeks.[50] In fact, as an a priori form, judgment, prior to both determinant and reflective modes, provides a link between the otherwise disparate legislations of the understanding (which generates concepts, in the realm of nature) and reason (which generates ideas, in the realm of freedom). However, it is clearly judgment in its reflective mode, as provident of a "subjective maxim," which for Kant provides the intellect with the "transcendental concept of purposiveness."[51]

Reflective judgment underwrites the explicitly *subjective* dimension of the transcendental unity embracing diverse imaginative presentations. Correspondingly, it is Kant's explicit or implicit attention to the dimension of reflective judgment in the third *Critique* that provides the focus for a *Darstellung* (of whatever kind) of the Kantian subject.

This dimension is evident in his treatment of both aesthetic judgments and judgments of the sublime. Aesthetically, reflective judgment prompts free play of the imagination, to the point where there is generated an event of harmony. This is a harmony between the understanding and imagination, or else between reason and imagination, which is real, though it falls short of being a concept or an idea. Works of art that stimulate this free play are, Kant tells us, said to have *spirit* [*Geist*]. This, as "an animating principle in the mind," is "no other than the faculty for the presentation [*Darstellung*] of aesthetic ideas."[52] Kant defines the *aesthetic idea* as

> that representation [*Vorstellung*] of the imagination which occasions much thought, without however any definite thought, i.e., any *concept*, being capable of being adequate to it; it consequently cannot be compassed or made completely intelligible by language. We see that it is the counterpart of a *rational idea*, which conversely is a concept to which no *intuition* (or representation [*Vorstellung*] of the imagination) can be adequate.[53]

Is the aesthetic idea here a *presentation*, or a *representation*? Kant seems to hesitate. If the passage is to be taken literally, aesthetic ideas undergo presentation to the mind. The use of the term *Darstellung* implies a sensibly mediated presentation, comparable to that associated with concepts. But, because no concepts are in fact achieved by the presentation, it remains on the level of a representation (*Vorstellung*)—one might say that the sensible, or "objective," aspect of the (re)presentation is discounted. In fact, however, the contrast that Kant draws with the rational idea (which, in Kant, is unrepresentable to the imagination precisely as having no sensible correlate) implies that the sensible "component" of the aesthetic idea is *not* being discounted here. Hence it might well be acceptable to interpret the *Vorstellung* of the aesthetic idea to the imagination as a "presentation."[54]

For the moment, we might compromise between these positions as follows. In the aesthetic idea we encounter an expression of the reflective judgment's "subjective" drive to purposiveness, issuing in a sensible presentation. This presentation is a *Darstellung*, lacking, however, an attendant definite concept or idea of which it is the presentation. We are led to a further question: In what way can such a *Darstellung* be said to be related to the subject itself?

Subjectal Presentational Absence in the First Two Critiques

First, it seems important to reiterate that Kant, when he uses *Darstellung* here, is unlikely to have in mind a direct presentation of the subject. In the two earlier *Critiques*, he has stressed the impossibility of a sensible detection or demonstration of the subject as such. I briefly rehearse these two arguments, which together generate the lacuna in subjectal self-presentation that the third *Critique* attempts to fill.

In the first place, and in the first *Critique*, Kant's First Paralogism argues that neither the substantiality of the theorizing subject nor the fact of its self-presentability can be derived from its capacity for thought, or from its actual thinking activity. Here, the subject is, one might say, merely the "locus of theorizing activity," corresponding to a transcendental unity of apperception:

> The unity of consciousness, which underlies the categories, is [by rational psychology] mistaken for an intuition of the subject as object, and the category of substance is then applied to it. But this unity is only unity in *thought*, by which alone no object is given, and to which, therefore, the category of substance, which always presupposes a given *intuition*, cannot be known.[55]

In simple terms, the paralogism argues that thought does not deliver its objects with that immediacy of apprehension required to confirm them as substance.[56]

Later, the second paralogism considers anew the unity of the thinking self, this time from the point of view of its simplicity (that is, its indivisibility). Kant argues that the "subject" associated with thinking, though it cannot be an object detectable sensibly (by "outer intuitions"), might yet be regarded as a *noumenal* subject. That is,

the something which underlies the outer appearances and which so affects our sense that it obtains the representations of space, matter, shape, etc., may yet, when viewed as noumenon (or better, as transcendental object), be at the same time the subject of our thoughts.[57]

"When *viewed* as noumenon. . . ." The hypothetical nature of the observation here is clear. In the remainder of the paralogism, Kant goes on to point out that, anyway, nothing distinct about such a subject, *as* subject, can be known. The bracketed observation further indicates that Kant is less than happy about introducing what we might call the "surrogate substantiality" of a subjectivity that is noumenal. He would prefer to locate a subject which is a "transcendental object," that is, the condition of the possibility of the intellectual functions performed by the self.

What is true of the theorizing subject is also, as I have already indicated, the case for the practical or moral subject. This subject, now the locus of the exercise of the will within the concept of freedom, is again described as a noumenon. Again, what is at issue is a "noumenal substantiality" of this subject—in this case, in order to save the premise of spontaneous subjectal agency because free agency is invisible in the world of appearances. Kant makes reference to an "intelligible substrate":

Lacking this intuition [that is, an intellectual intuition of the spontaneous subject], the moral law assures us of this difference between the relation of our actions as appearances to the sense-being of our subject and the relation by which this sensuous being is itself connected to the intelligible substrate within us.[58]

In other words, the moral law, by its a priori guarantee that there are things we *ought* to do and things we can freely choose to do, describes the free subject "within." The self is thus seen to enclose (I continue Kant's spatial metaphor) a "substrate" corresponding to spontaneity of agency, regardless of the natural determination that cannot but appear to rule the sensate "self."

Deconstructive Interplay between *Negative Darstellung* and the Aesthetic Idea: An Expansion

The foregoing places the third *Critique* in an interesting position at its very outset. To attempt the unification of the subjects of nature and freedom is one thing, but how might the new *Critique* confirm the unification through a subjectal *Darstellung* so effectively excluded by it precursors? Kant appears to hope that the subject can become presented in the process of exercising the faculty of *judgment as such*. It would then correspond to the *single* subject that mediates between those others. Kant speaks about this in terms of a connection [*Verknüpfung*] that judgment constitutes, between the legislations [*Gesetzgebungen*] of the understanding and of reason.[59] But this solution is compromised when an ambiguity or equivocation becomes evident in the conceptual link connecting *negative Darstellung* and the aesthetic idea, notions upon which the solution fundamentally relies. I turn now to this problem, which will variously require my revisiting all three *Critiques*. At several points, I will take my departure from Helfer's reflections.

I first anticipate, on the basis of what we have seen, the possibilities for a subjectal *Darstellung* in the third *Critique*. It can be expected that, against the romantics, the Kantian aesthetic idea will not turn out to canvas the possibility of a presentation (*Darstellung*) of the subject *itself*. Rather, a subject, in judging according to an aesthetic idea, will partially concretize aspects of itself while ultimately remaining invisible (or insensible), fully in line with the Kantian notion of an empty transcendental unity of apperception, allied to a merely "intelligible," *super*sensible, moral substrate.

This expectation is formally borne out within Kant's development of both the idea of the beautiful and the idea of the sublime. In the former case, concretization is *symbolically* of the moral good and refers to an "inner possibility in the subject."[60] And for the sublime, as we have seen, the "presentation" of self that accompanies our incapacity to attain the idea of humanity in our own subject is of limited immediacy: whatever concretization occurs is associated with the *feeling* of this incapacity.[61]

Sublime Presentation as Negative Darstellung, Distinct from the Aesthetic Idea

In what characteristic sense, then, can the sublime be regarded as occasioning a presentation of the subject? This question might be sharpened by means of two others. First, how does the mode of subjectal presentation associated with the sublime relate to that associated with the "aesthetic idea" arising in conjunction with the beautiful? The aesthetic idea certainly connotes *sensible* presentation; it would be interesting were this to be true of sublime presentation also. Second, and relatedly, what does Kant mean when he speaks of the sublime as a *negative Darstellung* (that is, a negative presentation) of "the idea of humanity in our subject"?

With regard to the first question, Kant does not employ the aesthetic idea in speaking of the sublime. The essence of the sublime is lack of form, that is, of what reason demands and imagination cannot supply. Conversely, what makes the aesthetic idea presentable, and what makes possible the judgment of beauty, is its *form*, albeit in the absence of a concept. In fact, the satisfaction of reason, through this presence of form, is what seemingly makes aesthetic appreciation restful for Kant, while in the experience of the sublime the mind feels itself moved (*bewegt*, stirred or disturbed).[62]

This apparently crucial gulf between the two modes must be narrowed before the second of my questions can be approached.

Sublime Presentation as Continuous with the Aesthetic Idea

It is interesting to see Helfer argue, against Hans Graubner (and following Nancy), that, despite contrary indications, Kant invokes the aesthetic idea, not only in connection with the beautiful but also in regard to the sublime.[63]

Certainly, in a formal sense, the sublime and the beautiful are opposed. The sublime is experienced as formless, thus unpresentable to the understanding. By contrast, the aesthetic idea facilitates the judgment of beauty through its component of form, which animates the imagination in relation to striving of the understanding. How, then, are the two connected?

For one thing, if the aesthetic idea *has* form, it also *lacks* form, and to this extent it recalls whatever formless presentation is afforded in the sublime. Aesthetic presentation involves an *indefinite* concept of the understanding; when Kant speaks about the natural sublime, a connection is drawn between this "indefinite" concept and the "like" concept of reason, which occasions the judgment of sublimity.[64] This is also how the mind connects beauty with goodness. Kant's description of the beautiful as the "symbol" of the moral good comprises the following line of thought. The aesthetic idea is attended by a *Darstel-*

lung (of an analogical sort) of the purposiveness of the intellect, itself part of a broader purposiveness of reason. The judgment of the beautiful analogizes that purposiveness of reason (toward the good) is expressed in desire. It is important for Kant that *spirit* [*Geist*]—that is, *an animating effect in the subject*, rather than mere formal perfection of the object—comprises the experience of a work of art as "beautiful." As Helfer says, following Rodolphe Gasché, "By animating the cognitive faculties, aesthetic ideas enable the mind to construct symbolic presentations of transcendental ideas."[65]

It is clear that the Kantian aesthetic idea, in mobilizing the imaginative faculties, achieves a subjectal *Darstellung*, which shares, at the very least, a touchpoint with that credited (negatively) to the natural sublime. This touchpoint is, formally, the purposiveness of reason itself. Now, if the *Darstellung* that elicits this purposiveness is identified with the *animation* of the presentational faculty, rather than with the presentation or nonpresentation of *form(s)*, then Kant's treatment cannot but imply that the *Darstellung* involved in the sublime is not sharply dissociable from that involved in the beautiful.

Helfer also makes this connection, but with an emphasis different from mine. In dialogue with Graubner, she argues that Kant's presentation of the moral good depends as much on his definition of the sublime as on his definition of the beautiful. She says:

> Like the beautiful [the moral good] appears to be a presentation of a concept of the understanding, and like the sublime it appears to be the presentation of an idea of reason.[66]

Negative *(Sublime)* and Indirect *(Aesthetic)* Darstellung: A Subtle Interplay

Though Helfer is right, my own purpose requires that I remain with the differentiation as well as with the continuity that is afoot in Kant's dually focused description. It is significant that the assimilation (of the beautiful to the sublime) evident in the third *Critique* is also ripely indicative of *difference*. At issue, here, is a delicate interplay—a battle for the definition of *Darstellung* played out via a definitional differentiation between the notions of indirect *Darstellung* (associated with the beautiful) and negative *Darstellung* (associated with the sublime). Seemingly, *indirect Darstellung*, involving as it does sensible presentation, has definitional priority or, at least, more in common with *Darstellung* than has *negative Darstellung*, since the latter is presentation of the impossibility (or limit) of presentation, that is, it is no presentation at all.

Nevertheless, there is a sense in which the ostensible priority is reversed. For example, Helfer points out that, in the analytic of the beautiful, Kant's treatment of *Darstellung* pales, for dynamism and depth, with its corresponding treatment in the analytic of the sublime. From this point of view, a *negative Darstellung* (of the limitless in interaction with the mind's demand for limitation) is the paradigm of pure presentation—of objects as they are and, what is more, of the subject as it might be self-intuited (independently from sensibility, comparably with the intuition of mathematical ideas in the first *Critique*).

So we have here a curious equivocation in the third *Critique*, which might reasonably be read as an unacknowledged contest between "sublime *Darstellung*" and aesthetic *Darstellung* for the right to signify subjectal purposiveness. Kant avoids the engagement of the two notions by virtue of describing both in terms of "improper" *Darstellung*: "negative" in the first case, "indirect" in the second. In other words, both the sublime and the aesthetic idea are presentations only by virtue of having external sensible correlates—they are occasioned by "outer sense" experiences—in which, however, it is impossible to say that presentation occurs as such. The presentation of the sublime is a presentation of unpresentability; the *Darstellung* of the aesthetic idea is presentation of something that for Kant is itself a *representation* [*Vorstellung*]. It is because Kant retains an almost formalized "arm's length" between the terminology of presentation and the identification of the presented as such that an equivocation within a generalized notion of subjectal *Darstellung* can here go unnoticed.

But this equivocation is highlighted as soon as it becomes clear that the frustrated purposiveness associated with the sublime is redescribed, and in fact redescribed *oppositely*, when Kant comes to discuss the aesthetic idea. As a consequence, what Kant means by representing the subject as frustrated purposiveness becomes radically undecidable—which is another way of saying that a deconstructive loss of the subject becomes evident within Kant's *Critique*. This point, essential to my argument, merits elaboration.

Deconstructive Interplay between *Negative Darstellung* and the Aesthetic Idea: A Mechanism

Subjectal purposiveness is "presented" in the sublime in terms of formlessness. When it comes to the beautiful, however, Kant almost clandestinely includes, under the rubric of the aesthetic idea, the presentation of this same purposiveness, but this time as the *sublime dimension* of the beautiful. Now, however, the purposiveness obtains as a *surfeit* of forms. (Forms, of course, cannot as such be excluded here, because such unity as is found in the aesthetic idea is engendered by the *understanding*.) The result of the dual description of subjectal *Darstellung* is this: excess, the excess of sensibility over presentability, simultaneously undergoes notional containment in two opposite ways, to yield the subject. But this surely means that whatever subjectal definition or presentation Kant hopes to achieve is lost or is split. In fact, it would not be difficult to trace this division to the old division that the third *Critique* was meant to heal: that between the subject of nature and the subject of freedom. Space constraints preclude that demonstration here; what does demand demonstration, however, is the claim that a deconstructive efficacy is inherent in the opposition.

A Derridean Deconstructive Economy: Supplementation and Supplanting

Most straightforwardly, the confrontation between oppositional subjectal motifs might be related to a Derridean deconstructive economy. This typically involves the supplementing of one theoretical construct by another, which, however, in turn supplants that which it supplements. This can be noticed in our reading of the third *Critique*, as follows. Initially, Kantian presentation is constructed as the (unfulfilled) purposiveness of reason, which demands a unity from all that sense encounters. Thus the inability of the understanding to determine the content of a sublime experience testifies to the "idea of humanity in our subject." Then, however, insofar as the same purposiveness presents as also informing the aesthetic idea, a supplementation of the above construct occurs. The aesthetic idea offers an additional interpretation of subjectal *Darstellung*, arrived at through a relating of reason's demand, experienced in the *natural* sublime, to the presentational excess manifest in art.

The effect of the supplementation is this: the previous construct, which involved limitlessness as *absence of form*, finds itself augmented by another: the form of the aesthetic idea. The supplement, though, supplants that which it was intended to supplement, by redescribing (purposively generated) limitlessness in terms of, not formal absence, but *formal excess*: the infinite multiplication of forms by which the imagination offers aesthetic presentations. In the very realm of the beautiful—of form—the aesthetic idea consists in a multiplicity of presentations of the imagination, one that cannot itself be "totaled" into an idea of reason or a direct *Darstellung* of the subject.

The supplementation was needed to extend the description of the sublime so that it could account for the "animated" presentation offered by art that has *Geist*. But the supplanting occurs here, equally irresistibly. The infinite production of imaginative forms becomes a *Darstellung*, not of the unicity of Reason, but of the propensity of imagination to supply forms ceaselessly to the understanding. Likewise, the subject becomes identified with *presentation*—insofar as this unending multiplicity of presentations can be regarded as presentation—rather than with the mere demand for presentation. It is thus that the supplanting by the supplement, by the subject of the aesthetic idea over the subject of purposive reason, triumphs, as the following will explain.

Supplemental Supplanting: The Mechanism Elaborated

The third *Critique* foregrounds reason as that faculty the activity of which results "reflexively," as it were, in a *Darstellung* of the subject. Reason has given the imagination the "destination" of "comprehension . . . of a given object in a whole of intuition." With both the beautiful and the sublime, this demand on the imagination is extended, impossibly but fruitfully, to one of comprehending the incomprehensible. This becomes a permission or license for the imagination to produce freely in keeping with an act of reflective judgment. So what is judged is apprehended as something that has form (but not to the point of being a concept) and thereby yields pleasure. Otherwise, the imagination offers matter for *comprehension* to the understanding, in keeping with determinant judgments corresponding to prior concepts of the understanding.[67]

Initially, this means the judgments of the beautiful and the sublime are linked as follows. Judgments of beauty are made when the imagination processes such sensory material as is capable of yielding form. This is done under the law of reason, implemented by the understanding. Judgments of the sublime, however, occur when the imagination, faced with an overwhelming quantity of material for apprehension, cannot satisfy the demands of the understanding but nevertheless remains under reason's demand to put its products together.[68] Here, what occurs is a "failure" that is nevertheless productive. The imagination races to infinity, feeling its inadequacy to its (impossible) task, and reason's demand is experienced as a "checking" of life's forces. Pain is occasioned because what fully occupies the imagination is not capable of satisfying reason. But at the same time there is an exhilaration at the unboundedness of the *effort* of the imagination, and a revelation of the very process of striving of the subject itself. This striving occurs under the law of reason and is oriented toward a limitless comprehension of sensory material. It is revealed through a (subrepted) feeling of respect for the "idea of humanity" in our subject.

Kant's approach here presents as an interesting bid to "totalize" the account of the sublime around the notion of the purposive reason, "presented" as the "idea of humanity in our subject." Nevertheless, "presentation" here is not direct sensible presentation of the subject. Here, as well as later, when Kant speaks of the sublime in (literary) art, he maintains that a *negative Darstellung* is involved. Helfer suggests that this repression of the visual is deliberate, in line with Kant's fear that any claim that ideas of reason can find sensible presentation could be used to support fanatical belief systems.[69]

Still, *negative Darstellung* is purposiveness become presentation— presentation characterized in and through the absence of sensible form. As presentation, it is *direct*—a "pure" presentation of a striving itself, independent of empirical aspects—but also *negative*, lacking formal sensibility. By contrast, the beautiful is also presentation: presentation characterized as an *indirekte Darstellung* of the moral good (read, rational purposiveness), which, however, does comprise formal sensibility. Given these alternative characterizations of subjectal *Darstellung*, it is unsurprising that the third *Critique*, with its unificatory intent, also offers an implicit characterization of subjectal *Darstellung* "itself," combining both purity and formal sensibility. The locus of this characterization is the presentation of the *aesthetic idea*, which offers formal sensibility, but without an attendant empirical concept. The effect is that of causing (limitless) presentational striving to display itself.

As I have said, this final characterization can also be seen as embodying Kant's need to supplement the "formless" (and thus insensible) subjectal *Darstellung* of the sublime with a "completive" description of a formally sensible *Darstellung*. In the end, however, this supplementing in terms of formal sensibility also effects a supplanting of the original presumption of a *Darstellung* of rational purposiveness that exceeds formal sensibility. That is, in light of the aesthetic idea, *Darstellung* "itself"—*Darstellung* of the subject as a striving—becomes the event of the production of sensible form "itself," in myriad and limitless quantities, independently of the telos of purposive and unifying reason.

It can be shown, though space precludes that demonstration here, that this production has significance, not only as a completive gesture but also as a supplanting. If the barrier separating the sublime from aesthetic experience is allowed to fall, the presentational *inadequacy* marked by the sublime becomes reinterpretable in light of the presentational *excess* attending the aesthetic idea. And this falling *does* occur, two marks thereof being visible in Kant. The first is the very possibility of the mediation of the sublime through art, which I pursue in Chapter 7. The second is the account of the aesthetic idea itself as *formal,* or definitive, formlessness. The aesthetic idea generates, as it were, an endless sum of forms that the imagination cannot cease to present. Here, Kant's description, in the third *Critique,* of the presentation of the aesthetic idea can be set against the type of presentation that, in the first *Critique,* made for aesthetic clarity. Kant says, for example, that

> even if [the poet] deals with things of which there are examples in experience—e.g., death, envy and all vices, also, love, fame and the like—he tries by means of the imagination, which emulates the play of reason in its quest after a maximum, to go beyond the limits of experience, and to present them to sense [*sinnlich zu machen*] with a completeness of which there is no example in nature. This is properly speaking the art of the poet, in which the faculty of aesthetical ideas can manifest itself in its entire strength.[70]

The aesthetic idea, then, issues from a striving for *completeness*. It seeks this completeness in terms of form, but form that must not, in the end, deliver that containment as a particular concept: that would amount to *incompleteness*, whether as presentation or representation.[71]

It is just here, however, that the supplement can be seen to supplant so that the rational telos that has hitherto determined the notion *Darstellung* is displaced in favor of a telos identified with experience itself, the experience of the excess of presentation over "itself." In short, "excess of formal sensible intuition" supplants "intuited intellectual form" as the telos and meaning of *Darstellung* in Kant.

Conclusion

This brings me to the end of the demonstration I have undertaken in this chapter. Taking as my point of departure the account of early

German romanticism that we find in Lacoue-Labarthe and Nancy's *The Literary Absolute,* I have sought to open a view onto the Kantian subjectal *Darstellung* as hyperbolic, and incipiently hyperbo*logical.* For Lacoue-Labarthe and Nancy, the *hyperbolic* dimension of literature is, in this romantic gesture in which our own era participates, at once recognized and retrained toward subjectal gain. They rightly say that "the massive truth flung back at us is that we have still not left the era of the subject." Later, I offer an exploration of Lacoue-Labarthe's elaboration of the contrary case: that the hyperbolic exhibits subjectal loss through a (yet to be explained) hyperbo*logic.* Anticipating that exploration, I have set out in this chapter to locate the seeds of this type of loss in the Kantian account to which the romantics respond.

It is to be hoped that those seeds have now been excavated for view: I have shown how deconstruction is at play within that structure of subjectal *Darstellung* by which Kant hopes to fix the subject in the third *Critique.* Because pure a priori (negative) *Darstellung* becomes supplemented and then supplanted by the *Darstellung* that yields the *aesthetic* idea, subjectal *Darstellung* itself undergoes a like reinterpretation. It now connotes direct sensible presentation of forms, generated endlessly and without the final unifiability that would attest the subject. In the end, then, *excess* triumphs, as the excess of *Darstellung* "itself." Its triumph is achieved over the presumed demands of reason that would reshape its meaning, and thereby over the possibility of an originary subjectal intuition.

There is here, then, a particular depiction of the subjectal loss incurred within the Kantian aesthetic as that aesthetic flowers into the romantic notion of literature. The early romantics, indeed, took up a veiled invitation in Kant to think of poetry as providing an aesthetic, pure (*rein*) negative presentation of the idea, equivalent to that of the a priori critical-stylistic presentation of mathematics. In doing so, they neglected to notice that the subjectal presentability attached to sublime *negative Darstellung* becomes subverted within Kant's own text when he comes to describe the aesthetic idea. The final bias of that text is toward the presentation, not of a unified subject, but of simultaneous representations, always multiple, of a never-present subject. In subsequent explorations of the link between literature and philosophy, Lacoue-Labarthe will draw heavily upon this depiction, exploring almost endlessly its effects and variants. This will become evident as I proceed, in Chapter 5, to further refine and characterize the account of representational subjectal loss that informs his work.

5

Subjectal Loss in Lacoue-Labarthe
The Recurrence of Hyperbology

Introduction: Representational Surfeit Pursued

I am ready now to probe the heart of Lacoue-Labarthe's characteristically complex explorations of subjectal loss. The *hyperbological* is the name and the concept that links the variety of his readings, and my preliminaries have been intended to lead carefully toward it, by eliciting, as it were, irrepressible occurrences of subjectal loss and gain wherever his analyses tread. In Chapter 2, I argued that his texts ought not to ignore the level on which a subject is always reinscribed. But this reinscription turned out, in Chapter 3, to be susceptible to a more profound dissipation, exemplified in the hesitation of the thespian and autobiographical subjects between two types of self-detachment: willed and unconscious. Within this hesitation, loss of the subject occurs through the events of interminable self-repetition, "otherwise," that accompany "its" attempts at self-gain. Chapter 4 discovered—in Kant's own *Critique,* antedating and withstanding the "literary absolute" initiated by the romantics—subjectal loss thus mediated, through a surfeit rather than a shortfall in subjectal representation.

I move now to seek an organizing motif behind these various expressions of "surfeit as loss." A question arises: How is "too much representation," in the case where it fails to deliver a unified subject, equivalent to "not enough representation" of that subject? And, indeed, it is this inherent capacity of the hyperbolical loss of the subject to exhibit itself as a transition between extremes that attracts Lacoue-Labarthe. He gives the process of hyperbolical transit attention under a new and inclusive name: the hyperbological. Hyperbology interests Lacoue-Labarthe in its delivery of subjectal loss through an alternation of subjectal representation. This alternation finally appears to paralyze the possibility of subjectal *presentation* as well.

Later chapters will attempt to suggest that this is not quite the case as I re-examine the *movement* that comprises this paralysis. For the present, however, I follow Lacoue-Labarthe, mostly in *The Subject of Philosophy*, as he demonstrates the futility threading itself through all attempts at recovering the subject of philosophy, entombed by literature.

Representation, Abyssal Subjectivity, and the Hyperbological

In investigating the hyperbological, I begin by anticipating the difference between the hyperbolical and the hyperbological, starting with the following observation. "Hyperbol*ical*" subjectal loss, in the absence of the further reflection entailed by hyperbo*logy*, does not elicit "duality" or "doubling" of subjectal representation, as I have described it. In fact, hyperbolical movement and representational doubling present as symmetrical opposites rather than as equivalents. The hyperbolical ostensibly refers to subjectal loss in terms of a "representation of excess." "Doubling" refers to the loss of the subject through an "excess of representation." The thought of the hyperbological locates the latter in the former. Within the hyperbolical, the hyperbological identifies pairings of opposed representations of the subject, and the transit between these. What is represented, and its opposite, become present simultaneously as alternative subjects. That is, the hyperbolic ceases to be simple excess and becomes excess theorized in a particular way.

To make this clearer, I now compare two different contexts in which Lacoue-Labarthe identifies the hyperbological. The idea is broached in his work on Hölderlin, "The Caesura of the Speculative."[1] Yet perhaps it is seen in clearer outline in "Diderot: Paradox and Mimesis," to which I have already referred (see Chapters 1 and 3). Drawing especially upon Diderot's comments on the "Rêve de d'Alembert," Lacoue-Labarthe recalls that for Diderot "paradox" is essentially "madness," an "extravagance." Paradox enacts the equivalence of logical contraries:

> The paradox is not only a contradicting or surprising opinion. . . . It implies a passing to the extreme, a sort of "maximisation" . . . by which the equivalence of ordinaries is established (probably without ever *establishing* itself)—the contraries themselves pushed to the extreme, in principle infinite, of contrariety. . . . Paradox is defined by the infinite exchange, or the hyperbolic identity, of contraries.[2]

What can be seen here is a shift in emphasis. Hyperbolic *as such* becomes hyperbolic as a *matrix of opposition,* the "hyperbolic identity of contraries." Paradox involves the representation of an extreme simultaneously with its contrary, the possibility of which it was thought to have excluded. Thus a truthful man pronounces all men liars. Or an actor remains devoid of emotion during a performance, enabling her stage character convincingly to be engulfed in emotion. In each case, one "pole" of the doubled representation is the enunciating subject, who "disappears" as hyperbole undoes the event of his or her subjectal agency in what has been enunciated or performed. If *all* men are liars, then there is *no (truthful) man* present as enunciator of this claim. Similarly, the actor retaining *complete* emotional detachment from a scene in which she portrays passionate emotions leaves a gap, an absence of agent-subject at the place of the mimetic event. I have shown how Lacoue-Labarthe finds the logic of this "mimetic hiatus" in the enunciation of the Paradox itself (that is, of Diderot's "The Paradox of Acting").

A particular logic of exchange or loss is implied here. Lacoue-Labarthe describes it as "abyssal," and also "unceasing, endless," and thereby "without resolution."[3] One "type" of the subject, that which is said or enacted, invalidates the presence of the other type, namely, the sayer/performer. It thereby also invalidates itself. If what has been enunciated or performed has lacked an agent-subject, then the "truth" of the enunciation/performance itself is lacking. It has no "responsible" author, no one who comes to answer for it.[4] Conversely, if one insists on asserting the presence of the agent-subject, then, equally, the truth of the *work* disappears, and consequently the subject *as* agent-enunciator is again no longer present. Abyssality, here, is the engulfing, "endlessly and irremediably," of the subject of the paradox, in both senses of the word "subject."[5]

Thus, then, hyperbo*logical* abyssality. Both within and beyond *Typography*, it is impossible to miss the recurrence of this notion in Lacoue-Labarthe. Derrida, introducing the collection *Typography*, does not. But his attention to hyperbologic *as such* comprises an almost conspicuously delayed and abbreviated outline of its connective function in the collection.[6] It is necessary, if both the specificity and the reach of the notion are to receive due attention, that time be spent with its elements as they emerge in the various texts. Here, I proceed by first comparing the hyperbologic abyssality just mentioned with that found in "The Caesura of the Speculative." In that essay, Lacoue-Labarthe invokes the hyperbological mechanism to nuance an analysis by Peter Szondi.[7]

Szondi identifies in both Schelling and the later Hölderlin a speculative-dialectic "philosophy of the tragic." Lacoue-Labarthe wants to add that not only does Schelling's "philosophy of the tragic" remain a version of Aristotle's philosophy of the cathartic tragic *effect,* but this same speculative-cathartic framework informs Hölderlin's hitherto neglected dramaturgical works: the unfinished *Empedocles,* his translations of Sophocles' *Antigone* and *Oedipus the King,* and the theoretical essays accompanying these three works.[8]

Here, the hyperbological makes its entry as follows. Hölderlin's speculative-dialectic mechanism, says Lacoue-Labarthe, betrays an intrinsic dislocation: "Hölderlin rigorously dismantles the speculative-tragic matrix he himself helped to elaborate," at the same time precluding "the resources for an 'other' thought [or] the possibility of instituting any difference whatsoever in relation to it."[9] So Hölderlin's thoroughly speculative matrix becomes simultaneously, subtly, and irremediably abyssal as regards the subject.

This abyssality is of a piece with that in Diderot's "The Paradox of Acting"; in both there occurs a dialectic of displacement of the enunciator by the enunciated, and vice versa. Again, the hyperbologic is associated with a mimesis that strives to display itself as Aristotelian "general mimesis," that is, as a poietic-productive effect. But again this notion "steps back" to become Aristotelian "restricted mimesis," mimesis as *imitatio.* Ultimately this is Platonic mimesis, haunted by a "proper" subject, whose loss is played out in the theatrical-mimetic event.[10] Hyperbology, a matrix that works by way of an exchange of opposites, is here highlighted by a particular contrast. Two modes of speculative resolution compete: the speculative dialectic that is part of Schelling's theory of tragedy, and the corresponding speculative-cathartic resolution in Hölderlin.

Schelling's analysis of tragedy takes its departure from the question "How was the reason of Greece able to bear the contradictions inherent in its tragedy?" With *Oedipus* in mind, says Lacoue-Labarthe, Schelling answers that tragedy realizes a speculative resolution between implacable opposites: human freedom and the power of the objective world. Enacting fate through the very sequence of events by which he attempts to escape it, Oedipus must bear a punishment that confirms the intrinsic and extrinsic in human agency as irrevocably linked. The Sophoclean resolution recognizes the thoroughgoing simultaneity of human freedom and natural necessity. In Schelling's terms, it reconciles *dogmatism* (the absolute "I") and *criticism* (the Not-I, or the absolute object). Lacoue-Labarthe notes that what is important for Szondi is Schelling's attention to the reconciliation of this central contradiction: "The subject *manifests* his liberty 'by the very loss of that liberty.'"[11] The logic here is not hyperbologic but something more familiar, and not per se an ally of deconstructive subjectal loss. It is constituted in what Schelling himself calls the "identity of identity and difference."[12]

But, probing further, Lacoue-Labarthe identifies a link between this resolving mechanism and Aristotelian catharsis. He notices the notion of "tolerance," or "bearability," that informs the latter and that can be brought to bear upon Schelling. The question is,

> Can we avoid seeing . . . that the question bearing upon the *tolerance* or the capacity for tolerance, in general, of the unbearable (death, suffering, injustice, contradiction) governs, in both cases, the entire interpretation?[13]

Both Schelling and Aristotle treat tragedy as a mode oriented to externalizing contradictions played out in the subject. In both, if one looks closely enough, the logic of this externalization lies in its use to further the reconciliation or tolerance of those contradictions. Ultimately, the subject retains its identity by purging its self-difference.

Now, turning to Hölderlin, Lacoue-Labarthe finds a dialectical mechanism apparently similar in its attempts cathartically to resolve contradictions between divine and human agency. But this mechanism is significantly different in the mode of its resolution.

The Hyperbological in "Der Grund zum Empedocles"

Lacoue-Labarthe argues that Hölderlin's engagement with Sophocles corresponds to his shift toward an "abyssal" mimetology.[14] This shift marks itself in his "violent" translation of *Antigone*, his translation and analysis of *Oedipus the King*, and his alteration of the plot of his own *Empedocles* to portray a tragic hero whose self-divinization is a fault. Lacoue-Labarthe finds the meaning of these moves illuminated by the theoretical work *Der Grund zum Empedocles*, in which Hölderlin "abruptly" introduces "the Platonic problematic of the mimetic (or dramatic) mode of enunciation."[15]

It must be noted in passing that Hölderlin has given this problematic a specifically romantic face. His premise is a paradox intrinsic to romanticism: that the artless quest for innocence is self-defeating. Nature is still sought, but no longer in the formally natural, since only a necessary artificiality of expression can return us to lost nature. Lacoue-Labarthe develops this point at length in the companion piece "Hölderlin and the Greeks."[16]

Scrutinizing *Der Grund zum Empedocles*, Lacoue-Labarthe finds a Hölderlinian subject of mimesis that is "Platonic" in being threatened with loss through writing—"The sentiment no longer expresses itself directly"—and concerned to preserve or recover itself.[17] Now, however, this self-preservation is represented as occurring by way of the necessary passage *through* mimesis, as through a "foreign material." Emblematically, this foreign material is the dramatic poem. Hölderlin says:

> Thus in the tragic dramatic poem as well, the divine is expressed which the poet senses and experiences in his world; the tragic dramatic poem is also an image of the living for him, one that for him is and was present in his life.[18]

This imaging of interiority must, in the very proportion in which the interiority approaches the *nefas*, or divine poietic essence, signal its own differentiation from that "interiority." That is, "the image must differentiate the human being from the element of his sentiment."[19] In other words, the more the (experiencing) subject is "one," undifferentiated from the poietic force that drives enunciation, the more the *content* of the enunciation portrays a *separation* of "the human being" from "the element of his sentiment." There is here a logic of the impossibility of the self-presentation of the subject.

This impossibility is represented in a "perfect" tragedy such as *Oedipus*. The poet's total *unity* with the poetic force has issued in a tragic work that portrays the truth of human agency: Oedipus as *separated* from the *nefas*. Within the drama, the cause of this separation is also evident, namely, Oedipus' "successful" attempt to be one in agency with the *nefas*. The message is paradoxical but clear: the attempt to achieve artistic subjectal integrity by merging with the *nefas* is manifest as a failure by the very process that, by another criterion, manifests its success.

For Lacoue-Labarthe, what is on display here is the "paradox that founded the speculative interpretation of tragedy,"[20] including, implicitly, Schelling's interpretation. His argument runs broadly as follows. Hölderlin's account exemplifies the paradox when it characterizes Oedipus as becoming himself only by way of "his" taking on a purely external agency. This agency brings him to himself, that is, manifests his "identity" *as* one who has occasioned irreparable rejection of the "natural" or "human" elements in that identity. In short, the paradox characterizes the appropriation of the subject by way of "its" passage through a "foreign material." The survival of this foreignness as such is what distinguishes Hölderlin from Schelling. In Schelling, representation of the free subject occurs through its being represented *as* free in the face of the thoroughly triumphant agency of fate. But what happens if the freedom and determination of the subject are allowed simultaneous play, as a *genuine* passage of the human through the "foreign" would demand? In that case, the neat recuperation of the two subjects into one unified subject is thwarted.

It is this further, subtle step that brings hyperbology to the foreground. A representation and its opposite are kept in view simultaneously so that, as it were, no sooner is the subject appropriated than it suffers disappropriation. Lacoue-Labarthe says:

Everything happens, therefore, as though we are dealing with (and with nothing more than) a kind of immobilized attenuation of a dialectical process that marks time in an interminable oscillation between the two poles of an opposition, always infinitely distant from each other.[21]

No longer is the speculative mechanism in service of any final appropriation. Lacoue-Labarthe isolates its key characteristic as *suspension*. It is clear from his accompanying description that this suspension takes the form of a hesitation between alternative (or alternating) representations:

The act of suspension is this: quite simply, the incessant repetition of the engaging of the dialectical process in the — never changing — form of *the closer it is, the more distant it is; the more dissimilar it is, the more adequate it is; the more interior it is, the more exterior it is*.[22]

This equivalence of opposites amounts to a paralysis of the speculative. It is here that Lacoue-Labarthe broaches definition of the *hyperbological*. The hyperbolic was canvased in *The Literary Absolute* as hyperbolization or excess: the infinite propensity for literature to complete itself by exceeding itself.[23] Now the term "hyperbologic" is coined to refer to an inner logic by which the hyperbolic might be seen to proceed, that is, by distancing what is near, and so on.

Lacoue-Labarthe must be read carefully here. Formally, this way of interpreting the hyperbolic and, in particular, of characterizing it as a paralysis between opposite representations, by which the subject of enunciation is lost, remains *inside* the conceptual framework that it *also* subverts:

> Nothing would prevent us from recognizing in this paralysis affecting (without end) the very movement of the dialectic and the ontologic, and beyond the evident gesture of conjuration, the return effect of mimetology within the speculative, and, consequently, within the general discourse of truth and presence.[24]

Again, I have already noted that Lacoue-Labarthe also recognizes that hyperbology presumes an affinity of Hölderlin's hyperbolic with Heideggerian *ent-fernung* (dis-distancing): a stepping back so as to come nearer—or, more accurately speaking, to allow truth, as *aletheia*, to come nearer, in unconcealment. Lacoue-Labarthe implies that this is an inevitable but limited understanding of the effect of the "logic" of hyperbologic. He "baptizes" the hyperbologic, "following Hölderlin's terminology" as

> the "logic" of the open-ended exchange of the excess of presence and of the excess of loss, the alternation of appropriation and disappropriation.[25]

But, noticing "everything that holds it still within the framework of the 'homoeotic' definition of truth," he is forced to ask, "Who knows if this is not the (paradoxical) truth of *aletheia*?"[26]

In other words, through hyperbologic there is elaborated a distance from the representation of truth as *adequation*. This lends itself, on a simple level, to confirming the possibility of approaching *aletheic* truth. Here, though, what is finally confirmed is the possibility of an (adequate) *representation* of *aletheic* truth. However, a more sophisticated understanding of the notion of hyperbologic, continuous with, say, the demonstration of alternating subjectal representations in "The Echo of the Subject," would notice that paralysis *of representa-*

tion itself occurs in this paralysis *between* representations so that the hyperbologic cannot be employed to bolster the notion of representational truth.

In sum, then, the definition extends as well as expounds the hyperbological we have encountered to date, as rendering subjectivity abyssal through provision of a simultaneous representation of opposites. Now we have a more dynamic abyssality, involving the *continuous passing of representations into their opposites.* In addition, the hyperbological contains the resources to prevent this interchange of representations from ever becoming the kind of *unified* representation that would constitute a classical subject. Where a text bids to offer the unification of previously separated representations, the hyperbological identifies itself in a distancing that occurs simultaneously with this unification, undoing it. For Lacoue-Labarthe's Hölderlin, the power of tragedy itself resides in the simultaneous representation of both this unification and its undoing. The undoing offers relief from what would otherwise be a totalization too powerful to bear.

The Hölderlinian hyperbological is now also ripe to be pursued as "catharsis," which Lacoue-Labarthe has earlier characterized in terms of rendering contradictions bearable. Now he takes up the reference to tragedy as *purifying,* from Hölderlin's "Remarks on Oedipus."[27] What Lacoue-Labarthe calls Hölderlin's "final definition of the tragic" is found here:

> The presentation of the tragic rests principally upon this: that the monstrous, the fact that God and man can couple, and the fact that without limit the power of nature and the innermost of man become one in fury, is conceived in that the limitless becoming-one is purified through limitless separation.[28]

"Purification" interposes itself as the theoretical connector between simultaneous subjectal opposites, in a move that for Lacoue-Labarthe confirms Hölderlinian tragedy as the "catharsis of the speculative."[29] In this new role, catharsis purges, not the unbearability of *separation,* but the unbearability of *unification,* that is, speculation. Separation, though, is no more final than is unification; Hölderlin offers, not the triumph of either, but the paralysis effected by their interplay. Lacoue-Labarthe once more engages the important figure of *rhythm,* hitherto almost pointedly absent from the argument.

I note first how Hölderlin uses the word. The representational rhythm within tragedy enables it to, as it were, display life schematically; tragedy is able to show how a sensuous system, man in his entirety develops as if under the influence of the element, and how representation, sensation and reason appear in different successions yet always according to a certain law.[30]

"Rhythm" signifies the pace and flow of alternating representations of the two kinds I have just identified: unification and separation. Within this rhythm, the respective representations are transported with a different "weight" or "rapidity," says Hölderlin. That is, within the alternation, one or the other is more emphasized. In the tragic plot, a caesura serves the function of preventing the dominant representation from accumulating so much momentum that it excludes its counterpart. In this way, tragedy displays what exists in life, but it does so "more as a state of balance than as mere succession."[31]

Quoting Hölderlin, from the "Remarks on Oedipus," Lacoue-Labarthe reminds his reader of how this theoretical framework operates, citing the process

whereby, in the rhythmic succession of the representations, in which the *transport* presents itself, *what in meter is called caesura*, the pure word, the counter rhythmic intrusion, becomes necessary in order to meet the racing alternation of representations at its culmination.

As the quotation continues, Hölderlin claims a more significant effect of this operation: "What appears then is no longer the alternation of representations but representation itself."[32]

Hölderlin sees much significance in this metaphorical caesura (analogous to a metrical caesura, or pause), in its provision of a "still point." Lacoue-Labarthe does not say here whether he joins Hölderlin in attributing this "phenomenal" capability to the caesura. Evidently, he at least accepts that, in Hölderlin's terms, the caesura is a *figure* of "representation itself." What does this figure show? His considered answer: that representation involves nothing more definitive than a perpetual oscillation between alternating hyperbological representations. The stillness at the caesura is to be understood schematically or *figurally*. It denotes, not an absence of hyperbological oscillation, but rather an absence of the resolution of this oscillation. The disarticulation that occurs with the caesura

does not do away with the logic of exchange and alternation. It simply brings it to a halt, re-establishes its equilibrium; it prevents it, as Hölderlin says, from carrying along its representations exclusively in one sense or another.[33]

Hallmarks of the Hyperbological: Hölderlin

It is now possible more carefully to locate elements within this cathartic hyperbological that relate to subjectal loss. First, there is the subjectal doubling that I have already mentioned. This is nowhere better seen at work than in the earlier, pivotal quotation ("finally" defining the tragic, says Lacoue-Labarthe), with its three subjectal couplings: God-man, nature-man, and unity-separation.

Second, the tragic offers unification of the "subject" of these couplings. Each pair comprises a representation of two-subjects-become-one. Accompanying this is a purification, a rendering bearable of the unbearability of such a representation. Otherwise, this representation would depict the *undifferentiated* activity of the divine in the living, an intolerable depiction of the divine through, or even in partnership with, a human *recognized in contradistinction to this divine*. The purification takes the shape of the "limitless separation" of the two spheres. The two-become-one becomes inevitably represented again *as* two (that is, as two-become-one-become-two) in terms of, as Hölderlin says and Lacoue-Labarthe underlines, a "categorical turning about of the divine."[34]

Lacoue-Labarthe takes up the challenge successfully to interpret this "turning about," this limitless separation, or "purification," as *loss* of the subject. For, under one understanding, and in a project that connects Schelling with Hegel, a duality of representations can be theorized as instead representing the *gain* by the subject of itself. The linkage between opposed representations allows one representation to be seen as a negation of the other, with both contributing to a sublative process that moves toward delivering an absolute subject. In this way, particular representations of the subject furnish, in view of their very diversity, the presumption of an overarching subject. This subject is constituted as a linkage, systematically or organically, of those representations.[35]

This subject, thwarting abyssality, finds reassertion by way of a "return of the figure," with a finality that Lacoue-Labarthe would not wish to concede. We saw, in the "The Echo of the Subject," that Lacoue-Labarthian subjectal *désistance* involves a simultaneity of self-representations that the subject views concurrently, and that it "'desists' because it must always confront *at least* [these] two figures."[36]

Now, though, it is interesting *both* that the subject appears under these conditions of oscillation *and* that this appearing does not finally amount to a staving off of *désistance*. Seemingly, this figure of oscillation contains both of the elements that we have noted in Lacoue-Labarthe's work to date, each failing to gainsay the other: the reassertion of the structure of subjectivity, and the abyssal loss of the subject itself. The reassertion implies a triumph of Hegel that cannot, under one reading, be resisted. Conversely, for the abyssal loss, Lacoue-Labarthe looks to an intrusion into the Hegelian schema of a "radical" other that is never better signified than in Nietzsche. Hegel and Nietzsche are brought into dialogue through a return to Heidegger's treatment of Nietzsche, and to Heidegger's tendency inadvertently to "Hegelize" Nietzsche.

The Nietzschean Subject: Its Metaphysical Rescue and Hyperbological Loss

As Lacoue-Labarthe presents Heidegger, the latter certainly does not avoid the question of the displacement of the subject in Nietzsche's texts. But Heidegger resolutely identifies the subject "Nietzsche" with Nietzsche's *thought*. He replumbs this thought by applying *thinking (Denken)* to the texts, in an effort to uncover the subjectal displacement that attends their *unthought*. In so doing, he fails to ask a question about the displacement of "Nietzsche" himself, namely, about the *subject Nietzsche* "who" *enunciates* Nietzsche's texts. At this juncture, the point involved here is worth generalizing, briefly and broadly; I shall return to nuance it later.

"Subjective" and "Objective" Dimensions of the Subject

Lacoue-Labarthe sees Heidegger's omission as avoiding the question of the subject in its most critical dimension. What is written or mimetically performed is always a *work*, the producing subject of which becomes represented *as* producer of the work and, moreover, as produced in the production of the work. But, as an *event*, each writing or mimetic performance also implies an authorial or enunciating subject who is "prior" to the work he or she produces. But this enunciating subject is inevitably deconstituted by its placement in relation to its "other," the subject produced in the event of production of the work. The enunciating subject is, as we have seen Derrida point out, either "early" or "late" in respect to "itself." It suffers *désistance*.

This distinction between two modes of subjectal representation might be framed from a slightly different angle. It might be said that a theoretical work bids to establish a subject both subjectively and objectively. Objectively, it represents the subject by way of a description or argument that gives an account of what a subject *is*, in general. The Cartesian subject "Nietzsche," to take only one historical example, would be the "Nietzsche who thinks," arguably reducible to a "Nietzsche" retrospectively produced as thinker of Nietzsche's thoughts. But there is also the "subjective" subject: the subject preceding and generating the (self)-representation (by which "Nietzsche" emerges): as its author or speaker, or as the actor involved in its presentation. Here, too, subjectivity is synonymous with identity: the claim is "I, and no other, am speaking to you."

As I track Lacoue-Labarthe's analyses, it will become clear that he often places subjectively and objectively delineated subjects in engagement with each other, the better to elicit a loss of the subject as occurring *between* them. What results is the subversion of the substantiality or identity of *both* these "types" of the subject.

The subversions are interrelated in the following way, which I will seek to expound as the Lacoue-Labarthian hyperbological. Any objective representation or self-representation of the subject remains a representation of the subject *as* divided, or a representation of "at least" two subjects. It follows that representing the subject is an impossible project. True, a relation between representations might be postulated whereby this "objective" subject, in its division, nevertheless amounts to a unified whole—through sublation, for example. But then there occurs the "disappearance" (or "withdrawal") of the subject under its *subjective* aspect. Having signaled this way in which subjectal loss, or subversion, is paralleled between the two modes and even shared between them, I now return to consider Nietzsche, using Lacoue-Labarthe as guide.

Hyperbology and the Nietzschean Fictive Subject

In terms of a displacement of the "objective" subject, the subversion engendered by writing emerges from deconstructive readings of Nietzsche, and of Heidegger's Nietzsche. In terms of a displacement of the "subjective" subject, and according to what might be described as Lacoue-Labarthe's peculiar interest in both Nietzsche and literature, this subversion emerges in the way in which Nietzsche "himself" fails to be fixed by his writings. To track Lacoue-Labarthe's engagement with Nietzsche through several early articles is to notice varying but convergent means by which Lacoue-Labarthe undermines subjectal representation in Nietzsche, or in readings of Nietzsche. There again results a subject both manifest and lost in a "hesitation" between dual or doubled subjectal representations.

Visiting the places where Lacoue-Labarthe canvases the subversion of the representational in Nietzsche, we encounter various kinds of "doubling" within which the Nietzschean subject "slips" away. In "Typography," where Lacoue-Labarthe observes Heidegger taking up the unthought in Nietzsche, what Heidegger "avoids," or at any rate attempts to "take from behind," is "the question of the *subject*," by which Lacoue-Labarthe means "the 'subject of enunciation,' . . . or of writing" as opposed to anything that might be in any way "*identified* with the subject of the 'metaphysics of subjectity,' under any form whatsoever."[37]

Heidegger conveniently seeks the "unthought" *content* of Nietzsche's writings (one representation of Nietzsche's "subject") while avoiding the question of *Nietzsche himself* (another representation). What is in play here is, in fact, *not* the metaphysicality of the former representation in comparison to the nonmetaphysicality, or nonsubstantiality, of the latter. Rather, what interests Lacoue-Labarthe is the *interplay* between the two representations. Or, one can say, it is the fact that the appearance of the former and of the latter can never "coincide." The content of Nietzsche's thought can never identify a subjective "Nietzsche" on whose account it *is* content. It is this displacement that, as it were, causes the disappearance of the subject to appear.

This becomes clearer in two further articles.

In "Apocryphal Nietzsche," Lacoue-Labarthe returns to the Nietzsche who has been displaced, or dispersed, as subject, by his act of writing "philosophy as literature."[38] Heidegger has not noticed that Nietzsche invents his Zarathustra as analogy to a particular characterization of Plato. We have already met this Plato. It is the Plato who subverts his own identity in subverting that of Socrates, by promoting, "in accordance with Plato's unfaithfulness to his own doctrine, . . . the *dissimulation* of the author (of the subject of writing) as a character."[39] Heidegger fails to read this clue. But it is in "Obliteration," a review of Heidegger's *Nietzsche*, that the closest scrutiny yet is made of the way Nietzsche's thought becomes susceptible to Heidegger's framing of it as metaphysics.[40]

"Obliteration": A (Non)subject "Who" Escapes (Dis)-distancing

"Obliteration" finds Lacoue-Labarthe observing as Heidegger approaches Nietzsche by way of a technique of *Ent-fernung/é-loignement,* or, as Lacoue-Labarthe's translator says, "(dis)-distancing": a stepping back so as to get closer to a presumed "unthought" in Nietzsche. This Hegelian move allows Heidegger to resolve (read, *evade*) the contradictions inherent in Nietzsche's self-representation, and to arrive at a unified representation of Nietzsche as the last victim of metaphysics. Heidegger thus "dismisses" the question of the "subject of philosophy," to the benefit of "the law of repetition."[41]

Lacoue-Labarthe sees in this dismissal Heidegger's avoidance of the evidence of a radical hesitation of the Nietzschean subject with respect to its own being. Heidegger, intent on exorcising Nietzsche's madness, turns a blind eye to the disappearance (or, desertion) of that which, in "Nietzsche's" subject, fails to correspond to the Nietzsche that is subject to representation. It is worth listening to Lacoue-Labarthe at some length on this. He says that

> what interests us here is neither the subject nor the author. Nor is it the "other"—whatever this may come to mean—of the subject or the author. Rather (and to limit ourselves for the time being to the question of the subject alone), what interests us is what is *also* at stake in the subject, while remaining absolutely irreducible to any subjectivity (that is, to any objectivity); that which, in the subject, deserts (has always already deserted) the subject *itself* and which, prior to any "self-possession" (and in a mode other than that of dispossession), is the dissolution, the defeat of the subject in the subject or *as* the subject: the (de)constitution of the subject or the "loss" of the subject—if, at least, it is possible to think the loss [*si du moins l'on pouvait penser la perte*] of what one has never had, a kind of "originary" and "constitutive" loss (of "self").[42]

Note the formulation "that which, in the subject, deserts (has always already deserted) the subject *itself.*" Lacoue-Labarthe is hardly saying that there "is" a subject that manifests itself in the hesitancy between inevitably doubled representations of the subject. Under that reading, the *désistant* subject would still be metaphysical, achieving presence in the very interaction between dichotomous poles of subjectivity. As a subject, it would link these poles, bridging "objective" and "subjective" subjectity, nature and freedom, science (theory) and art (practice). That claim would ultimately tie in to the idealist project that I have already discussed as originating with Kant; in Chapter 8 I shall recall echoes of this project as these inhabit even formally postmodern accounts of subjectivity.

Instead, Lacoue-Labarthe's claim seeks to remain subtly but clearly distinct from this. For him, what becomes "present" in the "subject's" hesitancy, oscillation, or division between representations is the *loss of the subject* or the *subject as loss*. The subject-in-desertion is "that which is lost" and as such is "something." But this "something" is, in fact, nothing, or at least not a subject. It is itself irreducible to any subjectivity, signifying radical and irremediable absence, something *always already lost* to the subject.

What is present *is* thus, as it were, *both* a represented but divided subject *and* an "other" (non)subject. The latter is delineated only in desertion; it is "that which in the [represented] subject deserts." More accurately, it is manifest *postdesertion*, since it has "always already deserted" the subject itself. This (non)subject of desertion is also explicated in terms of its "dissolution," or the "(de)constitution" of the subject. Within the structure that yields subjectivity, it is radically undermining, resistant to all recuperation.

Lacoue-Labarthe must pursue such a nonsubject carefully, since by definition it cannot bear investigation as a subject in its own right. Its identity, its destiny, is to be that by which any subject is (de)constituted in "loss." The form of writing, and the insinuation of the structure of writing into conceptualization and language, becomes the blueprint for this loss. The loss re-marks itself in the hesitation *between* two theorizations, one of which presumes the possibility of a pure representation, occurring prior to writing or language, while the other sees writing as purely fictive. Lacoue-Labarthe's "The Detour" allows me an excellent opportunity to demonstrate this.[43]

"The Detour": The Nietzschean Subject in Hyperbologic Hesitation between True and Fictive Identities

"The Detour" examines Nietzsche's discovery of rhetoric as a divided, nonconceptual, origin of language. Nietzsche's previous work on tragedy, including *The Birth of Tragedy*, looks to music for a pure representation of the will, and likewise to language, as Lacoue-Labarthe says, "on the basis of its musical essence."[44] Now Nietzsche explores the possibility of a musical component within language, considered either apart from rhetoric or (later) within it.[45] Both explorations characterize music as an "art," which, nonetheless, is "immediately" representational of the will, and therefore of the subject itself. Neither treatment finally resolves the paradox implied here: How can art, as representational, be presumed to represent something "immediately"—in other words, to *present* it as if without an intervening medium? Nietzsche's approach is to treat music as unique, following Arthur Schopenhauer (as recounted by Nietzsche in *The Birth of Tragedy*, and as recalled by Lacoue-Labarthe): "Music . . . unlike [other arts] . . . is not a copy of the phenomenon but an *immediate copy* of the will itself."[46]

Lacoue-Labarthe does not elaborate on the nature of the ambiguity here. But by implication it is this: Does music achieve what no other art can—*immediate* copying—*because of* its nature as an art, or *in spite of* this nature? In other words, is all art, and specifically the "art" within language, to be conceived on the basis of music, as beginning with "pure" representation? If so, the *rhythm* in rhetoric, as the Apollinian "formative" characteristic within language, is secondary to the Dionysiac harmony, melody, and flow, by which the will is represented wholly. Empirically, this corresponds to proposing a preferred order in which representations are held to be generated. Language seen as "musical" presumes a priority for the generation of its musical component, as a copy of primal reality, over the generation of images. So that the "son" might not "sire the father," this order must be preferred to that in language seen as "adequational": the generation of sensory stimuli, then images, then sounds.[47]

Nietzsche finds this schema, which is implied in *The Birth of Tragedy*, disrupted by his deeper exploration of rhetoric itself. There he encounters a separate, and ultimately incompatible, theorization of rhetoric as the force within language. A clash with music as originary is inevitable, since "rhetoric remains completely inaccessible unless one pays the price of entirely recasting the analysis of language (this is at least a risk taken)."[48] Rhetoric (as "play") now becomes cast as the essence of Greek *art*. Also, Greek *language*, in particular, becomes elevated as the "art par excellence." In this shift to according language a rhetorical or artistic essence, as play or metaphor, Nietzsche has ceased looking to it for immediate representation.[49]

In short, language (through its musical component) *was* immediate subjectal representation to the earlier Nietzsche but is now (in its artistic essence) mediate representation. Characteristically, Lacoue-Labarthe probes the hesitation between these representations of language, and especially the strength of the second, as a nevertheless implicit gesture in the direction of the hyperbological. The point is that the rhetorical origin of language cannot be reconciled with its musical origin.

Nietzsche recognizes, in effect, that even before formal rhetorical structures emerge, rhetoric informs language as an instinct, "a means of unconscious art."[50] The force—the *dunamis*—behind this instinct is one of persuasion, which "plays with," at the very origin, any presumed "pure representation" of the subject as will.

In other words, any presumed "musical component" at the heart of rhetoric is itself implicated in "play" and denied its own "musical" essence. Rather, as rhythm (the rhythm or repetition by which the subject persuasively creates the self it purportedly reports), this component reveals musicality itself as implicated in the *artistic* purposes of language. What is thus effaced is the alternative understanding of music as Dionysian, that is, as unified, pure representation of a state prior to the conceptual. It follows that

> Dionysus can therefore no longer appear: Apollo precedes him, and in preceding him—him whom he represented—he hides his face for good, he hides all hope that his true face (the face of truth) might one day reveal itself *as such*.[51]

Representation of the subject, then, is reduced to rhythm, that is, to the mere shell that is the intent to (mis)represent by repetition. "The Echo of the Subject" obviously finds its own echo here. Can the subject here similarly be said to be lost within a "doubled representation"? Yes, for the reason that rhetoric itself—art itself, language itself—is implicated specifically in the presentation of the self-as-other. The subject here appears *as* lost, but since language plays *at the origin*, no "alternative" subject can be said to be re-erected here; what appears, again, is not a lost subject but the (event of) loss of the subject. "That which in the subject never appears" fails to appear precisely as having never been present. For Lacoue-Labarthe, Nietzsche's loss of faith in the possibility of representation coincides with and perhaps explains his inability, after the "passage through rhetoric," to produce more than fragments. The "desired form" of the work is no longer possible. This form, says Lacoue-Labarthe, would have contained a "voice" through which the subject as will is absolutely represented.

Toward the conclusion of "The Detour," fragmentation of the work and doubling of the subject come jointly into view. The scene is the death of the last philosopher, from the second of two fragments in the first notebook of the *Book of the Philosopher*.[52] Lacoue-Labarthe observes that the philosopher's speech is no longer meant to instantiate, as in the first fragment, the "miraculous equilibrium and 'fraternal alliance'" between Dionysian and Apollinian dialogue with which *The Birth of Tragedy* credits the third act of Tristan. Instead, "[in the second fragment] the scene previously sketched is repeated in the *soliloquy* of the last philosopher, in the '*discourse* of the last philosopher with himself.'"[53]

Here, then, we have the mark of the passage through language: a loss of the original, a soliloquy that is unavoidably a discourse with an other (as) self. It is significant for Lacoue-Labarthe that in this second fragment, language (*soliloquy* and *discourse*) rather than music (crying or singing) carries the presentation. The identification with myth is also more direct: "the last philosopher is not *like* Titan, it is Oedipus 'himself.'"[54]

That the dying, plaintive Oedipus is doomed always to hear his "own" voice as the voice of a separate other demonstrates that even the last philosopher is doubled by discourse. He pleads to undergo the death that is loss of differentiation, in exchange for participation in "whole," undifferentiated truth. But this plea is in vain:

> This voice, which haunts the discourse of the last man on (the absence of) truth, which doubles that discourse and echoes its desolation (which defers its death), is perhaps already the one it will be given to "Nietzsche" to make heard.[55]

As it speaks, this voice encounters its "other," a presence to itself from outside itself (but presence in delay, in echo), inevitably subverting any closure effected by what has just been said, making it impossible for there to be a "last word." Even thus will Nietzsche's own "voice," after the encounter with rhetoric, be itself split, never speaking without also speaking (and hearing itself), after and alongside itself, as an "other to itself."

This duplication has spawned itself from the "original doubling," which Nietzsche's exploration has not been able to shake: that between language as immediate representation of the subject, as (prerhythmic) music, and language as artistic, mediate representation. Again, it seems, it is "between" these two divided representations (as "self" and as "other," or immediate and mediate representation) that a "third" subject becomes manifest—as recent absence, having already departed.

This analysis takes me some distance toward my task of identifying a generic mode of the loss "between representations" of the (never present) subject of philosophy. What finds itself thwarted in philosophy (couched within literature, or within art generally) is the representation of the subject "itself," or the unification of split Kantian representations of the subject. The "mode of loss" of the subject thus constitutes itself as a perpetual oscillation between representations, resulting in a hyperbological "passing into each other of extremes": self and other, nature and art, human and God. But this interchange is symmetrical so that the "passing over," far from effecting unification, restores the split. The hallmark of the mode is a priority of representation over that which is represented, that is, over the subject, which correspondingly becomes the product rather than the template of representation.

In Lacoue-Labarthe's explication of Nietzsche, this priority is manifest as that of language. As the fictive, as art, language is found at the origin of being, preceding it and dividing it. And, *within* language itself, what is determinative is rhetoric—mere form, as a "monstrosity" that sires that which is ontologically its father, namely, substance or life force itself. In Nietzschean terms, this is tantamount to the irreversible priority of the Apollinian over the Dionysian:

> For in art as it is now defined, Dionysus has practically disappeared. Or more correctly, he has become Apollo. There is henceforth no force that is not already weakened *as* form, that is, as language. Apollo is the *name* of Dionysus ("originary" metaphor). Apollo precedes him, and in preceding him—him whom he represented— he hides his face for good, he eliminates all hope that his true face (the face of truth) might one day reveal itself *as such.*[56]

Yet one must follow Lacoue-Labarthe closely here. Finally, it is not the priority of the Apollinian over the Dionysian that Nietzsche's discovery yields but the circularity that such a priority sets in train. Care must be taken precisely to identify the movement through which the loss of the subject emerges within this original triumph of the fictive. "Apollo replaces Dionysus," Lacoue-Labarthe seems to say. But if this were so, the subject would not be lost, but rather *found* as "Apollo," as the fictive itself, as *pure* production, analogously with the infinitized romantic subject that Lacoue-Labarthe and Nancy locate in *The Literary Absolute.* Literature, (re)presented solely and unconflictedly as "pure production," merely saves and reinscribes the subject.

By contrast, Lacoue-Labarthe's interest in the passage just quoted is in the juxtaposition of Apollo and Dionysus, of the true and the fictive, in which each is obliterated by the other, in an interminable exchange. If Dionysus can no longer be seen for Apollo, the replacement is nevertheless not pure. It does not offer total freedom from Dionysus, precisely because the obverse side of this truth is that Apollo can no longer be seen except in relation to Dionysus. Dionysus survives as the one who, having been replaced by Apollo, grants Apollo identity: "Apollo is the name of Dionysus." Were *either* Dionysus (the original) *or* Apollo (its figure) to emerge from this analysis as the truth of representation, representation would become the event of the manifestation of the subject, either as that which representation erects or as that which it copies and falsifies.

Instead, in Lacoue-Labarthe's reading, and much more subtly, the subject is lost precisely in an *interactivity* between the figures of Dionysus and Apollo. Subject *to* this interaction, each of the two (the original and the fictive) cannot but pass, and keep on passing, into the other. Apollo effaces Dionysus, but Dionysus equally effaces Apollo. He effaces him, as it were, from *behind* him, that is, by virtue of being the original, which the figure of Apollo cannot but be hiding. Once this is conceded, the "purely fictive" is robbed of its credibility as such.

So neither Apollo nor Dionysus remains free of the other. And it is within the "endless circulation" between these two figures that the subject emerges as lost. Seeking the mode of loss peculiar to the Lacoue-Labarthian Nietzschean subject, we have found it to occur through a communion between extremes that yields their equivalence. We have returned, in short, to the *hyperbological*: a movement whose force resides neither in the true nor, despite appearances, in the fictive but rather in the interminable propensity for each to become the other.

All this, and its thematic consistency in Lacoue-Labarthe's work, is appropriately enough on display in the essay that begins Lacoue-Labarthe's philosophico-literary corpus: "The Fable."[57] I now take up, in two stages separated by an interlude, Lacoue-Labarthe's exposition there, which I find ripe to be sifted for a blueprint of the Lacoue-Labarthian hyperbological. On offer is his typically sophisticated recourse to a particular mechanism by which hyperbology is protected from recuperation to metaphysics.

"The Fable" (1): Sameness without Substitutability

The question that "The Fable" explores—"What if philosophy is nothing but literature?"—is taken from the famous Nietzschean fragment that Lacoue-Labarthe reads here: "How the 'True World' Finally Became a Fable (The History of an Error)."[58] It broaches, with disarming naïveté, the site of the overlap of philosophy and literature, which overlap will preoccupy Lacoue-Labarthe for the remainder of his career as he maps and remaps its contours.

Taken together, the title and orienting question suggest that the latter can be paraphrased as follows: After Nietzsche, and particularly after the fragment at issue, might not the genre of "fable" be taken to include philosophy, to the point where philosophy is seen to be nothing but literature? Correspondingly, philosophy as such disappears, and literature becomes "all that there is" and can take for granted the "philosophical" truth of whatever it erects as subject. In fact, Lacoue-Labarthe begins where this oversimple point ends, and he engages with its key self-contradiction: any "substitution" of literature for philosophy springs the trap of re-erecting philosophy as that which literature replaces. It re-erects philosophy, *as* literature. The point of the article is its ambitious and constantly renewed attempt to circumvent this trap, and its several subtle variants, so as to signify the "genuine" triumph of the fictive that Nietzsche's piece intends. ("Genuine" is itself, of course, a word under erasure here.) This becomes a matter of keeping in play the duality of representation(s) that is philosophy-literature and of persistently resisting, on Nietzsche's behalf, a reductive substitution of either representational medium by the other.

"Fable" becomes the name reserved for the genre that promises escape from these substitutions. The Nietzschean fragment, well scoured by commentators, provides six theses, each identifying a phase in the history of metaphysics. Lacoue-Labarthe takes up the sixth and last, envisaging the final eclipse of metaphysics-as-truth and the beginning of the possibility of the radical revaluing represented by Zarathustra:

> 6. The true world—we have abolished. What world has remained? The apparent one perhaps? But no! *With the true world we have also abolished the apparent one.*
>
> (Noon; moment of the briefest shadow; end of the longest error; high point of humanity; INCIPIT ZARATHUSTHRA).[59]

The abolished world has, Nietzsche says, become a fable. But Nietzschean fable is envisaged as a very particular type of fiction, one that cannot draw upon a contrast with "reality." Thus is set up the key challenge, since

> to think fiction [in this text, as opposed to its predecessors] is not to oppose appearance and reality, since appearance is nothing other than the product of reality. To think fiction is precisely to think without recourse to this opposition, *outside* this opposition; to think the world as a fable. Is this possible?[60]

Lacoue-Labarthe senses that moving "outside this opposition" requires a move against *substitution* itself. Reading the world as fable involves undoing (as such) the myth of creation that yields the world. Could this involve replacing what is true with what *saying* establishes? If so, then *saying* becomes the decisive event: "the world is what is said about it."[61] But if that merely means that the event of saying, as *muthos*, now establishes what "is," then the move is counterproductive, for what "is" has once again been established as truth. Attempting to say that "the discourse of truth, *logos*, is nothing other than *muthos*, that is, the very thing against which it has always claimed to constitute itself," one is erecting *muthos*, the fable, in terms of a substitution that re-erects *logos*, reasserting its priority over *muthos*.[62]

Breaking this cycle of equivalence involves associating the "error" Nietzsche names with *substitution* itself, that is, with the presumption within language that the figure "stands for" something else. One might return to a notion of fable free from substitutive logic, that is, free from the logic of differences that substitution presupposes:

> For fable is the language with respect to which (and in which) these differences—which are not differences—no longer obtain: literal and figurative, transparency and transfer, reality and simulacrum, presence and representation, *muthos* and *logos*, logic and poetry, philosophy and literature, etc. Is such a language thinkable except as a kind of "eternal repetition" [*réassessement éternel*] in the course of which the same play of the same desire and of the same disappointment would indefinitely repeat itself?[63]

On Nietzsche's behalf, Lacoue-Labarthe is moving toward Heidegger's insight that difference itself correlates to the possibility of the metaphysical. The abolition of difference thus becomes a precondition for the "abolition" of the true (read, metaphysical) world, and the recharacterization of that world as fable.

But difference is not so easily abolished. Is Nietzsche's intention respected by Heidegger's claim that, for the pre-Socratics, *muthos* has an original equivalence with *logos*? Lacoue-Labarthe argues that it is not. Heidegger's point is that myth, as *true saying*, once referred to the unconcealment of truth (*logos*). But, later,

> *muthos* and *logos* become separated and opposed only at the point where neither *muthos* nor *logos* can keep to its original nature. In Plato's work, this separation has already taken place.[64]

For Lacoue-Labarthe, as we have seen, such attempts to find an "original" link between appearance and truth result, in general, in an absolutization of literature or language. This in turn re-erects the philosophical subject (that is, resurrects the subject of literature *as* an infinitized philosophical subject). Here he says the same: the Heideggerian identification reflects the Nietzsche who "rehabilitates" appearance and *muthos, as such*, not the one who would abolish them.

Instead, for the Nietzschean abolition to proceed, the identification of *muthos* with *logos* must be resisted while, paradoxically, their utter equivalence axiologically (that is, as values) must be signified. This necessitates that their axiological engagement should occur, on equal terms yet undecidably, by way of a third figure with which each equally identifies—the fable. Lacoue-Labarthe says that, for Nietzsche, it must be that

> *muthos and logos* are the same thing, but neither is more true (or more false, deceptive, fictional, etc.) than the other; they are neither true nor false; both are the *same* fable.[65]

So problem and solution are intriguingly set up in terms of this interplay between *logos* and *muthos*, held together in the figure of fable as entirely alternative subjectal representation. The problem is this: neither representation must be proposable as the truth *of the other* (for then *logos* becomes the sole truth, relativizing its counterpart). But this would be impossible were they to remain as *different* representations of the subject. In that case, the question of their comparative truth would immediately arise, the substitutive framework would be set in train, and so on. Therefore, we have Lacoue-Labarthe's solution: the two representations must constitute the *same* fable. I pause here to open this point into an anticipatory consideration of hyperbology, the better to be able later to reconnect with Lacoue-Labarthe's analysis.

Interlude: Hyperbological Disruption of Unified Subjectal Representations

In the last-mentioned quotation, the notion of sameness is remarkably characterized. Originating in contradistinction to difference, it is then required to operate independently of this origin. The freedom sought is from a Hegelian bind.[66] It is obtained by Lacoue-Labarthe in terms of, one might say, *différance*. At the origin of *muthos-logos* he finds a difference that differs from difference, or a sameness that differs from itself. While this approach obviously implies an appeal to familiar motifs of Derridean deconstruction, here I argue that in Lacoue-Labarthe they exhibit themselves within and through the hyperbological.[67] My contention is that hyperbology is what more or less explicitly catches Lacoue-Labarthe's eye in almost any text; it then incorporates and shapes deconstructive and other motifs, becoming the overarching mechanism within which they find scope.

A broad description of that mechanism is possible now, as we watch Lacoue-Labarthe, at the outset of his career, treating the simultaneous demands in "The Fable" for competing and yet noncompeting representations of *muthos* and *logos*. What already appears is his concern to point out that any "single" representation of the subject of mimesis, literature, or thought inevitably presents as dispersed into two opposing representations. He clearly also is at pains to question mechanisms that unify these representations, whether by dissolution of their differences or by sublation. His later texts convict the experience of writing and language as providing a site of "warm loss" of the subject, by delivering a subject always separated from itself. "The Fable" signposts these themes, anticipating their later generalization as hyperbology.

That anticipation is evident if one probes the *muthos-logos* formulation he has just offered: "*muthos* and *logos* . . . are the *same* fable." The formulation reasserts, in Nietzsche's interests, the requirement that the opposing representations *not* remain un-unified, for representations surviving in opposition are susceptible to theorization or Hegelian sublation, processes that promote the erection of the subject rather than its subtle loss. What instead *does* signal this loss is a passage of representations into each other, a passage that, as it were, careers helplessly *through* unification *to* a new and effective separation beyond. In this way, any mechanism that exhibits representations as unified has another mechanism as its shadow. This "other" interacts with its counterpart, rendering it impotent with regard to re-erection of a subject.

The demands made by this complex mode of "unification" invariably recur whenever Lacoue-Labarthe's readings canvas subjectal loss; the "mechanism" by which his account of lost subjectivity respects these demands gathers itself under the rubric of hyperbology. Hyperbology manifests the passing of extreme and opposite representations into each other, each representation continuously giving way to, or "passing into," its opposite, in a movement that continues incessantly. Here the impetus to unification, rhythm, or repetition remains an avatar of the post-Kantian desire for the subject. I have explained how this desire survives in Hegel, Schelling, and the romantics and also, in a more complicated way, in Heidegger. But the operation of the hyperbological means that this unification remains on the level of an orienting desire. Its poles are never themselves; each is always and already its other.

Within the hyperbological, then, no discrete representation of the subject survives as "fodder for sublation." Any "single" representation that hyperbology identifies is already in the process of giving way to its opposite representation. Admittedly, this process still demarcates the difference or space in which metaphysics, as a *dunamis* or drive for Being, the idea, or the subject, is housed. But the subject "itself" is always only present *as* lost between each alternating pair of representations: writer and philosopher, agent and theorizer, the necessary and the free, the divine and the human, actor and character, and so on.

It is this passing of opposing representations into a "single" representation, but then *beyond* it, that subverts the classical hope finally to represent the subject. In the essay at hand, for example, Lacoue-Labarthe is untroubled by the prospect of showing Nietzsche as collapsing the dual representations of truth and the fictive into what is apparently a single representation of both, for the representations have simultaneously, of their own accord, as it were, separated themselves again. I can now return to this point in Lacoue-Labarthe's exposition of Nietzsche's fragment. On display is the hyperbological, in the form of a radical unification that nevertheless must coexist with a peculiar and insurmountable disunification.

"The Fable" (2): Muthos and Logos in Interminable Hyperbological Exchange

Lacoue-Labarthe has offered an initial version of this unification of subjectal representations: the *substitution* of the metaphysical representation of fable for Nietzsche's sought-after representation so that "the world is what is said about it." But as we have seen, what Nietzsche seeks cannot be delivered so simply; the new formulation only restores "fable" to the realm of metaphysics. So Lacoue-Labarthe proposes, in effect, this altered version of what Nietzsche is attempting: to generate a subject of the fable precisely through the *interplay between the two representations*. In hesitating *between* those representations, this subject loses itself, and *thus* finds "itself."

To generate the first of these representations, one approaches the fable, on Nietzsche's behalf, as "true saying." The fable thus represents a turning of metaphysics against itself. It is "what metaphysics hereafter sees . . . of itself in a kind of mirror that it does not present to itself from the outside and that must be thought by repetition . . . without recourse to metaphysical reflection or self-consciousness"; to generate the second representation, and the hesitation between representations, one additionally approaches the fable "as the play of what today we call the text."[68] This play betrays the gap between the first, metaphysical representation, "the world is what is said about it," and another representation, metaphysical but under erasure, in which literature or reportage are seen as genuinely prior to philosophy, or to what is reported. This second representation is impossible to present without affirming its opposite.

More attention will be given below to the event of a representation passing irretrievably into its opposite. In this early text, Lacoue-Labarthe has dwelt at some length on that movement as such. What is just as important, there has come into view the process of which this exchange is a part, that is, the "template" of all hyperbological exchange. That template locates the deconstructive loss of the subject within a matrix of representational exchange. As Lacoue-Labarthe's overture suggests, the exchange will have as its constant context the eternal circularity that relates philosophy to literature. I will shortly glance both backward, to places in my argument where this template has been implicit, and forward, to anticipate subsequent exploration.

First, though, I must not neglect the way in which Lacoue-Labarthe both gathers and redirects the present consideration of subjectal loss, with its incipient hyperbology. The concluding portion of "The Fable" broaches the dimension of this loss that relates to *experience*: effectively, *sensible* experience. One of the defining and alluring aspects of Lacoue-Labarthian subjectal loss is that its description engages not only the thought of subjectal loss but also its felt experience. The "mechanism" that elicits the subjectal loss of *fictioned* subjects, such as the world, truth, and so on, obversely elicits the experience of self-loss in the *fictioning* subject itself. This experiential dimension of subjectal loss will lie at the heart of Lacoue-Labarthe's later work. So it is unsurprising that this first piece concludes by addressing it with a lyricism that betrays an almost poetic energy. Loss of the true world is related to a corresponding loss of the *writing* self.

The transition is made by way of a further reflection on logos. As the thought of truth, logos survives through the question of metaphysics, or of what *really is*. Lacoue-Labarthe has already canvased the power possessed by this thought to overpower the thought of pure fiction. Nevertheless logos as subject, necessarily triumphant, is hyperbologically subverted by the fictive. So too is its experiential counterpart, the self-identical ego.

At issue is the way in which logos, by returning all to relationship with itself, destroys, in an excess of power, anything *else* attempting to be born:

Logos is absolute mastery and there is nothing outside of it, not even literature, to which it has given a "meaning."[69]

But Lacoue-Labarthe immediately adds that, in the face of the play of the text, this excess as mastery becomes excess as a *lack*. Mastery cannot "truly" (re)present that which inherently suffers misrepresentation under mastery. Writing itself writes, with an in-built ambiguity that fails to surrender to the unifying power of the thought, consciousness, or will of the self that sets out to write. It divides this self, promoting the experience of "its" erosion, since

perhaps, not writing exactly what we wanted to write, we experience a weakness, a powerlessness that is no longer the effect of an excess of power, but rather like the obscure work of a force that is foreign to what we say, to the consciousness that we have of it, to the will to say it.[70]

Representations by means of which the "writing subject" attempts to convey "its" experience "faithfully" appear as their "others": excess as lack, powerlessness as power. These counterparts do not dissolve by passing into each other but hover together, convicting the subject of its own foreignness. Self-identical truth is again hyperbologically lost in the face of the possibility of "pure" fiction. But now the focus is the *experience* of this self-loss before the relentless fictiveness of writing:

> We write: we are dispossessed, something is ceaselessly fleeing [*ne cesse de fuir*], outside of us, slowly deteriorating.[71]

Facilitating reflection, writing at the same time works against this facilitation, implicating it in loss. So writing is

> first of all that reflection of experience wherein reflection (and hence experience) is incessantly undone [*ne cesse de se défaire*], because it is the most painful of failures and because, in it, the radical alterity of force "reveals" itself most painfully.[72]

In the work that writing makes of experience, what is done is also, by the same token, undone. The "force" behind writing always locates itself outside the self that seeks to write, displacing both the object and the subject of writing from themselves; the span of hyperbological subversion has here been caught at its widest. I now recapitulate and bring to a conclusion my own orienting description of the hyperbological, beginning with the thought that Lacoue-Labarthe has just offered.

Conclusion: Writing, the Playful Text, and the Loss of the Subject between Two Hyperbological Economies

First of all, "writing is . . . that reflection of experience wherein reflection (and hence experience) is incessantly undone." Writing is a *reflection* that is an *undoing*. This particular representation is an especially fruitful path to the hyperbological as a generic description of Lacoue-Labarthian subjectal loss. To exploit it, I now make a further distinction between those hyperbological elements that appear in thought and writing, respectively.

If part of hyperbology is "the passing of extremes into each other," then this is what reflective thought—the logos—effects, by endlessly returning that which is "not itself" to itself. As a unificatory "doing," a bringing near, a provision of the *work* or the subject, this dimension is a counterpart to hyperbological *distancing*, as Lacoue-Labarthe's analysis of Hölderlin showed. It will be recalled that Lacoue-Labarthe notes both aspects when he instantiates the interchange of extremes that is hyperbology. He mentions them in alternating sequence; nearing and distancing perpetuate a mutual undoing:

> The closer it is, the more distant it is; the more dissimilar it is, the more adequate it is; the more interior it is, the more exterior it is. In short, the maximum of appropriation . . . is the maximum of disappropriation, and conversely.[73]

At first sight, it is the second "half" of the hyperbological that can be most directly associated with *writing*: the movement *from* the near *to* the distant, from unification to disintegration, from interiority to exteriority. This structure of writing, as "Typography" showed, also takes over whatever is *said*, making it circulate endlessly, so that the immediacy of *saying* is thwarted. The distancing that belongs to writing appears to correspond exactly to the *undoing* of the unification that writing itself achieves in reflecting experience. Thereby, it appears to confirm the loss of the subject.

Such a description, however, does not totalize (or explain without remainder) the subjectal loss that writing effects. If it did, then the loss, as a "pure" loss, or a pure distancing of the subject from itself, would have achieved re-erection of a *new* subject: the unified or self-identical self that talk of dispossession reveals as having been *previously* present, as a standard against which self-loss is established. The simply theorizable experience of self-in-dispossession is clearly not where Lacoue-Labarthe's analyses come to rest. In his telling of it, self-in-loss is an experience as nebulous as it is inescapable, as resistant to theoretical reconstruction as it is recurrent:

> *Something* is ceaselessly fleeing. . . . It may have to do, for example, with a *certain confusion* in thought, a blurred insufficiency of consciousness, a *kind* of lethargy.[74]

This reinforces what ought already to have become strongly indicated: that Lacoue-Labarthian self-loss does not correspond to any simple representation of the self-loss or distancing that writing visits upon the writing self.

Instead, given what Lacoue-Labarthe has already said, this effect must correspond to the *overall* movement that is hyperbology, a more complex mechanism that mediates irreparable subjectal loss. First, "distancing," when ultimate, cannot survive as such but becomes a nearing. This is, after all, half of what the hyperbological thesis also accepts: "the more dissimilar it is, the more adequate it is." Second, in this light, it must be possible to invoke in the hyperbological the counterpart of this "distancing as nearing." That, of course, is *nearing as distancing,* namely, the first "half" of hyperbological exchange. Nearing as distancing is the movement that renders doing—or unification, or provision of the subject, wherever it is found—as simultaneously an undoing.

Taking the two parts together, we have the extended meaning and "mechanism" of the hyperbological, as a movement detected by Lacoue-Labarthe in a variety of texts and contexts. Drawing upon terminology with which Derrida makes a related distinction, I suggest the following: the hyperbological offers itself in both *restricted* and *general* economies.[75] The restricted hyperbological, as the "near becoming far," directly represents loss or undoing of the subject. However, it is the generalized hyperbological, as a sequential mechanism of the near becoming far, *and then vice versa,* ad infinitum, *that in fact effects* the loss of the subject. Restricted hyperbological loss is inevitably recuperated to subjectal re-erection. It requires a counterpart, in interaction with which it can comprise hyperbological loss, to "salvage" its efficacy in representing the loss of the subject.

This terminology can now be used to add a new layer of interpretation to my analyses of Lacoue-Labarthian subjectal loss in previous chapters. Both economies might now be found to inform those analyses, beginning with the residual "structure" of subjectivity that emerged in "Typography" (see Chapter 2, this volume). In writing, subjectal loss displayed itself *en abyme,* through the displacement of the writing self from its authorial persona. But this loss was restricted in its scope, allowing Plato's self-displacement as "his" mimetic persona Socrates to effect a recuperation of subjectivity. This limitedly efficacious evocation of subjectal loss corresponded to loss within a restricted hyperbological economy. The representation involved can be seen to have required juxtaposition with a new subjectal representation as hyperbological counterpart. In Chapter 3, precisely this was provided by way of my comparison of subjectal loss in Lacoue-Labarthe's "Diderot: Paradox and Mimesis" and his "The Echo of the Subject." It is evident that, by virtue of being placed "over against" an other, *consciously* desistant subject, the subject of *désistance* avoided recuperation to metaphysics. This "opposite number" introduced to *désistance* an undecidability that promoted further—deconstructive—subjectal loss. In my current terms, the consciously desistant subject provided a bridge to a general hyperbological economy, and a confirmation that the previous economy was indeed restricted.

In Chapter 4, a similar distinction can be discovered to have been operative. There, the hesitation of the subject was between twin depictions of Kantian *Darstellung*: representation of excess, and excess of representation. "Representation of excess" was implied by Kant's description of the sublime in terms of excess of sensible material over presentability. Such excess denoted absence of the presentable subject. But this absence also connoted *presence* of the subject under another understanding: as a striving (for form) that is *presentation itself,* or romantic *Selbstdarstellung.*

This failed restricted economy of recuperated self-loss can also now be seen to have been part of a general hyperbological economy, manifesting unrecuperable subjectal loss. The latter economy employed a new and opposed counterrepresentation of subjectal loss: *Darstellung* as *excess* of representation. Again, the confirmation of the unrecuperability of this loss utilized a Derridean deconstructive resource: the demonstration that the second representation begins as a *supplement* of the first, only to *supplant* it. Creating an endless circularity of priority between the representations, this effected the loss of the subject.

Here, the complicity between Derridean deconstruction and Lacoue-Labarthian hyperbology is not thoroughgoing; between the assumptions that fuel Derrida's deconstructive readings and those that inform Lacoue-Labarthe's investigation of hyperbological subjectal loss there remain certain differences. These differences relate mainly, but not entirely, to emphasis and point of departure; they are addressed in Chapter 8, where I consider the possibility of a Lacoue-Labarthian presentational subjectivity.

That development of hyperbology, and the further explication of its deconstructive efficacy, lie ahead. In this chapter, I have sought to explain the hyperbological and to establish it as central to a general account of Lacoue-Labarthe's descriptions of subjectal loss. As interim conclusion to this undertaking, a final point merits mention.

Hyperbology typically depicts subjectal loss as occurring through, as it were, a *surfeit* of subjects. Rather than becoming invisible to theory, subjects become *overvisible* in the multiplicity of "their" duplications: as near and far, interior and exterior, disappropriated and appropriated, and so on. Through each duplication, the unified subject is experienced as "in escape." None of its self-representations survives; each passes, at its extreme, into its "other" as part of an interminable sequence (nearing of the distant, followed by distancing of the near, and so on).

This being so, it is useful to ask whether this *sequence* becomes a new subject. I will argue later that, under one understanding, it does. This understanding must be hedged with several provisos, involving the meaning of *presentation*: granted these, I will suggest that the subject bids to be offered to sense in or as the presentation of "its" movement. But the hyperbological sequence *as such* does not presume a self-identical subject that the successive representations re-present. Hyperbological sequence is intended instead to express a simultaneity of opposites that is so thoroughgoing as to signify a prior instability of identity itself. The dynamic that drives this simultaneity allows no single subjectal representation any rest before its overflow into its opposite: the writer into the written, the artist into the scientist, nature into art.

Accordingly, we find that, in Lacoue-Labarthe, hyperbologically framed representation of a subject is always in the throes of "its" own dissolution. Opposites are present synchronously: what is nearest is already, and at the same time, what is farthest, and what is farthest is what is nearest, ad infinitum. Similarly what is most "interior" to myself is that which writing manifests as most exterior, and vice versa. And so on. However, a *sequential* view of the exchange of representations is more friendly to imaginative reconstruction, and this is what I have employed here, in outlining the typical interaction between restricted and general hyperbological loss. The former, even as it erodes the subject, effects a "doing" or representation of this eroded (or split) subject. "Then" the latter offers a ceaseless and simultaneous representation of this doing *as* an undoing of the subject. In the "end" (there being really no end to this), the subject is lost "through" this oscillation.

This is not to say that hyperbological oscillation itself retains the status of a subject. Rather, it is removed from this status insofar as it is, itself, theorization: of an already prior unavailability of the subject to "itself." This prior loss is nevertheless *sensed* as its effect in the *present*: "We write: we *are* dispossessed, something *is* ceaselessly fleeing, outside of us, slowly deteriorating."[76] Even if the subject has never been, its loss is ceaselessly with us and is endlessly in motion, since never complete.

6

The Political Subject Lost between Heidegger and Nietzsche

Introduction: The Quest for a Hyperbological Hesitation between Heidegger and Nietzsche

My study of Lacoue-Labarthe turns now toward the Lacoue-Labarthian political. In doing so, it turns also toward Heidegger, particularly the Heidegger of the 1930s. But I do not intend "yet another chapter" on Heidegger's Nazism, that is, on the question of his personal politico-philosophical acquiescence with Nazism as such. That proviso is meant equally to forestall what might be anticipated interest for some readers and anticipated irritation for others. Much has been written on Heidegger and National Socialism in recent years, and a good deal has been discovered, some of it unfavorable to Heidegger. What follows here works, I suspect, neither toward convicting or exculpating him further. If Lacoue-Labarthe's analysis probes Heidegger under the rubric of Doing Wrong, it also identifies that rubric with a structural failing proper to Western philosophy itself, of which Heidegger's Rectoral Address of 1933 becomes a significant articulation. Lacoue-Labarthe is tracking a deeper question, one that goes *to* but also *through* Heidegger—and then as much through Nietzsche as through Heidegger. It asks about the subject of philosophy in its political dimension. I, in turn, track Lacoue-Labarthe in the asking, with an eye to relating his analysis to my own argument.

In particular, if my exposition so far has been successful, the reader will want to hear more about hyperbology as a motif that bids to link various modes and contexts in which Lacoue-Labarthe notices the loss of the subject. To date, my conclusions regarding it are these. Hyperbology anatomizes the structure of writing as the ongoing event of an incessant passing of representations into their opposites. Thereafter, what this structure presents as most close, interior, and proper it simultaneously presents as most distant, exterior, and derivative. Thus we obtain these pairs: philosophy-as-literature, truth-as-mimesis, autobiography-as-allothanatography. Each testifies to the loss of the subject, at the very least insofar as a generalized writing makes it impossible for the subject to present itself except in and through its "other." Herein is written this loss. It is a loss, however, of something that never was—something, that is, which was always already lost, what Maurice Blanchot calls "something that has passed without being present."[1] Notwithstanding this, literature, mimesis, and autobiography emerge in Lacoue-Labarthe as places where the effort to *regain* the lost subject is vainly in full train. But finally these are witness to the impossibility of the quest that would restore the subject to "itself" or provide a demarcation that could exclude the other *as such*: as literature *rather than* philosophy, mimesis rather than truth, or allothanatography rather than autobiography.

Thus the implications of hyperbology. But how extensive, the reader might reasonably ask, is the reach of the motif, particularly in those texts where it receives little or no explicit mention? By way of answer, I turn in this chapter to its manifestation when Lacoue-Labarthe treats the *political*. I hope thus to exemplify the way in which hyperbological exploration might be seen to organize Lacoue-Labarthe's readings, even when it does so more or less clandestinely. This move into new territory is also intended to develop my account of the hyperbological while strengthening my case for generalizing, in its terms, a description of Lacoue-Labarthe.

Lacoue-Labarthe's incursions into the political span several texts.[2] Invariably, he is interested in the *philosophical* concern with the political, and the future of this concern.[3] This linkage of the political with the philosophical most often goes by way of Heidegger and Nietzsche, and hyperbology itself is rarely mentioned. But, given that the occasions of his specifically philosophical concern with their texts so often focus on hyperbolical subjectal loss, it can be confidently anticipated that hyperbology will figure wherever he is concerned to explore the philosophical-*political* dimension of subjectal loss.

Nevertheless, an imbalance that is curious, at first sight, is evident in the way in which Lacoue-Labarthe treats subjectal loss in the two authors. Although he employs Nietzschean thought to subvert the Heideggerian philosophical-political, he does not offer any corresponding subversion of Nietzsche in this regard. My analyses suggest that this is unlikely to be because Lacoue-Labarthe believes the Nietzschean subject impossible of subversion. More likely, he considers the demonstration of this unnecessary, precisely because Heidegger's commentary on Nietzsche already provides a vantage point, if limited, from which Nietzsche's thought can be subverted.

As far as I am aware, Lacoue-Labarthe nowhere says this explicitly. But if it is not his view, one is at a loss to explain why Nietzschean subjects, culminating in the *übermensch*, uniquely receive no subversive attention. In any case, I am going to presume here that a level of Heideggerian subversion of Nietzsche is *part* of what Lacoue-Labarthe takes for granted even while explicitly addressing the reverse, more urgent (and congenial) task: the demonstration of a Nietzschean (re)subversion of Heidegger. This leads me to ask, in terms of hyperbological analysis, how the presumed Heideggerian assimilation *of* Nietzsche might relate to the process that assimilates Heidegger *to* Nietzsche, for if these competing processes of assimilation (read, overdetermination, or subversion) could be shown to operate concurrently, then the overall process might well provide precisely the unending and paralyzing exchange of representations that I have steadily been developing as the Lacoue-Labarthian hyperbological.

In this chapter, I shall argue that this does in fact happen. Nietzschean overdetermination of Heidegger forms the backdrop for the analysis of the link between Heidegger and Nazism in Lacoue-Labarthe's *Heidegger, Art and Politics* and is also explicitly addressed by him in the essay that is the final chapter in *Typography*.[4] To find a Heideggerian overdetermination of Nietzsche, I go to Heidegger's own "The Word of Nietzsche: God Is Dead" while keeping in view some hints of this overdetermination from *Heidegger, Art and Politics*.[5] Having evoked the dimension of "representational exchange" that each of these overdeterminations separately effects, it will be possible for me to consider them together in concluding this chapter. In the conclusion, I explore the interacting exchanges for evidence of sequentiality and nonsublative oscillation, the hallmarks of Lacoue-Labarthian hyperbological subjectal loss.

Heidegger, Art and Politics: The Philosophical-Political Subject after Nihilism

The political is a topos that Lacoue-Labarthe visited early in his career, in relation to the specific question of Heidegger's political affiliation. The setting for *Heidegger, Art and Politics* is Heidegger's dialogue and confrontation with the National Socialist "aestheticization of the political": Hitler's attempt to create the State as a political work of art that accurately reflected the German subject. Lacoue-Labarthe's preface says that the book assumes the proportions of a "settling of accounts with Heidegger."[6] If this also finally gives it the aspect of a mitigated defense of Heidegger's involvement with National Socialism, it is by showing that Heidegger's aesthetic and political assumptions were intended to be the culmination of mainstream Western political. Heidegger's thought signals the distance between the Western aesthetico-political and Nazism as well as their inherent proximity. In a review of *La Fiction du politique*, the original French version of *Heidegger, Art and Politics*, Jean-Joseph Goux perceptively characterizes Lacoue-Labarthe's "most original and strongest" demonstration in regard to the debate or dialogue between Heidegger and Nazism as the insight that

> Heidegger's thought, far from coinciding with the discourse of Nazi ideology, "produces its truth," throwing a precise light on the essence of national socialism . . . and at the same time illuminating the modern essence of the political.[7]

The "modern political" here refers also to the *Western* political. Lacoue-Labarthe's argument is as follows. The history of the political—of the polis—becomes the history of the preservation of the Western subject, as the expression of a more basic attempt to preserve the subject itself. The attempt necessitates the identification of the subject as such, in contradistinction to an other, whose exclusion as such it correspondingly requires. The identification of the Jews as utterly "other" to the human economy (as "waste"), and the consequent project of their elimination, is thus available to be seen as continuous with the most fundamental Western philosophical suppositions concerning subjectivity. It is this unpalatable but unavoidable truth that makes the devastation of the Shoah a defeat for the Western political that essentially condemns the mode. And, of course, because the "other" as such is structurally unexcludable, the failed attempt at exclusion is doomed to perpetual repetition; more recently, Lacoue-Labarthe has informally discussed other problematic attempts to secure the subject by this mode: as the proletarian worker, or the consumer-subject, or the global-subject, and so on.[8]

The chief elements of the argument relating to the Shoah are put in the third and fourth chapters of *Heidegger, Art and Politics*: "The Political" and "Doing Wrong." Heidegger's engagement with Nazism was highlighted by the "commitment" constituted by his Rectoral Address of 1933. "The Political" proposes that this commitment was "neither an accident nor a mistake."[9] The commitment is best understood in the light of a statement by Heidegger in 1935 that "the *polis* is the historial place, the there *in* which, *out* of which, and *for* which history happens."[10] Far from being accidental, the commitment is in pursuit of the historial possibility of the founding of a State. Nor is the commitment an "error," since in 1933 National Socialism embodied that historial possibility or at least was the bearer of it.[11]

It is clear that for Lacoue-Labarthe, this "possibility" involves no less than the political salvaging of a Western subject threatened, by an ascendant technology, with an exhaustion of identity. At the "heart of his Rectoral Address," Heidegger invokes Nietzsche's phrase "God is dead" precisely because, Lacoue-Labarthe reminds us, this exactly captures "the situation, i.e., the 'forsakenness' (*Verlassenheit*) of 'man today, in the midst of what is.'"[12] This abandonment, however, corresponds to a necessary experience of *nothingness*, which prepares the way for the salvaging, through the realization that

it is philosophy's task to snatch man from a life that would be limited to using the works of the mind and . . . to throw him back up [in a way] against his destiny.[13]

It is because Nazism "contains" the possibility of this realization (Lacoue-Labarthe evidently means "contains notionally" or as intention) that Heidegger's commitment to it cannot have been an error.

Notwithstanding this, the category applicable to Heidegger's action is "doing wrong," as the chapter thus titled argues. Here, Lacoue-Labarthe widens the context of blame, far beyond the standard condemnation of Heidegger's continued association with Nazism after the moral odium attached to the concrete realization of the above "possibility" became clear. An isolation of the inner logic of the extermination of the Jews identifies it as a project of subjectal salvaging toward which the entire history of the West is oriented, and in which no less than the essence of the West is revealed.[14]

The subject, then, tries determinedly and destructively to salvage itself by means of the futile attempt, interminably repeated, to decide *against* what is *not* itself. There is clearly here a politically delineated version of Lacoue-Labarthe's account of the subject of philosophy-in-literature, doomed to try eternally to re-erect itself in the face of the loss that writing occasions. At the political level, the expressions of this self-protection are typically acts that seek to preserve personal identity through the assertion of the identity of a social or political unit. While the assertion comprises a suppression or denial of identities other than the desired identity, it cannot arrest the subjectal loss that is written into every representation. As I have noted, Lacoue-Labarthe elsewhere argues that Heidegger fails to recognize this power, possessed by the generalized writing that operates within language and thought, for dissimulation of the philosophical subject.[15] But in his case, the denial of this dissimulation corresponds to a thoroughgoing theorization that issues in a more profound error: the philosophical-political hope for the creation of a Western subject corresponding to the final unconcealing of Being itself, Being as it was given to the pre-Socratics.

This does not mean that Heidegger's own break with Nazism was less than philosophical. The Nazi ambition for a German subject elaborates itself in ways that deviate significantly from Heidegger's anticipation of the new German subject of aesthetic science. But, at a more basic level, Heidegger's situating of his account within that of the destining of Being accomplishes an understanding, by the West, of its own destiny, which encompasses the Nazi ambition. In this sense, Heidegger, ultimately as a representative of the West, supplies both the essence of that ambition and the deepest dimension of its philosophical, political, and moral failure.

The question of Heidegger's culpability, interesting as it is, cannot be followed further here; my purpose in tracking Lacoue-Labarthe's analysis is to expose to view the particular Heideggerian subjectal representation that Lacoue-Labarthe considers to be incapable of preventing subjectal loss. For this, it is necessary to observe, with Lacoue-Labarthe as guide, the thoroughness with which the Shoah represents an elimination of heterogeneity, in the interests of erection of the Western subject. It is then possible to see what Lacoue-Labarthe makes of this. Unsurprisingly, he sees this Heideggerian representation exchanged at its height for the very Nietzschean representation it was intended to supersede—nihilism. I shall now return to reading the relevant portion of the chapter titled "Doing Wrong."

Lacoue-Labarthe finds the essence of the West revealed through the insight that, uniquely among massacres, the German extermination was of Jews not as agents of social, political, or religious dissension but "as people *decreed to be* Jews."[16] Jewish identity here represented, precisely,

> a heterogeneous element, only for a nation that was painfully lacking an identity or existence of its own and which was, in fact, also facing very real threats, both external and internal.[17]

To this isolation of the exact nature of the perceived Jewish "threat"—admittedly "a projection"—Lacoue-Labarthe adds a second element of uniqueness:

> The Jews were treated in the same way as industrial waste or the proliferation of "parasites" is treated. . . . This purely hygienic or sanitary operation (which was not only social, political, cultural and racial etc., but also *symbolic*) has no parallel in history.[18]

Taken together, these elements indicate the essential "need" toward which the project of the salvation of the Western subject has arrived—the need for "simple elimination . . . [w]ithout trace or residue" of the heterogeneous as such."[19]

Thus the act that salvages the Heideggerian-Western subject. Yet now, without development, Lacoue-Labarthe passes an apparently Nietzschean verdict on this event—it is also the *accomplishment* of nihilism and the death of God:

> And if it is true that the age is that of the accomplishment of nihilism, then it is at Auschwitz that that accomplishment took place in the purest formless form. God in fact died at Auschwitz—the God of the Judeo-Christian West at least.[20]

This comment beckons investigation, notwithstanding that the view of Auschwitz as an "accomplishment of nihilism" is hardly radical from our historical vantage point. It signals a battle for overdetermination that trades upon and extends an ambiguity in the concept of nihilism. I explain this point in outline now; it will be developed and extended in all that follows.

Two notions of nihilism are in play in any text cognizant of Heidegger: Nietzsche's diagnosis of nihilism as the devaluation of all values, and Heidegger's understanding of nihilism, broadened to embrace the Nietzschean post-nihilistic itself—those values that grew in the wake of nihilism, and for which nihilism was preparatory. Thus the Nietzschean subject that represents the overcoming of nihilism is also the subject that Heidegger associates with its deepening. A "Heideggerian subject," corresponding to the overcoming of nihilism, will triumph through and after this deepening.[21]

But it is alternatively possible that Nietzschean nihilism overdetermines the Heideggerian so that Heidegger's new subject merely represents the erection of a value system that Nietzschean nihilism, as it were, pursues and razes preparatory to the erection of its own subject, namely, the subject of the will to power.

Correspondingly, the phrase "accomplishment of nihilism" is available to signify either in an original Nietzschean sense or in a Heideggerian sense (that is, through the "frame" or context that Heidegger allocates to Nietzschean nihilism). In the passage I am considering, *both* significations are in play. The Heideggerian signification is unavoidable, because, after all, Lacoue-Labarthe is explicating Heidegger; chillingly, however, Lacoue-Labarthe, writing from the far side of the moral and philosophical failure of the Shoah, knows that the phrase "bites back" in its *Nietzschean* signification. It overdetermines the putative Heideggerian surmounting of nihilism— now revealed as morally misconceived, philosophically futile—as the deepening of nihilism, that is, as the "accomplishment of Nihilism" in a Nietzschean sense, awaiting, if anything, the new (perhaps Nietzschean) subject of the will to power, which Western philosophy is intrinsically incapable of providing. This Nietzschean overdetermination is one vital half of the hyperbological subjectal loss I am exploring here. The other half is, of course, the Heideggerian overdetermination that, it can be shown, *also* survives. Both overdeterminations, each deconstructing the other, ought, in fact, to be demonstrable in *any* text in which either is formally canvased.

As *Heidegger, Art and Politics* proceeds, Lacoue-Labarthe indirectly pursues the interrelationship between the prospective overdeterminations, particularly through his attention to the subject of *technē* that Heidegger's Nietzsche presages. For the sake of simplicity, though, I now move to two other texts where the respective overdeterminations are *formally* pursued, so as to exemplify the way in which each, given the right perspective, succeeds in assimilating its counterpart. Lacoue-Labarthe's "Transcendence Ends in Politics" offers an intricate claim for the overdetermination of the Heideggerian subject by the Nietzschean subject of the will to power. Conversely, Heidegger's own "The Word of Nietzsche: God Is Dead" allows Heidegger to present the case for the opposite overdetermination.

"Transcendence Ends in Politics": Nietzschean Overdetermination of the Postnihilistic Heideggerian Subject

"Transcendence Ends in Politics" focuses on Heidegger's Rectoral Address of 1933. Lacoue-Labarthe intends to show that this address stands "in a direct line with the 'destruction of the history of ontology,'" which for Heidegger means, as Lacoue-Labarthe puts it, "the project of the . . . fundamental *instauratio*, or re-foundation [of metaphysics]." But, he argues, it also inscribes the return, in Heideggerian guise, of the Nietzschean subject of will to power—the very subject that Heidegger rejects elsewhere, as subsumed by metaphysics. [22]

In demonstrating this, Lacoue-Labarthe's first task here is to connect the Heideggerian political to its philosophical underpinnings. An interview given by Heidegger in 1966 identifies the point of a particular question in the Rectoral Address: "If there is to be science . . . under what conditions can it then truly exist?" [23] In the interview, Heidegger sees the question and the address itself as belonging to a "foundational gesture," intended as a repetition and radicalization of the Kantian foundation. [24] This (re)foundation of the university, "on the basis of a thorough determination of its essence"—an essence now understood "in terms of the *né-ant or Ab-grund*"—is intended to forestall "the *totalitarian* menace itself, that is to say, the project of the 'politicization' of the University, and of science." [25]

Heidegger paints the program of refoundation as a political expression of a particular philosophical—in fact, metaphysical—goal. [26] The *Fuhrung* (guiding, leadership) of the university is to serve "the spiritual mission that forces the fate of the German people to bear the stamp of its history." [27] This mission expresses itself in a "will to science" and is determined in the autonomous university—in fact, in the very capacity of the university for determining its own essence. (As we shall see, this essence is ultimately related to the unconcealing of Being). Heidegger says,

> The will to the essence of the German University is the will to science as will to the historical mission of the German people as a people that knows itself in its state. [28]

When he speaks of characterizing the refounding essence as "science," Heidegger has in mind a particular philosophical understanding of science—as a knowing that leads to Being. The essence of science itself is *Wissen*—knowledge, as it was initiated in Greece, as "the questioning holding of one's ground in the midst of the self-concealing totality of what is."[29]

For Lacoue-Labarthe, this recalls the association of this Heideggerian "science" with *Dasein* in its "finite transcendence," that is, as "the understanding or the pre-understanding of Being."[30] What is more, Heidegger identifies the essence of science as the "metaphysics of *Dasein*"; as Heidegger says, in "What Is Metaphysics?":

> What is happening [in the pursuit of science] is nothing less than the irruption [*Einbruch*] of an entity called man into the whole of what is, in such a way that through this irruption what is manifests itself *as* and *how* it is.[31]

Lacoue-Labarthe argues that it is in this very description of the "irruption of 'Man'" that we find the seed for an overdetermination of Heideggerian *Dasein* by the Nietzschean *overman*.

The argument must be advanced methodically, initially through a connection between the Heideggerian philosophical and the Nietzschean political by way of the Heideggerian politico-philosophical. To say that the "irruption . . . of man into what *is*" determines how "what is manifests itself *as* and *how* it is" is to say that scientific *Dasein* determines the gathering and assemblage of the world. In this context, "world" is the sociopolitical world, the world of Being-with-others. The philosophical essence thus becomes the political essence; in constituting the former essence, the German people constitute also the latter. In short, it is the irruption of the German subject that will create a new world coterminous with science as such. Heidegger says:

> If we will the essence of science understood as the *questioning, unguarded holding of one's ground in the midst of the uncertainty of the totality of what is, this* will to essence will create for our people its world.[32]

The "will to essence," which provides for a firm openness to life as such, that is, without mistaking metaphysics for Being, is already reminiscent of the Nietzschean will to power. But there is still the necessity of demonstrating its specifically Nietzschean antecedence.

Surprisingly enough, Lacoue-Labarthe does this by way of a Kantian predilection that he finds in Heidegger's modus operandi.

Lacoue-Labarthe notices why, in Heidegger's thinking, the *German* people have the privilege of providing the above essence. The reason is, of course, their unique connection, due to Kant, with (pre-Socratic) Greek philosophy.[33] Lacoue-Labarthe reminds us that, for Heidegger,

> Kant—and Kant alone—was recognized straightforwardly as the first thinker to have been able to reappropriate the positions and questions of the great age of Greek philosophy.[34]

Enter Nietzsche into the equation at this very point because the move toward the foundational Kant is a move toward Nietzsche. Lacoue-Labarthe says that "to claim Kant for oneself, in the context of the thirties and against the neo-Kantian interpretations, is also to lay claim to Nietzsche."[35]

This is important because Nietzsche, prophet of the death of God that will inaugurate the new metaphysics, is the "hero" of Heidegger's Rectoral Address. And for Lacoue-Labarthe, the Nietzchean overdetermination of Heidegger takes effect through Kant so that

> at a fundamental level it is Nietzsche's metaphysics itself—although within it, in fact, what comes above all from a certain interpretation of Kant—which overdetermines Heidegger's whole philosophical-political message.[36]

So Heidegger's overdetermination by Nietzsche is due to the indebtedness of his philosophical-political message to a Nietzschean version of Kant. How so? In the Rectoral Address, the turn toward Nietzsche announces itself when Heidegger identifies *energeia* with knowledge as *technē*. Aristotle's *energeia* is the productive force of metaphysics, being-at-work. Lacoue-Labarthe's point is that Heidegger follows Nietzsche (after Kant) in reading *energeia* as creative and *worldforming*. Kant becomes the bridge here by way of his definition of metaphysics (quoted by Heidegger in "What Is Metaphysics?") as "a natural disposition of man." In this adoption of Kant, Lacoue-Labarthe argues, Heidegger is led to figure *Dasein* in terms of the working of Being to keep beings close to itself. This *energeia* drives the passion for *technē* as knowledge, by which Being is both characterized and characterized inadequately, since knowledge never yields contact with Being as such. Thus metaphysics also comprises the working of Being against itself; here, metaphysics is "the essence of technique, which is understood as energy or creation and which is the 'combat' against the power of Being."[37] By this point, Heidegger's Kantian interpretation of metaphysics as "a natural disposition of man" has taken on a distinctly Nietzschean appearance. Being keeps beings close to itself by a necessary but inadequate mode of subjectal characterization that seeks constantly to overcome itself. The shape of Nietzschean "will to power" is clearly discernible.

What still separates Heidegger from Nietzsche is that for Heidegger it is *technē* as *knowing* that expresses "the passion to remain near to what is as such and under its constraint." For Nietzsche it is *technē* as *art* that plays this role in forming the world as the will to power. Nevertheless, Lacoue-Labarthe argues that the ontological superstructure here is still that of Nietzsche. What returns Heideggerian thought to the Nietzschean worldview are its underlying premises of determinant will and power:

> Being-in-the-world, in this sense (finite transcendence) is technique. . . . But this is a properly Nietzschean determination of "technique" (of "metaphysics"). Not only because it presupposes that knowledge is thought in relation to will . . . . [but above all] in that Being itself is thought as power.[38]

More specifically, Nietzschean thinking is implicated here in the involvement of will (albeit translated as knowledge) in the interplay between transcendence and finitude. This is so because

> the articulation of will and power (it is the power of Being that wills the powerless and creative will to knowledge of *Dasein*) is finitude itself: the finite transcendence of Dasein as the finitude of Being, whose power is subject to the superpower of destiny.[39]

Put simply, Lacoue-Labarthe's point is that the self-emanation of Being is here generated as will. Will therefore determines knowledge, rather than vice versa. It thus also determines the finite locus of knowing that is *Dasein*. More, the essence of the unconcealing of Being is will, rather than vice versa. In short, the Heideggerian "spiritual mission," in terms of which Being raises up that "subject of knowledge" that will keep beings close to Being, ultimately generates a thoroughly Nietzschean subject.

This essentially completes Lacoue-Labarthe's overdeterminative characterization of Heidegger's worldview in its Nietzschean representation. It raises several intriguing issues, but I retain my own focus by asking what, in this demonstrated overdetermination, is reminiscent of the hyperbological. Three responses come to mind.

First, in the process of demonstrating the overdetermination, Lacoue-Labarthe has shown us the Heideggerian postnihilistic worldview in motion *to its extreme point,* in quest of the subject. Heidegger's *Weltanschauung* has been transported toward its articulation of Being itself, Being as it proposes to unconceal itself purely, through a thoroughly nondistortive subject of experience. This transportation to the extreme is what Lacoue-Labarthe has identified in other contexts as the hyperbolical.

Second, the overdetermination delivers more than the hyperbolic. It delivers the mechanism of self-reversal inscribed in the hyperbolic and named specifically by Lacoue-Labarthe as the *hyperbological.* Hyperbology as reversal occurs at the height and culmination of the hyperbolical and yields the "other" of the representation under transport: here, a Nietzschean subject of the "will to power" that "essentially" substitutes itself for Heideggerian *Dasein.*

I have already offered evidence to the effect that the new German subject of the Rectoral Address corresponds to a culminating representation of *Dasein* as "provoker" of the unconcealment of Being. The function of its provocation will be to regain the "original Greek essence of science," which Heidegger expounds thus:

> All knowing about things has always been delivered up to overpowering fate and fails before it. Just because of this, knowing must develop its highest defiance; called forth by such defiance, all the power of the hiddenness of what is must first arise for Knowing really to fail. Just in this way, what is opens itself in its unfathomable inalterability and lends knowing its truth.[40]

The new *Dasein* constitutes itself as this culminating representation of knowing at its point of "highest defiance." But, as we have seen, at this very point the components of Nietzschean "will" and "power" take over the representation. *Dasein,* at the very apex of its representation as "provoker" of the hiddenness of Being, is, as it were, "forced" to cast Being as the *power* of this hiddenness, and thus as will. *Dasein* itself is then found at the "intersection" where Being as will meets its own finite, but transcendent, expression as power.

Third, this new representation cannot itself be absolutized. I develop presently a detailed account of its hyperbological "transport" into a *Heideggerian* representation. My account will utilize Heidegger's essay "The Word of Nietzsche: God Is Dead." First, however, the latter part of Lacoue-Labarthe's analysis in "Transcendence Ends in Politics" itself provides us with a glimpse of the mechanism of this hyperbological reversal, as follows.

The Nietzschean subject of the will to power formally figures the possibility of an original *enactment* of Being. But Lacoue-Labarthe's exploration reveals this figure itself as always presuming of a prior enactment of Being. In this sense, the Nietzschean and Heideggerian accounts of the history of Being share a common mythological framework. So it is no surprise that Nietzschean Being, at its extremity, becomes assimilable to Heideggerian Being. The assimilation becomes evident as Lacoue-Labarthe moves, with Heidegger, to locate Being at an *origin.*

Lacoue-Labarthe argues the following specific characteristic of the Nietzschean-Heideggerian subject that comes to be as the will to power of Being: it enacts *ontotypology,* the raising up by Being of a figure of itself. This ontotypology works through a particular mimetology, or logic of mimesis: it presumes an *original mimesis* according to which the world which *is,* is *created, but* always as an image "itself moreover imperceptible (unpresentable), of a possible presentation of what is."[41]

The ontotypology of original mimesis marks what *is* as bearing inevitably the image (or type, or stamp) of Being. This leads, inter alia, to an understanding of history itself as "originally mimetic," that is, as repetitive production of a succession of worlds in response to the self-giving (which is also the self-seeking) of Being. Under such an understanding, the succession is oriented toward a protection of tradition (whatever in the previous world has truly strained toward Being) by a repetition that alters what it duplicates.

The succession, then, is fundamentally *agonistic.* Each version of *Dasein,* as a subject-world, struggles to overthrow the subject corresponding to a previous attempt to come close to Being. This struggle is also that of the subject to become *one,* as a subject: the struggle for identification. As an agon, it is played out in its communal, political dimension. It is the struggle in this dimension that Heidegger anoints by speaking of the German (scientific) subject. This characterization of the struggle constitutes, says Lacoue-Labarthe, "the response that is properly the Heideggerian response to the German political problem par excellence: the problem of national identification."

But for Lacoue-Labarthe this Heideggerian characterization partakes of a specific matrix, which sees the future as repeating a past that, moreover, never occurred.[42] It is crucial that Heideggerian-

Nietzschean ontotypology presumes a historically realized self-giving of Being—the giving to the ancient Greeks. *Original mimesis*, has, in this agonistic setting, a further meaning: a striving to repeat, in a new way, the presumed original giving. But, what is most important for Lacoue-Labarthe's Nietzschean Heidegger, the repetition of the beginning means also its repetition *as* beginning. Thus Heidegger, from the Rectoral Address:

> For if indeed this primordial Greek science is something great, then the *beginning* of this great thing remains what is *greatest* about it. . . . The beginning still *is*. It does not lie *behind us*, as something that was long ago, but stands before us.[43]

What is significant about this claim for a new beginning is its *structural* relegation of that beginning to a point in the future. Because Being strives to repeat a past self-giving that never actually took place, its arrival as Being is structurally postponed. No actual dispensation of Being can be adequate to this arrival: the second coming always and irreducibly "stands before us." It is for this reason that any concretized present or future manifestation of Being is itself rendered provisional, pending a new "true" arrival.

In this picture, Nietzschean Being, as the will to power that overdetermines Heideggerian *Dasein*, has itself been overdetermined. It has become Heideggerian again, a representation of the concealment rather than the revelation of Being as such. *This* overdetermination, which corresponds to a hyperbological "tipping over" of the Nietzschean representation into its "other," is, as I have already suggested, more openly available to analysis. It emerges within one of Heidegger's closest readings of Nietzsche, to which I now turn.

"The Word of Nietzsche: God Is Dead": A Heideggerian Overdetermination of the Nietzschean Will to Power

There are several texts in which Heidegger places Nietzsche within the history of the dispensations of Being. While of course the claim for a Heideggerian overdetermination of Nietzsche should find support in any of these, "The Word of Nietzsche: God Is Dead" provides a distillation of Heidegger's Nietzschean thought that is ideal for my purposes here; it offers a thorough yet concise exposition of the view on nihilism advanced in *Being and Time*, in *Nietzsche* and in *An Introduction to Metaphysics*. Heidegger develops a description of the meaning and ontohistorical role of nihilism, as the "Nothing" or "forgetting" that "befalls" Being, including the forgetting that occurs with Nietzsche's own "surmounting" of nihilism.[44] It is also clear that he adopts and "overwrites" the Nietzschean framework rather than merely refusing it. Here, I follow his argument as it develops, but with a particular eye to the question of overdetermination.

From the outset, "The Word of Nietzsche: God Is Dead" seeks a framework that can enclose the framework of Nietzschean nihilism. Heidegger aims "to point the way towards a place from which it might be possible someday to ask the question concerning the essence of nihilism."[45] What is important for my question of overdetermination is that Heidegger suggests from the start that his exposition will accommodate the initial, and even culminative, success of Nietzsche's thought. It will attest "the overturning of metaphysics accomplished by Nietzsche," and which essentially precludes other possibilities of metaphysics in the West.[46] But this accommodation will at the same time contextualize Nietzsche within the more fundamental project by which Thought seeks

> to light up that space within which Being itself might again be able to take man, with respect to his essence, into a primal relationship.[47]

This *thinking* of nihilism, then, occurs in service of that unconcealing of the truth of Being which will relativize nihilism. Indeed, it will relativize Western thinking itself in its denial of that truth, and also the denial of the denial.

From here Heidegger proceeds to contextualize the emblematic declaration of nihilism, "God is dead," in terms of its essential point: the *killing* of God as the *destined* disempowering of the supersensory world in metaphysics. "Destining," here, will become a determination that subsumes the determination that Nietzsche himself envisages. In other words, it will become an overdetermination, the source of which is Being itself. As an inverting countermovement to metaphysics, Nietzsche's philosophy is both caught up in metaphysics and effective in paralyzing it. Thus paralyzed, metaphysics is separated from its own essence and unable to "think" that essence.[48]

The essence in question, as will emerge later, is the forgetting of Being, as the historical work of Being itself. Nihilism is an inherent part of this work: "Nihilism, thought in its essence, is, rather, the fundamental movement of the history of the West."[49] It is also both cumulative and culminative, absorbing within itself thought that bids to thwart its devaluation of all values: "Those who fancy themselves free of nihilism perhaps push forward its development most fundamentally."[50]

This last insight is particularly interesting from the point of view of the *mutual* overdetermination of Heideggerian and Nietzschehan versions of nihilism that is my larger task in this chapter, for it includes Heidegger's recognition of the following paradox: the arrest of nihilism can be effected only through remaining within its ambit of influence, since to seek freedom from nihilism is to advance it. Nihilism can be *brought down* only from within. Now, while this approach will be intrinsic to Heidegger's attempt to "trap" Nietzsche's attempted overcoming of nihilism, it will remain as a challenge for *any overcoming* of nihilism, including Heidegger's own, for its condition of success might be read from the opposite perspective: whoever would gainsay the triumph of nihilism (including by trapping it) eventually *surrenders* to its framework.

The relative positions of the two accounts become complicated because the Nietzschean framework itself foreshadows the completion and subsequent overcoming of nihilism, and Heidegger's exposition aims to turn Nietzsche against himself at this very point by pressuring Nietzsche's distinction between *incomplete* and *complete* nihilism.

For Nietzsche, incomplete nihilism merely overturns one metaphysics, corresponding to the explicit notion of "God," in favor of another value system that contains this notion implicitly. It thus becomes another metaphysics, grounded in the supersensory. By contrast, there is completed nihilism, which must, in addition,

do away even with the place of value itself, with the supersensory as a realm, and accordingly must posit and revalue differently.[51]

Heidegger's exposition of this notion accepts its possibility and inevitability while also exposing Nietzsche's own version of "completed nihilism" as inadequate to the term. For Nietzsche, "value" in the postnihilistic era will evolve through the revaluation of value itself as "the ideal of superabundant life."[52] Heidegger argues that this choice of ideal does in one sense "overturn" metaphysics in that the supersensory is no longer formally accorded value; however, it remains within the metaphysical ambit. Ultimately, this is because ideals are still involved in the Nietzschean dispensation.

Given the "ideal of superabundant life," values are determined as points of view that look to the preservation and enhancement of life. In turn, as the fundamental characteristic of life, the "will to power" becomes the essence of value. This will to power is what posits values and, "at the same time, the principle of the revaluing of all [previous] values."[53] Heidegger therefore parts company with Nietzsche. "The revaluation of values" itself implicates its products and its world in metaphysics. Heidegger summarizes the self-subversion in Nietzsche's approach thus: "Every overturning of this kind remains only a self-deluding entanglement in the Same that has become unknowable."[54] In other words, Nietzsche's revaluation is to be seen as *incomplete nihilism*. In turn, *completed* nihilism will involve an end to metaphysics that occurs *through* the Nietzschean revaluation, but beyond it, and by, as it were, "nihilizing" it.

Already it is not difficult to see the way in which Heidegger's approach here carries one trademark of overdetermination—subsumption. It subsumes or overwrites the Nietzschean framework rather than merely rejecting or refusing it. Underlining the interpretive power that this framework exerts over previous Western accounts of subjectivity, Heidegger's own interpretation then gradually assimilates it to metaphysics. In this way, it subsumes the subsuming Nietzschean subject.

I take up "The Word of Nietzsche: God Is Dead" at a point slightly farther along in its course. Heidegger has briefly addressed the matter of subjectivity, to which he will return later. He has recalled Nietzsche's demonstration of the will to power as the self-sufficient essence of willing, and as the essence of modern "subjectness." Nietzsche argued that it is in the light of the willing of life-preservation enhancement that there appears, for example, the Cartesian search for "certainty," which conditions the modern subject.[55] Now Heidegger identifies this Nietzschean willing as a *value*, found in a metaphysical structure or axiomatic hierarchy:

> Inasmuch as the essence of value proves itself to be the preservation-enhancement condition posited in the will to power, the perspective for a characterisation of the normative structuring of value has been opened up.[56]

It is here that the overdetermination drives itself by metaphysically framing the Nietzschean revaluation following nihilism. The will to power establishes value in a *fundamental* sense. Heidegger quotes Nietzsche: "The question of value is more *fundamental* than the question of certainty."[57] It thus establishes the subject that is the *fundamentum* of metaphysics; then, in an ultimately thoroughly traditional way, its "revaluing of values" becomes a metaphysical revaluing.

In fact, more explicitly, both Cartesian certainty and Nietzschean will to power answer to a prior condition of subjectivity, namely, justice. The "self-grounding" of the Nietzschean subject is exhibited in its automatically providing this justice, the value ultimately underlying notions of subjectivity throughout Western philosophy.

Heidegger's investigation proceeds in terms of essentiality. He is drawing out the hidden force corresponding to Nietzsche's "radical" revaluation. He will then show how traditional metaphysics subsumes that force under its banner.

The argument runs its course by assimilating the demand for certainty to metaphysics, drawing on the connection between justice and metaphysics. Heidegger recalls that justice, as "making secure," was the implicit demand behind Cartesian and Liebnitzian certainty. Similarly, Kant's transcendental deduction essentially concerned itself with the "making right" of the transcendental subject. But if the will to power is provident of this age-old value, the subject identified as will to power is not a unique, self-subsistent value. Instead, it represents the old value system, which grounds the subject outside itself, in justice:

> Just as in Nietzsche's metaphysics the idea of value is more fundamental than the grounding idea of certainty in the metaphysics of Descartes, inasmuch as certainty can count as the right only if it counts as the highest value, so, in the age of the consummation of Western metaphysics in Nietzsche, the intuitive self-certainty of subjectness proves to be the justification belonging to the will to power, in keeping with the justice holding sway in the Being of whatever is.[58]

Nor is it by chance that justice has represented itself so thoroughly in axiology. What *is* just has always been "what is in conformity with the right," that is, to paraphrase Heidegger here, "with what ought to be." Nietzsche interprets the "right" as the successful self-expression of the will to power. This merely completes the account of justice as the truth of whatever is.

In turn, this is why the metaphysicality of nihilism is invisible. Nihilism is essential metaphysics as justice, as "the truth of what is":

> As this truth, [nihilism] is metaphysics itself in its modern completion. In metaphysics as such is concealed the reason why

Nietzsche can indeed experience nihilism metaphysically as the history of value-positing, yet nevertheless cannot think the essence of nihilism.[59]

In short, Nietzsche hopes for a nonmetaphysical positing of value, but by pointing out the above implicit *justification* of nihilism, Heidegger overdetermines Nietzschean nihilism as metaphysics. Again, the overdetermination qualifies as such not only by refuting but also by subsuming and reframing Neitzsche's arguments; for example, it does not proceed *simply* by condemning the postnihilistic phase as metaphysical on the basis of the value positing involved in it.

To make this point more clearly, let us consider an oversimplistic argument of the "direct" type. It might run thus. Value positing occurs *after* the consummation of nihilism, that is, of the devaluing of all values. Hence, as fundamentally different from this devaluing, it involves a revaluing. Just as overcoming of the metaphysical was associated with devaluing, so is a revaluing necessarily associated with a return of the metaphysical. No further proof of the metaphysicality of Nietzsche's thought is required.

Heidegger, however, recognizes both the superficiality of this thought and what is implicitly overlooked by it. It is formally feasible, and indeed part of the Nietzschean bid to overdetermine all countertheories, that the exhaustion of all values that corresponds to the accomplishment of nihilism *is itself synonymous* with the rise of the one value that is not supersensory, namely, the sensory value "life." In this case, life would just be "itself," proceeding as its own preservation enhancement in enacting the will to power. It would answer to no "external" criterion of ideality or truth. As such, the will to power would not be *metaphysical,* arising "after" the consummation of nihilism and therefore contradicting this consummation. As nonmetaphysical, it could happily accompany the dispensation under which nihilism is consummated and metaphysical values are dissolved.

Nietzschean overdetermination of the theories that class it as metaphysical thus requires sterner counterargument if it is to be resisted. Heidegger feels the need to show this, even *pace* Nietzsche himself, as it were:

However, inasmuch as Nietzsche understands his own thinking—the doctrine of the will to power as the "principle of the new value-positing"—in the sense of the actual consummation of nihilism, he no longer understands nihilism merely negatively as the devaluing of the highest values, but at the same time he understands it positively, that is, as the overcoming of nihilism; for the reality of the real, now explicitly experienced, i.e., the will to power, becomes the origin and norm of a new value-positing.[60]

In the schema in which the will to power is a "new value-positing," any basis for it is arguably itself "new." Heidegger's reinterpretation of Nietzsche will be required to go further, by subsuming and reframing the Nietzschean revaluation understood in its strongest possible terms: as a revaluation by the will to power of the *realm* of value itself. Those terms in fact denote Nietzschean value positing as an utterly new notion of justice, as the centerpiece of a radically new, postmetaphysical, irruption of value. Can *this* irruption be assimilated to metaphysics as such? Heidegger must go "behind" metaphysics, as it has hitherto manifested itself, to its essence. He travels by way of the question crucial to Nietzschean value positing: the meaning and philosophical status of overman.

He does best initially to concede that the value positing which this new dispensation of Being encapsulates is continuous with the accomplishment of nihilism, in the Nietzschean sense:

Man hitherto would like to remain man hitherto; and yet he is at the same time already the one who, of all that is, is willing— whose Being is beginning to appear as the will to power.[61]

Indeed, it is not this essence of overman that Heidegger wishes to gainsay, but, as it were, the essence of this essence, which is there, but hidden to Nietzsche, so that

it thus remains obscure even to Nietzsche himself what connection the thinking that thinks overman in the figure of Zarathustra has with the essence of metaphysics.[62]

The connection with metaphysics is indeed not obvious but remains to be thought. Overman does not replace the dead God; notwithstanding this, however, its irruption, newly, within nihilistic soil in which God has died, is still a *metaphysical* one.

But before establishing itself with that point, the overdetermination waits, the better to triumph eventually. Heidegger allows a culminating establishment of Nietzsche's will to power as such. He accepts that overman initiates a radically new dispensation of Being, which is not to be assimilated to the old categories of the human and divine, or the sensory and supersensory. Overman opens up a place that is identical neither with the essential realm belonging to God, nor with that of man, but with which man comes once more into a distinctive relationship.[63]

This distinctiveness having been established, the thought turns to its hitherto unconsidered metaphysicality,

rather the place into which his willing enters is another realm belonging to another grounding of what is, in its other Being.[64]

What overman enters into is no less than—but no more than, either—a new dispensation of metaphysics, centered on itself. Heidegger says: "This other Being of what is, meanwhile—and this marks the beginning of modern metaphysics—has become subjectness."[65] Heidegger's nice use of "meanwhile" suggests not only that overman enter the new dispensation but also that, simultaneously, he effects its realization. The zenith of this realization is Nietzsche's anticipated "Great Noon," marked by a universal consciousness that engenders self-consciousness as "a knowing which consists in deliberately willing the will to power as the Being of whatever is." This life-focused hegemony of will succeeds in "rebelliously withstanding and subjugating to itself every necessary phase of the objectifying of the world."[66]

It is only now that Heidegger moves to establish the overdetermination of this radically new subjectness. He asks a simple question that survives even the "time of brightest brightness." The question:

What *is* now, in the age when the unconditional dominion of the will to power is openly dawning, and this openness and its public character are themselves becoming a public function of this will?[67]

It is this question that returns the new subject to a metaphysical superstructure, to "the truth of what is as such, which is coming to utterance in the form of the metaphysics of the will to power."[68] What "is," of course—whether as certainty, or justice, or will to power—cannot but find admittance to the realm of metaphysics, the revealed shape of Being wherein Being itself is concealed.

The overdetermination has thus proceeded by identifying *essential* metaphysics with that remembering of metaphysics which is a forgetting of Being. As William Lovitt puts this in a lengthy translator's note,

Being, in manifesting itself precisely as value through the thinking belonging to the metaphysics of the will to power, is, at the same time, concealing itself regarding that which it is as *Being*.[69]

Correspondingly, true or essential nihilism *is* this metaphysics as a forgetting. Essential nihilism overdetermines Nietzschean nihilism by overdetermining the apparent overcoming of metaphysics that Nietzschean nihilism entails, and which appears to beckon the rise of a new subject.

All this casts Nietzschean subjectivity itself as consummation and emphasizes that Heidegger's reading effects an overdetermination rather than merely a refutation or reversal of Nietzsche. Consummation here is reinforced by the notion of the historical *destining* of which it is the culmination: a self-concealing of Being itself within the history of Western philosophy from Plato to Nietzsche. With Nietzsche, this self-concealing reaches its apex in being recognized as such, only to attain a new concealment intrinsic to this very event of recognition. What is more, says Heidegger, this new concealment is confirmed as the truth of nihilism, as also of metaphysics. Nihilism *essentially* involves the historical "remaining wanting" of the truth of Being in the appearing of whatever is as such. But then metaphysics, "*as* the history of the truth of whatever is as such, is, in its essence, nihilism."[70]

Nietzschean nihilism thus exposes metaphysics as such to philosophy, only to be itself subsumed as forgetting, as metaphysics, because its own essence is also the essence of metaphysics. Heideggerian, essential nihilism, *as* metaphysics, is a destining of Being itself, and it means, for Heidegger, no less than this: that "nothing is befalling whatever is as such, in its entirety."[71]

This somewhat detailed reading of "The Word of Nietzsche: God Is Dead" has been necessary in order to demonstrate persuasively the Heideggerian overdetermination of the postnihilistic subject of the will to power. If the reader is by this point confused that successive perspectives (Lacoue-Labarthe's, on Nietzsche's behalf, and Heidegger's, on his own behalf) have yielded equally convincing but opposed overdeteminations — Nietzsche's of Heidegger, and Heidegger's of Nietzsche — perhaps that confusion itself might be taken to mirror the very hesitation, between two subjectal representations, by which hyperbology makes its mark, that of the lost subject. But because the demonstration of hyperbological interaction between representations involves more than a marking of this hesitation, it remains for me formally to locate hallmarks of the hyperbological that are evidenced when the two overdeterminative representations are brought into interactive juxtaposition.

Conclusion: Nietzschean and Heideggerian Overdeterminations in Mutual Exchange: The Oscillation of the Hyperbological

How might the overdeterminations be read as entering into (interminable and finally unresolved) engagement with each other? I work by way of three points.

The first involves my returning to Lacoue-Labarthe's notion of an ontotypology of original mimesis. This ontotypology, it will be recalled, construes Being itself as repeating a former self-sending, which, however, never occurred. The anticipated sending will yield Being as constituted originally, but also as a copy—herein lies its paradox.

What is important to point out is that both Nietzschean Being, as Will to Power, and Heideggerian Being, as forgotten in metaphysics, partake of this particular ontotypology. In my discussions of "Transcendence Ends in Politics" and "The Word of Nietzsche: God Is Dead" I have noted the elements of ontotypology as they contribute to the overdetermination of Nietzschean Being by Heideggerian Being. But Nietzschean Being is *also* envisaged by its proponent as, one might say, "once and future Being," under the paradoxical conditions I have described. Given this, it is likely that the Nietzschean overdetermination can reassert itself *over* the Heideggerian, employing the same logic as before, but with different terms.

In other words, precisely *because* the two overdeterminations share a common ontotypology of original mimesis, neither can permanently gainsay the other. Lacoue-Labarthe's focus only on Nietzschean "overdetermination" tended to mask the explanatory equality of the representations. But latent throughout his exposition is the hint of this equality. It is linked to the possibility that the representations of the respective overdeterminations can be shown as intimately entwined. To become plausible, this possibility required an exposition of Heideggerian overdetermination of Nietzsche at the points where their concepts are mutually reinforcing. The exposition was needed especially in relation to the competing representations of the philosophical-political subject.

Once established, the Heideggerian overdetermination of Nietzsche survives on an equal representational footing with the Nietzschean overdetermination of Heidegger. These become parallel and equal interpretations of the way in which the "Heideggerian" subject of science fulfils the demands of Being as destiny. This parallelism of opposites corresponds precisely to the ambiguity with regard to the accomplishment of nihilism that shadows Heidegger's own account.

Second, the opposing representations—of the subject of Nietzschean Heideggerianism, and of the subject of Heideggerian Nietzscheanism, respectively—pass into each other. This becomes a typical occurrence of the hyperbological that, admittedly, Lacoue-Labarthe has not himself pursued. I briefly present here an outline of this interchange, building on my previous development of hyperbology, and on the attention I have already accorded the individual representations.

The Nietzschean Heideggerian subject elicited in "Transcendence Ends in Politics" is born in the will to power. It is triumphant, in its self-erection, in expression of this will, which is the power of Being itself. In terms of this Nietzschean overdetermination, this subject is established through its own positing of the values of the preservation and enhancement of life.

This "revaluing of all values," while not constitutive of a new metaphysics, is an overcoming of nihilism. The postnihilistic subject is born of its own self-creation, following the thoroughgoing devaluation of all values that is the accomplishment of nihilism. As Lacoue-Labarthe implies in *Heidegger, Art and Politics*, it is in this sense that the aspect of clinicality that informed the Nazi extermination of Jews is to be related to the history of Being in the West. Nihilism is finally realized by the extermination of what is Other, not as valuable (for this would be to reaffirm the prenihilistic dispensation) but as waste. The accomplishment of nihilism, under the provocation of Being as will, here accomplishes the end of metaphysics, that is, the end of the life-inhibiting duality of the worlds of the sensible and supersensible.

However, at the height of its establishment, this Nietzschean-Heideggerian subject is unable to avoid being changed into its "other," a Heideggerian-Nietzschean representation. This representation corresponds to Heidegger's rejection of the post-Nietzschean subject of the will to power as itself implicated in nihilism. It requires substitution: by the newly scientific subject that allows Being to give itself as *technē*.

That representation, however, is again itself immediately liable to exchange: Lacoue-Labarthe's point in "Transcendence Ends in Politics" is that it cannot gainsay the Nietzschean overdetermination of the "postnihilistic" Heideggerian subject of the Rectoral Address. The nub of this overdetermination is the framing of Heidegger's address within the ontological superstructure corresponding to the will to power.

"Framing," here, might also be seen as exchange. It occurs as an "internal" wresting back of the Heideggerian overdetermination of the Nietzschean subject and its retransformation in terms of a Nietzschean overdetermination. The transformations might be seen as subsuming each other sequentially. But, as my first point has made clear, neither "overdetermination" is normative, and neither do the two exist on "different levels." Rather, it is as if each in turn survives to "have a say" when the other has done its worst.

This is also why the "accomplishment of nihilism" that coincides with the project of creation of the Western subject relates ambiguously to this subject. This subject is now the new Nietzschean-Heideggerian Western subject. In other words, it is Heidegger's "discredited Nietzschean" subject now overdetermined as Nietzsche's subject of the will to power, which represents the "overcoming of nihilism" in the Nietzschean sense of this term. Alternatively, and alternately, it is the new Heideggerian-Nietzschean subject, this being Nietzsche's subject now overdetermined as Heidegger's subject of metaphysics. This subject deepens nihilism as—this time in Heidegger's terms—the forgetting of Being. These two representations might be seen as interminably interchanging themselves for each other, in terms that Chapter 5 has made familiar.

Third, a remaining aspect of the *sequential* exchange of overdeterminations must be addressed. The reader will have noted that I have followed Lacoue-Labarthe in demonstrating the Nietzschean overdetermination of the "postnihilistic" Heideggerian subject who is the focus of the Rectoral Address. My demonstration of the corresponding *Heideggerian* overdetermination, however, worked on the "generalized" Nietzschean subject encountered in "The Word of Nietzsche: God Is Dead." How might Heidegger's ontology fare before the challenge of overdetermining the *particular* Nietzschean subject that Lacoue-Labarthe has erected while overdetermining Heidegger's "New German" subject?

This question may also be developed as a reply to the following objection by one who feels that this "mutual overdetermination" bespeaks some philosophical sleight of hand. Lacoue-Labarthe's demonstration has left the final Nietzschean overdetermination "triumphant" over Heidegger's most sophisticated subject, whereas my demonstration of Heideggerian overdetermination has operated on another, more "primitive" Nietzschean subject. But if, as hyperbology requires, the Nietzschean and Heideggerian overdeterminations are equal and oscillatory in scope, it ought to be possible to demonstrate a Heideggerian overdetermination of the final (Nietzschean) subject of "Transcendence Ends in Politics." In other words, it remains for me to establish the possibility of a hyperbological *return* of this *newly* Nietzschean subject to Heideggerian overdetermination.

The outline of such a return is in fact not difficult to sketch (and here a sketch will have to suffice): the overdetermination will of course again render metaphysical a subject whom Heidegger has implicated in metaphysics but whom Nietzsche (represented by Lacoue-Labarthe) has been able at least formally to overdetermine as a value-positing will to power.

In its barest terms, this demonstration follows. I begin with the Heideggerian subject of the Rectoral Address. This new German subject initially retains formal metaphysical-subjectal aspects. Embodying Heidegger's interpretation of *technē* as science, this subject is implicated in the general type of "response" to Being that comprises metaphysics and that yields Being as what "is" as such. For this subject, science will be the highest value.

There is only one thing in Heidegger's description of the new German subject that precludes its *final* complicity in metaphysics: the depiction of its scientific activity as an ultimately *defiant* determination of Being, designed to "provoke" the approach of Being in unconcealment. But Lacoue-Labarthe's scrutiny has seen this activity redescribed in terms of will to power. Its "provocation" has itself been overdetermined as Nietzschean, that is, as the *willful* and *powerful* expression of Being determining itself as such. Then Heidegger's characterization of such Being as metaphysical, in "The Word of Nietzsche: God Is Dead" and elsewhere, returns to thwart the escape of this subject from metaphysics.

So the postnihilistic subject is effectively subverted, not through a once-and-for-all overdetermination as metaphysical but by being unable to avoid an ongoing interaction with a metaphysical subject that is also, alternately, overdetermined *by* it. The alternative, a single and final triumph of metaphysics over nihilism, is tempting but unsustainable. As Heidegger himself reminds us, "Those who fancy themselves free of nihilism perhaps push forward its development most fundamentally."[72] And exactly the same is true when the hoped-for escape is from metaphysics, as "The Word of Nietzcshe: God Is Dead" patiently demonstrates.

This indication of how the Nietzschean and Heideggerian overdeterminations replace each other sequentially, ad infinitum, completes my demonstration of the hyperbological interaction between them. I recall the two previous points made in this section: that the Nietzschean and Heideggerian subjectal representations mutually pass into each other at their heights, and that they have equal status, made possible by their sharing an ontology wherein Being is both original and mimed. Taken in conjunction, these three characteristics clearly betoken marks of the hyperbological: equality of "opposing" representations, the passing of these into each other, and the interminability of their sequential exchange (or cotemporal opposition).

In all, between these representations of the Nietzschean subject as Heideggerian and the Heideggerian subject as Nietzschean, there is the loss or fatal hesitation of the subject. True to the essence of the hyperbological, the scope for sublation is eliminated here. Each representation opposes the other, but it has also already passed into this other so that this other is itself, and vice versa. Here, hyperbological oscillation ensures that neither can be effectively replaced by the other, or by a third that might reconcile their differences. This precludes, here, an operation of Hegelian negation, which might have provided a sublative path toward an absolute subject.

This observation appropriately concludes my task in this chapter: that of extrapolating, into the realm inhabited by the political subject, Lacoue-Labarthe's notion of hyperbology. There should be little surprise, once the connection between the philosophical and political subjects has been drawn, in seeing hyperbology implicated in the philosophical-political, evoking subjectal loss there. It does this clandestinely, but no less effectively than in other spheres, where the subject whose (de)constitution Lacoue-Labarthe pursues is more obviously marked by original mimesis.

7

Lacoue-Labarthe and Jean-Luc Nancy
Sublime Truth Perpetually Offered as Its Other

Introduction

Context

It is time to take stock of the journey with Lacoue-Labarthe that this book represents. I have attempted hitherto to trace a single "Ariadne's thread"—hyperbology—through the intricate, often labyrinthine, paths of his pursuit of subjectal return and loss, from Plato to Heidegger. Some will no doubt find this project unattractively paradoxical, in danger as it is of becoming reductive of a writer whose own texts aim subtly and patiently at subverting essentiality. Others will happily use the thread to locate the paths in Lacoue-Labarthe that offer continuity toward a single destination; this approach need not deny that there are other paths that invite dallying and are rewarding for other reasons. The latter is my own perspective in writing this book this way. Moreover, in the two final chapters, which I steer toward "extruding" Lacoue-Labarthe somewhat beyond himself, I will not discard the hyperbological thread. Instead I move cautiously, and cognizant of paradox, toward a reflection on what hyperbological loss might finally make possible in terms of subjectal return, albeit a return that is *otherwise*. I do this because I think that the ceaseless fleeing of the Lacoue-Labarthian subject permits the premise of this "subjectal otherness," which emerges as such when his texts are brought into interaction with those of his nearest contemporaries—Jean-Luc Nancy, of course, but also Jacques Derrida and Maurice Blanchot.

So I take up the comparison with Nancy in this chapter, and with Derrida and Blanchot in the next. "Hyperbology" will provide my center again, and I will keep in view the treatment of subjectal loss that links these others to Lacoue-Labarthe. But I will also gradually and provisionally elicit, as a suggestion for further inquiry, the possibility that these writings, taken together, entertain of a postmetaphysical subjectivity. The specific questions are these: In the deconstructive oeuvre that Lacoue-Labarthe broadly shares with his contemporaries, is there room for the thought of an "other" structural subject, that is, one that comes to be (re)presented *other* than as the now familiar reinscription attending deconstruction? And to what extent could this thought draw support from the very *necessity* associated with representations of subjectal loss, and which tends to render those representations as *presentations*?

In a generic sense, the question of "deconstructive subjectivity" has hardly been neglected, as Chapter 8 will recall. My own contribution to this question will be by way of proposing a particular placement of Lacoue-Labarthe in relation to his key contemporaries. I will suggest that Lacoue-Labarthian hyperbology identifies a mode of representation of the subject, *in and as its loss*, that might well pass for a subjectal *presentation*, appropriately construed. These hypotheses will emerge toward the end of the present chapter, in order properly to guide the explorations of the next.

Aim and Method: Lacoue-Labarthian Hyperbology Sharpened by the Comparison with Nancy

To speak about Jean-Luc Nancy, in the terms broached above, is to speak about one who has not only been Lacoue-Labarthe's closest colleague and authorial partner over these last thirty years but who has certainly also published more than Lacoue-Labarthe, and likewise been more critiqued. Selectivity, therefore, is in order. Moreover, I will continue to prefer close reading of fewer texts to wide reading of many. Given that it is sadly impossible anyway for me to do Nancy justice in the short space available here, this approach will at least provide some depth of exploration and do justice to my own task of scrutinizing subjectal loss, in both authors, in its subtler dimensions.

The chapter unfolds as follows. I begin by selecting points for consideration from a key text of Nancy's that, among his recent works, offers the broadest summary of that subjectal loss attending the openness to meaning.[1] But even here, Nancy's emphasis differs interestingly from Lacoue-Labarthe's, and sometimes from that on display in their joint writings.

I allow an initial examination of this difference to lead me, in the following two sections, to respective extended readings of the two authors' texts on the sublime.[2] Those readings, oriented to the comparison of the texts, form the bulk of the chapter. My purpose will again be to highlight Lacoue-Labarthian hyperbology by contrasting it with equivalent subjectal loss in Nancy.

Again, I confess, I will thus have bypassed some thought that is quite central to other parts of Nancy's corpus, notably the work relating subjectivity to community.[3] On the other hand, my approach will have indicated the ways in which Nancy's emphases support those of Lacoue-Labarthe. It will also have indicated, in precisely the places where their concerns overlap, which emphases are likely to be Lacoue-Labarthe's own. Finally, it will have evoked the important question of whether a *Nancian* hyperbology, by virtue of its mediation through *sense*, might support the notion of a subjectivity persisting in and through the loss of the subject.

Nancy's *The Gravity of Thought*: Sense and Writing in Interplay

My interest in *The Gravity of Thought* might be introduced as follows. The joint works by Lacoue-Labarthe and Nancy that have been analyzed heretofore investigate a subject lost through writing. In *The Literary Absolute*, literature becomes the place preferentially mined for the exhibition of this loss. In *The Title of the Letter*, that topos is supplied by psychoanalytic representation. However, in his solely authored works, Nancy focuses on the subjectal loss mediated by elements of experience.[4] He is less direct than Lacoue-Labarthe in associating this experience with writing, or with its structure. What distance, if any, does this place between the two authors' different approaches?

In *The Gravity of Thought*, if the subject, as self, is lost, it is in the event of thought itself. The "forgetting of philosophy," as a forgetting of the nature of thought, is also a forgetting of this loss of the self.[5] Thought is not, as it were, its own subject. It has never been *"that*

which happens," but rather, "the wonder before the fact that it happens."[6] Instead, *meaning* is what happens. Philosophy, as thought, is
the *opening* [*ouverture*] "to which and through which what belongs to
meaning is able to happen."[7] This description implies that an event
of thought corresponds to the impossibility of preserving the self:
"Thinking is presumably nothing other than the sensation of a 'self'
that falls outside of itself *even before* having been a self."[8]

"Loss of the self," here, stands in both comparison and contrast
with its Lacoue-Labarthian equivalent, mediated by writing: "We
write: we are dispossessed, something is ceaselessly fleeing, outside
of us, slowly deteriorating."[9] True, Lacoue-Labarthe does not mean
here to distinguish writing *from* experience, as the locus for loss of the
self. However, he seems to go beyond Nancy in consistently invoking
writing as *reflecting* experience:

> If writing has this privilege [of revealing our dispossession, it
> is] . . . rather because writing is first of all that reflection of
> experience wherein reflection (and hence experience) is inces-
> santly undone, because it is the most painful of failures and be-
> cause, in it, the radical alterity of force "reveals" itself most
> painfully.[10]

For Nancy, meaning "happens" in the "opening" which is reflection. Lacoue-Labarthe speaks of reflection-experience as undone by
a "radical alterity of force." He is evidently not far from Nancy's notions of reflection as opening, and meaning as "happening." Nancy,
however, is clearly more ready to explore *sens* (sense as "meaning,"
but also as "sensation") outside the context of the experience of
writing.

He seemingly intends thereby to avoid the thought of writing as
"containing" or "revealing" sense. Otherwise, sense and meaning, removed from their essence as "happenings," become assimilated to
writing. Thus Francis Fischer, in a short but insightful essay, remarks that, for Nancy, sense *is* writing, in its occurrence as "event,
dispersion, brilliance or shard, punctuation," but it is *not* writing as
"that metaphysics of the written which haunted theoretical reflection
in the 1970s."[11] Fischer quotes Nancy:

> It is a matter of holding oneself very precisely upon the very
> thin line where sense is proposed and dissolved, where it is dis-
> solved in its proposition.[12]

Writing, insofar as it proposes sense, also dissolves it. Or, to put
it another way: even if writing is the place where a "subject" of sense

occurs, this subject is not the subject of *philosophy*. Writing excises *that* subject, no less surely here than in Lacoue-Labarthe.

I have already examined Lacoue-Labarthe's way of saying this. For him, the subject is never cotemporal with the text but is always either "early" or "late" with respect to it. Writing is thus where the subject is both created and lost or is created *as* lost, that is, as noncoincident with itself. Nancy invokes this very notion when he speaks about inscription as the *exscription* of presence. Fischer quotes Nancy again:

> By inscribing meanings, one excribes the presence of what withdraws from all meaning, being itself (life, passion, matter, . . .). The being of existence is not unpresentable: it presents itself excribed.[13]

Fischer employs this text in speaking about the exscription of "existence." But the quotation is more explicitly about the exscription of the *being* of existence, that is, the philosophical subject.

Additionally, for Nancy, as for Lacoue-Labarthe, it is the constant *undoing* of experience (Nancy would say its "openness") that mediates or becomes the occasion for the loss of any "self" that might presume to ground itself through experience. This is due to that part of the structure of experience that corresponds to thinking. As we have seen, subjectal loss itself has first to do with the way in which thinking consigns the subject *in the present, to an undoing that has always already occurred*; the self is sensed as falling outside itself "*even before* having been a self."

It is specifically this *prior exteriority* of the self in regard to itself that constitutes its loss. I have already pointed out this same notion in Lacoue-Labarthe. His "something is ceaselessly fleeing outside of us, slowly deteriorating" describes a lost subject that, paradoxically, *except for* writing *and because of* writing, *never was*. The subject is constituted in and through this loss, this *désistant* "*I'm* late," as Derrida terms it.[14]

Clearly, then, the two approaches have points of convergence. Both finally gravitate toward identifying the self-dispossessive structure of writing with which thought is imbued. Nevertheless, Nancy, as it were, seeks the *sens* of the dispossession that is writing. In this he often seems to begin where Lacoue-Labarthe leaves off. One might say aphoristically that Lacoue-Labarthe probes sense (or meaning, or experience) for the structure of writing; Nancy prefers to probe writing for the structure of sense. In both cases, subjectal loss is signaled by the division, hesitation, or fissure within the representations obtained. For both writers, a past—a past that has never been present—becomes the locale for a subjectal exteriority or division. In turn, this division reflects the subjectal loss attending the structure of thinking (Nancy) or writing (Lacoue-Labarthe).

Equally, for both writers, the *future* becomes the locale of a sheer "openness" that manifests subjectal loss. For Nancy,

> the dimension of the open, then, is the one according to which nothing (nothing essential) is established or settled; it is the one according to which everything essential *comes to be*.[15]

But this does not mean that, for Nancy, the arrival of the essential is possible as such. Meaning cannot be finally fixed by a "closure upon itself"—thought of this closure merely helps one evoke the conditions of its (im)possibility, or, as Nancy puts it, helps one discern its "themes and structures." Then one may

> begin to make oneself available to the "open," to what comes—to that which, since it comes and since its essence lies in coming, in the yet-to-come, has no "self" upon which to close itself.[16]

Nevertheless, Nancy's continued use of the language of "essence" here is interesting. Is essence related to the possibility of describing a self that has regained itself as subject, but in a radically non-Cartesian way? Such an "open" subject would be neither self-possessed nor master of its own thinking. It would incorporate an anticipation of its own change in the face of an utterly dispossessing future, marked by the "happening" of meaning. By contrast, philosophical subjectivity has always presumed some degree of closure and self-possession. Under what description might subjectivity be reimagined, to be linked to radical "openness" of the self, and self-dispossession? This important question will return later to the center of my attention.

For the moment, though, the following seems evident. Nancy's conclusion here is of a piece with what he and Lacoue-Labarthe jointly assert in *The Literary Absolute,* where the "infinitized" or "organic" subject is at issue: to invoke the "closure" informing classical or even romantic notions of subjectivity is finally to fail to evade the radicality of subjectal loss. Instead, say the authors, drawing here on Blanchot (to whom I shall attend later), "this auto-manifestation of literature ought to be considered as a neutral manifestation, or as a *negative* [*pas*] of manifestation."[17]

How, in fact, does subjectal loss occur in *The Gravity of Thought?* "Ineradicable openness of the horizon of meaning" is one answer, but not a sufficient one; it must be coupled with the fact of *thought*, anatomized by Nancy as the subject's *impetus toward meaning*, through which is manifest its separation from itself. Eventually, this anatomy of thought becomes that writing. It is instructive to see how this occurs.

Nancy begins by observing that "the desire for meaning marks in every way the modern subject's access to itself."[18] But desire for meaning implies, of course, a distance from meaning. And as long as the subject is separated from meaning, it has also not yet become itself. In this sense, the desire for meaning marks the subject's *inaccessibility* to itself, and "the subject defines itself as the subject of its desire, and this desire is the desire to become a subject (such is the law of the *Verstellung*)."[19] In other words, awareness of "meaning-at-a-distance" also generates the subject's desire for itself, that is, a desire to "close the distance," that is, to become a subject. Such an argument ties the subject's self-displacement squarely to the displacement of meaning attending all signification. If this is so, then subjectal displacement in Nancy, as in Lacoue-Labarthe, is linked to generalized writing.

This power of signification is reiterated when Nancy comes to reflect upon the "project of the subject."[20] The term refers to the attempt by the subject, renewed throughout history, to appropriate the above-mentioned "presence-at-a-distance" of meaning. This appropriation always involves signification, whereby the "I am . . . ," the move by which the subject identifies itself, becomes a *projection* of self *as other*, entailing a renewal of self-distancing. Nancy puts the incessance of this projection thus:

> Ideas, values, even the idea and value of the subject itself, can only be projected onto the screen of representation since their status or nature is of the order of signification. . . . Projection is thus the true order of signified meaning. . . .[21]

Signification then, as subjectal projection, is that which, within the fabric of thought, cannot be avoided. It at once corresponds both to the subject's desire for itself and to its loss of itself.

At this point, what I designated earlier as the distinction between "sense as writing" and "writing as sense" is all but imperceptible:

there seems scarcely any distance at all between Nancy and Lacoue-Labarthe on the matter of subjectal loss. In fact, what Nancy has just offered is just what is evoked whenever Lacoue-Labarthe pursues the subject: a displacement of the subject by which, in the act of producing meaning—the writer writing, the mimetician acting, the psychoanalyst autoanalyzing—it inevitably produces itself as an "other."

Likewise, convergence is evident between Nancy and Lacoue-Labarthe on the notion of the "exhaustion of signification," to which Nancy's analysis tends.[22] *The Gravity of Thought,* and especially its first part, "The Forgetting of Philosophy," has the polemic intent of reasserting this exhaustion in the face of calls for a "return of meaning." The attempt to signify signification has been renewed constantly over Western philosophical history; metaphysics is the name of this attempt, now complete to the point of exhaustion. For Nancy, metaphysics

> represents the total accomplishment of what one might call the signification of signification, or the presentation—that is, the representation—of meaning present at a distance.[23]

This accomplishment as exhaustion signifies the end, in both senses of the word, of what grounds signification: ontology and/or theology. Rightly read, Nietzsche's account of the "death of God" implies the end of the possibility of a referent that is external to signification. This means the closure of signification upon itself:

> Signification becomes empty precisely because it imprisons [*boucle*] its subjective process; its only meaning is itself, in its inertia, that is, at once its own desire, its own projection, its own representational distance, and its own representation of distance, insofar as this distance constitutes its essential property: the ideality, transcendence, or future of meaning.[24]

Nothing that is said here concerning the "emptiness" of signification, or its consigning of the subject of meaning to "its own representational distance," has taken us very far from the conclusions of *The Literary Absolute,* or even from Lacoue-Labarthe's description in "The Fable," of writing as "first of all that experience of reflection in which reflection (and hence experience) is undone."[25] This seems to have razed my presenting distinction between "writing explored as sense" (Nancy) and "sense explored as writing" (Lacoue-Labarthe), the thesis collapsing precisely where the authors converge on the matter of the loss of the subject through signification. But the difference might yet raise itself as a difference in the *mode* of their respective investigations of this notion.

Broadly speaking, where Lacoue-Labarthe demonstrates how writing "unaccomplishes" sense, Nancy seeks "meaning" that "happens" in the wake of an unaccomplished sense.[26] Thus for both, it seems, the subversion that writing effects and expresses becomes (re)oriented *to* sense. But, particularly for Nancy, sense connotes something more primitive than philosophical "meaning." It is sense as in "a sense of," or even sense as sensation, as in, for example, the sense of touch.[27] Or it is even, perhaps, sense as the "feel" (or the "this feels right") that makes meaning meaningful while at the same time confirming its utter contextuality and unaccomplishment, its freedom to reconfigure itself in a new opening.

At any rate, this Nancian "faith in sense" in turn makes for the possibility of using sense itself, under suitable erasure, as a hermeneutic tool. It becomes a prospective "subject as sensation" associated with signification: with the *event* of producing it, with its subversion as writing, or with its general problematicity. More specifically, Nancian "faith in sense" highlights itself, and it allows of comparison with Lacoue-Labarthe on this topic, through a comparison between their respective discussions of the *exhaustion of signification*. This they both do often, but most directly when they treat the question that has been, since Kant, emblematic of the exhaustion of signification. This is the question of the sublime.

In the remainder of this chapter, I will focus on their treatment of this question, taking for comparison, as I have said, their respective contributions to the 1988 collection *Du Sublime*.[28] I mention again that I will treat Lacoue-Labarthe first and in more detail, and Nancy later and more selectively. My aim in comparing them will be to reinforce my description of Lacoue-Labarthian "hyperbology," while using Nancy's approach as foil and counterpoint, to cast Lacoue-Labarthe in bolder relief. As this occurs, the path to the question of a "presented" subject of sensation will also be seen to open itself to exploration, as I have promised.

Lacoue-Labarthe's "Sublime Truth": Hyperbological Loss between the Eidetic and the Noneidetic

"Sublime Truth" comprises a steady and intricate engagement with the notion of the sublime in Kant, Heidegger, and Longinus. Its aim is to keep in view what Lacoue-Labarthe calls, after Derrida, *heliotro-*

pism: "the motif of light, brilliance, refulgence, bedazzlement, and so on," which has been "from the start constitutive of the discourse of philosophy upon its object: the meta-physical."[29]

Any presumption of an "illumination of Being" inevitably threatens an absolutization of the subject. The focus on heliotropism has as its point the following question, designed to thwart this absolutization. Within heliotropism, might something "here or there . . . intrude or occur which would be completely foreign to the metaphysical assumption of sight and the unbroken coercion of the theoretical"?[30] Ultimately, Lacoue-Labarthe finds this something to be the mutual cancellation by which the motifs of veiling and unveiling encompassed by the (heliotropical) sublime interact with each other. The fact that one name for the mechanism of this "cancellation" is hyperbology explains how Lacoue-Labarthe's essay will feed my overall claim in this work. I now outline the course of the argument in "Sublime Truth" before going on to elicit, in several stages, its implicit references to hyperbology.

The Kantian Sublime as Noneidetically Overdetermined

"Sublime Truth" begins with Kant's attempt to extend previous notions of the classical sublime. These center themselves on the possibility that Reason might engage itself even with that which, exceeding thought, is not susceptible of determination as an idea. For Kant, supreme sublimity is historically exhibited in two dicta, which I have already had occasion to mention in Chapter 4. The first, from Jewish law, forbids the making of graven images or "the likeness of anything which is in heaven or in the earth or under the earth, etc."[31] The second, from an inscription on the temple of Isis (Mother Nature) declares: "I am all that is and that was and that shall be, and no mortal has lifted my veil."[32]

Lacoue-Labarthe does not directly pursue heliotropism in respect of these examples. But he does note that both involve presentation to sight. Thus both reiterate the "canonical definition" of the sublime [since Longinus] as "the presentation of the nonpresentable, or, more rigorously, to take up the formula after Lyotard, the presentation (of this:) that there is the nonpresentable."[33]

"There *is* the *nonpresentable*." Does the "is" in this formulation not undo the signification of nonpresentability? The remainder of Lacoue-Labarthe's exploration consists in showing that ultimately it does not. Neither, he argues, does it allow the sublime to be overdetermined as *eidos*, that is, to exhibit itself as merely a nonpresentable *idea*.

In the traditional account of the sublime, moving from Longinus through Kant to Heidegger, might there be a notion of sublimity as an excess that defies subjectal representation? If not, sublimity is a self-showing of the subject. This latter conclusion is one that the tradition has not been able to avoid, ever since Plato steered it toward only one of two possible interpretations of the beautiful as *ekphanestaton*. These alternatives are captured etymologically. *Ek-phanestaton* can mean "showing-out-of itself" but also "outside showing" or "without showing." It is the latter two understandings that Lacoue-Labarthe wishes to help revive. However, it is the former that has been ascendant ever since, "with Plato, the eidetic overdetermination of the *ekphanestaton* no doubt definitively introduces itself."[34]

At this point, Lacoue-Labarthe's interests effectively become one with my own. In terms that I have used hitherto, the question is whether the beautiful as such marks the "occurrence" of the subject. Alternatively, it might mark subjectal absence or loss. The initial field of investigation is the beautiful. But whichever of the two overdeterminations (eidetic or noneidetic) controls the Kantian account of the beautiful controls, in turn, the Kantian sublime. As we have already seen in Chapter 4, under classical readings of the third *Critique*, the Kantian account of the beautiful, in its eidetic connotations, not only precedes that of the sublime but also determines that account. By contrast with what is found in the beautiful—success in presentation of a figure—the feeling of the sublime corresponds to a vain striving by Reason to give form to that which the imagination generates as formless.

As Chapter 4 suggested, the *Critique*'s descriptions of the sublime and the beautiful conspire only unsuccessfully to link subjectal loss in the sublime with an *absence* of form. In fact, Kantian subjectal loss is equally, and undecidably, offered in the sublime (and in the sublime dimension of the beautiful) as an *oversupply* of form. This means that the subject here is lost hyperbologically. That demonstration, which was only incipiently possible in Chapter 4 (my description of hyperbology being then undeveloped), is now much more thoroughly capable of prosecution. Lacoue-Labarthe's description of the hyperbological exchange between *phusis* (nature) and *technē* (art) will be seen to converge nicely with the descriptions of exchange, between representations of *Darstellung*, found in my earlier chapter.

Still, in Lacoue-Labarthe's "Sublime Truth," hyperbology as a mechanism remains for the most part clandestine, surfacing explicitly only once, as I show below. Nevertheless, its elements become available to be extruded from the account by which Lacoue-Labarthe undermines certain readings of Kant. The readings in question are those that privilege the beautiful as presentation.

Elements of Hyperbology: The Beautiful-Sublime in Heidegger and Hegel

The most significant of these elements emerge when Lacoue-Labarthe takes up Heidegger's reading of Kant's third *Critique*. Lacoue-Labarthe notes "Heidegger's complex gesture with regard to the *ekphanestaton* and his equally complex gesture with respect to the Kantian determination of the beautiful."[35] Heidegger regards the beautiful as affording a shining forth of the truth (as *aletheia*, unconcealment) that reveals the object in its essence. He speaks, on Kant's behalf, of the object as a "pure object." At the same time, says Lacoue-Labarthe, the terms of praise for Kant imply a "nonaesthetic (non*eidetic*) determination of the beautiful."[36] Somehow, in Kant, the essence of art remains something apart from the ideas yielded by aesthetics, as reflection. The Kantian manifestation associated with the beautiful is not essentially that of the *eidos*.

Already in view here are opposing representations of the *essentially* beautiful, as eidetic and noneidetic, respectively. Having regard to all I have so far said concerning hyperbology, an interesting Lacoue-Labarthian interplay can be anticipated between these representations. The noneidetic is formally a representation of subjectal loss, but to accept its signification as such is to imply the *return* of the subject, either simply or sublatively, through its representation *as* lost. It can be taken for granted that Lacoue-Labarthe is wholly aware of this problem.

In any event, the prospective hyperbological elements here are different from those that I provisionally identified in the Kantian sublime in Chapter 4. Subjectal loss is now in prospect through oscillation between a representation of the *subject*, on the one hand, and another of the *loss of the subject*, on the other. Consequently, as will become evident, the scope here is more directly for the demonstration of hyperbology as present on its own terms as opposed to the "mere" Derridean undecidability that was on display in Chapter 4.

One sign that it might be thus present is that Lacoue-Labarthe sees Heidegger's Kant as unamenable to a sublative interpretation of art. As we have seen, such resistance is often explicated by Lacoue-Labarthe in terms of hyperbology. Here, he begins by showing how resistance to sublation is necessary if art is not to be assimilable to aesthetics *as* idea.

He first invokes Heidegger, writing on Hegel, as follows. Heidegger's Kant differs from Heidegger's Hegel, for whom the aesthetic-eidetic determination of art becomes dialectically inevitable. As Heidegger describes it, the inevitability follows from Hegel's demand for a resolution between art itself and aesthetics. In the first course of lectures on Nietzsche, Heidegger argues that for Hegel, the purpose of art is "to present [*Darstellen*] the absolute and install it [*stellen*] as such as measure in the domain of historical humanity."[37] By contrast, aesthetics involves production of the eidetic through reflection on art. Aesthetics must triumph, and then, says Lacoue-Labarthe, again recalling Heidegger on Hegel, "it's all over for great art."[38]

But how is Hegel's own reading to be read? As itself philosophy of art, *it* can never be other than enclosed *as* aesthetics, the very aesthetics it decries. Lacoue-Labarthe says, again speaking as Heidegger's proxy, that if the insight Hegel offers still survives, it does so only

> from the standpoint of a broader and deeper vision of aesthetics, from the standpoint of a more "archaic" end of art and a — totally — other interpretation of truth.[39]

Nevertheless, formally Hegel has committed the aesthetic "crime" that he himself has detected elsewhere, and that henceforth closes art off from a preaesthetic possibility of revealing the "truth of the being." Heidegger is aware that Hegel's aesthetics, as ultimately eidetic, has betrayed Kant's account of art, in the process generating an "other" of art: aesthetics. This, implies Lacoue-Labarthe, is why Heidegger never mentions Kant in relation to the history of aesthetics.

Lacoue-Labarthe follows this aesthetic-sublative determination of art as it becomes a counterpoint to noneidetic art. As an "other" to art, aesthetics cannot function to bring art into itself. It can function only to end art, by assimilating it to the idea, which is not art. Further, a mere *aesthetics* of the noneidetic cannot effect an exchange of the representation of art as eidetic for a representation of art as noneidetic. In this light, it will not be surprising to find that the demonstration of a noneidetic essence for art involves the identification of a more complex "mechanism of exchange" of the above representations. Eventually, in what follows, I hope to show that what is needed here, and what is provided by Lacoue-Labarthe's demonstration, is evidence of a hyperbological mechanism.

This point made, there is scope for a precise description of how Heidegger's own insights into Kant differ essentially from those of Hegel. Where, in Heidegger's Kant, is there evidence of a preservation of a nonaesthetic essence for art, one that remains outside the Hegelian closure? Lacoue-Labarthe finds that the work here is done clandestinely by Heidegger's notion of "showing/shining" (*Scheinen, Phainesthai*). Heidegger's "more or less secret re-evaluation of Kant and Schiller" means that

> above all . . . the comprehension of the beautiful in its essence as pure *Scheinen* translates a complete rupture with the eidetic apprehension of art.[40]

Such a rupture, says Lacoue-Labarthe, properly occurs with the Kantian sublime. The implication here is that Heidegger's notion of art allies itself with the noneidetic essence of art that the Kantian sublime proposes, and that is determinative of the Kantian beautiful.

Scheinen, therefore, will return us to the mechanism that delivers the Kantian noneidetic sublime. Before examining this mechanism for elements of hyperbology, I must follow Lacoue-Labarthe's reminder here regarding the clandestine nature of its operation. In fact, it will be seen that such hiddenness is part of the reason why it escapes assimilation to its "other," Hegelian sublation. The hiddenness arises because Heidegger's account retains a formal attachment to the notion of the beautiful as prior to, and determinative of, the sublime. Heidegger does not notice that an opposite movement occurs in Kant, giving the sublime priority and determinative status. (I have already had occasion to explore this movement in Chapter 4.) Consequently, says Lacoue-Labarthe, Heidegger ignores the sublime as such, treating it (in perpetuation of a mistake that occurs from Longimus to Kant) as merely "an exhaustion of the sense of the beautiful," and as falling short of the presentation of *eidos* as form.[41]

Lacoue-Labarthe, of course, is interested in precisely this radically "other" meaning for the sublime, one that occurs clandestinely in texts, such as those of Hegel and Heidegger, that ostensibly develop the Kantian "eidetic" sublime. This interest takes him back to Kant himself, and to pre-Kantian classical texts on the sublime, such as

that of Longinus. I shall follow him, allowing the elements of hyperbological subjectal hesitation to make their presence felt, while the
hyperbological itself draws Lacoue-Labarthe's explicit mention only
once, but at a significant juncture.

Eidetic Assimilation of the Kantian Examples by Hegel and Heidegger

We are following Lacoue-Labarthe's claim that the noneidetic essence of the Kantian beautiful, as originating in the Kantian sublime,
goes unnoticed by Kant's successors. Certainly this is so for Hegel,
whose dialectical sublime is "the incompletion of the beautiful, which
is, the beautiful seeking to complete itself," and, in a more equivocal
way, for Heidegger.[42]

Lacoue-Labarthe develops this point as follows. The first of Kant's
paradigmatic examples of the sublime had recalled the divine prohibition of representation. But because the prohibition cannot itself remain *un(re)presented, nonpresentability* itself emerges, clandestinely, in
its having to be shown. Nonpresentability *presents* as the "inner," *eidetic* truth of *the nonpresentable,* that is, as a *subject* that representation
strives to attain. In fact, Moses himself, speaking for God, becomes a
figure representing what he says ought not to be represented. Hegel
notices this, saying that the figure of Moses has "the value . . . of
an organ."[43] Freud, commenting on Michelangelo's Moses, valorizes
Moses' restraint (in not breaking the tablets of the law) as "the highest psychic exploit of which man can be capable," since he is able "to
defeat his own passion in the name of an end to which he knows
himself to be destined."[44] Figures of the absent God are created here,
and of the absent human.

Lacoue-Labarthe is concerned by the neatness of this escape from
the problem of negative presentation. In a manner strongly reminiscent of Schiller, it identifies the sublime effect with a contradiction
between formal sensible traits. This interpretation, however, once
more subsumes the sublime to the beautiful.

Can the account of the "beautiful-sublime" as (essentially) *presentability* be subverted? The problem, as the above examples show, is to
assert the sublime as "essential nonpresentability"—and already this
term displays inherent reversion to the eidetic!—without *presenting*
this nonpresentability as such. Otherwise, the beautiful becomes
controlling again, the sublime being determined in terms of the *eidos*

of the *beyond-form*. The sublime art or nature manifests itself as "the negation of the presentation."[45]

The alternative is the reverse dispensation: that essential sublime "nonpresentability" controls. In *this* case, the sublime, thus redefined, would determine anew the understanding of art so that the latter "is not *essentially* a matter of eidetic presentation."[46] Lacoue-Labarthe here comes implicitly to the question of a mechanism that might deliver an interplay, between eidetic (subjectal) presentation and subjectal loss, and that is resolved in favor of the latter. Formally, his question is this: "If art is nonetheless *presentation* (and how could one define it otherwise?) what does it essentially present other than form or figure?"[47]

This question leads him to Kant's second example—the self-presentation of Isis—and to the possibility of an answer in Heidegger. Here again, Lacoue-Labarthe works to rescue noneidetic elements from Heidegger's formally eidetic analysis, while I attempt to keep in view emerging elements of hyperbology.

Relating Heidegger to Kant, Lacoue-Labarthe points out that Kant's thought becomes accessible to Heidegger's own through a change in form from the first dictum to the second. The Mosaic saying was prescriptive; that of Isis is constative, claiming to present truth itself: "I am all that is and that was and that shall be, and no mortal has lifted my veil." A second entrée is provided by the form of the metaphor, since "the nonpresentable is conceived here as non-unveilable."[48] The figure of "veiling" has, "from time immemorial," had truth as its subject; here, the utterance is made both *by* truth and *about* truth. More significantly, a paradox is involved, of the following form: I, the truth, tell the truth about the truth—this truth being that the truth has never been told. Or in terms of veiling / unveiling, the utterance means that, in

> telling the truth about itself, telling the truth of the truth and unveiling itself as truth, truth (unveiling) unveils itself as the impossibility of unveiling or the necessity, for finite (mortal) Being, of its veiling.[49]

Thus Lacoue-Labarthe ties the Isis saying, which is formally about veiling and unveiling of Being, to "truth." He is relying here, unproblematically enough, on the classical equation of "Being itself" with truth, as that which finally "is" (in other words, of course, as the subject). He is now ready to connect Heidegger's discussion of the work of art, couched in terms of veiling and unveiling of truth, to the second Kantian dictum on the sublime.

Lacoue-Labarthe's Heidegger: Embryonic and Implicit Recourse to Hyperbological Exchange

"Truth (unveiling) veils itself as the impossibility of unveiling," says Lacoue-Labarthe. Already visible here, in silhouette, so to speak, is a hesitational loss of the subject (truth) between opposing representations: truth as veiling and truth as unveiling. Neither of the representations survives through sublimation, for each passes into the other. Truth *as* unveiled becomes veiling, the veiling that it itself "is." Equally, truth as veiled (as incorporating the "true" declaration of its own veiledness) becomes an unveiling of "the truth of truth." Truth, then, is unveiled *as* veiled and simultaneously is veiled *as* unveiled.

This, however, is anticipation. I rejoin Lacoue-Labarthe as he reads Heidegger. In his second lecture in "The Origin of the Work of Art," Heidegger explicitly examines the proposition "The truth, in its essence, is untruth" as a paraphrase of the Isis utterance.[50] Lacoue-Labarthe analyzes Heidegger with two aims in mind. On the one hand, he seeks to demonstrate how Heidegger's account of art formally resolves the opposition between the two representations of truth so that art delivers truth and a subject. On the other, he hopes to show that, simultaneously but clandestinely, Heidegger's account leaves the opposition unresolved so that art finally presents what "is" noneidetic: what is neither truth nor the subject, or rather is truth *as* untruth.

"The Origin of the Work of Art" sees Heidegger approach the sublime by transposing its elements into his reading of the Kantian *beautiful*, seen in terms of his own account of the Being of beings. The point seems to be that, for Heidegger, the Kantian beautiful corresponds, not simply to the essential appearance of the object, but to this appearance as an unveiling, against the backdrop of the simultaneous *veiling* of Being. Something appears, therefore, and, in its very appearing, marks that which does not appear. It marks that, the Being of which is inextricably bound up with nonappearance.

This nonappearance is the focus of Lacoue-Labarthe's probing of Heidegger. Truth occurs here or is unveiled, but not as a showing. Whatever *occurs*, as the appearance of truth, is also *not* an appearance of anything (since it is the appearing of truth precisely *as* concealment, *aletheia*). Asking, "So how does this occurrence signal itself?"

Lacoue-Labarthe answers, on Heidegger's behalf, in terms of the *uncanny*. This is the mode of estrangement by which the ordinary is revealed as extra-ordinary.[51]

Lacoue-Labarthe watches Heidegger argue that this uncanniness resists Hegelian sublation. "Uncanniness" is the means by which the object reveals itself as unfamiliar, and thereby as "given" against a self-concealing background that, for Heidegger, is Being itself as, effectively, a lost subject. But uncanniness does not announce itself as "negative presentation," in terms of the sublative project presumed by Hegel. There, presentation is at once the site of what is and what is not so that the resolution of this opposition moves dynamically toward the absolute idea. Lacoue-Labarthe quotes Heidegger: "['The truth, in its essence, is nontruth'] . . . also does not mean, in a dialectical representation, that truth is never itself but always also its contrary."[52]

The difference between Heidegger and Hegel here is that Heidegger begins with the (fact of the) presented, moving then to how "presentation itself (or the 'fact' that there is presence) comes, in an absolutely paradoxical fashion, to 'present' itself."[53]

How is this uncanniness to be investigated for signs of the hyperbological? Lacoue-Labarthe takes us a great deal of the way. He points out that the Heideggerian uncanny, as a "prior" excess over form, has touchpoints with the *essentially* noneidetic that the Kantian sublime strives to name, finally failing to do so. For Heidegger, the defamiliarizing of a work, yielding an awareness of its coming to be in the unconcealing of truth, occurs archetypally in art. But note what has happened here. Speaking about the beautiful, Heidegger has ventured into the vocabulary and experience associated with the sublime: defamiliarity, alienation and derangement, and so on. Lacoue-Labarthe observes: "What this text describes, in its own way and at a depth doubtless unknown before it, is the experience of the sublime itself."[54]

The essence of this description is its assumption that Being manifests "itself" at the edges of the work. Lacoue-Labarthe summarizes again:

> The work presents *a-letheia*, the no-thing luminous with an "obscure illumination," which "is" the Being of what is. And this is sublimity.[55]

It is possible now to probe the aspects of the hyperbological available here. As I anticipated earlier, what becomes evident in Lacoue-

Labarthe's pursuit of Heidegger is a delicate delivery of two demonstrations: respectively, of the resolution of opposing representations of truth/Being, and of their nonresolution. Thus how much of what is noticed by Heidegger assimilates the Isis declaration to an eidetic sublime? Under one reading, the answer is "all of it," since,

> above all, Heidegger thought of manifestation as the eidetic presentation of the being, that is, in accordance with an account that was only attentive to the *Washeit* or to the quiddity of the being.[56]

In this context, defamiliarization cannot *but* begin with *that which is* defamiliarized: "What the work de-familiarizes, or what the presentation of presentation nihilates (but precisely does not annihilate), is the presented being." This presented being cannot but have the aspect of the eidetic, framed against the pre-eidetic. It is, Lacoue-Labarthe continues, "the being such as it is, such as it presents itself ontically, such as it ceaselessly cuts a figure against the background of that which is in general.[57]

Under another reading, however, nothing that Heidegger says here finally assimilates the Kantian beautiful to the eidetic. This becomes evident if one continues to ask: What is the status of the *pre-eidetic* with respect to the establishment/loss of the subject, that is, Being "itself"?

I have already pointed out that the subject, as Being itself, hesitates here. The hesitation is between two representations. One involves its self-veiling, and thereby self-loss. The other involves its self-gain: its manifestation of itself *in* this very veiling, as *that which has concealed itself* in order that beings might appear. If the "mechanism" of this hesitation is examined, it exhibits the characteristics of hyperbology, though Lacoue-Labarthe does not invoke the term itself until a much later stage in his analysis, when he has left Heidegger. As I have indicated, the two representations in question are those of subjectal presentation and ("first level") subjectal loss, respectively. An *overall* effect of ("second level") subjectal loss is created by hesitation between these two representations.

The elements of hyperbology might be observed at work (or, more accurately, at play!) here as follows. First, the two representations exist, as it were side by side, that is, simultaneously. The veiling of Being that is the unconcealment of beings—hence, subjectal loss—is an occurrence that always simultaneously signifies subjectal "gain," that is, that there "is" Being, "which" conceals "itself." Truth declares that the truth of itself is its veiling.

Second, each representation passes into the other *at its extreme*, in the precise manner associated with the hyperbological. At the very culmination of the "assertion" of "itself" that is the manifest presentation of beings, Being itself is concealed. But, seen from an opposite side, this "concealment of Being" itself, at *its* very height, becomes a manifestation of Being, in the *Unheimlichkeit*, or defamilarizing, which signifies a "something behind" beings, rendering them as *given*. This is hyperbological loss of the subject, in the oscillation between the presented and lost versions of the subject. With *and* against Heidegger, one might say that this oscillation "happens" par excellence in the experiencing of a work of art.

Lacoue-Labarthe at this point merely indicates the hesitation, between the eidetic and noneidetic, that finally marks the Heideggerian concealing/revealing of Being.

He tells us that this experience of presentation becomes for Heidegger "the opening of this: that there are beings." This yields the conclusion that there is not, for Heidegger, the nonpresentable as such (that is, negative presentation) but only ever the presentation itself as veiled in (the moment of) presentation. Lacoue-Labarthe puts it thus:

For [the "phantic" apprehension of the sublime] does not posit any "negative presentation"; it posits simply that the *sublime is the presentation of this: that there is presentation.*[58]

In other words, the sublime only declares that there "is" showing (or "the shown"). It does not go as far as positing that there "is," "behind the shown," as it were, a "not shown." This constitutes no less than Heidegger's admission of the noneidetic essence of the sublime. Being "is," finally, *other than* an "is" that goes unpresented in the sublime. It is not the existent, but essentially hidden, "nonpresentable," presented *as such*, or even otherwise, in the sublime. And yet this representation of the sublime as noneidetic is still ambiguously inscribed. It emerges only when Heidegger approaches the Kantian sublime under the rubric of the beautiful, that is, only in interplay with the representation of the Kantian sublime as *eidetic*.

Thus far, then, Lacoue-Labarthe, implicitly courting the hyperbological while reporting on Heidegger's Kant. I now follow him as he invokes hyperbology explicitly, if still only in outline. "Sublime Truth" moves in a new direction, searching the history of the notion of the sublime for a trace of the noneidetic sublime *prior* to its recuperation to the eidetic. Lacoue-Labarthe glances backward to Kant himself, and further still, to the antecedents of the Kantian sublime in Longinus.

Lacoue-Labarthe's Kant and Longinus: Hyperbology Developed and Explicitated, Beckoning Analysis

When Laocue-Labarthe turns to inspecting philosophical history for a hint of the "noneidetic sublime," what, exactly, is being sought, and how? Lacoue-Labarthe frames the hope thus:

> It is in the thought of the sublime—a certain thought of the sublime—that the memory has been maintained, however vague or half-forgetful, of a comprehension of the beautiful which is more original than its Platonic interpretation in terms of *eidos-idea*.[59]

The search for this remnant necessarily proceeds subtly and indirectly, moving through, and yet beneath, Kant's structurally eidetic sublime. Lacoue-Labarthe goes behind Kant to Pseudo-Longinus (whom he abbreviates as Longinus, as I shall here), who provided "the initial thought of the sublime" upon which Kant has built.[60] Lacoue-Labarthe indicates the places in Kant where elements of Longinus' "noneidetic sublime" survive. He sometimes goes as far as showing how these elements are absorbed into an eidetic superstructure. More often, however, he prefers the more delicate course of indicating the ambiguity whereby they become available to be redirected toward the eidetic future to which they are eventually consigned by the history of philosophy.

Lacoue-Labarthe presupposes, in Longinus, "a precise philosophical intent," in two stages. These are, respectively, "to think the essence of art anew in terms of the sublime, the great," and "consequently to ask oneself under what conditions the great is possible in art."[61] In short, he is asking: What is sublime art, and how is it to be produced? Regarding the first part of the question, he sets out to prove that sublime art can in fact be associated with a particular *technē* as know-how. But, in answer to the second part, he moves towards identifying this *technē* as innate *phusis*, thereby invoking an altered sense of *technē* itself, one that equates to what Kant will later call *genius*. For Kant, "*Genius* is the innate mental disposition (*Ingenium*) through which nature gives the rule to art."[62]

In other words, genius is the *human* mental disposition that allows nature to produce art. Already discernible in Longinus, therefore, is the skeleton of Kant's problem: how artistic *technē* might be described so as to represent both a human expression and one of nature, *phusis*. For Kant, contradiction between *technē* and *phusis*, which are at work at the same time, is resolved thus: *technē* is that *disposition* which allows *phusis* to operate autonomously.

Can a trace be found here of a noneidetic *technē*, by dint of which *technē* also exhibits definitional priority over *phusis*? Returning to the precursor of the above account from Longinus, Lacoue-Labarthe finds that *phusis* is still autonomous and initiatory, with *technē* as its regulating force (a "bridle"). But in the ensuing, albeit disputed, passage, Longinus quotes Demosthenes, to the effect that technique is the indispensable "source" of learning "what in speeches and writings depends wholly on nature."[63] Here there is a hint, developed in conjunction with Longinus' further description, of what Lacoue-Labarthe calls a *necessary supplementarity* between *phusis* and *technē*.[64] Longinus is saying, Lacoue-Labarthe concludes, that,

> in other words, only art (*technē*) is in a position to reveal nature (*phusis*). Or again: without *technē*, *phusis* escapes us, because in its essence *phusis kruptesthai philei*, it loves to dissimulate itself.[65]

This encourages Lacoue-Labarthe to trace this same interaction back further, to Aristotle's *Poetics*, where it is through mimesis, as a "natural" mode of *technē*, that a person's "first knowledge" is produced.[66] Here, *technē* produces, shapes, or draws truth from nature. Lacoue-Labarthe reveals in the notes that his point of access to the *Poetics* is a sentence, from Heidegger's *Introduction to Metaphysics*, which says that "through knowledge [*technē*] wrests being from concealment into the manifest as the essent."[67] In turn, Heidegger's interpretation has Aristotle maintaining the strain in Longinus that contrasts with, or "resists," the Platonic interpretation of mimesis as imitative fiction.

To simplify—and perhaps oversimplify—this point, for Plato what "is" exists prior to *technē* and is changed by the *technē* that reveals it. On the other hand, when Longinus/Aristotle/Heidegger offer the insight that the essence of *phusis* is concealment, they imply that *phusis* is the *nothing* that paradoxically becomes "itself" through its other, *technē* (as knowledge, or art). *Technē*, in short, is *phusis*, but if each of these "is," it "is" only as its other; equally, it cannot but conceal itself as the other is revealed.

In the terms I have already broached, what is being developed here is the seed of a description of *technē* as both gain and loss of the "subject" that is *phusis*. Hyperbology, here, is "in the wind," but the "final" loss of the subject will in those terms be of a different order from "first order" loss characterized by the notion of subject lost *as phusis*.

Lacoue-Labarthe begins with this latter loss. For Plato, the fictive is the imitative, that which works from an idea by copying. Kant has designated *technē* as a gift, granted by *phusis* to humans, through *genius*, to enable itself to appear. Has he thus succeeded in preserving an understanding of *technē* as nonimitative and, in this sense, purely fictive? And—a further step—can this purely fictive be determined as noneidetic?

For answer to these questions, Lacoue-Labarthe looks to the "apophantic" notion of mimesis found in Longinus, with its apparently divergent possibilities. Here, "apophantic," a term Lacoue-Labarthe borrows from Emile Martineau, refers to mimesis in its capacity properly to reveal *phusis*.[68] Under one aspect, which Lacoue-Labarthe labels "restricted *technē*," *technē* is invoked to correct the excesses of sublime art. For example, it may be used to make a statue show better resemblance to the *human*. In this sense, *technē*—and, by extension, mimesis—is imitatively, and also eidetically, oriented.

Under a more fundamental aspect, however, mimesis is called upon to approach the workings of nature, understood this time as the *superhuman*. Lacoue-Labarthe follows Longinus as he invokes specifically the context of oratory, where the figure of *hyperbaton* "dissociates words or thoughts from their customary sequence" and thus "constitutes . . . the most true character of a violent passion."[69]

The elements of Lacoue-Labarthe's description here can be translated into those I have already linked to hyperbological loss and gain. *Phusis* is a subject gained for view as, and through, *technē*. As "itself," however, *phusis* is not visible and as such is "lost." One might say: art always declares itself *as* art, rather than nature, even when it is exhibiting nature more essentially than nature herself could. Correspondingly, it might seem that the subject is here gained *as technē*. In this case, *technē*, as the very "method" that produces *phusis*, would be what finally "is."

However, at issue here is, equally, the effacement of *technē*. Following Longinus further, Lacoue-Labarthe finds him Heideggerian in this respect:

In deciphering *phusis*, in other words, *technē* ciphers itself: as Longinus indicates in a word, it is the very play of *aletheia*; and this is why, moreover, the sublime *logos* is for Longinus the true *logos*, that is, the unveiling.[70]

The exposition has thus brought Lacoue-Labarthe to the hyperbological mechanism properly so-called, and at this point he invokes the term explicitly. Here, *technē* is the (disappearing) subject of hyperbological movement, visible in a proper, if specific, mode: "The more *technē* accomplishes itself, the more it effaces itself."[71]

In the terms Longinus uses, this means that the produced effect (*phusis*) *shines* the more brightly, the more the rhetorical figure producing the effect is concealed; in fact, it is precisely the light cast by the figure—the effects of emotion and sublimity—that hides the figure as such:

> Just as a faint gleam is almost made to disappear when the sun radiates all around it, so rhetorical devices grow faint when greatness is poured over them from all sides.[72]

As an experience, this "radiation" or "outpouring of light," hiding form and figure, is, of course, quintessentially the sublime. At this point, what has been gained by the incursion into Longinus is the following: in the sublime there is revealed the essence of *technē*, and this essence is revealed as noneidetic.

Now that all the elements of Lacoue-Labarthe's investigation have been elicited, I can extend his outline of a hyperbological "mechanism" that delivers *technē* from assimilation to the eidetic, to yield the fuller description of the hyperbological that I have been steadily building. The subject of *technē* is lost between *phusis* and *technē*: that is, between a representation of *technē* as, on the one hand, lost *phusis* and, on the other, gained *phusis*. At its extreme, each of these representations passes into the other. The more *phusis* "itself" fails to appear, through the failure of the representing figure to efface itself, the greater does the clearly appearing form of the figure confirm *phusis* as an invisible "reality" of which it itself is mere imitation. Equally, the more *phusis* is "gained," through the *success* of the figure in effacing itself, the more there is nothing—no subject—*that* is gained. Or, one might say, *phusis* is thereby gained only as *nothing which is*, and it is in this sense lost. The first of the above representations obviously corresponds to art possessed of an eidetic essence, while the second corresponds to art understood in terms of a noneidetic essence.

I have already pointed out, however, that the picture is not so simple. In the end, if the subject is not to make good its return, the hyperbological mechanism that delivers loss of the subject must offer an endless interchange of eidetic for noneidetic, and vice versa. The fact that Lacoue-Labarthe refers to hyperbology in the context of, as it were, "establishing" a noneidetic essence for art must not be allowed to mislead. Hyperbology provides the mark of a noneidetic essence of the beautiful, but it can do so only because hyperbological loss occurs *between* the essences. It is also for this reason that the term "noneidetic essence" is not self-contradictory: essence here escapes determination as an idea, precisely because it is *two* ideas at the same time, oscillatingly and interchangeably.

Thus the hyperbological dissolves the identity between *phusis* and the figure. The content of the foregoing demonstration also becomes available to extend my previous description of the hallmarks of hyperbological subjectal loss. I return once more to Lacoue-Labarthe. He takes his insights into Longinus toward a reflection on the effacement of the subject within the sublime.

Hyperbological Subjectal Loss Confirmed in the Incessant Interchange between Technē *and* Phusis

Corresponding to the fact that the essence of the figure lies in its own nonfiguration is the fact that *that which* it "is," *as* art, is no longer *essentially* a figure. Nature has thus, one might say, employed art dazzlingly to reveal the following as its (nature's) truth: *that* there is, without a *what*. Lacoue-Labarthe says:

> And this is of course why great art cannot be seen—the light it throws casts it into shadow. It makes essentially no "form," figure," or "schema" come into presence. It presents, while impresenting itself, that there is the being-present [*de l'étant-prés-ent*]. And it is a bedazzlement.[73]

To explain Lacoue-Labarthe on Longinus here: what "occurs" or "becomes present" in the experience of sublime art *as* art—in, say, the painting of the Last Supper or a great speech—is not the idea, or the representation of an idea (say, the "meaning" of the Last Supper, or "the virtue of courage," and so on). Rather, what becomes present is the sublime itself: nature manifest *as* noneidetic, in inverse proportion to the brightness of the figures that accompany this shining.

The sublime, then, is *ekphanestaton* in a double sense. As a showing "out-of-itself," it is a "self-showing." But it is also a showing that indicates that what is being shown (as *eidos*, figure) is not all that is there to be seen, and that what is "really" being indicated, but without being shown, is the *ek-phanestaton* (this time, the "beyond showing").[74]

Phenomenologically speaking, subjectal loss is mediated here through the conjunction of opposing representations, of subjectal loss and subjectal gain, occurring in endless mutual exchange. The declaration of Isis captures this, in its incessant implicating of truth with untruth, and vice versa. So too does the concatenated quotation from Walter Benjamin with which Lacoue-Labarthe concludes "Sublime Truth." The quoted sentences play around twin points: that beauty is inseparable from appearance, and that, equally, beauty is not appearance. The key sentences read:

> Beauty is not an appearance [*Schein*], a veil covering something other than itself. Beauty itself is not appearance [*Erscheinung*], but essence, an essence that remains the same as itself only when veiled.[75]

"An essence that remains the same only when veiled." The characteristic form of the hyperbological, in evidence here, might be read once more in Kantian terms, thus: *technē* must disappear as *phusis* appears, and vice versa. If for *technē* (mimesis) we read "representation," and for *phusis* (Being, nature), "the subject," hyperbology here yields the following: representation disappears as the subject appears. And, conversely, the subject disappears as representation appears.

Does this mean that, in Lacoue-Labarthe's thinking, the subject *can* appear? No, because hyperbological oscillation or hesitation dictates that neither of its poles can exist undisturbed by the movement that is *simultaneously* exchanging it for its other: subject for representation, representation for subject. That the explanation of hyperbology is facilitated by its explanation in terms of sequentiality must not remove from the inherent *synchronicity* of the elements of exchange that comprise it. This synchronicity is nowhere better evidenced than in the ongoing interchange between *phusis* and *technē*, and veiling and unveiling, that Lacoue-Labarthe has just explored.

In this light, I can now elaborate upon my earlier remark that a "simple" exchange between *phusis* and *technē* does not effect hyperbological loss. The point here that "loss" (or effacement) of *phusis* (as the subject) is, under an eidetic interpretation, not "truly" loss, since phusis (read, the subject) survives (or the subject returns) as that which has been lost. It is for this reason that hyperbological exchange must be seen to involve exchange between two simultaneously present subjects (or, as I have hitherto put it, *too many forms*): for example, *technē* present together with the *phusis* it has just effaced, but which nevertheless survives, so that the subject hesitates between alternative descriptions, and so on. In this light, it can also be seen that "oscillation" and "hesitation," the two terms that have carried my explanation of the hyperbological, remain complementary rather than competing or inconsistent descriptive notions. The hyperbologically lost subject is lost precisely through a hesitation between alternative subjectal identities that hyperbological oscillation creates.

In the end, it is this full hyperbological effect that differentiates Lacoue-Labarthe's Longinus from one plausible interpretation of Longinus' text: that a perfectly self-effacing *technē* can reveal "original" Being. Instead, the movement of effacement must be seen to point toward Being as *ekphanestaton*, understood in the sense of "beyond revelation." Given some nuances, this latter interpretation correlates with Lacoue-Labarthe's account of mimesis as providing a subject as loss, or, one might say, "the subject in its loss."

The foregoing analysis is now ripe to contribute to the main purpose of this chapter: the use of Jean-Luc Nancy to highlight, through comparison and contrast, the Lacoue-Labarthian hyperbological. As I have already suggested, the account of the hyberbological sublime in "Sublime Truth" is thrown into greater relief by Nancy's "The Sublime Offering," but the comparison will also allow me to locate a particular strain of implicit hyperbology that might be said to be Nancy's own.

Jean-Luc Nancy: "The Sublime Offering"

Nancy's Argument in Outline

Before letting the two essays engage one another, I shall briefly outline the argument of "The Sublime Offering." Nancy proposes the following. The sublime is a "derangement" of art, by which art is offered to "another destiny." Art thus becomes itself by becoming other than itself, but not sublatively. In so doing, it escapes an alternative fate, that of being assimilated to that *other* "other" by which it is lost to itself: philosophy. Through philosophy, art is sublated but is sublated *as* its other, philosophy. In Kant, the sublime, defined in terms of the "pure" giving of form, misfigures beauty, assimilating it to the service of reason. Beauty thus comes into itself by coming into form.[76] But, being thus appreciated as itself, it is also paradoxically lost to appreciation as its *essential* self, that is, as its other, the sublime. In short, art (the beautiful) is destined to *lability*—to becoming itself by becoming other than itself. More specifically, it is destined to transformation into *two* others, philosophy and the sublime, the latter being its true destination.

Nancy implies that what is essential to bring art into itself, and what the sublime supplies, is the very dimension of "transportation." The sublime is both destination and transportation toward destination. It takes art, not toward the *infinite*, but toward the *unlimited*. The former is in principle assimilable to form but prevented by its sheer magnitude from being encompassed *as* form and is thus "beyond the limit." By contrast, the latter is lacking a line or border that could genuinely serve to demarcate that which is form (or susceptible to presentation) from that which is not. Through the sublime, presentation, as it were, "drags" what is formally beyond presentation to a position "this side" of the presentational limit, in which case that limit ceases to function as such. In what has undertones of a phenomenological exploration, Nancy identifies the sublime with presentation *as* movement—the movement whereby presentation is "approached from the side of" or "presents itself as" removal of a prior unlimited.

Thus transported by and as the sublime, presentation is in contact with "union" beyond the limit of apprehensible or comprehensible experience. It thus "unborders" this limit while not providing a contact with any "something" beyond the limit (so its movement is not dialectical). Equally, any "sense" of this sublime must be associated with a touching of the limit on its "near" side, there being now "nothing" on the other.

In the context of subjectivity, this unbordering also renders the feeling of the sublime as an unbordering of the self. This self in one sense corresponds to acts of presentation of form to reason. Within these presentations, it cannot feel itself, except indirectly and reflexively, in association with the feeling of beauty occasioned by such judgments. However, the sublime presents the nonpresentable as such, as the movement of form toward the formless. In so doing, it occasions the "presentation" to the self of a subject that is not the (feeling) self and is itself nonpresentable.

As Nancy reads Kant, the attendant feeling occurs *in* the self, as it were, but is not feeling *by* the self or *of* the self. It occurs, he implies, in a "self" that is "other" to itself. This other self occurs (or slips away?) "between" the dimensions of the self as "thing" (delivered by presentation), on the one hand, and subject (delivered by representation), on the other. The sublime is the "mutual offering" of form to formlessness, and vice versa. In this sense, it precludes representation from delivering the subject. For Nancy, this is also what is implied when Kant associates the sublime with the prohibition of representation. The prohibition expresses the dimension of (human) freedom from the demands of representation.

The skeleton of this argument, and its flesh as well, provide the several points of comparison and contrast with Lacoue-Labarthe that I have already anticipated. I now focus on the more important of these, taking them toward a reflection that situates Nancy in relation to Lacoue-Labarthian hyperbology, and then in relation to the question of a presentational subjectivity.

The Argument Retraced: The Sublime as Movement

Like Lacoue-Labarthe, Nancy is interested in the sublime as it bids to displace the subject of (re)presentation by producing the "other" of this subject. In fact, the heart of his reading here is the identification of the sublime itself with displacement, or *movement*, under various descriptions. The sublime, precisely in its status as a current "fashion," *offers* itself as a *derangement* of art. This derangement is, in fact, "positive" in effect, since thereby art itself, which "deranges our history," is redirected as offering:

> In the sublime, art itself is deranged, offered to yet another destiny; it has its own destiny in a sense outside of itself.[77]

The alternative is a displacement in the opposite direction: the offering of art toward *philosophy*. Here, a Kantian reduction of art to philosophy occurs in the name of the truth of art. Thereby "art . . . shudders, as Adorno says, . . . giving itself as its task something other than art."[78] There is sublation here, but not sublation of *art*. Thinking the sublime *as* philosophy, *as* the *end* of art, does not accomplish a Hegelian sublation. Therein art would realize itself by means of an assimilation to an opposite that accomplished its own conservation. Instead, in thinking the *end* of art, rather than its *destination*, Hegel consigns himself, in fact, to thinking the sublime as the sublation of *philosophy* rather than of art.

There are obvious touchpoints here with Lacoue-Labarthe's exploration of the effacement, by *technē*, of the figure (which it itself "employs"), in the interests of letting *phusis* shine. Like Lacoue-Labarthe, Nancy is concerned to highlight the reduction of beauty to form involved in the opposite course, which formally proceeds by prioritizing the sublime over the beautiful. He elicits the inevitability of this course, linked as it is to the "birth of form" that the imagination provides. However, such an "aesthetic schematism" supplies a logic that can function only by failing to distinguish the sublime as such.[79] For beauty itself is here temptingly (mis)figured as the full explanation of the schematism, becoming the figuring that anticipates figuration. Its essence is now a "presentational anticipation" that is no less than what Nancy calls "the hidden secret character of the schematism."[80] As such, however, it is the hidden essence of a technique that serves reason. Equally, the disinterested pleasure linked to the beautiful is attributed to the conformity with reason that form itself exhibits.

We have here, then, as with Lacoue-Labarthe, the sublime as providing a representation of the subject (of art) which is an "opposite" of that provided by philosophy. The net result is a subjectal "hesitation," between representations, which displays some key elements of hyperbological loss. I shall develop this point further below. Bracketing it for the present, I pursue the *mode* of Nancy's reading. I first recall some of my earlier observations in this area.[81]

Nancy often takes his reader in the direction of a "birth" of meaning as "happening sense." "Sense," here, conveys its full range of meanings, from "meaning" itself to the various connotations of "touch." But if sense is "what occurs," Nancy's interest in the loss or reversal of classical subjectivity seems at least embryonically in service of the possibility of a new subjectivity, associated with this occurrence. The question here is whether his affirming the occurrence of sense might not itself correspond, on some level, to an affirmation of the subject. Or, if the simultaneous indications of *loss* of the subject are to be taken seriously, perhaps "happening sense" nevertheless corresponds to a *structure* of subjectivity, which can persist through subjectal loss.

At any rate, there is here a point of contrast with Lacoue-Labarthe. Appropriately enough, given the above, Nancy investigates the sublime through its own sense: the mark, somewhere between sensation and meaning, that it makes on the psyche. Lacoue-Labarthe, in pursuing the mark of writing, or signification, seems to settle upon more developed representations. True, he emphasizes the exchange between these, and the effacement of one by the other: the nearer by the farther, and so forth. But it is, as it were, the *result* of this effacement—the transformation of *phusis* into itself through *technē*, and vice versa—that he dwells upon. Nancy, by contrast, appears determined to dwell upon "shift" itself. Its results or subjects, while mentioned, remain incidental. He pursues the sublime *sensed* as movement, the shifting of form toward the formless, and of the formless toward form.

Thus, for him, the effect is the sensed movement itself. Sensation itself remains a component of the various dimensions of this sensed movement, all of which fall short of delivering a "meaning of the sublime." The twin displacements of art—toward philosophy and/or the sublime—are characterized as the destination of Art (the beautiful) to *lability*—to becoming itself by becoming other than itself. Only one of these movements additionally brings art *into* itself, that is, into beauty rather than agreeability:

If a transport of the beautiful into the sublime is indeed the counterpart or reversal of its sliding into the agreeable . . . then . . . the beautiful becomes the beautiful only beyond itself, or else it slides into the space this side of itself.[82]

Sensed movement is again at the heart of the "unbordering" of form in the sublime, through the union of form with the formless. Again, this unbordering toward the formless is the way in which art regains itself by losing its definition. It is evident here that presentation takes its place on *both* sides of the limit that is form so that presentation becomes unlimited, and the limit becomes unbordered. More precisely, however, this manifestation is one of *movement*—the movement of traversal across the limit:

The beautiful and the sublime *are* presentation but in such a manner that the beautiful is the presented *in its presentation,* whereas the sublime is the presentation *in its movement*—which is the absolute re-moval of the unlimited along the edge of any limit.[83]

Here again, the "absolute re-moval" (*l'enlèvement absolu*) of the unlimited effects its absorption into a union with what is limited, so that there is now nothing outside the limit.[84]

The most direct elaboration of the Kantian sublime in this sensory mode occurs when Nancy turns toward the question of subjectivity itself. The gist of this elaboration, which I shall develop in detail in a moment, is as follows. Hitherto, the reading has elicited the following suggestion. The feeling of the sublime no longer corresponds to the painful-pleasurable recognition by the intellect of the thwarted telos of its faculty of presentation, that is, the telos of presenting all sensory material to reason, *as* form. Described thus, the feeling of the sublime became identified with a type of negative presentation of the faculty of presentation, equivalent to a negative presentation of subject to itself. Instead, now having been exposed as properly including the nonpresentable within its "subject matter," the faculty of presentation becomes, as it were, nonpresentable to itself.

The subject is thus no longer the proper, or unambiguous, referent for sublime feeling. How, then, might its association with that feeling be characterized? Nancy eventually makes a point that my attention to hyperbology has already rendered familiar: that the "loss of the subject" manifest in the sublime has to do with an *essential* nonpresentability of the subject. This nonpresentability has finally little to do with the subject's nonappearance. It seems, however, to have everything to do with the inherent *movement* within which the subject is presented.

I now read the final portion of "The Sublime Offering," with a view to giving the above points more detailed attention.

The Nancian Hyperbological Sublime: Movement as (Self-)Offering

The offering that takes art toward the unlimited, and thus toward itself as other, is identified as subjectal loss in a particular way: as the sublime *feeling* that is no longer a self-feeling. The sentiment accompanying the Kantian sublime, with its admixture of pain and pleasure, no longer marks the presence of a "feeling" subject:

> If feeling properly so-called is always subjective, if it is indeed the core of subjectivity in a primordial "feeling oneself" . . . then the feeling of the sublime activates itself [*s'enlève*] — or affects itself — precisely as the reversal of both feeling and subjectivity.[85]

Nancy is speaking here of that Kantian unrequited striving for presentation, which succeeds in presenting nothing but the purposiveness of presentation itself. In Lacoue-Labarthe and Nancy's *The*

Literary Absolute, this sublime feeling corresponded to the "reflected" but "conceptually open" Kantian subject by which the third *Critique* implicitly resolves the tension between the subjects of the previous two *Critiques*.[86] Here, Nancy emphasizes that it is not a feeling *of* the subject:

> This feeling is not a feeling-oneself, and in this sense, it is not a feeling at all. One could say that it is what remains of feeling at the limit, when feeling no longer feels itself, or when there is no longer anything to feel.[87]

Feeling, that property most intimate to the subject, here becomes housed outside the self. It becomes a feeling "through or by the other."[88] What Nancy seems to be referring to here is the feeling of the sublime as a feeling *of* oneself from "outside the border" of the self marked by the (broken) limit of the capacity for presentation. This matches the experiencing of any aesthetic object from "inside the border." Everything felt by a self "reflected" to itself as by-product of an event of formal presentation becomes a feeling *by*, or *inside*, the self but of, or *about*, something "outside" the self.

The above includes feeling *of* the self as such. This also, insofar as it is presentation, is a sensation of an external object. But what can one make of a "feeling" experienced in the absence of an event of formal presentation? One such feeling is that attached to a presentation of the nonpresentable, in the indeterminate manner in which the sublime provides this experience. Might not this feeling, uniquely "lodged" at a vantage point *outside* the self, be directly associable with presentation itself (presentation as faculty, presentation of the presentable and the nonpresentable alike)? It might thereby be an experience by the subject of "itself," but from outside the self. Here, it is still the self—that is, the self associated with formal presentation and attendant self-alienation—that is "doing the feeling." But it is doing so this time from "outside itself" (from the zone, one might say, of the "real nonpresentable"). Nancy puts it thus:

> Can one feel through the other, through the outside, even though feeling seems to depend on the self as its means and even though precisely this dependence conditions aesthetic judgement? This is what the feeling of the sublime forces us to think.[89]

His suggestion is that the self feels itself most closely under these conditions. Thus it is the intimacy of the "to feel" and the "to feel oneself" that produces itself here, paradoxically, as exposure to what is beyond the self [*exposition hors de soi*], passage to the (in)sensible or (un)feeling limit of the self.[90]

Thus sense, as movement, and more particularly as the sensed movement that is feeling, is the determinant of "self" here. But Nancy is not here assimilating subjectivity to the psychological "self," or to sublated extensions of this self. He is not implying that, in the experience of the sublime, "I" find "myself," from outside myself. If the "self" here is a subject, it is so as something other than, and *in between*, the self as subject or object. Akin to the "lost" subject in Lacoue-Labarthe, it is something that flees or escapes subjectivity and objectivity alike.

Hyperbological Subjectal Loss: The Offering of Form to the Formless

It is possible now to see how the hyperbological within this Nancian sublime mediates subjectal loss, in a manner entirely compatible with the Lacoue-Labarthian hyperbological yet also unique. As the locus of the capacity of the self of experience to feel itself through its outside, the Nancian sublime is an *offering* that "comes to pass" at the limit. It does not therefore confirm the subject, either as subject of representation or object of presentation. Nancy is here doing nothing less than pointing to a continued "hollowness" or loss of the Kantian subject, even as an infinitized reflected subject of the judgment of taste. The locus of offering is neither presentation nor representation:

> The offering takes place between presentation and representation, between the thing and the subject, elsewhere.[91]

Nevertheless, the offering *does* "take place." I have suggested that this correlates to the "gain" of a subject of sense, as counterpart of the lost subject of writing or signification. At the conclusion of this chapter, I will reflect generally on this "gained subjectivity." Its final dimensions in Nancy are complex, communal, and beyond the scope of this study. But its connotations, even as found in the text in question here, might in the end be what is most significant about hyperbological loss.

These connotations become apparent if the Nancian subjectal loss is probed for its connection to the Lacoue-Labarthian hyperbological. Two motifs relating to loss of the Nancian subject—its movement and its perpetual "in-betweenness"—culminate in Nancy's theme of the sublime as *offering*. Here, "offering" is not meant to suggest the presence of a single subject as "offerer." The offering itself is what remains in focus, as a movement that is "two way," slipping between one and the other of the two classical subjects, form and the formless:

> The aesthetic always concerns form; the totality always concerns the formless. The sublime is their mutual offering.

Mutual offering is not allowed to come to "rest" at either form or formlessness. It does not orient itself to either but to a dissolution of the limit as border. Nancy continues:

> It is neither simply the formation or formalization of the formless nor the infinitization of form (which are both philosophical procedures). It is how the limit offers itself to the border of the unlimited, or how the limit makes itself felt: exactly on the cutting edge of the figure the work of art cuts.[92]

In this "mutual offering," between the aesthetic as form and the totality as formless, it is not difficult to see the very pattern of representational exchange that marks the Lacoue-Labarthian hyperbological. Admittedly, Nancy here uses other terms for what Lacoue-Labarthe has explicitly identified as the hyperbological exchange between *phusis* (as the totalizing formless) and *technē* (as limiting figure).

A simplifying observation of the equivalence between the authors might run as follows. In Nancy, the sublime, as offering, marks the gesture by which art as a *presentation of form* becomes instead a presentation of formlessness, that is, of the formlessness that presentation brings into the "region" of form. This removes the conceptual barrier sharply distinguishing "formal" from "formless" presentation. It renders artistic presentation—presentation at its limit—as a way of representing form as the essentially formless. Formlessness itself is now no longer a "frustrated striving for form." Then the subject, as "presentation itself," becomes perfectly suspended between the two overarching representations of presentation, exhibiting a version of the hyperbological that Lacoue-Labarthe finds, in other variants, in other places.

An observation such as the above would, I think, be substantially accurate. It draws together the various elements of the Lacoue-Labarthian hyperbology that this chapter has sought to locate in

Nancy. But it requires for completeness a revisitation of two aspects that formally render the hyperbological in Nancy somewhat different from its Lacoue-Labarthian counterpart. I have already signaled the direction in which these aspects might take the Nancian hyperbological, namely, that of a "structural subjectivity," albeit revisioned. In this regard, they complement Lacoue-Labarthian hyperbological subjectal loss, confirming its inner but unspoken possibilities. I now conclude this chapter by developing that thought.

Conclusion: The Nancian Sensate Hyperbological: Subjectivity Restored as Movement?

The aspects are linked, and they are jointly evoked by this impression: if, in Lacoue-Labarthe, it is the exchange of representations that marks the hyperbological, in Nancy it is the *sensed movement* of this exchange that remains in focus. Both elements of this term are important, and they respectively generate the aspects I wish to highlight. I treat them in reverse order, since the second takes us usefully toward the final chapter.

First, hyperbology in Nancy *is* movement—the movement that shifts every artistic form toward the formless and simultaneously shifts the formless which borders that form back toward form itself. So pronounced is this emphasis on movement that Nancy devotes virtually all of "The Sublime Offering" to an observation of this movement itself rather than to the representations of form or formlessness that it "unites." Not only is the sublime explicitly movement—"the beautiful is the presented *in its presentation*, whereas the sublime is the presentation *in its movement*"—but the reading obtains its impetus from notions almost invariably synonymous with movement, or carrying its connotations: lability, derangement, destiny, offering.

As I have pointed out, this movement to some extent implicates *itself* as a subject—the subject that "takes place" in the experience of art as the sublime, or of presentation as such. If it finally avoids this implication it is only because Nancy presents it as a movement *between* subjects. The subjects in question are the familiar alternatives offered by classical philosophy: form and the unified formless. In any case, Nancy provides an emphasis on the *process* that is hyperbology, and, in this, usefully complements Lacoue-Labarthe's emphases on its *effects*.

Not that there is any lack in Lacoue-Labarthe of descriptors that indicate hyperbology as process: exchange, hesitation, oscillation, and so forth. But these lead his reader toward the *representations* that form the poles of the indicated movement. Nancy, by contrast, recalls the reader from those poles and toward the "no-man's land" that is the proper territory of the hyperbological. He does so by remaining with the hyperbological movement itself, steadfastly traversing the sublime as an "unbordering" along the "edge" of presentation.

Second, this hyperbological movement is *sensed*. I have already noted that when, as here, an experience of "movement" is treated meditatively, as in itself an object of meaning (in isolation from the destination of movement), the meaning of this movement becomes "meaning as sensation." Or, at least, it resides in the sensate, or apprehensive, component of comprehension rather than in the conceptual. As we have seen, Nancy's tracking of the Kantian sublime along these lines takes him inevitably to the *feeling* of the sublime, as marking the experience of the unbordering of the self that the sublime entails. Again, this yields a perspective on hyperbological movement that is underemphasized in Lacoue-Labarthe's own explorations. Those instead focus on the conceptually verifiable destinations, or results, of the movement: the disappearance of the figure in the refulgence of *phusis*, and vice versa.

In sum, then, the Nancian hyperbological distinguishes itself from the Lacoue-Labarthian hyperbological, both by emphasizing the movement that comprises the sublime experience and by underlining a further, sensate, dimension of the "movement." One might say that where Lacoue-Labarthe allows us to *think* the subjectal loss that is hyperbology, Nancy encourages us to *sense* it. He encourages us to *feel* it, as an experience of that "presence of absence," as it were, by which a viewed work of art is present only by virtue of having removed itself to a place and a meaning outside the confines of its form.

Whether this sensate hyperbological, as I have sought it in "The Sublime Offering," promotes *sens* as a subject is a question too large to be included in my considerations here. If *sens* is a type of subject, as *The Gravity of Thought* invites us to think, it might properly be located in a communally shared "sense," short of meaning, that survives the exhaustion of signification. Minimally, what has been demonstrated here opens up the possibility of a subjectivity constituted in sensed, incessant, hyperbological movement. Such a subjectivity would survive as the "structural" counterpart of the subjectal loss which that movement promotes.

Lacoue-Labarthe between Derrida and Blanchot
Movement as Marking the Subject-in-Loss

Introduction: My Purpose and Plan in Engaging
Lacoue-Labarthe with Derrida and Blanchot

My exploration has now brought me to one of the most interesting and fruitful, if also somewhat vexed, issues to present itself to recent continental philosophy—the possibility of describing a new, nonclassical subjectivity cognizant of the insights of deconstruction. I began the present work with the hope of showing that a single motif—hyperbology—might be capable of organizing, without reducing, the unique, largely untapped, complex and yet rigorous contribution that Lacoue-Labarthe has made to continental philosophy, and particularly to the question of the loss of the subject, in these past thirty years. That demonstration is now practically complete. But it has left itself on the brink of a large issue, concerning a new subject that hyperbology itself might constitute. In closing this work, addressing that issue allows me finally to contextualize Lacoue-Labarthe among his closest contemporaries (after Nancy)—Jacques Derrida and Maurice Blanchot.

The question in point arises simply, if polemically, from my preceding exposition, as this: Might not hyperbology, as a "mechanism," offer *itself* as a subject, or at least a "structure of subjectivity"? And how would this subject resist being cast in classical terms, as a grounding or founding truth of experience?[1] In the previous chapter,

I mentioned that Jean-Luc Nancy's "hyperbological," as the sensed movement that attends subjectal loss, might point the way to a "structure of subjectivity," one to which Lacoue-Labarthian analyses might not be inimical.[2] Now I build upon, rather than retrace, the steps traversed earlier. I do this by bringing Lacoue-Labarthe into dialogue with Derrida and Blanchot.

I find it helpful to engage these authors with Lacoue-Labarthe in different ways. In Derrida's case, I take up at greater length his previously mentioned dialogue with Lacoue-Labarthe in the extended essay "Introduction: Desistance," which introduces *Typography*.[3] I notice the places where the assimilation of Lacoue-Labarthe to Derrida is formally resisted, occurs nevertheless, and is finally seen to be resisted again. Lacoue-Labarthe's mode of operation exhibits an all but imperceptible hesitation before the farthest reaches of Derrida's subversion of subjectivity. It remains open to elaborating the (non)-experience of the subject, which is also the experience of its loss, as a new account of subjectivity. Correspondingly, in the case of Blanchot, I seek out texts and contexts in which this possibility might be seen to echo, and to become "positively" inscribed.[4]

Derrida and Blanchot have been chosen here because Lacoue-Labarthe has specifically mentioned their thought as a significant part of the motivation for his literary-philosophical efforts. It is relevant here to quote him at length:

> And when you say that I speak of subjectivity as something which, so to speak, always seeks to secure itself but never succeeds in that — that is a formulation to which I can subscribe, in effect, and that refers for me to a principal experience, which is the experience of literature. I thought — I think today, upon reflection — that, when one writes, something is produced that breaches, attacks, threatens always to destroy the subject who writes — that the experience of literature is the experience of a sort of dispossession of self. And I have always tried to speak of this experience, in echo of some preoccupations that I have encountered in others. And, in particular — I don't hide this from myself — it's without a doubt the reading of Blanchot that has been decisive for me. And then, of course, the reading of Derrida — and the encounter with Jacques Derrida, and the work that, in short, around the time of the seventies, we were able to do together.[5]

A context, if not entirely a genealogy, is evident here: historical encounters with the thought of Derrida and Blanchot, leading Lacoue-

Labarthe to "echo" their preoccupations in his own. Indeed, the interests of both Derrida and Blanchot continue to resonate within Lacoue-Labarthe's account of the interplay between writing and subjectivity. My aim in exploring this resonance is to render audible what in Lacoue-Labarthe is only hinted at or even left unsaid. This concerns his tacit gesture toward what I have been calling a revisioned "structural subjectivity."

Like Lacoue-Labarthe, Derrida reads seminal philosophical and literary texts in order to trace *loss* of the subject and the absence of the self. He does not formally pursue the gain of any "other" self, or the inscription of any "alternative subjectivity," in any traditional sense of these last two terms.[6] Blanchot, while crediting this loss, often begins where Derrida leaves off, exploring the nature of a clandestine self of experience.

In relating Lacoue-Labarthe to Derrida first, and to Maurice Blanchot only later, I have two thoughts in mind. First, I hope to emphasize the empathy that Derrida's oeuvre shares with Lacoue-Labarthe's account of hyperbological subjectal loss. As is particularly apparent in "Introduction: Desistance," Derrida implicitly sees the Lacoue-Labarthian hyperbological as extending his own notion of the dead or absent self of writing. Second, consideration of Derrida prepares the ground for relating Lacoue-Labarthe to Blanchot. Derrida's analysis recalls a thought of subjectivity that links Lacoue-Labarthe with Blanchot. This occurs when Derrida links the notions of *désistance* and the hyperbological. The *désistance* by which the subject is delayed from any "coming into itself" is *relentless*; perhaps, then, the possibility of a subjectivity found in (or as) the very inevitability ("ineluctablity") of this movement of delay. "Subjectivity," in these terms, is marked as what Lacoue-Labarthe would call the "necessary representation" of a subject: *as* displaced away from "itself," or to a position beside "itself." I will raise this possibility in discussing Lacoue-Labarthe's links to Derrida, and I will confirm it, with appropriate caveats, in addressing his continuity with Blanchot.

**Jacques Derrida on Lacoue-Labarthian *Désistance*:
Intimations of an Incipient Subjectivity?**

How does Derrida's general approach to deconstructive loss of the subject stand in relation to the Lacoue-Labarthian description of hyperbological subjectal loss? Derrida's considered comment on *Typography* ought to give some clue to this. As I have pointed out, in his introduction to that book, Derrida gathers Lacoue-Labarthe's diverse explorations of the subjectal, using the rubric of *désistance*. I have already explored in some detail his explication of this term, which refers to the ineluctable earliness or lateness of the subject in relation to itself.[7] In the same place, I also indicated that while Lacoue-Labarthe does not himself use the term *désistance*, he has subsequently indicated his broad acceptance of it as an accurate characterization of the subjectal loss that his analyses typically demonstrate.

Having developed the notion of the Lacoue-Labarthian hyperbological, I am finally ready to address a key question: How, if at all, does the Derridean notion of *désistance* connect (or even assimilate) Lacoue-Labarthe to Derrida? That is, to what extent does *désistance*, used in relation to Lacoue-Labarthe's readings, confer on those analyses the superstructure of Derridean deconstruction? One can hardly miss the echoes of *différance* to be found in both the word *désistance* and its concept. And I have shown in Chapter 3 that for Derrida, *désistance* marks a middle voice between active and passive withdrawal of the subject. Plausibly, this "middleness" marks a putatively deconstructive *undecidability* of subjectal loss.[8]

Derrida is also seen to bridge deconstruction and hyperbology in another, rather intriguing, manner. In his essay, *désistance* is linked to *désistement* as depropriation (loss by the subject of its "propriety," or identity), but then Derrida points out that, in *Typography, désistement* as depropriation is invariably broached in terms of the hyperbological. It follows that Derrida sees *désistant* subjectal loss as hyperbologically mediated.

Yet the single extended comment with which Derrida draws this entire connection is nothing if not puzzling in the manner of its making. For one thing, he offers the comment at the very end of "Introduction: Desistance." Does this mean that it is meant to culminate the essay? Probably not, since the lateness of its appearance reduces its force, making it seem like an afterthought. This impression is reinforced by its form: that of a footnote. To boot, this is the *first* expository reference to hyperbology to be found in the essay: some three paragraphs from its end. By that stage, there is no time to treat it in the text; Derrida—having, as he says, to "cut things short, too late or too early"—has room for a single observation on "The Caesura of the Speculative," and, for the rest, must rely on the note itself.[9]

In Chapter 5, I have already mentioned the salient points of this note. Derrida's hypothesizes a connection between the *de-* of Derridean *désistance* and the nondialectical depropriation implied in various expressions of Lacoue-Labarthian hyperbology. I merely note the attempt at the connection, and the modesty of its manner. His enthusiasm for the notion of hyperbology seems muted. One has the impression that this tardy and almost apologetic manner is designed to forestall a particular conclusion: that Lacoue-Labarthe's depropriational *modus operandi* is a version of Derridean deconstruction.

An observation I made earlier might well throw light on Derrida's approach here, or even on the speculative explanation just offered for it. In "Introduction: Desistance," Derrida affirms his intention to acknowledge his links to Lacoue-Labarthe and Nancy but also reiterates that their work is "absolutely different" from his own. His pre-emptively stated aim is "to break with the family atmosphere, to avoid genealogical temptations, projections, assimilations, or identifications."[10] This is perhaps why Derrida has given the note on hyperbology its specific position and tenor in the text. But the "break" is not so easily achieved. The note notionally encourages the reader to range back over the text, with the following question in mind: To what extent is Derrida's stated intention belied by his very employment of the term *désistance,* and of the deconstructive presumptions underlying it, to read Lacoue-Labarthe? Answering this question becomes a matter of delicate judgment.

Happily, the note in question is not the "final" — in the sense of conclusive — place in "Introduction: Desistance" where scope for this judgment is offered. In several other ways, the essay bids, innocently or otherwise, to make the point that *désistement* of the subject, especially when it goes by way of hyperbologic, involves its deconstruction, and that this is because hyperbologic is assimilable to *désistance,* which is itself deconstructive in its mechanism.

Thus, tracking Lacoue-Labarthe's exploration of the *Ge-stell,* Derrida comments:

> [Lacoue-Labarthe] does not propose to restore, rehabilitate, or reinstall "the subject"; rather, he proposes to think its *désistance* by taking into account *both* a deconstruction of a Heideggerian type *and* that about which he thinks Heidegger maintained a silence.[11]

Two deconstructions are invoked here, the first explicitly Heideggerian. Is the second Derridean? Derrida does not say explicitly. But the course of his text invites the reader to think that the "deconstruction" which Lacoue-Labarthe finds lacking in Heidegger is not finally a deconstruction (in the Derridean sense). I shall come to this presently; first I call attention to, as backdrop, something Derrida omits in another note, immediately preceding this part of the text.

In itself, this note provides good insight into Lacoue-Labarthe's use of the word "(de)constitution," instead of "deconstitution," in a passage from "Obliteration" that I have already considered. Lacoue-Labarthe has said:

> What interests us here . . . is the dissolution, the defeat of the subject in the subject or *as* the subject: the (de)constitution of the subject or the "loss" of the subject—if, at least, it is possible to think the loss [*si du moins l'on pouvait penser la perte*] of what one has never had, a kind of "originary" and "constitutive" loss (of "self").[12]

Derrida focuses on both the "(de)" in "(de)constitution" *and* Lacoue-Labarthe's choice to emphasize the *"as."* In regard to the former, he says:

> The placing in parentheses of the "de" in "(de)constitution" signifies that one must not hear it (any more than in the case of *désistance*) as a negativity affecting an originary and positive constitution.[13]

This is clear enough: Derrida offers the same emphasis on the "(de)" as in the previously mentioned note. But there the emphasis served in part to link hyperbology with Derridean deconstruction; here, notably, there is no mention of hyperbology. The effect is to remove this comment on the "(de)" from the context of hyperbology and/or deconstruction. Is this separation significant? Indeed it seems so, when there follows this comment on the *"as"*:

> The italicizing of the *as* signifies that the "subject," as such, (de)constitutes itself in this movement of *dé*sistance and is *nothing other than* the formation of this movement. For this reason it also signifies that the subject cannot be simply omitted or dissolved, or passed over in silence in the name of a deconstruction of subjectity.[14]

The insight here has to do with the Lacoue-Labarthian subject-in-deconstitution as *movement*. Earlier, I came to the subject-as-movement by another path, involving the hyperbological content of this movement. But Derrida's point reaches farther and more strongly. It omits consideration of hyperbology and speaks specifically of the "de-" component of the movement that is *désistance*. Derrida speaks of Lacoue-Labarthe's subject as the *formation* of this movement.

Now, I think that to speak thus is to offer less than Lacoue-Labarthe's full picture; that picture would have become evident had Derrida recalled, as Lacoue-Labarthe inevitably does, the hyperbological context of the movement concerned. Hyperbology does not constitute a *formation* as such—the "movement" that it comprises, involving an oscillation, paralysis and exchange, requires a different description. So too, then, does any "subjectivity *as* movement" that it might connote.

Derrida's focus on the "formation" of this movement ignores, as it were, its simultaneous "de-formation." Does Lacoue-Labarthe's single phrase "the defeat of the subject *as* the subject" justify this reduction? Perhaps. But, I repeat: both aspects—formation and de-formation—would have remained in sight had Derrida explicitly recalled the notion of the hyperbological here. In that event, there would have accrued to this description the same connection as obtained before (in the other note): of hyperbology as *effectively* deconstructive, in Derridean terms.

What is raised here, if the two notes are considered, and if their mutual nonengagement rectified, is the following possibility: Lacoue-Labarthian subjectal loss is *both* hyperbological *and* deconstructive, and it is so because hyperbology *is* deconstructive. But it is deconstructive in a broadly, rather than narrowly, Derridean sense. That is, it effects the escape of the subject from metaphysical totalization, but by a unique process, finally unrecuperable to the "classic" modes of Derridean deconstruction, though exhibiting some of the aspects of these, such as undecidability, simultaneous transcendental possibility and impossibility, and so on. The key to the hyperbological "process" is the *combination* of doubling and exchange, the necessary representation by which opposites are not only simultaneously present (as undecidability demands) but also *always carried toward each other, in a movement—hence, neither formation nor de-formation—that (de) constitutes a subject.* Instead, Derrida's comment in the note at hand tends to equate the subject-in-deconstitution with its own attendant (metaphysical) reinscription as a "hole," that is, as *that which* has been deconstituted. As I have shown, however, this "automatically" reinscribed subject (equivalent to the automatically reinscribed subject of deconstruction) is only one pole of the hyperbological oscillation by means of which loss of the subject occurs.

"Introduction: Desistance" contains another—this time direct—observation to match the footnoted comment. Again, the context is the subjectal deconstruction about which (in Lacoue-Labarthe's opinion, as recalled by Derrida) Heidegger remained silent. Derrida says that, having removed "the question of the subject" from Heidegger's deconstruction, Lacoue-Labarthe

> leads back into its unicity. . . . He does this with the best justification in the world, . . . but it is not without confirming in passing the fundamental axiom according to which the un-*thought* of a thought is always single, always unique . . . . [And this in turn involves privileging] a "primary *destination* of the un-thought" . . . I won't make a critique out of my uneasiness, but . . . I will continue to wonder whether the very "logic" of *désistance*, as we will continue to follow it, should not lead to some dispersion of this "unique central question," as question of the subject—to its dis-identification, in some sense, its dis-installation.[15]

Again, it is an "effective metaphysicality" of the Lacoue-Labarthian subject that is at stake here. In effect, Derrida is asking: Is not the search for the subject under a *single* rubric, be it "Heidegger's omission" *or* "the defeat of the subject *as* the subject," simply a re-erection of the metaphysical subject, as a subject that *is* missing? Now he immediately broadens the point:

> And I will continue to ask whether the "subject" in question, even if it exceeds the limits of the "metaphysics of subjectity" or onto-typology, does not continue to reflect, or to collect in its gathering force, in the unicity of its question, something of the Heideggerian unthought.[16]

Derrida's observation is well made, but to my thinking it begs the question of the possibility of a subject that can exceed metaphysics. For if such a subject can be described, what will decide the validity and coherence of the description will not be the unicity or otherwise of the *interrogative* path. The trappings of unicity attend every interrogative process, as the thought of deconstruction itself must concede: after all, deconstruction works through looking, within a text, for *specific* play or "effects": undecidability is one of these, and I shall discuss simultaneous transcendental possibility and impossibility below. Regardless of the unicity that this specificity entails, the success of the deconstructive process corresponds to another demand: that nonunifiable representations *result* from the play or "mechanism." Now, in the terms in which I have described the Lacoue-Labarthian subject of loss, precisely such a case can be made for the hyperbologically lost subject, so long as its "final" metaphysicality is not reductively presumed in advance.

In any case, what might be most telling in these considerations is the lack of "fit" between hyperbology and those terms that bid to assimilate this notion to Derridean deconstruction. (As I have said, this is probably because hyperbology is a type of deconstruction, but not a Derridean one.) In particular, this seems to apply to the term *désistance*. Here, the following dilemma, in itself almost hyperbological, confronts the reader "caught" between Derrida and Lacoue-Labarthe: to the extent that *désistance* becomes assimilable to Derridean deconstruction, it fails effectively to explicate hyperbology; equally, when it is described so as to accurately explicate hyperbology, *désistance* fails to be coterminous with Derridean deconstruction. This is evident as I pursue Derrida's text to show how *désistance* betrays—in both senses of this word—the marks characteristic of Derridean deconstruction.

I have already noted that Derridean *désistance*, as this temporally cast subjectal withdrawal, occurs as the experience of the *ineluctable*, in two specific senses: as that which cannot be eluded, and/or as that which has "happened before happening, . . . always in a past, in advance of the event."[17] There is no doubt that these connotations can be found in Lacoue-Labarthe's critique of Heidegger's notion of the withdrawal of Being. Lacoue-Labarthe's critique is explicitly concerned with the subjects of *enunciation* (Nietzsche, Plato) to be sought behind, as it were, the figures that represent their metaphysical counterparts.[18] One dimension of this concern is an affirmation of the withdrawal of these subjects, in *désistement* (or *désistance*) and as ineluctability. In this sense, there can be no quarrel with the term *désistance*, and with its characterization of the present subject as lost, postponed infinitely forward to a "future," or backward to an "always already past."

Of course, "infinite postponement" is an operative strategy reminiscent of the triumph of *différance*, and of the play of deconstruction, and perhaps even of the *ineluctability* of these, as triumphs over the present. For Derrida, evidently, the *désistance* of the subject expresses the play of *différance* that corresponds to the deconstruction of the subject. One way in which Derridean deconstruction works to subvert self-identicality in a discourse is by demonstrating that the conditions of the *possibility* of the self-identicality of a key term in the discourse are simultaneously the conditions of the *impossibility* of the self-identicality of this term.[19] Derrida is aware that in "Typography," the subject Lacoue-Labarthe seeks, that is, the "subject" in inevitable "delay" in relation to itself, is the subject Heidegger avoids.[20] Again, initially, Derrida relates his observations on this "subject" to Heideggerian deconstruction: "Once again, the subject as thus written (in quotation marks) is not the one Heidegger deconstructs."[21]

And from here it is again a small step to moving to assimilate this *désistant* subject to a more original deconstruction: Derrida's own. Derrida notes that Lacoue-Labarthe's subject both marks itself *and* marks itself in its withdrawal, and in delay from itself. Hence,

> this "subject" does not identify itself. . . . [But also] it does nothing other than identify itself. . . . If the subject identifies itself, it is because it can never be identical, never identify itself—with itself or with the other.[22]

But this means that

> the condition of the possibility of identification is nothing other than its impossibility, both of them ineluctable.[23]

In other words, Derridean deconstruction *ought* to be readable into Lacoue-Labarthe's account here.

Now, undeniably, what Derrida is saying is eminently reasonable as a characterization of the sought "subject," once its nonself-coincidence, as self-delay, is established. The condition for the possibility of the "subject" is the occurrence of its noncoincident "avatars." These elicit the question of the subject, as the *one* that might integrate these *two*. But the noncoincidence of the avatars becomes also the condition for loss of unity, and thus the condition of the subject's impossibility.

Derrida neatly relates the self-unraveling of this subject to mimesis. What makes for the "appearance" of the subject in the first place—the effect that is *désistance*—is also what makes it appear as self-displaced:

> The subject, which is thus de-subjectivized, would not have to identify itself were it not for the *désistance* that makes absolute identification absolutely impossible for it.[24]

This seems comprehensively to reaffirm the assimilation of *désistance* to *différance*, and to Derridean deconstruction. And yet, here as elsewhere, Derrida *also* tends to give the impression that he is refraining from this assimilation. Again, he deliberately underplays the move deconstructing the subject, consigning it to a note. He forbears explicitly to mention *différance,* or indeed deconstruction. He has—to borrow a Lacoue-Labarthian expression, which Derrida himself appears to appreciate—avoided deconstruction without avoiding it.

Further evidence of this is found in the extraordinarily rich and highly complex parenthetical comment (fifteen pages long!) that constitutes the beginning of "Introduction: Desistance."[25] Derrida is at pains to emphasize the uniqueness of the maneuver by which, in Lacoue-Labarthe, Platonic typology returns to haunt Heideggerian and Nietzschean deconstructions of it. But it is the incessant *return* of the "Platonic *apprehension* of mimesis," and its reinscription under the most foreign figures, that catches his attention.[26]

Significantly, Derrida here acknowledges Lacoue-Labarthe's own reticence in invoking the notion of deconstruction to explain the relationship between Platonic mimesis and its later inscription(s):

> Lacoue-Labarthe does not oppose [this Platonic ontomimetology] and does not criticize it; he is not even sure that he is deconstructing it, or that "deconstruct" is the best word for describing what he does with it by reinscribing it in another structure: *abîme, Unheimlichkeit, double bind, hyperbology.*[27]

Of these structures (they cannot exactly, without further explanation, be called synonyms for a *single* structure), the one that once more interests me is hyperbology, which I have argued to be the most dominant and inclusive among the group. I have followed Lacoue-Labarthe as he evokes hyperbological subjectal loss, and subversion of the "return" of Platonic typology, in various ways: the oscillation of the subject between modes, its doubling, its paralysis between modes. It would be surprising were we to find Lacoue-Labarthe willing simply to gather all these under the rubric of deconstruction. For one thing, while all these modes involve the subject's noncoincidence with itself, what is also common to them is a *simultaneity* of "opposing," reinscribed, figures of the subject. There is not here, at least immediately, the *delay* of the subject with respect to "itself" that is the hallmark of Derridean subjectal deconstruction as *désistance.*

More interesting still is Derrida's recognition of the *insistence* of the return that yields ontotypology. Once all provisos acknowledging the *inability* of this return to deliver a subject are exhausted, *the return itself,* as *gesture,* must still be acknowledged. We have seen Derrida acknowledge it, albeit modestly and somewhat equivocally, when commenting on the passage in "Obliteration"; again he now does so here. So far, this return has been something to be "explained away," with an apparent view to preserving a force of (Derridean) deconstruction that is presumed to underlie Lacoue-Labarthe's work. But perhaps it is now time to acknowledge the return, somewhat in its own right, by conceding that the return (or stay) of the (de)constituted Lacoue-Labarthian subject is final in a way that distinguishes hyperbological loss-return from Derridean deconstruction, and thereby, if necessary, from *désistance* also.

Lacoue-Labarthe's analyses of subjectal loss invariably offer themselves *obversely* as insistent explorations of continuous loss sustained by continuous *return*. This is why each new investigation is newly dedicated to identifying the individual, delicate moments of the *loss* of the subject of enunciation—rather than pronouncing on the finality of that loss, as the notion of *désistance* would presume. Strangely, then, the notion of *désistance* might—not because it does not accurately characterize experience, but rather in the very event of its framing as such, in its character *as* characterization— correspond to a theoretical overlay that avoids the thrust of Lacoue-Labarthe's enterprise. And this avoidance, this overlay, might equally correspond to a certain premature closure that can be heard when Derrida praises Lacoue-Labarthe for taking up the question of the subject,

> now for almost fifteen years, with discretion, patience and rigor, in a kind of solitude, and without engaging in the "return of the subject" which has recently been animating Parisian conversations.[28]

Minimally, the overlay closes off an alternative direction toward which each of Lacoue-Labarthe's enterprises might be seen to face. This "alternative" thought is that of a "present," and yet barely perceptible, self of enunciation or writing, a self "other" to the subject in, or as, *désistance*. This other "self" would be present, but always in a nearly clandestine manner, as the barely perceptible *other* of the self who is caught (in the act of) escaping.

Lacoue-Labarthe stops short of thus "positively" describing this "self." He is content, as it were, to mark the loss of its other, a loss evident in the hyperbology that attends self-representation. But his account is nevertheless open to the possibility of this self, and its concomitant subjectivity, *unless we subsume that account to its other, that is, to an account totalized by* désistant *subjectal loss.* It is perhaps the danger of this totalization, rather than the thinking associated with the notion of *désistance* itself, that constitutes a perversely theoretical closure which Derrida's account bids to bring to Lacoue-Labarthian *désistement.*

More description needs to be given of this "other" self toward which I am claiming Lacoue-Labarthe's account might remain open. There also remains the question of in what sense, and to what purpose, this "self" might be called a subject or at least related to a possible "(post)deconstructive subjectivity" about which I have also spoken.

I summarize, then, the point to which the investigation in this chapter has brought me. Derrida argues (as I explained in Chapter 1) that self-experience is mediated as self-representation marked by original difference, which postpones infinitely, that is, into absence, the presumed "subject" preceding experience. Lacoue-Labarthe's investigations cannot but confirm this; it is nevertheless impossible, given Derrida's own premises, to present that account as totalizing the description of experience, including self-experience. Lacoue-Labarthe's account, if not overtheorized, opens to an account of "experience" perhaps freshly defined, taking its meaning from other than self-representation. In this light, experience would continue to promise a worthwhile end to the quest for the (admittedly always lost) subject of enunciation. This "self," and perhaps as part of a new notion of the subject, is offered by Maurice Blanchot, to whom I now turn.

Maurice Blanchot and Philippe Lacoue-Labarthe (1): The Self Hollowed by Thought and Writing

Blanchot: The Withdrawal of Self into Silence

In the short space available here, I am able to do a writer such as Blanchot even less justice than I can Derrida or Nancy. Now in his tenth decade of life, and having published for more than six of those decades, Blanchot stands to be regarded as the pioneer, if not (because of his famed reclusiveness) the doyen among writers on subjectal loss and the defamiliarization of the self with itself. Here I must allow my present purpose to direct and limit my approach to his infinitely interesting and elusive writings; I also often make use of the excellent lenses provided by two recent expository critiques authored by Kevin Hart and Leslie Hill, respectively.

For Blanchot, as for the others canvased here, the subject of self-experience, sought in philosophy or literature, is lost within the philosophical-literary acts that mediate experience: thought, language, and writing. One mark of this loss in speech and writing is that it occurs as "losing the power to say 'I,'" the theme and title of the above-mentioned extended essay by Hart.[29] The "I" is lost in and through its accompaniment by a clandestine *other* self, in relation to which it is inevitably exterior and late. Does subjectivity, seen as agency, survive the interaction between these selves? I will take thought, language, and writing in turn, keeping in view comparable reflections by Lacoue-Labarthe.

With regard to thought, we find, in Blanchot's *The Infinite Conversation*:

> Research—poetry, thought—relates to the unknown as unknown. This relation discloses the unknown, but by an uncovering that leaves it under cover; through this relation there is "presence" ["présence"] of the unknown; in this "presence" ["présence"] the unknown is rendered present, but always as unknown. This relation must leave intact—untouched—what it conveys and not unveil what it discloses.[30]

"... there is 'presence'": In what sense is Blanchot using the word "presence"? Hill comments on Blanchot's use of "'présence'" (that is, the word *with* quotation marks, indicating *so-called* presence, and thus cognizant of Derrida), replacing the word "présence" of 1963. That the replacement was so smoothly possible, Hill argues, suggests that Blanchot's notion of "presence," had, from the first, borne the connotation of self-withdrawal that later Derridean vocabulary explicitated. That is, "présence," no less than "'présence,'" connoted, and connotes,

> not in fact the fullness and immediacy of the present at all, but rather the withdrawal of presence from itself and the movement of self-differentiation that made such withdrawal possible."[31]

Corresponding with this "withdrawal of presence from itself," we experience thought and speech as hollowing out whatever subject or object they *name*, effecting a withdrawal of this subject as such. This hollowing removes, as it were, the inner being of an object from the presence of its namer. In "Literature and the Right to Death," Blanchot says:

For me to be able to say "This woman" I must somehow take her flesh and blood reality away from her, cause her to be absent, annihilate her. The word gives me the being, but it gives it to me deprived of being. The word is the absence of that being, its nothingness, what is left of it when it has lost being — the very fact that it does not exist.[32]

Hart and Hill both notice that Blanchot does more here than repeat the Hegelian thought of naming as negation, which Hart summarizes thus: "When an existent is classified as a member of general category, it loses its absolute singularity."[33] In Blanchot, this erasure of the being of the named extends to an erasure of the being of the *namer* (thinker or author), who himself has self-presence through a name, if only the name he calls himself. Hill argues that "what is at stake here is in fact the status of [Blanchot's own proper] name and of all names in general." Hart sees Hegelian naming (as loss) as antecedent to Blanchot's characterization of writing as dealing several deaths: of the self, of man, of the author, and of God.[34]

It is evident that writing, thought, and speech share in this loss of the named, occasioned by naming. In fact, *literature* arises in the quest for what writing, thought, and speech, in the act of conceptualization, produce as always already overlooked, namely, absolute singularity, or originary experience. Literature wants

the cat as it exists, the pebble *taking the side of things*, not man but the pebble, and in this pebble what man rejects by saying it, what is the foundation of speech and what speech excludes in speaking, the abyss.[35]

Literature here is writing, but also more than writing. Admittedly *as* writing, in demarcating the conceptual, it becomes structurally implicated in the subjectal loss that writing and thought effect, the writing of the *disaster*.[36] But is there a possibility that, *as* "literature," it can also move beyond this disaster, or death? Certainly, Blanchot's emphasis sometimes falls on the side of noticing literature as a *quest* for the lost subject rather than merely *marking* its loss. Hill notes that, for Blanchot, literature

dedicates itself, not to the resurrection embodied in conceptual thought, but to the unthinkable singularity that precedes the concept as its simultaneous condition of both possibility and impossibility.[37]

Hill's observation, however, must be complemented by another—the "dedication" above is forlorn. When Blanchot says, in specifying the nature of literature, that "the language of literature is a quest for this moment which precedes literature," the "moment" in question has been *structurally* emptied of the presence it seems to mediate.[38] This structurality corresponds to the temporality of experience as loss:

> How can I recover [the something that dies, that has disappeared, in speech], how can I turn around and look at what exists *before*, if all my power consists in making it into what exists *after*?[39]

So (at least thus far) structured subjectal loss reigns, as something beyond which literature seeks to go but cannot. Literature can at most be represented as a failed quest for the subject *as such*. Perhaps, though, this does not preclude it—as I shall show shortly—from the infinitely more complex and delicate search for what might eventually be called the subject *otherwise*. In that regard, closer attention will have to be paid to Blanchot's probing of the complicity of literature with writing. But I pause now to turn to Lacoue-Labarthe's own exploration of that complicity, and his engagement with the question of writing and literature. He, too, is interested in the loss of subjectal power that literature, as writing, occasions; his setting for the problem, however, explicitly includes philosophy.

Lacoue-Labarthe: Writing as Originally Fictive

I have already watched Lacoue-Labarthe refer to *writing* as "undoing experience," in a context where he is discussing the link between literature and philosophy.[40] This happens from the first in "The Fable," where it is writing, as "first of all that reflection of experience in which reflection (and hence experience) is ceaselessly undone," that corresponds to the loss of the self-subject: "We write: we are dispossessed, something is incessantly fleeing, outside of us, slowly deteriorating."[41] It is apparently from this earliest point, too, that Lacoue-Labarthe makes the general decision to speak of writing rather than literature. "The Fable" begins by canvasing the possibility that all writing might be included within the *fictive* status accorded literature. It ends by both accepting this possibility *and* settling for a formally opposite descriptive dispensation: the inclusion of literature within writing. Let us see how Lacoue-Labarthe traverses that distance.

He begins by considering whether he should treat literature in contradistinction to writing:

> Everything depends, in fact, on what we mean by *literature*. Do we mean the letter (*gramma*, trace, mark, inscription . . . writing), or do we mean *only* literature, in the most conventional, the most decried sense . . . [the sense in which] *literature* signifies above all what has for a long time been conventionally called *fiction*.[42]

Literature might well be taken in this second sense. But this would problematize Lacoue-Labarthe's guiding question for the essay, "What if, after all, philosophy was nothing but literature?" For, as we saw earlier, directly to invoke the notion of philosophy as "pure fiction" is to draw upon, and establish the very notion of "original truth" that one is seeking to replace. The failure here can be put down to the "replacement" motif itself, with its self-defeating point of departure, namely, "substitution or transfer in general, that is, a belief in origins that even the discovery of an 'originary difference' would not be able to correct."[43] This is why, Lacoue-Labarthe implies, it is as well to avoid the term "literature" itself in trying to pose the philosophy-as-literature question fruitfully, since "it is obviously no longer a question of 'literature.' Fiction, myth, and fable are provisional words. It would doubtless be better to speak of *writing*."[44]

This bracketing of literature in favor of writing finds interesting comparison in "Obliteration," where Lacoue-Labarthe relates subjectal loss to the question of "authorship." Here, overlapping understandings blur of the author as, on the one hand, "merely" a writer and, on the other, as a producer of what Blanchot would call "the language of literature." When Lacoue-Labarthe questions Heidegger's failure to treat Nietzsche as an *author*, as distinct from a subject identifiable purely with his thought, it is not the distinction between writing and literature that is on display; rather, it is Heidegger's failure to notice a subjectal *loss* made manifest whenever the subject Nietzsche, as *thinker*, comes under consideration. Lacoue-Labarthe asks, "What is entailed by the refusal to take the author into account, and by the desire to refer thought only to itself?" He then moves to recall, in terms entirely reminiscent of Blanchot, but with a particular Lacoue-Labarthian accent, the *ongoing* event of loss, to which the events of thinking, speech, or writing call attention, as

> that which, in the subject, always deserts (has always already deserted) the subject *itself* and which, prior to any "self-posses-

sion" (and in a mode other than that of dispossession), is the dissolution, the defeat of the subject in the subject or *as* the subject: the (de)constitution of the subject.[45]

Here, Lacoue-Labarthe's examination of the event of loss requires formal contradistinction from any project of subjectal salvage. He reasserts that what attracts his interest here will be "neither the subject nor the author"; it will also remain "absolutely irreducible to any subjectivity (that is, to any objectivity)."[46]

How, then, do the two approaches engage each other? The foregoing considerations, albeit limited, show that the respective treatments are in fact complementary and extend each other. Lacoue-Labarthe might be taken as reminding us that Blanchot's "language of literature" is produced as *writing*, after all, with the connotation of ongoing and irreversible subjectal loss that writing entails: equally, Blanchot encourages us to pay attention in literature to the endemic dimension of *quest* — or yearning for the subject — as the obverse side of that sustainment of loss upon which Lacoue-Labarthe's analyses focus. This quality of quest can now be sought in "writing" in the sense in which Lacoue-Labarthe understands it, that is, as "originally" fictive.

This last point is germane to my question of whether Lacoue-Labarthian hyperbological subjectal loss might, against the backdrop afforded by Blanchot, be related to a notion of deconstructive subjectivity, structural or "otherwise." I can now pursue this question in two steps. The first involves asking whether Blanchot's account of literature as originary quest has room for the subject of experience, albeit radically nonoriginary and unpresentable as such. Supposing it does, the second step will involve my relating Lacoue-Labarthe's account of hyperbological subjectal loss to the description of this subject. It is possible that Lacoue-Labarthian hyperbology will be seen to amplify, without essentially disturbing, a presumption of hyperbological loss already intrinsic to Blanchot and yet supportive of a subjectivity delineated "otherwise."

Subjectivity in Blanchot: Does a "Subject of Experience" Survive Hegelian Loss?

We have seen this: in Blanchot, the language of literature marks a quest for a subject that naming has always already bypassed. With Hegel, Blanchot notes this capacity for language to negate being, by overlooking absolute singularity. But Blanchot, unlike Hegel, does not presume the identity of language with the conceptual, in negation of the immediate, and in provision of a dialectical path toward the subject as Absolute Idea.[47] In fact, Blanchot's explorations do not gainsay that path or even its goal. But Hart, as we shall see, points out that Blanchot's explorations patiently prize free from the dialectic a parallel possibility for the operation of language. Blanchot returns incessantly to the "death" that language deals the singularity preceding being. But there he identifies a register in which words and their combination beckon rather than kill this prebeing, allowing its approach through a *dying* that is not death.

This is the register of the *neuter*, deriving through an affinity with the grammatical neuter, "in the most simple way, from a negation in two terms [*negation: en deux termes*]: *neuter*, neither one nor the other."[48] In this register, words associate with being in a dimension characterized by withdrawal. But only formally is it so characterized, because the withdrawal itself withdraws:

> The neuter, would it be neuter, would it be that which conceals itself [*serait-il neutre, serait-il ce qui se dérobe*] in concealing and concealing even the act of concealing, with nothing of what disappears in this way appearing, an effect reduced to the absence of effect. . . .[49]

Blanchot is typically complex, elusive, and allusive in his reflections on this relation. I content myself here with this summary: the essence of language as neuter is its passivity, its designation of "difference in indifference." Implied is the withdrawal, in the neuter, of language from its dialectical function. The dialectic works precisely by *not* being indifferent to difference: within it, the concept is engaged to negate singularity. The neuter remains *passively* other to the singulars it conceptually marks. Language thus retains a dimension in which it refrains from referring what it marks to the economy involving singularity and conceptuality:

> The Neuter that would mark "being" does not thus refer it back to the crudeness of non-being, but has always already dispersed being itself as that which, giving itself neither as this or that, also refuses to present itself in simple presence, letting itself be grasped only negatively, under the protective veil of the no.[50]

Language thus remains "other" to being(s), but in an other than dialectical way. It is, as Hart says, "left with a negative charge in excess of what is required of it."[51]

It is useful to follow Hart for some distance here.[52] He argues persuasively that, in Blanchot's terms, this excess over the dialectic allows language to escape the identification that Hegel makes between the possibility of death and the possibility of word-concepts as such. Again, this involves a nuancing of Hegel's claim rather than its rejection. Death as *finitude* is what gives words dialectical force, by rendering concepts as distinguishable from their singular exemplars. Yet this event, in which "the other annihilates the same," takes on more problematic dimensions when death as an *experience* is contemplated: I cannot experience my own death.[53] So death becomes the impossible possibility that accompanies the dialectic: "possibility" here refers to the fact that conceptuality is annihilative, while "impossible" reminds us of the absence of the annihilated subject *as such*, prior to conceptualization.[54] But language might also be engaged, in its passive register of the neuter, to yield the "possible impossibility" of *dying*.[55]

Do Hart's reflections permit a self-subject to be located in Blanchot? It is necessary to move cautiously here. Hart rightly observes that in Blanchot, death is approached by a self that is other (but not dialectically so) to the Cartesian "cogito," itself already subject to the annihilation of the dialectic. Even the word "self," here, suggesting as it does an entity that achieves continuing and bounded identity as the owner of its experiences, is an inadequate designator for Blanchot's "subject" of dying. Nevertheless, I shall continue to refer to the "I" and the "self" while understanding that, for Blanchot, what is engaged by *dying* "is" more primitive than these. Though determined within experiences such as these, it finds location, if at all, in a dimension other to the "Cogito," which precedes the "Cogito." Blanchot speaks in *The Infinite Conversation* of the "shaking" of the "Cogito" by the "unsatisfied exigency of a beginning still more beginning." He adds, "When, in a word, the beginning has spoken, we see it still illuminated by the light of the 'Cogito.'"[56]

One possible meaning, or dimension of meaning, of this last claim is that Blanchot sees language, perhaps as the neuter, as itself constituting the beginning, as a subject. He values Novalis's insight to the effect that "Speech is the subject," and also to the effect that, as Hart says, "poetic language already *is* matter, like nature."[57] He agrees with Novalis that writing (literature) is

> not produced under the sign of *Repräsentation* or *Vorstellung*, both of which presume a mental content prior to inscription, but rather of *Darstellung*, the sensible presentation of a figure.[58]

The ramifications of this are that writing itself precedes the "Cogito," which also becomes presented as "the absence of what it was intended to capture." However, Blanchot

does not actually conclude that there is no subject, let alone no self. The "lesson" of *Thomas l'obscur* is that when one says *cogito* one discloses an "invisible inexpressible, nonexistent Thomas" who does not coincide with the living Thomas.[59]

This, along with a reading by Blanchot of Michael Leiris, suggests to Hart that Blanchot is not averse to crediting the self with two dimensions, "one of negativity and power (the 'I') and one of neutrality and powerlessness (the selfless self of dreams)."[60] Hart quotes Blanchot again, on how we live each of life's events as this double relation:

We live it one time as something we comprehend, grasp, bear, and master . . . we live it another time as something that escapes all employ and all end, and more, as that which escapes our very capacity to undergo it, but whose trial we cannot escape. . . . The experience of non-experience.[61]

Blanchot is here describing a self that is vicarious: I live as something else that is suffering, that is passive before whatever it is undergoing. At the same time, this vicariousness of self is not characterized by vicarious *experience* as such. It is not I who am suffering in that other's suffering—in fact, what is suffered is too close to me for it to be experienced by my self. Blanchot calls it a suffering that is "almost indifferent," that is unexceptional, "behind each [experience] and as though its other dimension."[62] Hart comments: "This suffering must be common to everyone, approaching us at all times, while not something we can actually undergo."[63]

Under this description, as we have seen, suffering is also the mark of the possibility of the impossibility (as powerlessness) that is *dying*. Dying is not of the nature of death, the creative labor of the negative that produces an "I." Rather, it is interminably undergone by this other, too near to me, as the *approach* of death.

Blanchot and Lacoue-Labarthe (2): Lacoue-Labarthian Hyperbology and the Survival of Subjectivity in Blanchot

Hart's reflections provide an excellent exposition of the "self" to be found in Blanchot, and an opportunity for evaluating the touchpoints, if any, that link this self to "subjectivity," however drawn.

In closing his essay, Hart beckons and initiates a characterization of subjectivity in Blanchot:

Blanchot may tell us that there is no self-present, unified subject but in fact he shows us something else. First, if there is a transcendental subject of knowing, it cannot be presented to consciousness. And second, the presence and presentability of a *cogito* are not necessary conditions for subjectivity: a subject of action is created by being summoned by another person, not by virtue of possessing intentional consciousness.[64]

The criteria that are met by Blanchot's self-as-other here—its non-presentability to consciousness, and its dependence, not on intentional consciousness, but on the initiative of an other—meet those of a broad range of descriptions of experience that are postphenomenological, or cognizant of the deconstructive play on the premise of self-presence. I am thinking particularly of the accounts of Derrida, Georges Bataille, and Emmanuel Levinas; Blanchot's account has in fact been developed in dialogue with their accounts, though I cannot follow them further here. Levinas attempts to describe subjectivity determined otherwise; Derrida and Bataille do not. In Derrida's case, I have attempted to cast light on the "angle" at which he places himself in relation to both Blanchot and Lacoue-Labarthe, and I will presently attempt to cast more light on it. More immediately, I will further explore the sense in which Blanchot's self-as-other constitutes an account of subjectivity that affirms a "subject of experience." In turn, I will be interested in the continuity, and contribution, that the Lacoue-Labarthian hyperbological provides for that account.

First, I perhaps need to point out that a "deconstructive" subjectivity seen in terms of self-as-other cannot *simply* imply a subject of experience, for presumably such an account accepts the Hegelian thesis of the *loss* of unified, originary experience in naming but does not accept that there can be a path to ultimate *restoration* of this experience. That is, it accepts neither the prospective success of the Hegelian dialectic nor the claim of the later Heidegger that a patient *thinking* of this difference, as it is manifest to *Dasein*, is oriented fruitfully to allowing Being to disclose itself.[65] Rather, it projects difference itself as originary, not even itself the subject, since it differs even from itself. As I have already pointed out, Derrida's account of the play of *différance* has been pivotal to this approach. This account would lean toward an affirmation of the loss of the subject of representation, and within this loss, a loss of the subject of experience, since this latter subject would always exhibit originary difference from "itself."

Blanchot accords with this. As Hart points out, he is initially amenable to tracking, in Novalis, a prospective subject of speech, that is, speech *as* the subject—a subject becoming lost, however, in language, which has its own ends.[66] But later, it is writing, as literature, that interests him. Evidently this is because literature offers the substantiality of a sensible *presentation* (*Vorstellung* in Novalis' sense), which at the same time *marks* (Blanchot says literature "knows") the radical subjectal absence behind the ruse of representation in thinking and speech. Under a representational/mimetic dispensation, such an absence is covered over; at best, representation "admits," not that there is *no* self, but that it is offering a "self-as-other."[67] Hart's point, in short, can be taken as this: Blanchot's interest lies in a subject marking itself presentationally by a self-absence that is radical and not dialectically recuperative to a premise of self-presence.

In what sense might a "subject" "appear" here? If it is "presented," then what occurs cannot be presentation *of* a prior subject, since "presentation of a prior subject" is another name for *representation* of a subject. And, as we have seen in both Lacoue-Labarthe and Blanchot, "purely fictive" (re)presentation is also fated to be reducible to classically subjectal representation. This situation is not changed if it is the self-as-other that is (re)presented, since, as we have seen Lacoue-Labarthe point out earlier, once self is (re)presented as object, it is also represented as subject.[68]

It seems necessary that presentation, if it is to yield such a subject, must be described so as not to be presentation of *anything as such*. In the terms I have employed above, the presentation associated with *hyperbology* bids to provide this requirement. Hyperbology does more than describe the movement through which a "self-beside-itself" comes to manifestation. Also, in undoing the objects (representations) that accompany this subject, it first undoes *them* as subjects, and secondly undoes *itself*, in and through the very movement by which it constitutes itself. It is only with this proviso that hyperbological movement can be suggested as "providing" the "subject" that Blanchot and Lacoue-Labarthe commonly explore, and that is affirmed alongside the subjectal loss they describe.

As I have already suggested, the accounts of subjectivity in Lacoue-Labarthe and Blanchot complement each other in emphasizing subjectal loss and subjectal gain, respectively. How this happens can be seen precisely in terms of the motif of the hyperbological upon which both writers draw. I therefore briefly revisit the generalized development of Lacoue-Labarthian hyperbology, which has formed the burden of this book, and extend it to include its implicit and explicit points of contact with Blanchot. In so doing, I want also further to characterize the notion of subjectivity as hyperbologically *presented movement*. I think that this bids to comprise a structural subjectivity which can, without undue difficulty, include affirmations of subjectal loss.

Lacoue-Labarthian Hyperbology Recapitulated

My development in this work of a generalized account of Lacoue-Labarthian subjectal loss as hyperbology might be recapitulated as follows. In "Diderot: Paradox and Mimesis," paradox comes under notice as a "passing to the extreme, a sort of 'maximisation,'" defined by "the infinite exchange, or the hyperbolic identity, of contraries."[69] Here, as with Plato in "Typography," Lacoue-Labarthe finds, in the very movement that identifies the subject-enunciator of an enunciated (or written) work, a disappearance of the *subject of enunciation*. That is, there is a withdrawal or detachment of the speaking/writing "self" that this enunciator would identify as itself.

Similarly, Lacoue-Labarthe finds Hölderlin aware of the hyperbology by which a poet cannot incontestably be "as one" with the divine element that works through him. The more he and the element are thus united, the more the work depicts the opposite: God and man as irreconcilably separate so that, ultimately, "the image must differentiate the human being from the element of his sentiment."[70] Neither Heidegger nor Nietzsche "himself" can get behind the *figure(s)* of Nietzsche the "thinker" or writer, to the prior Nietzsche "himself" who is thinking or writing.[71] But this *é-loignement/ent-fernung*—(dis)distancing, or "distancing so as to get nearer"— simultaneously works in reverse, so as to again lose Nietzsche "himself" in the substitution that is *obliteration*.[72] In these and other cases, including that of the proposed (post)nihilisitic Heideggerian-Nietzschean political subject, I showed hyperbology to be operative. Developing and integrating both the explicit and implicit content of these characterizations, I obtained a generalized account of hyperbology as the incessant passing of representations into their opposites so that the subject is lost between these.

A further consideration of the hyperbological in Jean-Luc Nancy enabled me to isolate an important aspect of the Lacoue-Labarthian hyperbological that might easily have become lost in the talk of "exchanged representations." What the hyperbological most properly pertains to is not the poles of representation between which hyperbology operates but the *movement* that transports representations into each other. In this sense, whenever the "self" defines itself by producing or experiencing a work of art, it is simultaneously and irretrievably marked by the experience that corresponds to the priority of the sublime over the beautiful in art. This experience corresponds to a displacement of self as subject, through the movement between *phusis* and *technē* (Lacoue-Labarthe), or as "presentation *in its movement*—which is the absolute removal of the unlimited along the edge of any limit" (Nancy).[73]

The Subject: Presentation in Its Movement?

These points, and particularly this last, are crucial. They can be used to relate hyperbology to what I earlier identified as the survival in Blanchot of subjectivity as "subjectal experience." I pointed out that when Blanchot speaks of "experience," he does not mean primarily to refer to the experience had by a self-present self, that is, to the experience which "I" have, as the "I" of "possibility" (or of power). That "I" corresponds to the death that accompanies representation, as its obverse side.

The experience to which Blanchot *does* refer corresponds to that had by a self which is *beside* this "I." That self corresponds to a passive, "impossible" experiencing, one that is undergone but which it "itself" does not *undergo*, because it lacks the power to do so. Such a self is marked by *dying*, that is, by *approaching* death, and thus, as Hart suggests, by "losing the power to say 'I.'" It is also a self corresponding to experience as presentation rather than representation.[74] Of course, this occurs side by side with Cartesian, representational experience—Blanchot does not mean to deny that particular sine qua non of human consciousness.

Where might the effects of hyperbology correspond to, or enlighten, the account of such a self? One obvious point suggests itself: the dimension of transformation corresponding to the experience by the self of its passive companion. The transformation here is of interiority into exteriority, or nearness into distance, or familiarity into strangeness. This experience, it will be recalled, is undergone as "a suffering that is almost indifferent, not suffered, but neutral."[75] It is subjectless in Cartesian terms, since "the one who is exposed to it, precisely through this suffering, is deprived of the 'I' that would make him suffer it."[76] But the deprivation here corresponds to an experience of strangeness, which is not, however, due to the experience as *distant*: "On the contrary, it is so close that we are prohibited from taking any distance from it—it is foreign in its very proximity."[77] Paradoxically, this experience is best captured by the word, "immediate," "a word which designates what is so close that it destroys all proximity."[78]

It is not difficult to see here the explanatory marks of the hyperbological, which Lacoue-Labarthe develops in the first place by echoing Hölderlin.[79] But what is significant here is not the transformation of one representation into its opposite; rather, it is the *simultaneous* occurrence of each representation in pairs (familiarity-strangeness, interiority-exteriority, proximity-distance), in the midst of which the subject is lost. Equally, and for this reason, it is not the representations themselves that constitute the hyperbological effect, but the *movement* that ceaselessly transports one into the other, in each case.

Presentational Movement Manifest in the Sphere of Representation, as Hyperbolical Excess and Hyperbological Paralysis I have now arrived at the point of scrutinizing more closely a prospective "subject of presentation" continuous with Lacoue-Labarthe's explorations of hyperbology. Inter alia, I need to clarify the connection between "presentation in its movement," hyperbology, and subjectal loss. In an all-important sense, hyperbology is a paralysis that occurs between *representations*. Formally, there come under consideration here representations of the self as *both* exterior and interior, familiar and strange, one with the element and divided from it, and so on. In turn, this formal presence of representations exhibits the hyperbolic movement by which each "becomes" or "tips over into" its opposite.

Within this movement, in its incessance, there is also furnished a logic whereby alternative representations of truth, or Being "itself," are juxtaposed. Were they not juxtaposed *as such*, there could be no interrelating them, nor could there be a characterization of this interrelating as a "mechanism" that delivers paralysis of the subject. Hyperbology itself, as a descriptive rubric, is thus in fee to a presumption of representation, and thus, inevitably, to a presumption of mimesis as *imitatio* or *adequatio*. Nevertheless, hyperbology subverts representation from within—paralysis between representations occasions a paralysis of representation itself, effected by the incessant movement through which representations arise and perish and exchange themselves for each other. Correspondingly, room is created for noticing that the hyperbological corresponds to a lost subject of representation, but also, possibly, to a "gained subject" of *presentation*, as sensible movement that precedes representation but need not give way to it.

Evidently the connections among presentation, representation, and the hyperbological are as follows: presentational movement is manifested, in the sphere of representation, as hyperbolical excess and hyperbological paralysis. The paralysis amounts to subjectal loss: in Lacoue-Labarthe's terms, the loss *in* literature, *of* the subject of philosophy, insofar as this subject bids to be the subject of experience. By contrast, we have seen in Blanchot that literature, experienced as presentation, also bids to furnish a "subject," associated with the self of the "experience of non-experience." The "space" of this clandestine subject is, one might say, cleared by "presentation at work," generating hyperbolical excess and hyperbological movement. This excess and this movement empty representational experience of the self-certainty possessed by the (Cartesian) subject.

The Passive Other Self as a Clandestine (Non)subject of Presentation: Blanchot In *The Space of Literature*, while discussing Hölderlin's *Oedipus*, Blanchot attends in other terms to the hyperbologic identified by Lacoue-Labarthe.[80] He, too, finds that Hölderlin's reading of the tragic emphasizes an internal paralysis besetting the quest for an originary, "Greek" poetic experience, in which God and man unite. Consequently, the categorical "turning about" of the gods is to be met only by a similarly resolute human version. Blanchot says, ostensibly approvingly, of Hölderlin's Oedipus,

He must keep [this double separation, as split] pure, must fill it with no vain consolations. He must maintain there something like an in-between, an empty place opened by the double aversion, the double infidelity of gods and men.[81]

It is evident here that Blanchot, on Hölderlin's behalf, offers poetic production as, *first of all*, presentation. But it is presentation in a dimension unburdened of the expectation of an experience of immediacy raised by its accompanying character as representation. The maintenance of "something like an in-between" corresponds to the retention of a gap, produced by literature, between any self-subject and "itself" so that there is always a something that, as it were, is "me" but, because of writing, escapes me. This offers a representational experience of the clandestine companion, the equivalent of the companion presented nonrepresentably, unnameably, in literature.

Thus presentation as movement—the movement that prevents any representation from settling as itself—has evidently a great deal to do with marking the clandestine (non)subject. In this minimal sense, at least, it corresponds to a "structure of subjectivity" that I suggested might be a correlate of hyperbological subjectal loss.

If one is willing to say more about the clandestine (non)subject (as Blanchot is, but Lacoue-Labarthe is not) it is possible to go further in characterizing the "structure of subjectivity" corresponding to presentation in its movement.

I can now, for instance, refine my suggestion, in Chapter 7, that hyperbological movement might "itself" constitute this subject. Blanchot's hyperbologically marked subject would be marked by presentational movement insofar as this movement became its own "site," as it were, independent of the Cartesian subject "in" whom, on the representational model, the movement occurs. As I have shown, language—as the *neutre*—might be taken to correspond to this site, if care is taken to bracket the return to a traditional subjectivity that accompanies the notion of site. To avoid reduction of Blanchot here, I recall that the *neutre* itself is "neither one nor the other," so whatever "situation" it achieves as subject becomes also a "desituating" of the subject. In *Thomas the Obscure*, Thomas is "read" by the words on the page; he

> perceived all the strangeness there was in being observed by a word as if by a living being, and not simply by one word, but by all the words that were in that word.

This extension of "reading agency" outside of Thomas then spreads to an ever larger number of words, and ultimately to what presents as an undifferentiated "seeing" Other, "like a procession of angels opening out into the infinite to the very eye of the absolute."[82] Given that "Thomas" is reading the words, even as they are reading him from a vantage point in which they coalesce, it would not be unreasonable to conclude that subjectivity, here, becomes located at two sites—"Thomas," and language. The subject then "occurs" in an interplay between the site that is Thomas as "Cogito" and whatever site language provides, from which Thomas can be referred to in the third person. This is emphasized by the pronominal slippage (between "he" and "I") that Thomas experiences as he continues reading.[83] Of this, Philip Beitchman says aptly:

If the "he" is inauthentic because it hides an "I," then the "I" is no more satisfactory since it also sends us back to the "he": in Rimbaud's glorious formulation, "I is another."[84]

I note in passing that Lacoue-Labarthe has commended this same formulation and mused informally upon whether a Lacoue-Labarthian "subject" might be characterizable along the same lines. He says that, in that case, the connection of the "I" to "otherness" would need to be less sharply specified. Thus, while Rimbaud's expression has "remained very famous," Lacoue-Labarthe would prefer to explore " 'I' is of the other"; in other words, what disperses the "I" would be "not necessarily an other; perhaps many, perhaps no one."[85] In both Blanchot and Lacoue-Labarthe, this plausible plurality in the dispersion of the "I" must remain understood, even though I will continue to speak about an other or the other. Lacoue-Labarthe's comment protects the other in its otherness, preventing its recuperation to sameness, to the extent, at least, that such protection is possible.

In any case, Rimbaud's formulation finds clear echoes in the "structure of subjectivity" that Blanchot offers, corresponding to this "split" (non)subject that reading or writing alike produce. I am suggesting that this subject becomes manifest in presentational movement. It is perhaps inaccurate to say that Blanchot's passive "clandestine companion" is the subject of this presentational movement. In any case, such a bald assertion would require an accompanying self-erasure, so as to preclude its direct recuperation to metaphysical subjectivity. That would certainly contradict Blanchot's intentions here. More exactly, the "subject of experience" that Blanchot describes has its "impossible" identity in a tension between the "Cogito" and its clandestine other—the "to-ing and fro-ing," as it were, that presentational movement generates: "I is an other."

Experience, in this setting, corresponds to an "experiencing" that is split between experience had by an "I" and experience had by, and "in," an infinitely passive other. To the extent that this bespeaks subjectivity, it bespeaks a "tensile" structure of subjectivity. I have rehearsed in some detail the complexities of the tension involved. Its hyperbological dimensions come to light in a situation that analogizes tellingly to "everyday" experience: that of the insensible actor of "Diderot: Paradox and Mimesis." Lacoue-Labarthe's Diderot canvases the possibility of an "active" mimesis, as a movement allowed to operate in a passive human "subject." This thespian subject takes on "deliberate and voluntary alienation, originating from the gift of nature," so as to allow mimetic catharsis thorough productive efficacy.[86] Against Plato, Diderot is defending Aristotle's view of the beneficial moral function of mimesis, by showing that its cathartic "takeover" can occur in a subject "outside itself." Hyperbology manifests itself in the *nearness* to authenticity (read, to mediating the force of mimetic [re]presentation) that an actor achieves by *distancing* himself from his theatrical character, as the site of activity of this force.

Space precludes a detailed return here to the argument of "Diderot: Paradox and Mimesis." I note, though, Lacoue-Labarthe's observation that Diderot means to describe the world, and not just the theater.[87] This suggests that Lacoue-Labarthe's elicitation of hyperbology in that context can find an affinity with Blanchot's general account of a "passive" subject of transcendental experience that is other than the Cartesian subject. Of course, for Blanchot, this "other" becomes manifest, if at all, only through presentation rather than through mimetic representation. Nevertheless, Lacoue-Labarthian evocation of a hyperbologically lost subject in "Diderot: Paradox and Mimesis" might be regarded as broadly preparatory of the possibility of the "clandestine companion" that Blanchot offers as an other to the subject-self. [88]

This thought seems to reinforce the impression that Blanchot's "subject" offers itself as a subject of presentational movement, located itself in the tension *between* representation and presentation, between the Cartesian "I" and "its" unrepresentable other. Thus this "new" subject, or this new structural subjectivity, is not simply determined by presentation in contradistinction to representation. Still, it seems true to say that what maintains it in the space between presentation and representation—the space of literature—is *presentational* movement.

Here, "subjectivity" becomes the movement by which a represented self is always referred to an experience that subverts both the subject and experience. Well might this "experience" be termed the "experience of non-experience." Correlating to this newly described subjectivity, one might also speak about a new subject—one that is armed, however, with all the provisos that distinguish it from the metaphysical subject. This new subject corresponds intimately with the very movement that calls into question the subject of representation. What is also to be understood here is that this subject calls into question putative representations of itself.

Conclusion: The Subject in Hyperbological Self-Loss

The Subject in Suspension between "Who" and "Who?"

Will Lacoue-Labarthe himself ever move to training his exploration of subjectal loss on a "positive" description of postsubjectal subjectivity along the lines just described? All things considered, perhaps not. Given this book's aim, I can think of no better way to end it than by comparing the responses of Blanchot and Lacoue-Labarthe to the question "Who comes after the subject?"[89] Blanchot's almost pointedly abbreviated answer suggests that the form of the question (*"Who* comes . . . ?") itself restricts the terms of its answer.[90] "Who" expects a personal subject, a "who" rather than a "what," while "comes" signifies an imminence, an anticipation by virtue of which who(ever) comes has always already arrived. He says to an imaginary interlocutor, who is himself ("me perhaps"):

> "Who comes" has perhaps then always already come (according to the misfortune or fortune of the circle) and "Who," without claiming to once again put *the ego* into question, does not find its proper site, does not let itself be assumed by Me: the "it" that is perhaps no longer the it of it is raining, nor even the it of it is, but without ceasing to be not personal, does not let itself be measured by the impersonal either, and keeps us at the edge of the unknown.[91]

As happens almost always with Blanchot, this passage tends to resist unambiguous interpretation. The "who" that has always already come is by that fact prevented from offering itself in the shape of a future coming. Nevertheless, and in contradiction of this, Blanchot seems to propose a "who" that, because it "does not find its proper site," presents indeed as a subject that straddles the territory between the personal and the impersonal. "It" relates to the "who" who is Me by transporting this "who" to the "edge of the unknown." As it were, this new "who" obtains its own (non)identity—its openness, however incompletely, to representation—by virtue of its capacity for putting Me into question. For want of a better designation, and bearing in mind its noncoincidence with itself, it might be called, with due attention to the interrogative form, "Who?"—the title of Blanchot's essay, and presumably also a simplified version of his answer to the original question. Through or as this "Who?" and in its remaining impersonal but not exactly impersonal, "I" shifts to "us," retained at "the edge of the unknown."

Lacoue-Labarthe's own contribution makes a comparable point regarding the limitations and subjectal loss associated with the discussion of the subject as a "who."[92] He argues that treating a subject as a "who" is finally no different from treating it as a what—the distinguishing nomenclature marks no more than a failed intent to allocate a subjectal uniqueness to the human agent. This interchangeablity of "who" and "what" explains why the Ulysses of the *Odyssey* can call himself "no one" (a what) in answer to a question demanding a "who." It also means that the wondering question proper to literature ("Why is there someone rather than no one?") is obscured by, and conflated with, that proper to philosophy: Heidegger's "Why is there something rather than nothing?"[93]

But there is difficulty even in asking the former question, without its terms being subsumed as the latter. Here, Lacoue-Labarthe, converging with Blanchot, points out that *Who* is always marked by philosophy as having been already overlooked by philosophy:

> *Who* therefore cannot come after the subject. *Who* (enigmatically, and always according to the same enigma) is ceaselessly prior to what philosophical questioning installs as a presence under the name of subject.[94]

Lacoue-Labarthe, while patient and rigorous in pursuing the history of this obscuration from Descartes through Kant to Heidegger, stops there, however, less interested in naming a path to the lost "who." As I have said, it is ultimately the identification of subjectal loss, rather than the exploration of a new subject, that is his concern. His conclusion remains philosophical:

> Perhaps, then, one should leave to "literature" (I would willingly say: to writings, with no more identification than that) the effort of sounding that call: "Who?"—the effort of giving itself up to that call and of being summoned by it—so that the feeling "that there is someone" can tremble again, even if it were anonymous, and that from this *lethargy* there might arise the admiration for existence.[95]

This end is where, in general, Blanchot begins. In these terms, it is *as* literature, and in radical search of *Who*, that his own writings take flight.

Lacoue-Labarthian Hyperbology: A Subject Presented in and as the Necessary Representation(s) of Its "Own" Self-Loss?

The foregoing completes the project undertaken in this chapter: that of approaching a prospective Lacoue-Labarthian "subjectivity" by keeping in view the relationship between Lacoue-Labarthe's reflections on insistent subjectal return and loss, and comparable treatments in Derrida and Blanchot. In bringing these reflections to a conclusion, I return to a point in Derrida's "Introduction: Desistance" where he explores the insistence, within *Typography*, of the ontotypological mimetic return. To describe its mark, he seizes on Lacoue-Labarthe's own terms, "imprint" and "caesura"—terms that, taken in conjunction, signify its interruptive return in the history of Western thought. Most evocatively, however, Derrida settles on the figure of a "besieged force":

> The besieged force remains impregnable because it has no figurable site, no single site, no single figure [*parce qu'elle n'a pas de lieu figurable, un seul lieu, une seule figure*]; it has no proper identity, properly proper. Unstable and destabilizing, it presses and harries out of its *désistance* all the others in turn, without letting up [*sans relâche*], without granting them the least respite.[96]

Here Derrida comes close to the heart of the emphasis that is Lacoue-Labarthe's own. Lacoue-Labarthe's preoccupation with mimetic return becomes, in the end, neither a preoccupation with the subject nor a preoccupation with subjectal loss, though he addresses both of these. Rather, what repeatedly catches his eye is the *marking and remarking of subjectal loss*—something that is subtly but significantly different from either the subject or its loss.

If there is an essence to Lacoue-Labarthe's work, it is probably mimesis as the return of repetition, style, character. These are the "as if" of a subject that is admittedly never representable as itself. Mimetic return is the particular vehicle for the demonstration of a (re)-marking, the favored mode of which is hyperbology. I have proposed that it is here that Lacoue-Labarthe's work opens to a thought of subjectivity, as the unified but unpresentable *experience* associated with this remarking of subjectal loss. The experience is sensible rather than phenomenological: Lacoue-Labarthe is not canvasing the givenness of the subject in a phenomenal realm notionally separable from that of self-experience. Insofar as it *is* experience, it is transcendental experience with a sensible edge, marking the passage from *Er-*

fahrung to *Erlebnis,* but marking this passage as the loss or undoing of experience, and thereby of the subject. This is experience, not as constituted through self-representation, but as made possible by an experienced hyperbological paralysis of this self-representation. On the relatively few occasions when Lacoue-Labarthe has addressed this experience, in its "positive" dimensions, it has become the experience of the self as lost in and through its own remarking.

If experience that is centered on a Cartesian-style subject can be described only in terms of the self-representation that accompanies each of that subject's representational acts, then how might one begin naming an experience that relativizes such self-representation? Blanchot has his own term, upon which we have seen Hart reflect: "experience of non-experience."[97] Crucially for the possibility of a "new subjectivity" here, one might ask: "If such an experience is being had, who is it that is having the experience?"

Derrida, Lacoue-Labarthe, and Blanchot are all aware of the danger that threatens if this question is ever answered unequivocally: one might well return to an undifferentiated subject. In this light, their responses are interesting and show a telling gradation. Blanchot proposes the clandestine companion of "non-experience." Derrida, as we have seen, tends merely to see in the question no need for an answer; for him, the question merely elicits an original division in the subject, and in experience. Lacoue-Labarthe implicitly goes further than Derrida, but not so far as Blanchot. It is almost as if his exploration of hyperbological subjectal loss has determinedly reserved a middle ground between these positions. Derrida insists on the always prior *loss* of the subject in its own original nonself-identity. Blanchot seeks and describes an other "self"—arguably present, but certainly unrepresentable—that accompanies self-loss. Derridean *désistance* assimilates Lacoue-Labarthian *désistement,* but not quite. Equally, Blanchot's self of the "experience of non-experience" is one that Lacoue-Labarthe seems open to exploring; in the end, though, he marks it only implicitly. He remains with the experience of loss *of* the self, without naming a new self that might thereby be implied. Neither does he find a new location for the subject, one from which such loss might be experientially eradicated.

Finally, though, it might well be this very hesitation in Lacoue-Labarthe that marks in his work a thought of *subjectivity* that neither the Derridean "lost self" nor Blanchot's "self as other" (and the versions of these selves in Lacoue-Labarthe) attain. I have suggested that the insistent hyperbology which he highlights would allow, in conjunction with Nancy, the outlines of a subject as *sensed presentational movement*. The "subject" here would accord with, or favor, neither the Derridean "self" nor that of Blanchot. Instead, "it" would be delivered to sensible experience, but only inadequately, as its avatar: self-subverting, endless hyperbological exchange between self-representations.

The representational other of this recurrent presentation, inseparably associated with it, is in one sense always capable of assimilating it to itself. Movement itself then becomes a subject of philosophy, one whose incessant return hyperbology also marks. Perhaps, as Hart points out, the prospective "subject" in Blanchot, too, "hovers" between representation and a presentational "other self" of dying. In the end, though, in the very "positivities" of its designation—as *neutre*, as an "it"—it arguably "tips over" into assimilation to a represented subject, the very "other" that Lacoue-Labarthe refrains carefully from anointing as successor to the subject, or even as "Who?"

Admitting that "something is always escaping outside me," Lacoue-Labarthe forbears formally to pursue that something, knowing that to locate it is merely to initiate again the cycle of its restless escape. He permits it instead to depart, since in departing it might become perceptible, as a sensation of powerlessness before the mobility of representation. There is engendered, then, through the hyperbology that mediates loss, the mark of the subject. This is, as ever, its presence elsewhere.

Notes

1. Representation and Subjectivity: The Kantian Bequest Onward

1. Benjamin's essay on the origin of German tragic drama begins thus: "Es ist dem philosophischen Schrifttum eigen, mit jeder Wendung von neuem vor der Frage der Darstellung zu stehen" ("It is characteristic of philosophical writing that it must continually confront the question of representation"); see Walter Benjamin, "Ursprung des deutschen Trauerspiels," in *Gesammelte Schriften* (the translation here is from Walter Benjamin, *The Origin of German Tragic Drama*, 27). Seyhan renders the quotation rather more forcefully: "It is characteristic of philosophical writing that at every turn it must confront the question of representation anew"; see Azade Seyhan, *Representation and Its Discontents*, 1.

2. Philippe Lacoue-Labarthe, interviews with the author conducted at the Université de Strasbourg on June 2 and June 10, 1997. Initially recorded as informal conversations, the interviews deal with the story of Lacoue-Labarthe's involvement with literature and philosophy. They explore some specific questions concerning his characterization of the representation-subjectivity link (June 2 interview) as well as the historical evolution of the notion of subjectivity in the West (June 10 interview). With Lacoue-Labarthe's cooperation, texts and translations of the interviews are now being edited for publication by the author. Lacoue-Labarthe has kindly given permission for use here of excerpts from the current drafts, provided that their initial and provisional status is acknowledged.

3. Martha B. Helfer, *The Retreat of Representation*, 24. A note on citation: Helfer uses the texts of the three *Critiques* found in the *Immanuel Kant Werkausgabe* edited by Wilhelm Weischedel, and she refers to them by using the

pagination, indicated in that edition, of the first (A) and second (B) editions as given in the standard twenty-two-volume Akademie-Ausgabe edition published between 1900 and 1942 in connection with the Royal Prussian Academy of Sciences (see Immanuel Kant, *Kants Gesammelte Schriften*). I refer to Helfer's work at some length here and in Chapter 4. Therefore, I have, where applicable, reproduced her method of referring to Kant. Hereafter, I will refer to Kant's *Critique of Pure Reason* by citing the page number(s) of the standard A or B edition, followed by a solidus and the page number(s) of Norman Kemp Smith's 1965 translation, which I quote throughout. Helfer's translations sometimes vary from the standard translations she invokes; where this variation is significant, I have so indicated with the phrase "Helfer's translation." Here, Helfer's reference is to Immanuel Kant, *Critique of Pure Reason*, B194 (translation slightly altered by Helfer) / 192–93.

4. Kant, *Critique of Pure Reason*, B195 (Helfer's italicized interpolations) / 193.

5. Helfer, *The Retreat of Representation*, 24.

6. Mark C. Taylor, *Erring: A Postmodern A/theology*, 48. The included quotations are from Jacques Derrida, *Of Grammatology*, 203, and from that volume's preface by Gayatri Chakravorty Spivak, lxxi. Spivak is quoting the French edition of Jacques Derrida, *Positions*, 107–8, as translated in the 1973 publication by *Diacritics* of Jacques Derrida, "Positions," 40 (Derrida's emphasis). See also, for this quotation, the 1981 Alan Bass translation of Jacques Derrida, *Positions*, 81.

7. The book in question is Philippe Lacoue-Labarthe, *La Poésie comme expérience*, published in English as *Poetry as Experience*. This reading of three of Celan's poems evokes many of the themes plumbed by Lacoue-Labarthe's complex readings elsewhere. Lacoue-Labarthe's voice is heard behind and alongside Celan's, the philosopher coaxing from both the words and the silence of the poetry thoughts on the relationships among poetry, experience, and subjectal loss. In keeping with its genre, the book does not "bed" these thoughts in intricate argumentation, and I will not offer a reading of it here. By the same token, it frequently names ideas with a directness often unmatched elsewhere in Lacoue-Labarthe, and I draw upon it several times in that regard.

8. Seyhan, *Representation and Its Discontents*, 7.

9. My emphasis.

10. Lacoue-Labarthe, interview with the author, June 2, 1997.

11. Aristotle, *The Complete Works of Aristotle*, 1017b, line 14.

12. With this proviso, concerning the essentialism that *substantia* contributes to *subiectum*, one can take Lacoue-Labarthe's general point: "Aristotle himself had only a single word to say that: *hupokeimenon*—that which is under, that which is lying under, under-lying—and it is this that one translates in Latin by 'substance' or by 'subject'" (Lacoue-Labarthe, interview with the author, June 10, 1997).

13. Modern times, here, clearly date from Descartes: "And in particular, in the tradition that Descartes covers, what Descartes was thinking, still, through the Latin word *ego* — 'I' — is designated as 'subject'" (ibid.).

14. Ibid.

15. In the syntactically complex parenthesis appropriate to a conversation, Lacoue-Labarthe itemizes some of these ontological forms of the subject. It occurs "under the form of 'I think,' or under the much more general form of 'mind,' for example — there I invoke Hegel; or, again, under the from of 'will' — if I think of Schopenhauer or of Nietzsche; or under different forms: for example, of the 'subject of history' or of the 'subject of work' — I'm thinking also of Hegel, I'm thinking of Marx" (ibid.).

16. Ibid.

17. Thus Aquinas includes the premise that God "is his own invariable existence" and "is identical with his own nature"; see St. Thomas Aquinas, *Summa Theologiae,* 1a Q.10 art. 2.

18. "But when I see, or think I see (I am not here distinguishing the two), it is simply not possible that I who am now thinking am not something"; see René Descartes, *The Philosophical Writings of Descartes,* 22.

19. Thus Hume, in response to the description of the soul as an immaterial, simple and indivisible thinking substance, says, "Neither by considering the first origin of ideas, nor by means of a definition are we able to arrive at any satisfactory definition of substance; which seems to me a sufficient reason for abandoning utterly that dispute concerning the materiality or immateriality of the soul, and makes me condemn even the question itself," and on the impossibility of direct self-perception, which might evidence a thinking substance, he says, "If any succession gives rise to the idea of self, that impression must continue invariably the same, thro' the whole course of our lives. . . . But there is no impression constant and invariable"; see David Hume, *A Treatise of Human Nature,* 234, 251.

20. I discuss this concession at some length, especially in Chapter 4. Lack of an originary intution by the subject opens subjectal self-division as the space within which Lacoue-Labarthian subjectal loss can be seen to be elaborated.

21. Sarah Kofman, "Descartes Entrapped," 180.

22. Friedrich Nietzsche, *Nachgelassene Fragmente* (1885), cited in Kofman, "Descartes Entrapped," 178 (my ellipsis).

23. Kant, *Critique of Pure Reason,* A348 / 333.

24. Ibid., A349/333.

25. Ibid., A348/333 (Kant's emphasis).

26. Ibid. (Kant's emphasis).

27. See Chapter 4, this volume.

28. Hegel argues that "conceptual comprehension . . . knows natural existence when cancelled and transcended"; see Georg Wilhelm Friedrich Hegel, *The Phenomenology of Mind,* 780.

29. In Chapter 8, I develop Kevin Hart's reflections of this thought. These take their departure from Alexandre Kojève's development of Hegel, which expands in part upon the quotation in n. 28, above.

30. Martin Heidegger, *Sein and Zeit*, 46; Martin Heidegger, *Being and Time*, 43. Hereafter, references to *Being and Time* will include bracketed German-edition page numbers and unbracketed English-edition page numbers (for example, *Being and Time*, [46], 43). I retain the conventions of the English-language translator, Joan Stambaugh, except by referring to *Dasein* (which she renders as "Da-sein") and by capitalizing the word "Being" where it translates, or would be translated by, *Sein* (capitalized). I do this to avoid confusion between the noun "Being" and the present participle "being," both in English and in German (*seiend*); however, I take Stambaugh's point, in her preface to the English-language edition, that Heidegger "does not want to substantivize ['being']" (xiv).

31. Critchley comments thus on the Heidegger contemporaneous with the "Letter on Humanism": "For the later Heidegger, the human is no longer a subjective master but rather the Shepherd of Being ('Der Mensch ist nicht der Herr des Seienden. Der Mensch ist der Hirt des Seins')"; see Simon Critchley, "Prolegomena to Any Post-Deconstructive Subjectivity," 20. Critchley is quoting Martin Heidegger, *Wegmarken*, 338. He rightly takes this reflection (and Heidegger's associated reflections linking *Dasein* with the *Ereignis*) as implicating subjectivity, such as it is found in Heidegger, with metaphysics. Critchley stops short of explicitly linking *Dasein* with a Cartesian-style subjectivity, but Marion does trenchantly develop that train of thought in the same volume; see Jean-Luc Marion, "The Final Appeal of the Subject," in Critchley and Dews, eds., *Deconstructive Subjectivities*, 85–104.

32. See Chapter 6 and especially Chapter 8.

33. Interestingly, Derrida says that, had the French word "destruction" exhibited "structural" or "architectural" connotations (so as to imply, he appears to mean, the "de-structuring" of traditional metaphysics), he might well have chosen it to signify an adapted notion of *Destruktion*. But, in French, "destruction" is closer to Nietzschean "demolition" than to Heideggerian *Destruktion*. Thus Derrida explains, "Quand j'ai choisi ce mot [deconstruction]. . . . [e]ntre autres choses, je souhaitais traduire et adapter à mon propos les mots heideggeriens de *Destruktion* ou de *Abbau*. . . . Mais en français le terme 'destruction' impliquait trop visiblement une annihilation, une réduction négative plus proche de la 'demolition' nietzschéenne, peut-être, que de l'interprétation heideggerienne ou du type de lecture que je proposais," and turning then to the *Littré*, he found that "deconstruction" had, fortuitously, a mechanical (or, as he says, "machinic"—"machinique") significance well suited to his purposes; see Jacques Derrida, "Lettre à un ami japonais," 388.

34. Hugh J. Silverman, "Derrida, Heidegger, and the Time of the Line," 165–66.

35. The key texts are Jacques Derrida, *De la grammatologie*; Jacques Derrida, *L'Ecriture et la différence*; and *Marges de la philosophie*. Thus, for example: "It is because of *différance* that signification is possible, only if the so called 'present' element . . . is related to something other than itself"; see Jacques Derrida, *Margins of Philosophy*, 13.

36. Bass's comments are made in his translator's introduction to Jacques Derrida, *Writing and Difference*, xi (Bass's emphasis).

37. Thus Derrida, subverting Saussure, says, "If by hypothesis, we maintain that the opposition of speech to language is utterly rigorous, then *différance* would not be only the play of differences within language but also the relation of speech to language, the detour through which I must pass in order to speak"; see Derrida, *Margins of Philosophy*, 15.

38. Rudolf Bernet, "The Other in Myself," 178 (Bernet's emphasis).

39. Lacoue-Labarthe, interview with the author, June 2, 1997.

40. See Chapter 7, this volume.

41. See Chapter 8, this volume.

42. Originally published in French in 1975, with publication in English in 1989. See Philippe Lacoue-Labarthe, "Typographie"; Philippe Lacoue-Labarthe, "Typography."

43. Originally published in French in 1980 and 1979, respectively, with publication of both in English in 1989. See Philippe Lacoue-Labarthe, "Diderot, le paradoxe et la mimésis"; Philippe Lacoue-Labarthe, "L'Écho du sujet"; Philippe Lacoue-Labarthe, "Diderot: Paradox and Mimesis"; Philippe Lacoue-Labarthe, "The Echo of the Subject."

44. Originally published in French in 1978, with publication in English in 1988. See Philippe Lacoue-Labarthe and Jean-Luc Nancy, *L'Absolu littéraire: théorie de la littérature du romantisme allemand*; Philippe Lacoue-Labarthe and Jean-Luc Nancy, *The Literary Absolute: The Theory of Literature in German Romanticism*.

45. Originally published in French in 1981, with publication in English in 1989. See Philippe Lacoue-Labarthe, "La Transcendance finie/t dans la politique"; Philippe Lacoue-Labarthe, "Transcendence Ends in Politics."

46. Originally published in French in 1987, with publication in English in 1990. See Philippe Lacoue-Labarthe, *La Fiction du politique*; Philippe Lacoue-Labarthe, *Heidegger, Art, and Politics*.

47. Thomas, in Maurice Blanchot's *Thomas the Obscure*, is the paradigmatic, if complex, example; see Chapter 8, this volume.

2. Plato Pursued: Mimesis, Decision, and the Subject

1. "Typographie" is not Lacoue-Labarthe's earliest published work. That status must be accorded "Littérature et philosophie," later collected as "La Fable (littérature et philosophie)" and included with "Le Detour" (see n. 42 to Chapter 5, below) and other essays in Philippe Lacoue-Labarthe, *Le Sujet de la philosophie (Typographies I)*. (Hugh J. Silverman's English

translation, which appears as "The Fable" in Philippe Lacoue-Labarthe, *The Subject of Philosophy*, is of the essay collected in *Le Sujet de la philosophie*.) However, as Christopher Fynsk says, referring to a comment by Lacoue-Labarthe himself, "'Typography' gathers and reformulates the questions broached in the previous essays"; see Christopher Fynsk, editor's preface to Philippe Lacoue-Labarthe, *Typography: Mimesis, Philosophy, Politics*, x.

2. Todd May, "The Community's Absence in Lyotard, Nancy, and Lacoue-Labarthe."

3. See Daniel T. O'Hara, review of *Typography*, 298; Jacques Derrida, "Introduction: Desistance"; Jacques Derrida, "Désistance." Derrida's essay was written and published first in French, in 1987, but specifically as an introduction to the 1989 English-language edition of Lacoue-Labarthe's collection *Typography*. This intriguing set of circumstances allowed Derrida to set up in the essay itself the problems attending the translation of the word *désistance*. He introduces the term as an improvement upon Lacoue-Labarthe's *désistement*. Derrida writes, "How are they going to translate the word *désistement*, its discreet and at the same time insistent recurrence in Lacoue-Labarthe's work? . . . *Désistance* is better [than *désistement*] for marking the middle voice. Before any decision, . . . the subject is desisted without being passive; it desists without desisting itself, even before being the subject of a reflection, a decision, an action, a passion. Should one then say that subjectivity *consists* in such a *désistance*? No, that's just the point—what is involved here is the impossibility of *consisting*, a singular impossibility, something entirely different from a lack of consistency"; see Derrida, "Introduction: Desistance," 4–5 (Fynsk's translation altered to leave the word *désistance* untranslated; I attend to this word and its problematicity extensively in Chapter 3 and thereafter).

4. Lacoue-Labarthe, "Typography," 138.

5. Ibid.

6. See Martin Heidegger, "The Question Concerning Technology"; Martin Heidegger, *"The Question Concerning Technology" and Other Essays*. Lacoue-Labarthe ("Typography," 63–69) also makes references to Martin Heidegger, "Science and Reflection"; Martin Heidegger, *Essais et conférences*; and even Martin Heidegger, "Who Is Nietzsche's Zarathustra?" Here, Lacoue-Labarthe's tracking of Heidegger is typically thorough, intricate, and persuasive: I have no quarrel with it or, as such, with Lacoue-Labarthe's later subversion of Heidegger's equation between *aletheia* and *Unverstelltheit*. My point is that subjectivity corresponding to truth as *Unverstelltheit* (for Lacoue-Labarthe, not "non-dissimulation," but the installation or remaining-standing of Being in beings) does nevertheless mark itself here. It is marked, even if not as itself, by the structure of the "occurrent" decision that characterizes mimesis as falsification.

7. Lacoue-Labarthe, "Typography," 68, 64.

8. Ibid., 64–67.

9. Lacoue-Labarthe then traces the proper development of this link in Martin Heidegger, *Nietzsche*. Here, I follow the translations of passages from the German-language edition as found in Lacoue-Labarthe, "Typography"; these are Christopher Fynsks's English renderings of Lacoue-Labarthe's French translations of Heidegger and are not critical to my argument at this point. Equally, I follow David Farrell Krell's direct German-to-English translation as found in Martin Heidegger, *Nietzsche*, vol. 1: *The Will to Power as Art* when, occasionally, Krell's translation is used in "Typography." I identify the respective versions of Heidegger's *Nietzsche* as "German edition" and "English edition."

10. Lacoue-Labarthe, "Typography," 68.

11. Ibid., 73.

12. Ibid., 73ff. Heidegger's analysis is in *Nietzsche*, 162ff (German edition).

13. Lacoue-Labarthe, "Typography," 77.

14. Ibid.

15. Plato, *The Republic*, Book X, 596 (e). Here and throughout, Lacoue-Labarthe's references to this work cite the Paul Shorey translation found in the 1961 collection edited by Edith Hamilton and Huntington Cairns. For simplicity, I too shall use the Shorey translation when referring to Lacoue-Labarthe's citations of *The Republic*; in other contexts, I shall refer to Desmond Lee's 1987 translation and indicate such references as follows: "Plato, *The Republic* (Lee translation)."

16. I here follow the argument in Lacoue-Labarthe, "Typography," 87–89.

17. Ibid., 88.

18. Ibid., 87.

19. Ibid., 89 (Lacoue-Labarthe's emphasis).

20. Ibid., 86.

21. Ibid., 89–90.

22. Plato, *The Laws of Plato*, Book VII, 817, quoted here in Christopher Fynsk's English translation (Lacoue-Labarthe's bracketed interpolation); see Lacoue-Labarthe, "Typography,"108n. Fynsk's translation, presumably from Lacoue-Labarthe's prior French rendering of the Greek original, is uncontroversial, differing only in minor ways from standard versions; cf. Plato, *The Laws of Plato*, 208–9, in Thomas L. Pangle's 1980 translation.

23. Lacoue-Labarthe, "Typography," 98.

24. Ibid., 129.

25. Ibid., 132 (Lacoue-Labarthe's emphasis).

26. Ibid., 135 (Lacoue-Labarthe's emphasis).

27. Ibid., 134.

28. Jacques Derrida, *Dissemination*, 265n. Lacoue-Labarthe finds support more generally in Derrida's text, likening the "constitutional undecidability" of the *pharmakon* in "Plato's Pharmacy" to the "reversibility" that

constitutes "the trick of the mirror." His point here is that Plato, in *The Republic*, Book X, 595 (b), also refers to the need for a *pharmakon* (antidote) to "things of the mimetic kind" that "corrupt the judgment [dianoia] of *listeners*." But, as a "specular" *pharmakon*, mirroring cannot escape the implications of Derrida's demonstration of the above-mentioned undecidability. It is curious that Lacoue-Labarthe does not attempt more specifically here to explain the "reversibility" that becomes imputed to the "trick of the mirror" through its characterization as *pharmakon*. Instead, he refers the reader broadly and inclusively to "Plato's Pharmacy" and "The Double Session"; see Jacques Derrida, "Plato's Pharmacy," and Jacques Derrida, "The Double Session," both cited in Lacoue-Labarthe, "Typography," 100–101.

29. Lacoue-Labarthe, "Typography," 136 (Lacoue-Labarthe's emphasis).

30. Ibid., 137.

31. Ibid., 136 (Lacoue-Labarthe's emphasis).

32. Martin Heidegger, *Being and Time*, 15 / 2. For a reminder about my system of citing this work, see n. 30 to Chapter 1, above.

33. Hubert L. Dreyfus, *Being-in-the-World*, 45–46 (Dreyfus's emphasis).

34. Perhaps it is through such representation that *Dasein* itself, once its role in or interactivity with the world is specified, is recuperated toward subjectivity. As Dreyfus notices, Heidegger seems to recognize this, at least insofar as it applies to the *world* that is co-structured with *Dasein*: "There is world only insofar as *Dasein* exists. But then is world not something 'subjective'? In fact it is! Only one may not at this point reintroduce a common subjectivistic concept of 'subject.' Instead, the task is to see that being-in-the-world . . . fundamentally transforms the concept of subjectivity and of the subjective"; see Martin Heidegger, *The Metaphysical Foundations of Logic*, 195, cited in Dreyfus, *Being-in-the-World*, 99. Whether this hope for a transformed subjectivity for the world—and correspondingly for *Dasein*—is sustainable becomes an important question. I have already mentioned, and later in this volume will further explore (see Chapters 6 and 7), claims that *Dasein* is susceptible to overdetermination by the metaphysical subjects it was intended to supersede.

35. See Chapter 5, this volume.

36. Thus Lacoue-Labarthe finds that in Celan's poem *Tübingen* a punctuational division signifies the division between an unrepresentable experience and the idiom that follows to translate it: "I propose to call what it translates 'experience,' provided that we both understand the word in its strict sense—the Latin *ex-periri*, a living through danger—and especially that we avoid associating it with what is 'lived,' the stuff of anecdotes. *Erfahrung*, then, rather than *Erlebnis*"; see Philippe Lacoue-Labarthe, *Poetry as Experience*, 18.

37. It is effectively the *passage* itself, with its connotations of mobility, that will be seen to catch Lacoue-Labarthe's eye in many of the texts I ex-

amine. This passage *as such* is worthy of attention as regards the possibility of a Lacoue-Labarthian subjectivity that might attend subjectal loss. Relevant here is a brief but evocative work created jointly by Lacoue-Labarthe and a French painter; see Philippe Lacoue-Labarthe and François Martin, *Retrait de l'artiste, en deux personnes / "Retrait" of the Artist, in Two Persons*. Faced with the experiment (*expérience*) of making an autographical statement that combines writing with painting, Lacoue-Labarthe again evokes the passage through danger as the chief facet of the experiment-experience. In fact, within his sentence, either of the alternatives "experiment" and "experience" is equally possible: "Expérience, toutefois, implique danger, et risque: l'expérience est littéralement la traversée d'un péril" (7). One might say the experience *is* the experiment *is* the passage. This also occasions (*à la* Blanchot) the delocalized *pain* of the self-exceeding or exteriorized autographical passage "into" oneself: "l'expérience du mal apprend . . . que s'il y a un 'moi' (quelque chose comme du 'sujet'), celui-ci n'a en propre que de s'excéder ou de s'outrepasser" (16).

38. Derrida, "Introduction: Desistance," 7 (Derrida's emphasis).

39. Lacoue-Labarthe, "Typography," 47–53.

40. See René Girard, *"To double business bound": Essays on Literature, Mimesis and Anthropology*. My summarizing description draws in large part on this text's lucid concluding interview, "double business" (199–229), originally conducted by *Diacritics* and published there in 1978 (see René Girard, "Interview: René Girard").

41. Girard, *"double business,"* 205.

42. "Pretextual substantiality" is at this stage intended to connote, as an initial hypothesis, the way in which the anthropological mimetic itself bids to become constituted as the subject for Girard. See, for example, Gunter Gebauer and Christoph Wulf, *Mimesis: Culture, Art, Society*: "Girard conceives the mimetic structure of consciousness as a blind mechanism that, given the irreducibly mimetic nature of human action, constrains people to orient themselves according to models. Mimesis, interpreted in this way, becomes an inescapable fatality, a determining factor of human history" (256).

43. René Girard, *Violence and the Sacred*.

44. Lacoue-Labarthe, "Typography," 105; Girard, *Violence and the Sacred*, 295–96.

45. René Girard, "Delirium as System," 91. In the references made to this article in Lacoue-Labarthe's "Typography," its title is found inverted as "System as Delirium," a transposition perhaps explained by the French title of the essay that it translates (see René Girard, "Système du délire"). Upon reflection, "Delirium as System" appears the more accurate of the two renderings.

46. Girard, *"To double business bound,"* 204 (Girard's emphasis).

47. See Chapters 3 and 5, this volume.

48. Lacoue-Labarthe, "Typography," 138.

3. Describing the Subject of Paradoxes and Echoes

1. Philippe Lacoue-Labarthe, "Diderot: Paradox and Mimesis."
2. Philippe Lacoue-Labarthe, "The Echo of the Subject."
3. See n. 3 to Chapter 2, above, for bibliographical details about Jacques Derrida, "Introduction: Desistance," and Jacques Derrida, "Désistance," the French original. I continue throughout to avail myself of Christopher Fynsk's translation, with exceptions that I will indicate and that mainly pertain to the use of the term "desistance" itself. But I have of course retained this word in citing the title of this essay in English.
4. Derrida, "Introduction: Desistance," 4–5.
5. Ibid., 4–5.
6. Ibid., 5 (Derrida's emphasis; translation modified). Here, Derrida's word is *désistance*, not "desistance." The translator's task is clearly unenviable here, but Fynsk's use of "desistance" goes against the sense of all Derrida has said to this point. In response to Derrida's injunction against transcribing *désistance*, "without further precautions," as "desistance," Fynsk has announced his "standing down" (*désistement*). In other words, he will continue to translate *désistance*, and implicitly also sometimes *désistement*, by "desistance" while taking Derrida's caveat as understood. That is possible elsewhere, but not here. In any case, I do not see why use cannot be made of Derrida's exposition by using *désistance* for *désistement* when the occasion arises, and with due indication of Lacoue-Labarthe's original French. My own approach in this regard is indicated in the text.
7. Speaking of the Freudian subject, Lacoue-Labarthe says that "what Freud himself tries to say is that the identification precedes the constitution of the subject. Well, it is this difficulty that has, if you like, forced me to speak of *désistement*—and then later, in reusing the lexicon of Derrida, of *désistance*—in regard to the process of identification" (Philippe Lacoue-Labarthe, interview with the author conducted at the Université de Strasbourg, June 2, 1997).
8. When I say that *désistance* is "effectively involuntary," I mean that it presents as an event of "play" over which a subject has no control, that is, play *to which the subject is subjected*, and within which it is lost, regardless of what it might will. This becomes clearer as I proceed with Derrida's exposition of the notion.
9. See Chapter 8, this volume.
10. Derrida, "Introduction: Desistance," 2 (Derrida's emphasis).
11. Ibid.
12. Ibid., 6–42. Derrida is unfailingly insightful in eliciting the way in which Lacoue-Labarthe achieves deconstructive distance from his quarries precisely by reading so closely *with* them in their attempts to approach the forever elusive subject. In the end, though, as I eventually suggest in Chapter 8, Derrida's attentions to Lacoue-Labarthe may have a similar thrust, with his talk of *désistance* in Lacoue-Labarthe effecting a preemptive refusal

of whatever Lacoue-Labarthian subject might be found *in* (that is, within the very event of) subjectal withdrawal.

13. Philippe Lacoue-Labarthe, "Typography," 136.

14. Philippe Lacoue-Labarthe, "The Echo of the Subject," 195.

15. "Mimesis" here, as in Lacoue-Labarthe, refers to external or sensible representation, of the kind that occurs in the arts of acting, painting, and writing.

16. Gunter Gebauer and Christoph Wulf, in *Mimesis: Culture, Art, Society*, 25–59, adequately discuss the received contours of this debate, fought out in such texts as Plato's *Republic* and Aristotle's *Poetics*. In broad terms, art for Plato constitutes an imitation of nature that is ipso facto derivative and distortive. For Aristotle, by contrast, aesthetic mimesis is oriented toward a perfecting and changing that represents the actual or particular by the possible or universal, and so "mimesis is thus copying and changing in one"; see Gebauer and Wulf, *Mimesis*, 54.

17. See especially the discussion of mimesis as original doubling in Jacques Derrida, *Dissemination*, 191–95.

18. Philippe Lacoue-Labarthe, "Diderot: Paradox and Mimesis," 248. Gebauer and Wulf point out the incompletely established origins of Diderot's *Paradoxe sur le comédien*, first published in 1830, long after the author's death, and composed, according to Paul Vernière, over the ten years beginning in the autumn of 1769; see Gebauer and Wulf, *Mimesis*, 174. As regards the text's English translation, I here follow Christopher Fynsk, editor of Lacoue-Labarthe's *Typography*, in using Denis Diderot, "The Paradox of Acting," in the 1957 translation by Walter Herries Pollock. In referring to those passages of Diderot's *Paradoxe sur le comédien* that Lacoue-Labarthe employs, I will simply use the pagination in Lacoue-Labarthe, "Diderot: Paradox and Mimesis."

19. Lacoue-Labarthe, "Diderot: Paradox and Mimesis," 248.

20. Ibid. (Lacoue-Labarthe's emphasis).

21. Ibid., 249.

22. Ibid., 250.

23. Ibid.

24. Ibid., 251.

25. Lacoue-Labarthe, "Typography," 132 (Lacoue-Labarthe's emphasis).

26. An implication from my reflections below will be the following. What might well raise its head here is the complicating dimension of *ethics*, of how one "ought" to be, not only as an actor but as an agent in general. Is "value," in either its pre- or post-Nietzschean senses, to be had from consciously detaching "oneself" from one's actions, in order to mirror one's *involuntary* withdrawal? A fascinating question, which no doubt returns us toward Enlightenment theories on the detached use of reason, but with an entirely different focus.

27. Lacoue-Labarthe, "Diderot: Paradox and Mimesis," 252.

28. Ibid., 252–53.

29. Diderot, "The Paradox of Acting," 14, quoted in Lacoue-Labarthe, "Diderot: Paradox and Mimesis," 257.

30. Harold Bloom speaks of sensibility in this context as the receptive dimension attaching to the sentimental, itself associated with a celebration of feeling: "Martin Price, one of its foremost expositors, calls [the sentimental]: 'a vehement, often defiant assertion of the value of a man's feelings,'" and, in turn, "this self-conscious, overtly dramatic manifestation, sincere despite its theatrical overtones, was taken as the demonstration of a receptive spirit, compassionate and humane, and then was named 'Sensibility'"; see Harold Bloom, ed., *Poets of Sensibility and the Sublime*, 8. The eighteenth-century notion of "sensibility" is tolerably continuous with our own today. For its pejorative use, here is, for example, Hume, writing in 1741: "Some people are subject to a certain *delicacy of passion*, which makes them extremely sensible to all the accidents of life, and gives them a lively joy upon every prosperous event, as well as a piercing grief, when they meet with misfortunes and adversity. . . . And when a person that has this sensibility of temper, meets with any misfortune, his sorrow or resentment takes entire possession of him"; see David Hume, *Essays Moral, Political, and Literary*, 3–4.

31. Lacoue-Labarthe, "Diderot: Paradox and Mimesis," 257 (Lacoue-Labarthe's emphasis).

32. Ibid., 258 (Lacoue-Labarthe's emphasis).

33. Ibid., 259. See Chapter 2, this volume, for further discussion of the mimetic "impropriety" involved here.

34. Ibid., 257.

35. "For Diderot . . . actually moves back behind Aristotle, and constantly has recourse, whether he knows it or not, to a more ancient, more archaic determination of mimesis" (ibid.). Only elliptically, in the passage preceding the one just cited, does Lacoue-Labarthe suggest that this is a fate of Aristotelian "cathartic" mimesis per se, by emphasizing the comparable recognition that Aristotle and Diderot accord the *actor*'s art. The suggestion is made more directly and forcefully in Lacoue-Labarthe's essay on Freudian psychoanalysis and theatricality; see Philippe Lacoue-Labarthe, "The Scene Is Primal." See also Chapter 5, this volume.

36. Lacoue-Labarthe, "Diderot: Paradox and Mimesis," 259.

37. Ibid., 260 (Lacoue-Labarthe's emphasis).

38. Ibid.

39. It is certainly true that ultimately an equivalence might be adduced between Diderot's position and that of Plato, in the following terms. Both canvas the implications of subjectal absence in the thespian sphere, and the problem of arresting this absence in "real life." Plato thinks the absence can be countered at source by a ban on mimesis; Diderot, in the account here,

appears to disagree. In any case, Plato would agree with Diderot's prescription for a "good mimetician" but consider that good mimesis makes for bad living. "Living," good or bad, is outside the ambit of Diderot's considerations here. My point is simply that Lacoue-Labarthe's failure to distinguish between *initial* descriptive and prescriptive stances of the authors here corresponds to a missed opportunity to mark obverse sides of a single coin.

40. Lacoue-Labarthe, "Diderot: Paradox and Mimesis," 260–61.

41. Ibid., 264 (Lacoue-Labarthe's emphasis).

42. Ibid., 266.

43. Ibid.

44. Ibid.

45. Philippe Lacoue-Labarthe, "The Fable," 12.

46. See Chapter 5, this volume.

47. As a still point at which the subject becomes undecidable between either of two opposing representations of subjectal agency (that is, the human and the divine), the caesura becomes a figure of the loss of the subject through a hyperbological paralysis. I develop this point in Chapter 5.

48. Philippe Lacoue-Labarthe, "The Echo of the Subject," 140 (Lacoue-Labarthe's emphasis). This musical haunting is also one point of departure for Philippe Lacoue-Labarthe, *Musica Ficta (Figures of Wagner)*, originally published as Philippe Lacoue-Labarthe, *Musica Ficta (Figures de Wagner)*. There, too, the subject is the issue. Lacoue-Labarthe's concern is with Wagner's music as historically emblematic of the possibility that music can offer the subject self-appropriation, either as *feeling* or as *figure*. All further references to this work are to Felicia McCarren's English translation.

49. Theodor Reik, *The Haunting Melody: Psychoanalytic Experiences in Life and Music*, 217–376.

50. Lacoue-Labarthe,"The Echo of the Subject," 155.

51. Ibid., 153–89.

52. Friedrich Nietzsche, *Beyond Good and Evil*, 13, quoted in Lacoue-Labarthe, "The Echo of the Subject," 142.

53. See Lacoue-Labarthe, "The Echo of the Subject," 147–207. I follow here the main thread of Lacoue-Labarthe's argument in these pages, relating to Reik's *The Haunting Melody*. Typically Lacoue-Labarthe detours, never irrelevantly, to draw Nietzsche, Lacan, and especially Freud into the exploration—not to mention Reik, from his other writings. I can mention these sallies only sparingly, and only where they are essential to my purposes here. Ultimately, the thought under contestation is Wagner's, put thus by Lacoue-Labarthe in *Musica Ficta*, 11: "Literature cannot, in any way, accede to the rank of the *art of the subject*: language prevents the subject from overtaking or reappropriating itself. There is only one means of subjective appropriation, and that is music" (Lacoue-Labarthe's emphasis). Lacoue-Labarthe will argue that this hope is ultimately vain—music, as *rhythm*, is as much *allothanatographical* as is "autobiography" itself.

54. Lacoue-Labarthe, "The Echo of the Subject," 173 (Lacoue-Labarthe's emphasis).

55. Ibid., 175 (Lacoue-Labarthe's emphasis).

56. Ibid., 173–74. The reference is to Theodor Reik, *From Thirty Years with Freud*, 9.

57. Here, specifically, *en abyme* refers to presentation by means of an artistic depiction, the subject matter of which becomes, explicitly or implicitly, the event of the depiction itself. My use of the term is of a piece with that in Lacoue-Labarthe, "Typography," 92 (see Chapter 2, this volume): Plato, in dismissing mimeticians from the State through "his" persona, Socrates, is placing theorization itself *en abyme*, in a (vain) attempt to counter its abyssality. Similarly, Lacoue-Labarthe develops at a further level the following notion, which he takes for granted in Diderot's *Paradoxe sur le comédien*: that in the "interlocutive soliloquy," following the dialogue in which the paradox is delivered, there is contained, *en abyme*, the dialogue itself; see Lacoue-Labarthe, "Diderot: Paradox and Mimesis," 251.

58. This break is also designated, in passing and in brackets, as a caesura of the subject—again, Lacoue-Labarthe clearly has Hölderlin's notes on theory in mind. See Chapter 5, this volume.

59. Lacoue-Labarthe, "The Echo of the Subject," 190–91. Lacoue-Labarthe points out that the two programs are "contradictory" in form, the first being formally "straight" third-person narrative of the life and destiny of a hero, while in the second, Mahler has graduated to *allobiography*—discussion of "his" own life as that of another. Reik notes the elements in this shift, but their import for him is autobographicality on Mahler's part. By not going further in noting that the autobiographical here is allobiographical, Reik misses an opportunity to identify the form of allobiography in all autobiography, including his own. Even more precisely, autobiography as allobiography is allo*thana*tography—the writing of a *dead* other. I explore this further below.

60. It is particularly important to Lacoue-Labarthe that Reik chooses here to cite Mahler from the *first* program (with its otherwise third-person narration). He argues that Reik here fails to notice a transportation, *between* biography and auto- or allobiography, that is even more marked than in the second, allobiographical, narration. See Lacoue-Labarthe, "The Echo of the Subject," 193.

61. Ibid.; Reik, *The Haunting Melody*, 253.

62. Reik, *The Haunting Melody*, 253; Lacoue-Labarthe, "The Echo of the Subject," 193.

63. Pickstock, for example, appears to go too quickly when, omitting any contextualization of the quotation from Mahler, she says, "It is notable that Lacoue-Labarthe claims that if one sees a configuration of dancing couples through a soundproof window, one will 'see' no rhythm; only the music will provide the key to their movements"; see Catherine Pickstock, "Music:

Soul, City and Cosmos after Augustine." As I see it, Lacoue-Labarthe claims nothing of the sort. The point of the scene for Lacoue-Labarthe, as for Mahler's mourner, is that it figures the refusal of the past to recede, so that "past" and "present" figures of the subject become cotemporal. This is itself a disruption of rhythm. Rhythm works by repetition, but there can be no repetition without "death"—for example, without one drumbeat fading before the next one comes along. In the scene this disruption is manifest by images of contrast and exclusion: dark night and lighted dance hall; an observed dancing "to music" coupled with the absence of heard music. The disruption, experienced by the would-be subject as self-withdrawal (from "real life," from its "own" self-identicality), confirms as "normal" the opposite state of affairs, namely, the occurrence of the subject through rhythming. But, *pace* Pickstock, Lacoue-Labarthe is not implying in "The Echo of the Subject" that rhythm cannot be seen; rather, it appears as *mimed*: "the movements and figures are themselves performed *in imitation* of an (inaudible) music" (194; Lacoue-Labarthe's emphasis). This "infinitely paradoxical" appearance of "the mimetic itself" (195), that is, of subjectal withdrawal concurrent with the withdrawal of rhythm, suggests an obverse conclusion, namely, that rhythm is "the condition of the possibility for the subject," as is explained further in the present volume. Further, it is not that this "dull beat of impersonal pulsional rhythm," as Pickstock calls it, is proposed by Lacoue-Labarthe as an alternative to "expressive Romantic melody." Instead, Lacoue-Labarthe's point, in (de)constituting essences, is to recall to his reader that the constitution of a subject through *art*, in music as elsewhere, must always be remembered as such. This is because, as his preface to *Musica Ficta* recalls pointedly in the context of Wagner, "no aesthetic or artistic practice, for fundamental reasons that derive from the determination of the very essence of art, can declare itself politically innocent" (xxii). For Pickstock's criticisms, see Catherine Pickstock, "Music: Soul, City and Cosmos after Augustine," 252–55, 260–61.

64. Lacoue-Labarthe, "The Echo of the Subject," 193.

65. Ibid., 193–94.

66. Ibid., 194.

67. Ibid., 179.

68. Ibid., 202. The notion here, a Platonic one, is of musical rhythm as able to represent "truly" the *character* of diction, and, relatedly, the (ethical) character—order, virility, and so on—of a subject of the diction. Within this picture, the *rhythm* of the diction within a poem is seen as corresponding "truly" to, and even "stamping" itself as, the character of the person in the poem. See Plato, *The Republic*, 399e–400c (Lee translation), where there is mentioned, inter alia, the "need to find which rhythms suit a life of courage and discipline." This also implies the opposite possibility, namely, combinations of rhythms "suitable to express meanness, insolence, madness, and other evil characteristics"; see Plato, *The Republic*, 101 (Lee translation).

69. My paraphrasing and emphasis.

70. Lacoue-Labarthe, "The Echo of the Subject," 193; Reik, *The Haunting Melody*, 253.

71. Lacoue-Labarthe, "The Echo of the Subject," 195 (Lacoue-Labarthe's emphasis).

72. Lacoue-Labarthe discusses this also in *Poetry as Experience*, 48–49, where death or loss within the *unheimlich* is sourced more broadly than writing, to language itself: "The *Unheimliche*, despite what Celan's formulations imply, does not open up an *other* domain. . . . [That *discoursing* precedes dramatization] means that the *Unheimliche* is essentially a matter of language. Or that language is the locus of the *Unheimliche*, *if* indeed such a locus exists. In other words, language is what 'estranges' the human"; see Philippe Lacoue-Labarthe, *Poetry as Experience*, 48 (Lacoue-Labarthe's emphasis). The implication here is that the *unheimlich* mediated by writing is already "lodged" in language, insofar as language exhibits itself as a *"writing before the letter"* by virtue of which what can be said is always already hollowed out, and its subject *"disinstalled"*; see Lacoue-Labarthe, "Typography," 137 (Lacoue-Labarthe's emphasis).

73. See Lacoue-Labarthe, "The Echo of the Subject," 193–94.

74. "Going to sleep" is my gloss, justified by the tenor of Lacoue-Labarthe's overall interpretation here.

75. Lacoue-Labarthe, "The Echo of the Subject," 194.

76. Ibid., 195.

77. Ibid. In *Musica Ficta*, Lacoue-Labarthe argues that this correlation is also the basis and extent of Heidegger's complicity with the Nietszchean critique of Wagner. Rather than providing the properly musical *rhythm* by which the subject is figured, Wagnerian music offers itself as art, as mimetic theater in which the subject is caught up as *feeling* and thereby de-figured (109).

78. Lacoue-Labarthe, "The Echo of the Subject," 195 (Lacoue-Labarthe's emphasis).

79. Ibid., 193; Reik, *The Haunting Melody*, 253.

80. This return and robustness are in focus in Lacoue-Labarthe's first book-length authorial collaboration with Nancy; see Philippe Lacoue-Labarthe and Jean-Luc Nancy, *Le Titre de la lettre: une lecture de Lacan*; Philippe Lacoue-Labarthe and Jean-Luc Nancy, *The Title of the Letter: A Reading of Lacan*. Lacoue-Labarthe and Nancy offer a deconstructive reading of, inter alia, the account of subjectivity emerging from Lacan, "The Agency of the Letter in the Unconscious or Reason since Freud." Here, space precludes my considering *The Title of the Letter* except with respect to taking up the following point, made in James DiCenso's 1995 review of the book. DiCenso notes that the deconstructive thrust of the authors' reading of Lacan is *reconstructive* of a center, and a subject, that they find to be only illusorily deconstructed within Lacan's reading of Freud. Their decon-

structive reconstruction might seem puzzling or perverse, given its application, as DiCenso says, to a text that "already appears as de-sytematized, fragmented, exhibiting lateral and metaphorical levels of meaning irreducible to a single linear argument" (164). From another angle, however, here, as later, when they critique romanticism in *The Literary Absolute*, the authors are aiming to deconstruct a "deconstruction" that, while destabilizing one metaphysical framework, unwittingly finds itself in fee to another, in the shape of a formula of deconstruction that itself bids to becomes a center, or *arché*. By contrast, subjectal loss, when demonstrated *hyperbologically*, is exhibited, not in terms of an infinite deferral of subjectal representation, but more subtly—by virtue of an *excess* of representation(s), undergoing endless exchange.

4. Literature: Hints of the Hyperbological

1. See Immanuel Kant, *Immanuel Kant Werkausgabe*, vol. 10: *Kritik der Urteilskraft*. The Wilhelm Weischedel edition of Kant's third *Critique* indicates the pagination of the second (B) edition, published in 1793, as given in the standard twenty-two-volume Akademie-Ausgabe edition (see Immanuel Kant, *Kants Gesammelte Schriften*). See n. 33, below, for further details of German editions and English translations used here, and for the conventions of citing Kant's third *Critique* that I follow in this volume.

2. See n. 44 to Chapter 1 for information about this work's publication history.

3. Indeed, in separate essays in Jean-François Courtine et al., *Of the Sublime: Presence in Question*, both Lacoue-Labarthe and Nancy attend to the relationship between art and the Kantian sublime, and thereby to the subjectal loss attending aesthetic representation. *Of the Sublime* was originally published in 1988 as *Du Sublime*; in Chapter 7, I compare and analyze the articles contributed to that volume by Lacoue-Labarthe and by Nancy.

4. See Walter Benjamin, "Der Begriff der Kunstkritik in der deutschen Romantik"; Walter Benjamin, "The Concept of Criticism in German Romanticism."

5. Philippe Lacoue-Labarthe, "Introduction to Walter Benjamin's *The Concept of Art Criticism in German Romanticism*," 428.

6. See Chapter 1, n. 3. Martha B. Helfer, in *The Retreat of Representation*, 9–50, indirectly addresses, in the Kantian and romantic contexts, my general question here regarding the subjectal subversion implied within any subversion of representation as such.

7. Philippe Lacoue-Labarthe and Jean-Luc Nancy, *The Literary Absolute*, 17.

8. "Ersatz" is my word but, I think, a fair one. Thus Lacoue-Labarthe and Nancy speak about the project, in Kant's third *Critique*, of "the *Darstellung* . . . of the never-substantial 'substance' of the subject"; see Lacoue-Labarthe and Nancy, *The Literary Absolute*, 31. This striking turn of phrase

identifies a substantiality that underwrites Kantian transcendentalism, in the shape of the presumed *loss* of the originally intuitable self. In its very absence, this self becomes presence-in-absence, absence awaiting filling— "never substantial substance" has weight as substance, not as emptiness.

9. This "subjectivity as typology" is the thematic not only for the various essays in *Typography* but also for those in *The Subject of Philosophy*; see Chapter 5, this volume.

10. Again: "One must set out from this problematic of the subject unpresentable to itself . . . in order to understand what romanticism will receive . . . as its 'own' most difficult and perhaps insoluble question"; see Lacoue-Labarthe and Nancy, *The Literary Absolute*, 30. "Subject," here, connotes the ultimate agency behind theoretical and moral determinations, the question then being whether this agency can incorporate determinative experience of itself as such.

11. Ibid., 31–32.

12. Ibid., 32. The authors are very concise here. The "tension" to which they refer, insofar as it is historical, evidently means the following: Kant's referral of a historical telos to infinity obviates the possibility that historical-aesthetic evolutional presentation of the subject can reach its conclusion within history itself and thus present an "arrival" of the subject in any particular era.

13. *The Earliest System-Programme of German Idealism* can be found in H. S. Harris, *Hegel's Development: Toward the Sunlight, 1770–1801*, 510–12 (Harris's translation). For the debate on attribution, see Lacoue Labarthe and Nancy, *The Literary Absolute*, 131n.

14. Lacoue-Labarthe and Nancy, *The Literary Absolute*, 35 (authors' emphasis).

15. Ibid., 7. *The Earliest System-Programme of German Idealism*, with its admittedly contested origin, is included in this list.

16. Lacoue-Labarthe and Nancy, *The Literary Absolute*, 121 (authors' emphasis).

17. Ibid., 115 (authors' emphasis). They are commenting on a fragment that interprets a character of Ludwig Tieck's as "the romantic spirit [seemingly] pleasantly fantasizing about itself."

18. Ibid., 121.

19. Ibid., 15.

20. Ibid., 16.

21. Quoted in ibid., 92 (my ellipses).

22. Ibid., 93 (authors' ellipses).

23. Philippe Lacoue-Labarthe, "Sublime Truth."

24. Martha B. Helfer, *The Retreat of Representation*, 1–50.

25. Ibid., 182n. See also Jean-Luc Nancy, "Logodaedalus (Kant écrivain)"; Jean-Luc Nancy, "L'Offrande Sublime"; Hans Graubner, "Kant."

26. For the terms of this problem in Kant, see Chapter 1, this volume; see also Lacoue-Labarthe and Nancy, *The Literary Absolute*, 30–32. For an

outline of its romantic solution, see the translators' introduction to Lacoue-Labarthe and Nancy, *The Literary Absolute,* where Philip Barnard and Cheryl Lester find that the romantic theory is symbolized in the quest of the narrator in Mary Shelley's *Frankenstein* to create a companion in whom his own self-perfection could proceed so that "he would become what Lacoue-Labarthe and Nancy call the 'subject-work,' the paradigmatic model of the romantic subject's auto-production in the (literary) work of art" (xi).

27. See Chapters 2, 3, and 5, this volume. This absolutization, itself paradoxically under erasure, is in one sense the leitmotif of virtually every Lacoue-Labarthian exploration.

28. Helfer, *The Retreat of Representation,* 4–5.

29. Ibid., 4.

30. Ibid., 5.

31. Azade Seyhan, *Representation and Its Discontents,* 7–8.

32. Helfer, *The Retreat of Representation,* 5.

33. I refer to the third Kantian *Critique* as follows: Immanuel Kant, *Critique of Judgment,* with the title (or "ibid.," as the case may be) followed by the section number, the second-edition (B) pagination from the standard twenty-two-volume Akademie-Ausgabe edition, and, usually, page references to J. H. Bernard's 1951 translation. Thus, for example: Immanuel Kant, *Critique of Judgment,* sec. 27, B97 / 96 (Bernard translation). Helfer also uses the Bernard translation, but where she varies from him, she does not always cite the original German or Bernard's equivalent. Because her work in places involves considerable summary of Kant's text, some scrutiny has been necessary to determine the origin of the specific portions of text that have occasioned her retranslations. Where these determinations are mine, I have, for consistency, always placed the citation to Bernard in brackets; sometimes it has even seemed useful to add, from his translation, the phrases or terms to which I think Helfer's reference(s) correspond. Also, in several cases, I have turned for more modern idiom to the 1987 translation by Werner S. Pluhar.

34. Kant, *Critique of Judgment,* sec. 59, B125 / 198–200 (Bernard translation). "Originally determining" constitutes Helfer's rather insightful abbreviation of the following observation by Kant, regarding the judgment of taste as being both free and determined: "Hence, both on account of this inner possibility in the subject and of the external possibility of a nature that agrees with it, [this judgment] finds itself to be referred to something within the subject as well as without him, something which is neither nature nor freedom"; see Kant, *Critique of Judgment,* 199 (Bernard translation).

35. Ibid., sec. 27, B97 / 96 (Bernard translation).

36. Helfer, *The Retreat of Representation,* 45.

37. Ibid., 177.

38. This claim is developed and illustrated in quite different contexts in Kant, *Critique of Judgment,* secs. 29 and #49, respectively. Below, I pursue the significance of this variance.

39. "Kant a *évité* d'écrire la *Critique* en vers"; see Jean-Luc Nancy, "Logodaedalus (Kant écrivain)," 50. See also Helfer, *The Retreat of Representation*, 46n.

40. Helfer, *The Retreat of Representation*, 46–47.

41. Ibid., 47. This conclusion is supported by an accompanying diagram, in which Helfer labels poetry (presumably under its Kantian understanding) as "pure negative presentation."

42. Kant, *Critique of Judgment*, sec. 27, B97 / 96 (Bernard translation).

43. Ibid.

44. Ibid. / 114 (Pluhar translation).

45. Helfer, *The Retreat of Representation*, 48.

46. Kant, preface to the first edition of *Critique of Judgment*, 6 (Pluhar translation). The full title of the preface as it appears in the second (1793) edition is "Preface to the first edition, 1790." Hereafter, it will be cited as "Kant, preface, *Critique of Judgment*."

47. Ibid., 6 (Pluhar translation).

48. Kant, introduction, *Critique of Judgment*, iv / 18–19 (Pluhar translation).

49. Ibid. / 20 (Pluhar translation).

50. Ibid., v / 23 (Pluhar translation).

51. Ibid. / 25 (Pluhar translation).

52. Kant, *Critique of Judgment*, sec. 49 / 157 (Bernard translation, slightly altered).

53. Ibid. (Kant's emphasis). Here, Bernard's translation is more literal than Pluhar's (see text of Chapter 4).

54. Pluhar, differing from Bernard, does in fact thus translate the two occurrences of *Vorstellung* in this passage; see Kant, *Critique of Judgment*, 182 (Pluhar translation).

55. Immanuel Kant, *Critique of Pure Reason*, B422 / 377 (Kant's emphasis). For a reminder about my system of citing this work, see n. 3 to Chapter 1, above.

56. Kant makes an equivalent observation in the corresponding section of the first (A) edition of his first *Critique*: "The 'I' is indeed in all thoughts, but there is not in this representation the least trace of intuition, distinguishing the 'I' from other objects of intuition"; see Kant, *Critique of Pure Reason*, A350 / 334).

57. Ibid., A358 / 339.

58. Immanuel Kant, *Critique of Practical Reason*, 104; the page number of this citation corresponds to Immanuel Kant, *Kritik der praktischen Vernunft*, 100, as published in the twenty-two-volume Akademie-Ausgabe edition (see Immanuel Kant, *Kants Gesammelte Schriften*).

59. Kant, introduction, *Critique of Judgment*, ix / 35 (Pluhar translation).

60. Kant, *Critique of Judgment*, sec. 59, B125 / 198 (Bernard translation). See also n. 34, above, regarding Helfer's interpretation of this section.

61. Ibid., sec. 27 / 96 (Bernard translation).

62. Ibid. / 97 (Bernard translation).

63. Helfer emphasizes that, for Kant, the aesthetic idea is an *expression* [*Ausdruck*] of the beautiful; she argues that one can also, even against Kant himself, determine this idea as the expression of the sublime. See Helfer, *The Retreat of Representation*, 40; Kant, *Critique of Judgment*, sec. 51, B203 / 164 (Bernard translation).

64. Kant, *Critique of Judgment*, sec. 23, B75/82 (Bernard translation).

65. Helfer, *The Retreat of Representation*, 39; the reference is to Rodolphe Gasché, "Ideality in Fragmentation," xxvii.

66. Helfer, *The Retreat of Representation*, 40.

67. See Kant, introduction, *Critique of Judgment*, iv–vii / 15–29 (Bernard translation). Here, it is probably better to speak, not of a prior "requirement" of the understanding, which the imagination then "fulfills," but of a dialectical cooperation between the two faculties oriented toward the production of concepts, with the whole operation being directed by reason.

68. Kant, *Critique of Judgment*, sec. 27 / 96 (Bernard translation). It will be evident that here, and in the account of the Kantian sublime that follows, I am loosely paraphrasing Kant's description in this section.

69. Helfer, *The Retreat of Representation*, 49; she has in mind Kant, *Critique of Judgment*, sec. 29 / 116 (Bernard translation).

70. Kant, *Critique of Judgment*, sec. 49 / 157–58 (Pluhar translation).

71. We have seen from Kant's use of both *Vorstellung* and *Darstellung* in respect of the aesthetic idea that its occurrence has aspects of both "subjective" representation and "objective" presentation. One might say that Kant intentionally hesitates in confirming whether it is realized "internally," in the mind's eye, or rather externally and sensibly, in the "form" provided by the work of art—it is in fact important for his *Critique* that both aspects are affirmed. What can be said is that the aesthetic, *as* presentation, and therefore as having form, falls short of being a presentation of a "complete" idea of reason, since, by definition, Kantian rational ideas cannot be presented.

5. Subjectal Loss in Lacoue-Labarthe: The Recurrence of Hyperbology

1. See Philippe Lacoue-Labarthe, "The Caesura of the Speculative," published in Robert Eisenhauer's translation first in *Glyph* and later in Philippe Lacoue-Labarthe, *Typography*; see also Philippe Lacoue-Labarthe, "La Césure du spéculatif," originally published in Friedrich Hölderlin, *L'Antigone de Sophocle*, and later collected in Philippe Lacoue-Labarthe, *L'Imitation des modernes (Typographies II)*. Except where otherwise indicated, I have used the translation in *Typography*, based on Eisenhauer's 1978 translation.

2. Philippe Lacoue-Labarthe, "Diderot: Paradox and Mimesis," 252 (Lacoue-Labarthe's emphasis).

3. Ibid., 252, 253.

4. There are clearly echoes here of Plato's mimetician (non)subject. See Philippe Lacoue-Labarthe, "Typography," 132; see also Chapter 2, this volume.

5. Lacoue-Labarthe, "Diderot: Paradox and Mimesis," 251.

6. See Jacques Derrida, "Introduction: Desistance," 41n. The mention of hyperbologic here cannot but present as an afterthought, being confined to this extended note at this late point. Admittedly, Derrida is characteristically insightful in locating the essence of the hyperbologic, though the general territory he assigns to its disappropriative effects is noticeably that of deconstruction. Thus he says that, in the "precise context" of the actor, "this hyperbologic regularly converts the gift of everything into the gift of nothing, and this latter into the gift of the thing itself." More widely speaking, though, this "gift of impropriety" is "a matter of appropriation and (de)propriation in general." Derrida goes on to say, in this deconstructively oriented exposition, "The play of the *∂e-*, on which I have been working since the beginning of this essay, might well belong to this hyperbologic. Without being negative, or being subject to a dialectic, it both organizes and disorganizes what it appears to determine; it belongs to and yet escapes the order of its own series." He then lists various essays in Lacoue-Labarthe's *Typography* (notably excluding "Transcendence Ends in Politics") where variants of this radically nondialectical *∂e-* are instantiated as *∂isarticulation, ∂isappropriation, ∂isinstallation,* and *∂econstruction.* (He also mentions *∂e-constitution* in this group; its ascription to Lacoue-Labarthe's essay "L'Oblitération" is correct, but his apparent further assignment of that essay to "Typography" [*sic*] is erroneous: the intended reference is probably to Philippe Lacoue-Labarthe, *Le Sujet ∂e la philosophie (Typographies I),* a separate collection. (See n. 40, below, for the publication history of "L'Oblitération.") He concludes by noting Lacoue-Labarthe's continued appreciation of the durability of the word "deconstruct." Here, Derrida's highly abbreviated *résumé* of the hyperbologic leaves unaddressed key elements of the notion, as well as its overall reach. The elements involved are notably those related to the exchange, oscillation, and paralysis of figures within the hyperbologic "mechanism." These might admittedly be found within the territory belonging to deconstruction; but, even so, they at least remap it significantly. Then, of course, there is the *experience* of hyperbological subjectal loss (as distinct from its *effect*), emphasized in other of Lacoue-Labarthe's texts. This is territory that the Lacoue-Labarthian hyperbological shares with the work of Blanchot and Nancy, more so than with that of Derrida, as suggested in Chapters 7 and 8 of this volume.

7. Peter Szondi, *Versuch über ∂as Tragische.* Lacoue-Labarthe engages with Szondi over the latter's analysis of a text from the tenth and last of Schelling's *Letters on Dogmatism and Criticism.* I follow the rendering of portions of that text in Lacoue-Labarthe, "The Caesura of the Speculative," where, as indicated on p. 215 of that essay, this rendering does not signifi-

cantly differ from that in, say, F. W. J. Schelling, *The Unconditional in Human Knowledge: Four Early Essays, 1794–1796,* 192–93.

8. My discussion here follows the argument in Lacoue-Labarthe, "The Caesura of the Speculative," culminating in the author's definitive exposition of the hyperbological on pp. 230–35 of that text.

9. Ibid., 211.

10. Ibid., 227. The corresponding reference to this "step back" in Diderot is found in Lacoue-Labarthe, "Diderot: Paradox and Mimesis," 257.

11. Lacoue-Labarthe, "The Caesura of the Speculative," 216.

12. Ibid., 217.

13. Ibid., 218.

14. Lacoue-Labarthe's discussion here employs his own translation of this difficult essay; see Friedrich Hölderlin, "Der Grund zum Empedocles." I shall usually refer to quotations by using the pagination in Lacoue-Labarthe, "The Caesura of the Speculative," followed by the pagination in Hölderlin, "Der Grund zum Empedocles," and then by the pagination in Friedrich Hölderlin, "The Ground for Empedocles" (and, where useful, I quote Thomas Pfau's translation for comparison).

15. Lacoue-Labarthe, "The Caesura of the Speculative," 229.

16. Philippe Lacoue-Labarthe, "Hölderlin and the Greeks," 236–47; see also Philippe Lacoue-Labarthe, "Hölderlin et les grecs," first published in *Poétique* and later collected in Lacoue-Labarthe, *L'Imitation des modernes (Typographies II)*.

17. Lacoue-Labarthe, "The Caesura of the Speculative," 230; Hölderlin, "Der Grund zum Empedocles," 571; "The Ground for Empedocles," 51 ("The sensation is no longer expressed in an immediate manner").

18. Lacoue-Labarthe, "The Caesura of the Speculative," 229–30; Hölderlin, "Der Grund zum Empedocles," 572; "The Ground for Empedocles," 51.

19. Lacoue-Labarthe, "The Caesura of the Speculative," 230; Hölderlin, "Der Grund zum Empedocles," 572; "The Ground for Empedocles," 51.

20. Lacoue-Labarthe, "The Caesura of the Speculative," 230.

21. Ibid.

22. Ibid. (Lacoue-Labarthe's emphasis).

23. Philippe Lacoue-Labarthe and Jean-Luc Nancy, *The Literary Absolute,* 92–93.

24. Lacoue-Labarthe, "The Caesura of the Speculative," 231.

25. Ibid.

26. Lacoue-Labarthe, "Typography," 231.

27. See Lacoue-Labarthe, "The Caesura of the Speculative," and Hölderlin, *Werke und Briefe.* See also Friedrich Hölderlin, "Remarks on Oedipus."

28. Lacoue-Labarthe, "The Caesura of the Speculative," 231–32; Hölderlin, *Werke und Briefe,* 735–36; Hölderlin, "Remarks on Oedipus," 107.

29. Lacoue-Labarthe, "The Caesura of the Speculative," 231.

30. Hölderlin, "Remarks on Oedipus," 101.

31. Ibid.

32. Lacoue-Labarthe, "The Caesura of the Speculative," 234; Hölderlin, "Anmerkungen zum Oedipus," 730; Hölderlin, "Remarks on Oedipus," 102.

33. Lacoue-Labarthe, "The Caesura of the Speculative," 235. Andrzej Warminski offers a critique of "The Caesura of the Speculative" that I can address here only in passing. For Warminski, it is only a skewed reading of Hölderlin that enables Lacoue-Labarthe to reconstruct Hölderlin's theoretical texts as a mimetology at all. Inter alia, he offers the following reasons why Lacoue-Labarthe's interpretation rings false: for Hölderlin, the "alternation of tones" in a poem is an animating principle, not one of paralysis; Hölderlin's caesura has more to do with self-signification (the appearance of "representation itself," as Hölderlin says) than with "any 'catharsis' conceived on a sacrificial, ritualistic mimetic model of tragedy"; mimetology is intrinsically incapable of dealing with "textual processes and a 'negative' peculiar to language that it [mimetology] can by definition not account for." If Warminski's criticism of Lacoue-Labarthe's interpretation of Hölderlin's caesura can be taken as emblematic here, Warminski appears to be at cross-purposes with Lacoue-Labarthe: arguably, the appearance of "representation itself," by way of the "balance" (Hölderlin's term) between alternating tones effected by the caesura, corresponds to an appearance of the fact that *representation* does not represent anything (prior). On this point, Warminski and Lacoue-Labarthe would presumably concur; as I see it, Warminski's position achieves genuine distance from Lacoue-Labarthe's only if, when Warminski interprets Hölderlin's text as saying that "representation represents itself *as* representation," he means that "representation itself" can appear *self-identically*. Now, Hölderlin and the romantics might well have believed this, but Warminski's own account of the "death of consciousness" and the "death of writing" ought not to allow *him* to accept it. See Andrzej Warminski, *Readings in Interpretation: Hölderlin, Hegel, Heidegger*, 39–41.

34. Lacoue-Labarthe, "The Caesura of the Speculative," 232. See also Hölderlin, "Remarks on Oedipus," 108: "Inside [the utmost form of purificatory suffering] man forgets himself because he exists entirely for the moment, the god [forgets himself] because he is nothing but time, and either one is unfaithful, time, because it is reversed categorically at such a moment, no longer befitting beginning or end."

35. Rowan Williams presents this Hegelian economy well: "Because there is no moment of pure, unmediated identity in the actual world, there are no discrete and simple objects for thought to rest in. . . . [In the *Logic*] the point is that thought is bound to dissolve the finite perception, the isolated object, as such, moving from the level of diversity . . . to that of complementary opposition. . . . Everything is what it is because of what it is not; it is what it is by *excluding* what it is not; being what it is entails exclusion of what is in fact intrinsic to it. . . . And this [self-denial within thinking] is

why dialectic can be conceived as power, as that which outlives and 'defeats' stable, commonsense perception, not by abolishing it from outside, but by the penetration of its own logic and process." See Rowan Williams, "Logic and Spirit in Hegel," 117–18.

36. Philippe Lacoue-Labarthe, "The Echo of the Subject," 175.

37. Lacoue-Labarthe, "Typography," 62 (Lacoue-Labarthe's emphasis).

38. See Philippe Lacoue-Labarthe, "Apocryphal Nietzsche"; Philippe Lacoue-Labarthe, "La Dissimulation (Nietzsche, la question de l'art et la 'littérature'")"; Philippe Lacoue-Labarthe, "Nietzsche Apocryphe."

39. Lacoue-Labarthe, "Apocryphal Nietzsche," 54.

40. See Philippe Lacoue-Labarthe, "Obliteration"; see also Philippe Lacoue-Labarthe, "L'Oblitération," first published in *Critique* as a review of Heidegger's *Nietzsche* and later collected in Lacoue-Labarthe, *Le Sujet de la philosophie*.

41. Lacoue-Labarthe, "Obliteration," 81.

42. Ibid., 81–82 (Lacoue-Labarthe's emphasis). Two translators — Thomas Trezise here, and Christopher Fynsk in Derrida, "Introduction: Desistance," 16n, where this passage is quoted (see Chapter 8, this volume) — render the bracketed phrase differently, though not significantly so. For consistency here, I have retranslated, varying from both translators, and in favor of literality.

43. See Philippe Lacoue-Labarthe, "The Detour"; see also Philippe Lacoue-Labarthe, "Le Détour," originally published in *Poétique* and later collected in Lacoue-Labarthe, *Le Sujet de la philosophie*.

44. Lacoue-Labarthe, "The Detour," 29.

45. "The Detour" is an analysis introducing the first French translation of a group of Nietzsche's notes and course fragments that date from 1872 to 1875 and that relate to rhetoric, the history of Greek eloquence, and the origin of language (this last as an introduction to a course on Latin grammar). I rely here on the English translations of portions of these texts found in Lacoue-Labarthe, "The Detour."

46. Lacoue-Labarthe, "The Detour," 30 (My emphasis). See also Friedrich Nietzsche, *The Birth of Tragedy*, 78. For the original quotation, see Arthur Schopenhauer, *The World as Will and Representation*, 262.

47. Lacoue-Labarthe, "The Detour," 30.

48. Ibid., 19.

49. Ibid., 22.

50. See Nietzsche, *Gesammelte Werke*, 297–98 (sec. 3 in course on rhetoric), and Nietzsche, *Friedrich Nietzsche on Rhetoric and Language*, 21, quoted in Lacoue-Labarthe, "The Detour," 22.

51. Lacoue-Labarthe, "The Detour," 33 (Lacoue-Labarthe's emphasis).

52. See Lacoue-Labarthe, "The Detour," 35. The fragments are numbers 85 and 87 from Friedrich Nietzsche, *Das Philosophenbuch*, 35–36; Lacoue-Labarthe works from Friedrich Nietzsche, *Das Philosophenbuch / Le Livre du philosophe*.

53. Lacoue-Labarthe, "The Detour," 35; quotation from Nietzsche, *Das Philosophenbuch / Le Livre du philosophe,* fragment 87 (Lacoue-Labarthe's emphasis).

54. Lacoue-Labarthe, "The Detour," 36.

55. Ibid.

56. Ibid., 33.

57. See n. 1 to Chapter 2, above, for this work's publication history.

58. From Friedrich Nietzsche, *Twilight of the Idols,* reprinted in Walter Kaufmann's translation in Friedrich Nietzsche, *The Portable Nietzsche,* 485–86.

59. Lacoue-Labarthe, "The Fable," 5 (he is quoting Nietzsche); cf. "How the 'True World' Finally Became a Fable," 486.

60. Lacoue-Labarthe, "The Fable," 5 (Lacoue-Labarthe's emphasis).

61. Ibid., 8.

62. Ibid., 7.

63. Ibid., 9 (translator's square brackets).

64. Ibid., 7, quoting Martin Heidegger, *What Is Called Thinking?,* 10 (translation modified; when quoting Heidegger, Lacoue-Labarthe uses *mythos* rather than *muthos.*)

65. Lacoue-Labarthe, "The Fable," 7 (Lacoue-Labarthe's emphasis).

66. Hegel says that "identity is the reflection-into-self that is identity only as internal repulsion, and is this repulsion as reflection-into-self, repulsion which immediately takes itself back into itself. Thus it is the identity as difference that is identical with itself"; see Georg Wilhelm Friedrich Hegel, *Science of Logic,* 413.

67. Particular modes of which recur at several points in my elucidation of Lacoue-Labarthe. In Chapter 4, I referred to the subject lost through a substitutive representational event that begins as supplementation but ends as supplanting. That mode also shadows Lacoue-Labarthe's reading of Nietzsche here; so do others, such as the identity between the respective conditions of possibility and impossibility for the experience of subjectal loss.

68. Lacoue-Labarthe, "The Fable," 11. (The final phrase continues immediately from the previous quotation, linked to it by the emphasized conjunction "and"; thus, "without recourse to metaphysical reflection or self-consciousness *and* as the play of what today we call the text.")

69. Ibid.

70. Ibid.

71. Ibid., 12 (translation altered). I have preferred "ceaselessly" (and likewise, in the next quotation, "incessantly") over Hugh J. Silverman's "constantly," in order to evoke the content of hyperbological *movement* that Lacoue-Labarthe's description carries. Movement can be incessant without thereby being constant. It seems to me that this, to a great extent, forestalls implications, such as Derrida's, of a return of the substantial subject *as* "a

constancy," or as the "formation" of deterioration or (de)constitution. That argument is developed below and in Chapter 8.

72. Lacoue-Labarthe, "The Fable," 12.

73. Lacoue-Labarthe, "The Caesura of the Speculative," 230.

74. Lacoue-Labarthe, "The Fable," 12. (my emphasis).

75. See Jacques Derrida, "From Restricted to General Economy: A Hegelianism without Reserve." Derrida is reading Georges Bataille, to investigate the possibility of freeing deconstruction from recuperation to the Hegelian dialectic of negativity.

76. Lacoue-Labarthe, "The Fable," 12 (my emphasis).

6. The Political Subject Lost between Heidegger and Nietzsche

1. See Maurice Blanchot, *The Writing of the Disaster*, 117. Blanchot says earlier in this book, and at greater length, "If there is a relation between writing and passivity, it is because both presuppose the effacement, the extenuation of the subject: both presuppose a change in time, and that between being and not-being, something which never yet takes place happens nonetheless, as having long since already happened" (14). I explore the connection between Lacoue-Labarthe and Blanchot in Chapter 8.

2. Five books might meet this description. Of the first mentioned here, Lacoue-Labarthe is the sole author; see Philippe Lacoue-Labarthe, *La Fiction du politique*, available in English as Philippe Lacoue-Labarthe, *Heidegger, Art, and Politics: The Fiction of the Political*. There are also Philippe Lacoue-Labarthe and Jean-Luc Nancy, *Le Mythe nazi* (the argument of which is represented in summary form, as "The Fiction of the Political," in Lacoue-Labarthe, *Heidegger, Art and Politics*); Philippe Lacoue-Labarthe and Jean-Luc Nancy, eds., *Les Fins de l'homme: à partir du travail de Jacques Derrida*; and two collections proceeding from the first two years (1980–81) of the Centre de Recherches Philosophiques sur le Politique, cofounded and codirected by Lacoue-Labarthe and Nancy. The latter are Philippe Lacoue-Labarthe and Jean-Luc Nancy, eds., *Rejouer le politique*, and Philippe Lacoue-Labarthe and Jean-Luc Nancy, eds., *Le Retrait du politique*. In English, Philippe Lacoue-Labarthe and Jean-Luc Nancy, *Retreating the Political*, draws from the three last-named works.

3. The project of interrogating "the essence of the political" was in fact the raison d'être for the Centre de Recherches Philosophique sur le Politique. It was explicitly when they felt that this project could no longer be advanced—because, as Nancy Fraser relates it, "a certain facile, taken-for-granted consensus [had] settled in and closed off the opening in which radical questioning had, for a time, been possible"—that, on November 16, 1984, Lacoue-Labarthe and Jean-Luc Nancy announced the indefinite suspension of the activities of the Centre. See Nancy Fraser, "The French Derrideans," 74.

4. Philippe Lacoue-Labarthe, "Transcendence Ends in Politics."

5. Martin Heidegger, "The Word of Nietzsche: God Is Dead."

6. Lacoue-Labarthe, *Heidegger, Art and Politics*, ix.

7. Jean-Joseph Goux, "Politics and Modern Art: Heidegger's Dilemma," 19.

8. For example, he says that perhaps "one could go as far as saying that the imperialist essence (not in the sense of Lenin, but in the Athenian sense of the term) — the imperialist essence of the West was fulfilled in the autorecognition of the West as absolute subject. With, for example, some phenomena that are not 'subsidiary': I mentioned to you the European catastrophe, no, the *world* catastrophe : the colonizations, the exterminations during the eighteenth century of a large part of the indigenous populations discovered on the new continents. I was thinking always in particular of the drama of the American Indians, but this is not the only thing. One could see very well how the Occident defined itself as a sort of pure subject, itself identified as a pure will, and how this will that willed itself, finished by dominating absolutely and exploiting the world, and by destroying all that did not resemble the West" (Philippe Lacoue-Labarthe, interview with the author conducted at the Université de Strasbourg, June 2, 1997).

9. Lacoue-Labarthe, *Heidegger, Art and Politics*, 17–29. This phrase was in fact the title of the article from which that chapter derives; see Philippe Lacoue-Labarthe, "Neither an Accident nor a Mistake." Here and throughout, I have for consistency refrained from following Lacoue-Labarthe's practice of enclosing the term "Rectoral Address" in quotation marks. For the text of the Rectoral Address, see Martin Heidegger, *Die Selbstbehauptung der deutschen Universität*, available in English as Martin Heidegger, "The Self-Assertion of the German University" (this translation, by Karsten Harries, is the one used in Lacoue-Labarthe, "Transcendence Ends in Politics"; a more recent translation by William S. Lewis, one that is cognizant of Harries's work, appears in Richard Wolin, ed., *The Heidegger Controversy: A Critical Reader*).

10. Lacoue-Labarthe, *Heidegger, Art and Politics*, 17. Heidegger's comment is unsourced, but the translator notes that, in the French original, Lacoue-Labarthe rendered Ralph Manheim's "place" as "historial site."

11. Lacoue-Labarthe, *Heidegger, Art and Politics*, 18–19.

12. Ibid., 20 (Lacoue-Labarthe's parentheses); quotations from Heidegger, "The Self-Assertion of the German University," 474.

13. Lacoue-Labarthe, *Heidegger, Art and Politics*, 18–19. The quotation is from a comment made by Heidegger to Cassirer; for details on its debated interpretation, see ibid., 25n.

14. One must wait for Philippe Lacoue-Labarthe, *Poetry as Experience*, 122, to find the author naming what, within this attribution of essence, cannot exculpate the perpetrators of the Shoah, or the silent Heidegger: "Herein lies Heidegger's irreparable offense: not in his declarations of 1933–34, which we can understand without approving, but in his silence on

the extermination. He should have been the first to say something. And I was wrong to think initially that it was enough to ask forgiveness. It is absolutely *unforgivable*. That is what he should have said." Lacoue-Labarthe thus belatedly counters what Critchley rightly identifies as an ignoring of the "sheer facticity" of the Holocaust, which even risks "criminally ennobling" it, as "a destinal historical necessity"; see Simon Critchley, *The Ethics of Deconstruction: Derrida and Levinas*, 214.

15. See particularly Philippe Lacoue-Labarthe, "Obliteration," 57–98.

16. Lacoue-Labarthe, *Heidegger, Art and Politics*, 36 (Lacoue-Labarthe's emphasis).

17. Ibid.

18. Ibid., 37 (Lacoue-Labarthe's emphasis).

19. Ibid.

20. Ibid.

21. As I use the term here, "Heideggerian subject" designates the "subject of metaphysics" to which the Nietzschean will to power becomes assimilated under Heidegger's scrutiny in Heidegger, "The Word of Nietzsche." The term "Heideggerian subject" does *not* refer to *Dasein*. In his attempt to overdetermine will to power, it would be counterproductive, and it would also go against all that Heidegger formally says about *Dasein*, for him to concede *Dasein* a subjectal character. At another level, though, the metaphysicality or subjectity of *Dasein* is at issue within my overall demonstration here because the "reverse" overdetermination—the Nietzschean overdetermination of *Dasein*—operates on a "metaphysical" *Dasein*. That is, it operates at the point where *Dasein* has those dimensions of metaphysicality/subjectity formally denied it by Heidegger. This makes the two overdeterminations mutually and hyperbolically interactive: Heidegger converts Nietzschean will to metaphysics, and Nietzsche converts Heideggerian "metaphysics" to will. Is the attribution of a metaphysically related subjectivity to *Dasein* sustainable? I pursue this point in Chapter 7. *Dasein* is not, of course, formally a subject. But it arguably cannot escape connotations of subjectivity; I pointed these out in Chapter 1, in conjunction with the later Heidegger's description of *Dasein* as "shepherd of Being," and with Marion's notion of the "autarky" of *Dasein* (see Jean-Luc Marion, "The Final Appeal of the Subject"). Heidegger seems to envisage, in the latter days of the unconcealment of Being, a role for what might be called a cryptometaphysical subject, *as* that locus of the self-giving of Being by which metaphysics, and thus the subject itself, is overcome. More to the point, at the time of Heidegger's Rectoral Address (1933), *Dasein*, as a mode of apprehension of Being, is already envisaged as a fundamental determination of Being and as a locus of *decision*; this is a significant part of Lacoue-Labarthe's argument in "Transcendence Ends in Politics." It is thus that *Dasein* becomes open to Nietzschean overdetermination as a German *political* subject of will. This is the subject that—in what Heidegger's Rectoral

Address calls the "questioning unguarded holding of one's ground" (Heidegger, "The Self-Assertion of the German University," 474,) and what *Being and Time* calls "our Being-with-one-another in the same world and in the resoluteness for definite possibilities" (Martin Heidegger, *Being and Time*, [384], 352; see n. 30 to Chapter 1, above, for a reminder about my system of citing this work) — can correspond to the "mission of completing science," as Lacoue-Labarthe puts it in "Transcendence Ends in Politics," 284–85.

22. Lacoue-Labarthe, "Transcendence Ends in Politics," 268.

23. Heidegger, "The Self-Assertion of the German University," 471, quoted in Lacoue-Labarthe, "Transcendence Ends in Politics," 273. The interview was given to *Der Spiegel*; the translation cited in "Transcendence Ends in Politics" is by David Schendler and was published in 1977 (see Martin Heidegger, "'Only a God Can Save Us Now': An Interview with Martin Heidegger"). Further citations of this interview are to Maria Alter and John D. Caputo's more recent translation; see Martin Heidegger, "Only a God Can Save Us: *Der Spiegel's* Interview with Martin Heidegger."

24. Lacoue-Labarthe, "Transcendence Ends in Politics," 273. In raising the question, Heidegger in part intended, proactively as it were, to forestall threats to the self-understanding of the university, arising from Nationalist Socialist attempts to reinterpret science as fundamentally "political," in the sense of being oriented to "the practical needs of the people"; see Heidegger, "Only a God Can Save Us," 95.

25. Lacoue-Labarthe, "Transcendence Ends in Politics," 274–75. Heidegger's project is also aimed at preventing the scientification of philosophy, a threat arising with neo-Kantianism. The key text is Martin Heidegger, *Kant and the Problem of Metaphysics*. Bourdieu says that Heidegger's "'foundational thinking' (*das wesentliche Denken*) [uses] the capital of philosophical authority held by the Kantian tradition [to attack Reason as the enemy of thought]. . . . This masterly strategy enables the neo-Kantians to be attacked, but in the name of Kantianism"; see Pierre Bourdieu, *The Political Ontology of Martin Heidegger*, 58–59.

26. Or the goal is metapolitical. The curious hesitancy, in the Rectoral Address, between philosophical and political foundationalism — or, from another angle, between whether the essence of *metaphysics* is provided by *will*, or vice versa — is, in one sense, the theme of this chapter. Löwith puts it well: "Measured by philosophical standards, his discourse is from beginning to end of a rare ambiguity, for it manages to subordinate existential and ontological categories to the historical 'moment' so that they create the illusion that their philosophical intentions have an a priori applicability to the political situation . . . so that by the end of the lecture the listener does not know whether to turn to read Diels on the 'the Pre-Socratics' or join the S.A."; see Karl Löwith, "Les implications politiques de la philosophie de l'existence chez Heidegger," cited by Bourdieu, *The Political Ontology of Martin Heidegger*, 5.

27. Heidegger, "The Self-Assertion of the German University," 470, quoted in Lacoue-Labarthe, "Transcendence Ends in Politics," 277. Jacques Derrida tracks the mention of the spiritual in this address as signaling Heidegger's unwitting retreat from the steadfast refusal of metaphysical subjectity that formally characterizes his thought. He argues that in the Rectoral Address, "spirit" (*Geist*) loses its quotation marks, becoming the mark of a metaphysical subject, to the realization of which *Führung* is oriented. He examines the decisive appeal to *Geist* in the key paragraphs of the address—the people's "true spiritual world," "spirit is the being-resolved to the essence of Being," "the spiritual world of a people is . . . the deepest power of conservation of its forces of earth and blood," and so on—and concludes that there is here, "for the first time to my knowledge . . . [Heidegger's] definition of spirit. It is certainly presented in the form of a definition: S is P." Furthermore, spirit is conveyed here as an imprint (*Gepräge*); as such, it cannot but affirm the totalitarianism that is the essential evil of biologism, naturalism, and genetic racism, even when it condemns these. That is, one cannot thereafter oppose these "except by reinscribing spirit in an oppositional determination, by once again making it a unilaterality of subjectity, even if in its voluntarist form." See Jacques Derrida, *Of Spirit: Heidegger and the Question*, 31, 36, 39–40. Derrida does not take up the question of whether the voluntarism in the address is Nietzschean. However, what his argument *does* imply is that *if* (Nietzschean) will is the subject of the address, then this Nietzschean overdetermination is wrested back to metaphysical subjectity by Heidegger's appeal to *Geist*. This suggests, by another route, the metaphysical overdetermination (of the Nietzschean subject of the Rectoral Address) that forms the second half of my demonstration of the hyperbological loss occurring "between" Heideggerian and Nietzschean subjectal representations.

28. Lacoue-Labarthe, "Transcendence Ends in Politics," 279, quoting Heidegger, "The Self-Assertion of the German University," 471.

29. Lacoue-Labarthe, "Transcendence Ends in Politics," 281, quoting Heidegger, "The Self-Assertion of the German University," 473.

30. Lacoue-Labarthe, "Transcendence Ends in Politics," 282.

31. Martin Heidegger, "What Is Metaphysics?," 243 (Heidegger's emphasis). As Heidegger presents this thought in "The Self-Assertion of the German University," humanism, as the irruption of knowing, is identified essentially with mankind as a whole, and then surrogately, as it were, with the German people. Subtle contravention of official Nazism is already implied here. By 1940, the same thought, from "Plato's Theory of Truth," repeated in a university journal, *Jahrbuch für geistige Uberlieferung*, was found to contradict the reviewer Wilhelm Brachmann's dictum, adopted quasi-officially by the party, that "the term 'humanism' will have to give way to the term 'Indo-Germanic intellectual history' . . . [which] stands guard for the genetically determined intellectual inheritance of Indo-Germanic culture in

general"; it was only upon Mussolini's intervention that Heidegger's article escaped excision. See Hugo Ott, *Martin Heidegger: A Political Life*, 285–88.

32. Heidegger, "The Self-Assertion of the German University," 474–75, quoted in Lacoue-Labarthe, "Transcendence Ends in Politics," 284 (Heidegger's emphasis).

33. This affinity is ultimately one of language. In 1966, Heidegger retains this hope for the German people as the locale for a future thinking that will revisit and transform the origin and calling of the technological world so that it undergoes a transcending (Hegelian) reversal: "I have in mind especially the inner relationship of the German language with the language of the Greeks and with their thought. . . . When [the French] begin to think, they speak German, being sure they could not make it with their own language. . . . We would do well . . . to finally consider the grave consequences of the transformation which Greek thought experienced when it was translated into Roman Latin. Indeed this today, even this, blocks the way to an adequate reflection on the fundamental words of Greek thought." See Heidegger, "Only a God Can Save Us," 113.

34. Lacoue-Labarthe, "Transcendence Ends in Politics," 286.

35. Ibid., 290.

36. Ibid., 292.

37. Ibid., 294.

38. Ibid., 294–95.

39. Ibid., 295.

40. Heidegger, "The Self-Assertion of the German University," 472, quoted in Lacoue-Labarthe, "Transcendence Ends in Politics," 294.

41. Lacoue-Labarthe, "Transcendence Ends in Politics," 297.

42. Lacoue-Labarthe is again here reminiscent of Blanchot.

43. Heidegger, "The Self-Assertion of the German University," 473, quoted in Lacoue-Labarthe, "Transcendence Ends in Politics," 298–99 (Heidegger's emphasis).

44. "Thought from out of the destining of Being, the *nihil* in 'nihilism' means that *Nothing* is befalling Being. Being is not coming into the light of its own essence. In the appearing of whatever is as such, Being itself remains wanting. The truth of Being falls from memory. It remains forgotten"; see Heidegger, "The Word of Nietzsche," 109–10 (Heidegger's emphasis).

45. Heidegger, "The Word of Nietzsche," 53.

46. Ibid.

47. Ibid., 55.

48. Ibid., 61.

49. Ibid., 63.

50. Ibid.

51. Ibid., 69.

52. Friedrich Nietzsche, *The Will to Power*, aphorism 14, 1887, quoted in Heidegger, "The Word of Nietzsche," 70.

53. Heidegger, "The Word of Nietzsche," 75.
54. Ibid.
55. Ibid., 79–82.
56. Ibid., 83.
57. Ibid. (Heidegger's emphasis); the quotation is from Nietzsche, *The Will to Power*, aphorism 588, 1887–88.
58. Heidegger, "The Word of Nietzsche," 91.
59. Ibid., 93.
60. Ibid., 95.
61. Ibid., 97.
62. Ibid.
63. Ibid., 100.
64. Ibid.
65. Ibid.
66. Ibid., 102.
67. Ibid.
68. Ibid.
69. Heidegger, "The Word of Nietzsche," 103.
70. Ibid., 109 (my emphasis).
71. Ibid., 111.
72. Ibid., 63.

7. Lacoue-Labarthe and Jean-Luc Nancy: Sublime Truth Perpetually Offered as Its Other

1. Jean-Luc Nancy, *The Gravity of Thought*.
2. See n. 3 to Chapter 4, above. The texts in question, originally published in Jean-François Courtine et al., *Du Sublime*, are Philippe Lacoue-Labarthe, "La Vérité sublime," and Jean-Luc Nancy, "L'Offrande sublime." See also Jean François Courtine et al., *Of the Sublime: Presence in Question*; Philippe Lacoue-Labarthe, "Sublime Truth"; Jean-Luc Nancy, "The Sublime Offering."
3. Jean-Luc Nancy, *La Communauté désoeuvrée*, available in English as *The Inoperative Community*; and Jean-Luc Nancy, *L'Expérience de la liberté*, found in English as *The Experience of Freedom*. In Bridget McDonald's translation of the latter, Nancy says: "We share what divides us: the freedom of an incalculable and improbable *coming* to presence of being, which only brings us into presence as the *ones* of the *others*. This is the coming to presence of our freedom" (95; Nancy's emphasis). But, coming to presence as communal being, in *factual* freedom, being is itself precluded from the possibility of constituting a subject. It remains unconstrained by identity, and so do its participant units of will or decision. Here, Nancian freedom is, as Librett puts it, "the freedom of the subject from itself, in the sense of the freedom of the subject from the obligation not to be other than it is at any given moment"; see Jeffrey S. Librett, "Interruptions of Necessity: Being between Meaning and Power in Jean-Luc Nancy," 136n.

4. *L'expérience*, more than *vécu*; see n. 41 to Chapter 8, below, which relates this to *Erfahrung* and *Erlebnis*.

5. "The Forgetting of Philosophy" is the title of the formerly independent work that comprises the first half of the book.

6. Nancy, *The Gravity of Thought*, 10 (Nancy's emphasis).

7. Ibid.

8. Ibid., 2 (Nancy's emphasis).

9. Philippe Lacoue-Labarthe, "The Fable," 12 (translation altered).

10. Ibid. (translation altered).

11. Francis Fischer, "Jean-Luc Nancy: The Place of a Thinking," 35.

12. Jean-Luc Nancy, "De l'écriture: qu'elle ne révèle rien," 107, quoted from Richard Stamp's translation in Fischer, "Jean-Luc Nancy: The Place of a Thinking," 35 (Nancy's emphasis).

13. Jean-Luc Nancy, *Une Pensée finie*, 62, quoted from Stamp's translation in Fischer, "Jean-Luc Nancy: The Place of a Thinking," 35.

14. See Chapters 2 and 8, this volume.

15. Nancy, *The Gravity of Thought*, 10 (Nancy's emphasis).

16. Ibid., 11.

17. Philippe Lacoue-Labarthe and Jean-Luc Nancy, *The Literary Absolute*, 123. In Chapter 8, I further explore this aspect of "neutral manifestation" in Blanchot as it interacts with the possibility of a subject that "is" language.

18. Nancy, *The Gravity of Thought*, 31.

19. Ibid. As Nancy describes it, the "law of *Verstellung*" corresponds to an automatic displacement of any meaning in the subject's attempt to grasp it. This displacement introduces distance into the subject's grasp of "itself," that is, of the self that is the subject of the desire for meaning.

20. Ibid., 31–36.

21. Ibid., 35.

22. Ibid., 43–45.

23. Ibid., 43.

24. Ibid., 44 (translation adapted).

25. Lacoue-Labarthe, "The Fable," 12. As used here and elsewhere in this chapter, "experience" is *l'expérience*, corresponding to *Erfahrung*, but with the proviso mentioned in Chapter 2, regarding the representational passage into *Erlebnis*, understood. Generally speaking, this latter notion corresponds, in Nancy, Lacoue-Labarthe, and Blanchot, to *vécu* (real-life experience).

26. I use the word "unaccomplishes" here to encapsulate Lacoue-Labarthe's description of what writing does to experience in "The Fable." The word itself (*inaccomplir*) is used by him in a comparable way to describe how politics supplements/supplants philosophy; see Philippe Lacoue-Labarthe, "Transcendence Ends in Politics," 270.

27. See the translator's note in Fischer, "Jean-Luc Nancy: The Place of a Thinking," 37.

28. Philippe Lacoue-Labarthe, "Sublime Truth"; Jean-Luc Nancy, "The Sublime Offering."

29. Lacoue-Labarthe, "Sublime Truth," 73.

30. Ibid.

31. Immanuel Kant, *Critique of Judgment*, sec. 29 / 115 (Bernard translation)/135 (Pluhar translation), quoted in Lacoue-Labarthe, "Sublime Truth," 71.

32. Kant, *Critique of Judgment*, sec. 49/160 (Bernard translation)/185 (Pluhar translation), quoted in Lacoue-Labarthe, "Sublime Truth," 72.

33. Lacoue-Labarthe, "Sublime Truth," 74: "qu'il y a de l'imprésentable." Throughout "Sublime Truth," *l'imprésentable* is translated as "the nonpresentable" rather than as "the unpresentable," and its cognates are rendered likewise. Obviously, the word "nonpresentable," as opposed to "unpresentable," has the virtue of not characterizing the absence of presentability as a lack. It thus at least *suggests* the nonpresented as a *radical* other to the presented, though, as Lacoue-Labarthe would readily acknowledge, and as several of my readings in this work are intended to emphasize, the unpresentable is not so easily saved from recuperation to presentability. In any case, for consistency in this chapter, I follow the terminology associated with nonpresentability. Elsewhere I have reverted to "unpresentability" and its cognates, the better to recall the above recuperation, which provides a setting for *hyperbological* (as opposed to more simple) subjectal loss.

34. Lacoue-Labarthe, "Sublime Truth," 76.

35. Ibid., 79.

36. Ibid., 78 (Lacoue-Labarthe's emphasis).

37. Martin Heidegger, *Nietzsche*, 100 (German edition)/84 (English edition).

38. Lacoue-Labarthe, "Sublime Truth," 81.

39. Ibid., 82.

40. Ibid., 83.

41. Ibid., 84.

42. Ibid., 86. His point of reference here, as it has been for Heidegger's analysis also, is Hegel's *Aesthetics*; see George William Friedrich Hegel, *Aesthetics: Lectures on Fine Art*.

43. Lacoue-Labarthe, "Sublime Truth," 86; quotation from George William Friedrich Hegel, *Lectures on the Philosophy of Religion*, vol. 2: *Determinate Religion*, 137.

44. Lacoue-Labarthe, "Sublime Truth," 87; quotation from Sigmund Freud, *Character and Culture*, 103. The original is found in Freud, "Der Moses des Michaelangelo," 217.

45. Lacoue-Labarthe, "Sublime Truth," 89.

46. Ibid. (Lacoue-Labarthe's emphasis).

47. Ibid., 90.

48. Ibid.

49. Ibid., 91.

50. Martin Heidegger, "Der Ursprung des Kunstwerkes," available in English as "The Origin of the Work of Art."

51. Lacoue-Labarthe, "Sublime Truth," 93–94. The interplay emphasized here is between the *Geheure* (the familiar, ordinary), the *nicht geheuer* (the unfamilar, nonordinary) and the *Ungeheure* (the uncanny). Lacoue-Labarthe again exploits, under another name and context, the resources of the uncanny (*Unheimlichkeit*) that have been in evidence earlier (see Philippe Lacoue-Labarthe, "The Echo of the Subject," 189 ff.; see also Chapter 3, this volume). The same implication however, is present here as there: of an interruption of meaning. When Heidegger says, "Das Geheure ist im Grunde nicht geheuer," the *nicht geheuer* fails to be referable without remainder to the *Geheure*; this is emphasized by its variant repetition almost immediately as *das Ungeheure*. Equally, in "The Echo of the Subject," *Unheimlichkeit* fails to signify a *specifiable* absence of the subject.

52. Lacoue-Labarthe, "Sublime Truth," 93; quotation from Heidegger, "The Origin of the Work of Art," 55/"Der Ursprung des Kunstwerkes," 40.

53. Lacoue-Labarthe, "Sublime Truth," 94 (Lacoue-Labarthe's emphasis).

54. Ibid., 95.

55. Ibid.

56. Ibid.

57. Ibid.

58. ". . . *le sublime est la présentation de ceci qu'il y de la présentation*"; see Lacoue-Labarthe, "Sublime Truth," 96/"La Vérité sublime," 131.

59. Lacoue-Labarthe, "Sublime Truth," 96.

60. Ibid. The text now followed in "Sublime Truth" is Longinus, *On the Sublime*; the French edition used by Lacoue-Labarthe is *Du Sublime*. Hereafter, I follow the practice of Lacoue-Labarthe, "Sublime Truth," in referring to the French edition by section and chapter, followed by the page number(s) in the English edition.

61. Lacoue-Labarthe, "Sublime Truth," 97.

62. Kant, *Critique of Judgment*, sec. 46/150 (Bernard translation), quoted in Lacoue-Labarthe, "Sublime Truth," 97 (Kant's emphasis).

63. Longinus, *Du Sublime*, sec. II, chap. 3/*On the Sublime*, 14, quoted in Lacoue-Labarthe, "Sublime Truth," 99.

64. The quotation from which Lacoue-Labarthe derives this "necessary supplementarity" asserts that "the fact itself that there should be one among the things which one finds in discourses which depends only on *phusis*, from no other place than from *technē* we have to learn it"; see Lacoue-Labarthe, "Sublime Truth," 99.

65. Lacoue-Labarthe, "Sublime Truth," 99.

66. Ibid., 100. See also Aristotle, *Poetics*, 47.

67. Courtine et al., *Of the Sublime*, 234n. The reference is to Martin Heidegger, *Introduction to Metaphysics*, 160. In Chapter 6 of this volume, the same thought attracted notice when it occurred in the setting of Heidegger's Rectoral Address. There, Lacoue-Labarthe found it to be overdetermined by a Nietzschean account of Being as the will to power. Here, he appears to have more confidence that Heidegger, perhaps free from the constraints of negotiation with Nationalist Socialist thought, is answering to Aristotle alone.

68. Lacoue-Labarthe, "Sublime Truth," 100. The author is referring in particular to Emmanuel Martineau, "Mimésis dans la 'Poétique': pour une solution phénoménologique."

69. Longinus, *Du Sublime*, sec. XXII, chap. 1/*On the Sublime*, 119–20, quoted in Lacoue-Labarthe, "Sublime Truth," 103.

70. Lacoue-Labarthe, "Sublime Truth," 103.

71. Ibid., 104.

72. Longinus, *Du Sublime*, sec. XXVII, chaps. 2–3/*On the Sublime*, 105–20; quoted in Lacoue-Labarthe, "Sublime Truth," 104.

73. Lacoue-Labarthe, "Sublime Truth," 104 (translation adapted).

74. Ibid., 105–6.

75. Ibid., 107 (Lacoue-Labarthe's translation). Benjamin's original says, "Nicht Schein, nicht Hülle für ein anderes ist die Schönheit. Sie selbst ist nicht Erscheinung, sondern durchaus Wesen, ein solches freilich, welches wesenhaft sich selbst gleich nur unter der Verhüllung bleibt"; see Walter Benjamin, "Goethes Wahlverwandtschaften," 1, 195.

76. Mention can be made here of a disagreement between Lacoue-Labarthe and Nancy over the scope of the noneidetic in Kant. For Nancy, Kant fundamentally eschews the claim that art is *representation*. Nancy says, "For Kant, the beautiful and the sublime have in common that they have to do with presentation and only with presentation. . . . [When the imagination presents an image] . . . [it] presents to itself this: that there is a free accord between the sensible . . . and a unity. . . . The image here is not the representative image, and it is not the object. It is not the placing-in-form of something else, but form forming itself, for itself, without object: fundamentally, art, according to Kant, represents nothing in either the beautiful or the sublime"; see Nancy, "The Sublime Offering," 28–29. Now, this stance on the part of Kant might be construed as an aesthetics (of nonrepresentation), or a nonaesthetics (if by "aesthetics" one means a theory of art as representation) or, again, as a "suppressed aesthetics" (if one considers art as being refused representational status by virtue of being accorded another end). Curiously, Nancy later seems to combine all three assessments. But he has in mind a definitional framework of the aesthetic that is other than representational. He says, "On the one hand, it is aesthetics as a regional philosophical discipline that is refused in the thought of art seized by the sublime. Kant is the first to do justice to the aesthetic at the heart of what one can call a

'first philosophy': but he is also, and for this very reason, the first to sup-
press aesthetics as a part or domain of philosophy. As is well known, there
is no Kantian aesthetics. And there is not, after Kant, any thought of art (or
of the beautiful) that does not refuse aesthetics and interrogate in art something other than art" (27). Clearly, there is here an implied and reasonable
definition of aesthetics as that which interrogates, in art, not "something
other than art," but art itself. Under this definition, Kant's third *Critique*
would comprise an *attempted* aesthetics that fails, or an aesthetics that is not
an aesthetics because it refuses aesthetics. This sidestepping of the definition of aesthetics in terms of representation has its own problems, however.
Lacoue-Labarthe indicates this when he suggests, *pace* Nancy, that Kant—
and even Hegel, who refuses art as aesthetic-eidetic—cannot help having,
by dint of *whatever* reflection on art they provide, an aesthetics. Equally, he
insists that aesthetics *is* refused here. He says that "to 'interrogate in art
something other than art' is not perhaps a sufficient criterion [for 'refusal of
the aesthetic']: the more Hegel grants art the function of the presentation of
truth . . . the more he confirms the autotelic character of art, and the more
he consecrates aesthetics to the grasping of art in its essence"; see Courtine
et al., *Of the Sublime*, 230–31n. Lacoue-Labarthe's point is that *every* interrogation of "art itself" becomes an interrogation in art of *something else*, and
thus, in Nancy's terms, a refusal of aesthetics. This means that *no* aesthetics
remains an aesthetics, a point that is precisely supported by Nancy's account of art as seized by the sublime. But, for this very reason, it is pointless
to deny the use of the term "aesthetics" to an enterprise such as Kant's, or
to successive aesthetic enterprises. In my view, Lacoue-Labarthe's point is
finally valid because the question of what art *represents* cannot be avoided,
if only as the question of what art represents "in itself." Or, to make this
reply in Nancy's terms: to "interrogate" art (say, with any question beginning with the word "what") is already to presume it as representational. The
challenge is to seek an account of art whereby its capacity to represent (a
subject) is *both* given credence *and* denied essential status. This is what the
hyperbological "mechanism," rightly understood, effects.

77. Nancy, "The Sublime Offering," 26 ("positive" is my word).
78. Ibid., 27.
79. Ibid., 29.
80. Ibid., 31.
81. See "Nancy's *The Gravity of Thought*: Sense and Writing in Interplay,"
above.
82. Nancy, "The Sublime Offering," 33–34.
83. Ibid., 38.
84. Nancy says, "Unity comes to [a multiplicity] from its limit . . . , but
that there *is* this unity . . . comes from the external border, from the unlimited raising and razing of the limit"; see ibid., 37–38 (my ellipses).
85. Ibid., 46 (translation adapted).

86. Lacoue-Labarthe and Nancy, *The Literary Absolute*, 29.
87. Nancy, "The Sublime Offering," 46.
88. Ibid., 47.
89. Ibid.
90. Ibid. (translation adapted).
91. Ibid., 48.
92. Ibid., 50.

8. Lacoue-Labarthe between Derrida and Blanchot: Movement as Marking the Subject-in-Loss

1. At one level, this casting cannot fail to occur. See below, and see Philippe Lacoue-Labarthe, "The Caesura of the Speculative," 231. The logic of *entfernung*, or dis(distancing), remains an attempt at "exiting *from within* the onto-theo-logic." Here, the "from within" points to the reinforcement of traditional subjectivity whenever *entfernung* is explicated as "hyperbologic"; the question is whether the dimension of *exit* from ontotheology, which the hyperbologic also effects, can be included within the account of an alternative *subjectivity*, one for which hyperbological exchange is not, however, a *ground*.

2. To shadow my reflections in this chapter, here is Lacoue-Labarthe writing on Celan and extrapolating Celan's "wholly other" as disrupting the same from within: "The same (the Subject) does not, as speculative logic believes, go outside of the self and pass into its other, with a view to turning and relating back to the self so as to establish itself as such. But under the (original) gift of the other to which it already always relates itself, the same is the *pure movement* that allows the intimate gaping—which is, within the self, its 'original outside self' (time)—to hollow itself out, to open and spread"; see Philippe Lacoue-Labarthe, *Poetry as Experience*, 61 (my emphasis). This thought, of a subject disrupted by an already inner exteriority, is not in itself new. But what is additionally proposed here is a subject as *movement* corresponding to this exchange; in these terms, this movement is clearly consonant with hyperbological loss of the metaphysical subject. Is this, then—with all due provisos regarding inevitable metaphysical return—a (radically) postmetaphysical Lacoue-Labarthian subject?

3. See Chapter 1, this volume.

4. "Positively," here, takes its departure from Lacoue-Labarthe's reference to "something like a (de)-construction . . . more positive than critical, something, as it were, *not very negative*"; see Philippe Lacoue-Labarthe, "Typography," 123. For Derrida, Lacoue-Labarthe means thereby to note the survival of the philosophical, even in its very lapsing; see Jacques Derrida, "Introduction: Desistance," 27. I ask here and explore later whether something even more "positive," even radically nonphilosophical, might survive in Lacoue-Labarthe, *à la* Blanchot.

5. Philippe Lacoue-Labarthe, interview with the author conducted at the Université de Strasbourg, June 2, 1997.

6. See below. Here, a brief emblematic statement must suffice: "The step 'outside philosophy' is much more difficult to conceive than is generally imagined by those who think they made it long ago with cavalier ease"; see Jacques Derrida, *Writing and Difference*, 284.

7. See Chapter 3, this volume.

8. Avatars of this deconstructive loss have already appeared in several of my analyses of Lacoue-Labarthian hyperbology. As yet, though, I have carefully refrained from implying any thoroughgoing equivalence between the two, and the reason for that becomes clear in this chapter.

9. Derrida, "Introduction: Desistance," 42.

10. Ibid., 7.

11. Ibid., 17 (Derrida's emphasis; translation altered to leave the word *désistance* untranslated).

12. Philippe Lacoue-Labarthe, "Obliteration," 81–82 (Lacoue-Labarthe's emphasis; translation altered).

13. Derrida, "Introduction: Desistance," 17n.

14. Ibid., 16–17n (Derrida's emphasis; translation altered, to leave the word *désistance* untranslated).

15. Ibid., 19–21 (Derrida's emphasis). I have not been able to find, *as such*, in Lacoue-Labarthe, Derrida's formulation "primary *destination* of the unthought"/"*destination* majeure de l'impensé(e)"; see Jacques Derrida, "Introduction: Desistance," 20/Jacques Derrida, "Désistance," 616. Lacoue-Labarthe speaks of the "order of the *unthought*"/"de l'ordre de l'*impensé*"; see Philippe Lacoue-Labarthe, "Typography," 60/Philippe Lacoue-Labarthe, "Typographie," 187. He speaks also of the Heideggerian requirement that "thought, in its most intimate essence, in its own destiny, thinks itself as the *unthought*"/"la pensée, dans son essence la plus intime, dans son destin propre, se pense comme l'*impensé*"; see Philippe Lacoue-Labarthe, "Obliteration," 85 (translation amended)/Philippe Lacoue-Labarthe, "L'Oblitération," 157. And again, in "Obliteration," quoting Heidegger, he speaks of "'loss' as nothing other than *appropriation* itself, the *Verwindung* of the unthought" (87). So I take the formulation and emphasis to be Derrida's, though I agree that the thrust of Lacoue-Labarthe's critique of Heidegger involves construing the "unthought" as directional and unitary.

16. Derrida, "Introduction: Desistance," 21.

17. Ibid., 2.

18. I have discussed Plato in this context in Chapter 2, and Nietzsche in Chapter 5; see also below.

19. A well-known illustration of this is found in Jacques Derrida, "Plato's Pharmacy" 95–105; I refer to this in n. 28 to Chapter 2, above. Writing is invented as a *pharmakos*, or drug, to aid memory, but the meaning of *pharmakos*, as also of English "drug," becomes undecidable between "medicine" and "poison."

20. Derrida, "Introduction: Desistance," 30n, referring to Lacoue-Labarthe, "Typography," 138.

21. Derrida, "Introduction: Desistance," 30n.
22. Ibid.
23. Ibid.
24. Ibid. (translation altered to leave *désistance* untranslated).
25. Ibid., 1–15. This choice of the extended parenthetical for the purpose of investigating the "translatability" of Lacoue-Labarthe's *se désister*, with *désistance* "hovering off-stage," as it were, provides its own eloquence on the matter of Derrida's "avoiding without avoiding" an assimilatory comment on Lacoue-Labarthe.
26. Ibid., 7 (Derrida's emphasis).
27. Ibid., 8 (Derrida's emphasis).
28. Ibid., 16–17.
29. Kevin Hart, *Losing the Power to Say "I": An Essay Celebrating the Four Hundredth Anniversary of the Birth of René Descartes*.
30. Maurice Blanchot, *L'Entretien infini*, 442; Maurice Blanchot, *The Infinite Conversation*, 300 (bracketed interpolations in original of the English translation).
31. Leslie Hill, *Blanchot: Extreme Contemporary*, 130.
32. Maurice Blanchot, "Literature and the Right to Death," 42 (Lydia Davis's translation).
33. Kevin Hart, "The Blanchot Experience," 17–19.
34. Hill, *Blanchot*, 130; Hart, "The Blanchot Experience," 17.
35. Blanchot, "Literature and the Right to Death," 327 (Charlotte Mandell's translation; Blanchot's emphasis). Hill (*Blanchot*, 112) translates this passage as "the cat as it is, the pebble seen *from the side of things*, not man in general, but this man and, in this man, what man rejects in order to speak of him, which is the founding of speech and which speech excludes in order to speak, the abyss." Blanchot's idiom is typically fragmented and complex here; nevertheless, Hill's translation appears idiosyncratic in its focus on "*this* man"; Lydia Davis's translation of this passage is in virtually complete agreement with Mandell's and against Hill's.
36. See Chapter 6 for my reference to Blanchot's book bearing this title. Writing marks and finally respects the silence and passivity, the "extenuation of the subject," to which every disaster bears infinitely painful witness.
37. Hill, *Blanchot*, 112.
38. Blanchot, "Literature and the Right to Death," 327 (Mandell translation).
39. Ibid.
40. See Chapter 5, this volume.
41. Philippe Lacoue-Labarthe, "The Fable," 12 (translation altered). "Experience," as it is referred to here, is both formed *and* lost in the passage from *Erfahrung* to *Erlebnis*. In fact, as I shall explain below, Blanchot tends to explore experience *as* that passage, that is, as "the experience of non-experience." In such terms, experience might perhaps be called "transcen-

dental," to distinguish it from phenomenal experience; the divisions involved would be roughly those dividing *Erfahrung* from *Erlebnis*, though "transcendental experience," spoken of *as* the passage between the two, cannot but have some faint phenomenological dimensions. These would pertain to an awareness of the failure of, or division in, or derivative nature of, one's self-awareness. In both Blanchot and Lacoue-Labarthe, this experience dislocates the experiencing self by sourcing the self simultaneously "outside" itself (for example, in language), or anteriorly to itself (for example, in a past that has never been present). These possibilities I have to some extent already explored; they will be further explored below. For the moment, there is the following specific sense in which the experience that the two authors explore is "transcendental": it is the experience of the dislocation of self accompanying every phenomenal experience of the "I," as its condition of possibility. For discussion of the distinctions here (but not for the specific descriptions I have employed), I am indebted to Kevin Hart, "The Experience of Poetry."

42. Lacoue-Labarthe, "The Fable," 2 (Lacoue-Labarthe's emphasis and first ellipsis; second ellipsis mine).

43. Ibid., 9.

44. Ibid. (Lacoue-Labarthe's emphasis).

45. Lacoue-Labarthe, "Obliteration," 81.

46. Ibid.

47. Blanchot quotes Hegel himself on this divine function of language: "It immediately overturns what it names in order to transform it into something else"; but then he gently asks whether this experience (which yields being as lost) might not also evade the economy of being, by marking "impossibility, neither negation nor affirmation [indicating] what in being has always *preceded* being and yields to no ontology?" See Blanchot, *The Infinite Conversation*, 35, 47 (Blanchot's emphasis).

48. Maurice Blanchot, *Le Pas au-delà*, 104; Maurice Blanchot, *The Step Not Beyond*, 74 (translation altered).

49. Blanchot, *Le Pas au-delà*, 107; Blanchot, *The Step Not Beyond*, 77.

50. Blanchot, *The Step Not Beyond*, 75–76.

51. Kevin Hart, *Losing the Power to Say "I,"* 6.

52. The remainder of this section constitutes a rehearsal of and, in places, a dialogue with the argument in Hart, *Losing the Power to Say "I."* Hereafter, I will not repeat Hart's footnoting where this involves points I have already made; my footnoting of Hart or Blanchot will refer to as yet uncanvased points made by Hart, and/or to direct quotations from Hart or Blanchot.

53. Hart, *Losing the Power to Say "I,"* 33.

54. Ibid.

55. Ibid.

56. Blanchot, *The Infinite Conversation*, 176–77. Hart's entire reflection in *Losing the Power to Say "I"* takes the extended quotation leading to this thought as its point of departure.

57. Hart, *Losing the Power to Say "I,"* 21. His summary pertains to Blanchot, *The Infinite Conversation*, 356–57, where the reflection is upon a French translation of Novalis's *Monologue*, including the comments that "only a writer is inhabited by language, inhabited by speech," and "to speak for the sake of speaking is the formula for deliverance"; see Novalis, *Monologue*, 84. Language as "matter" or "nature" is certainly canvased there: "The particular quality of language, the fact that it is concerned only with itself, is known to no one . . . ; it is the same with language as with mathematical formulae. . . . They play only with themselves, express nothing but their own marvellous nature, and just for this reason they are so expressive—just for this reason the strange play of relations between things is mirrored in them"; see Novalis, *Monologue*, 83.

58. Hart, *Losing the Power to Say "I,"* 21–22.

59. Ibid., 22.

60. Ibid., 27.

61. Blanchot, *The Infinite Conversation*, 207, 210; Hart, *Losing the Power to Say "I,"* 31 (Hart's ellipses).

62. Blanchot, *The Infinite Conversation*, 44, 45.

63. Hart, *Losing the Power to Say "I,"* 31.

64. Ibid., 37.

65. As I have pointed out, *Dasein*, as Being-in-the world, is the site for the manifestation of the difference between Being and beings and is formally contrasted to masterful Cartesian subjectivity; finally, however, it might well be assimilable to this subjectivity (Marion's attribution of autarky applies here). To go in another direction: Heideggerian Being, which conceals itself (in giving itself in difference), also bids to become an absolute subject, by way of the unicity associated with its unconcealment *through and in* Dasein—especially as it looks to a once and future "definitive" self-giving by this means, repeating its unconcealing to the pre-Socratic Greeks; see Chapter 6, this volume. Derrida, too, notes that "the entity exemplary for a reading of the meaning of Being, is the entity that *we* are, . . . we who . . . have this relation to self that is lacking in everything that is not *Dasein*. Even if *Dasein* is not the subject, this point of departure . . . remains analogous, in its 'logic,' to what he inherits in undertaking to deconstruct it"; see Jacques Derrida, "'Eating Well' or the Calculation of the Subject," 104 (my ellipses).

66. Hart, *Losing the Power to Say "I,"* 21.

67. By contrast, as Hart says on Blanchot's behalf, "What Literature presents is, in all rigour, the unpresentable *as* unpresentable"; see ibid., 22 (Hart's emphasis).

68. Lacoue-Labarthe, "Obliteration," 81. Lacoue-Labarthe's confirmation here—that what interests him in the subject is "irreducible to any subjectivity (that is, to any objectivity)"—must be taken seriously. This is crucial, if a prospective Lacoue-Labarthian subjectivity identified with his

interest in the "defeat of the subject in the subject or *as* the subject" is to remain distinguishable from "classical" subjectivity, which renders the subject objectively. As I have pointed out, Derrida is reluctant to go past Lacoue-Labarthe's use of the word "*as*" here, considering that it generates a Lacoue-Labarthian subject as "formation" of the movement of its (own) deconstitution. But, given the above disclaimer, it is unlikely that Lacoue-Labarthe would envisage an explanation of that type here.

69. Lacoue-Labarthe, "Diderot: Paradox and Mimesis," 252.

70. Lacoue-Labarthe, "The Caesura of the Speculative," 230; Friedrich Hölderlin, "Der Grund zum Empedocles," 572; Friedrich Hölderlin, "The Ground for Empedocles." 51.

71. Lacoue-Labarthe has mentioned, as significantly motivational for his own explorations, Heidegger's curious keenness to dismiss the question of the "Nietzsche" of Nietzsche's "life" in favor of a much more manageable subject: the Nietzsche of Nietzsche's "thought" (Philippe Lacoue-Labarthe, interview with the author conducted at the Université de Strasbourg, June 2, 1997). In one or more of its expressions, this displacement haunts virtually all of Lacoue-Labarthe's early discussions of Heidegger, Nietzsche, and subjectivity itself. Recollection can be had of the following explicit or near-explicit occurrences of this theme in Lacoue-Labarthe, all of which I have already had occasion to mention (see Lacoue-Labarthe, "Typography," 62; Lacoue-Labarthe, "Obliteration," 84; Lacoue-Labarthe, "The Echo of the Subject," 142–44).

72. Lacoue-Labarthe, "Obliteration," 93. See also Chapter 5, this volume.

73. Jean-Luc Nancy, "The Sublime Offering," 38 (Nancy's emphasis).

74. "For Blanchot, the experience that matters to an author does not precede composition; rather, it occurs in and through writing"; see Hart, "The Blanchot Experience," 17. This does not, of course, mean that this experience is to be associated with representations that *succeed* writing, that is, which writing "produces." Rather, as I understand it, it is the presentational effect had "within" the event of reading and writing (corresponding to the interplay *between* formless and formal experience) to which Hart is alluding. I have spoken about this, above, as the passage between *Erfahrung* and *Erlebnis*.

75. Blanchot, *The Infinite Conversation*, 44–45.

76. Ibid., 45.

77. Ibid.

78. Ibid.

79. As I point out below, these marks are also present in Blanchot's reading of Hölderlin; see Maurice Blanchot, *The Space of Literature*.

80. Maurice Blanchot, "Hölderlin's Itinerary," 269–76.

81. Ibid., 272.

82. Maurice Blanchot, *Thomas the Obscure*, 25.

83. Ibid., 26: "And even later, when . . . he recognized himself with disgust in the form of the text he was reading, he retained the thought that (while, perched upon his shoulders, the word *He* and the word *I* were beginning their carnage). . . ."

84. Philip Beitchman, *I Am a Process with No Subject*, 105.

85. "Je est de l'autre, pas forcément un autre, peut-être plusieurs, peut-être personne" (Philippe Lacoue-Labarthe, interview with the author conducted at the Université de Strasbourg, June 2, 1997). The setting of Rimbaud's *mot* is a letter to his poetry teacher, Georges Izambard, written on May 13, 1871. Rimbaud explains that he is "corrupting" himself as much as possible, seeking to arrive at the unknown by "derangement of *all of the senses* [le dérèglement de *tous les sens*]." He then says: "Les souffrances sont énormes, mais il faut être fort, être né poète, et je me suis reconnu poète. Ce n'est pas du tout ma faute. C'est faux de dire: Je pense: on devrait dire on me pense. — Pardon du jeu de mots. JE est un autre." See Arthur Rimbaud, *Oeuvres complètes*, 248–49. The comment perhaps begins to describe a subject that is "poetic speech," and also one that correlates to the Lacoue-Labarthian subject enabled by the ceaseless hyperbological (de)constitution of all subjectal self-representations. The correlation could occur if the Rimbaudian "derangement," corresponding to the abstraction of the ego, was linked to a hyperbological multiplicity of self-representations and an incessant exchange between them.

86. Lacoue-Labarthe, "Diderot: Paradox and Mimesis," 265.

87. Thus Lacoue-Labarthe, ibid. (his emphasis): "Against the Platonic tradition, [and against the Socratic] . . . Diderot *plays* the theatre: a second theatre within the theatre of the world, a re-theatricalisation of the 'comedy of the world.'"

88. Blanchot "doubles," and so subverts, what he sees as the "clandestine companion" that Immanuel Levinas is proposing: philosophy, which accompanies all attempts to erase or supersede it. But Blanchot also hints that philosophy might be only a response to an always *prior* companionship offered by (radical) nonpresence attested by literature. He muses that what might ultimately be attractive about literature is that "it promises (a promise it both does and does not keep) to clarify what is obscure in all speech — everything in speech that escapes revelation, manifestation: namely, the remaining trace of nonpresence, what is still opaque in the transparent"; see Maurice Blanchot, "Our Clandestine Companion," 49–50.

89. See Eduardo Cadava, Peter Connor, and Jean-Luc Nancy, eds., *Who Comes after the Subject?*

90. Maurice Blanchot, "Who?," 58–60.

91. Ibid., 59 (Blanchot's emphasis).

92. Philippe Lacoue-Labarthe, "The Response of Ulysses."

93. Ibid., 200. Heidegger's question, from the *Introduction to Metaphysics*, is all but explicitated when, before posing his own question, "Why is there

someone . . . ," Lacoue-Labarthe refers to "Heidegger's reworking, from the most buried foundation of philosophy, of *Daßheit* (*quoddítaß*) on the *Waßheit* (*quiddítaß*), of the *oti estin* upon the *ti estin.*"

94. Lacoue-Labarthe, "The Response of Ulysses," 202 (Lacoue-Labarthe's emphasis).

95. Ibid., 205 (Lacoue-Labarthe's emphasis).

96. Derrida, "Introduction: Desistance," 9 (translation altered).

97. In addition to my citation of the occurrences of this formulation, here is Blanchot: "An experience that is not a lived event [*événement vécu*], and that does not engage the present of presence, is already nonexperience (although negation does not deprive it of the peril of that which comes to pass already past). It is just an excess of experience, and affirmative though it be, in this excess no experience occurs"; see Maurice Blanchot, *The Writing of the Disaster*, 50–51.

Bibliography

Works by Philippe Lacoue-Labarthe

Lacoue-Labarthe, Philippe. "Apocryphal Nietzsche." In *The Subject of Philosophy*. Trans. Thomas Tresize et al. Minneapolis: University of Minnesota Press, 1993.

———. "The Caesura of the Speculative." Trans. Robert Eisenhauer. *Glyph: Textual Studies* 4 (1978): 57–84.

———. "The Caesura of the Speculative." Trans. Robert Eisenhauer. In *Typography: Mimesis, Philosophy, Politics*. Ed. Christopher Fynsk. Trans. Christopher Fynsk et al. Cambridge, MA: Harvard University Press, 1989.

———. "The Detour." Trans. Gary M. Cole. In *The Subject of Philosophy*. Trans. Thomas Tresize et al. Minneapolis: University of Minnesota Press, 1993.

———. "Diderot, le paradoxe et la mimésis." *Poétique* 43 (1980): 267–81.

———. "Diderot, le paradoxe et la mimésis." In *L'Imitation des modernes: Typographies II*. Paris: Editions Galilée, 1986.

———. "Diderot: Paradox and Mimesis." Trans. Jane Popp. In Philippe Lacoue-Labarthe, *Typography: Mimesis, Philosophy, Politics*. Ed. Christopher Fynsk. Trans. Christopher Fynsk et al. Cambridge, MA: Harvard University Press, 1989.

———. "The Echo of the Subject." Trans. Barbara Harlow. In *Typography: Mimesis, Philosophy, Politics*. Ed. Christopher Fynsk.

Trans. Christopher Fynsk et al. Cambridge, MA: Harvard University Press, 1989.

———. "The Fable." Trans. Hugh Silverman. In *The Subject of Philosophy*. Trans. Thomas Tresize et al. Minneapolis: University of Minnesota Press, 1993.

———. *Heidegger, Art, and Politics: The Fiction of the Political*. Trans. Chris Turner. Oxford: Basil Blackwell, 1990.

———. "Hölderlin and the Greeks." In *Typography: Mimesis, Philosophy, Politics*. Ed. Christopher Fynsk. Trans. Christopher Fynsk et al. Cambridge, MA: Harvard University Press, 1989.

———. "Hölderlin et les grecs." *Poétique* 40 (1979): 465–74.

———. "Hölderlin et les grecs." In *L'Imitation des modernes (Typographies II)*. Paris: Editions Galilée, 1986.

———. "Introduction to Walter Benjamin's *The Concept of Art Criticism in German Romanticism*." Trans. David Ferris. *Studies in Romanticism* 31 (1992): 421–32.

———. "La Césure du speculatif." In Friedrich Hölderlin, *L'Antigone de Sophocle*. Ed. and trans. Philippe Lacoue-Labarthe. Paris: Christian Bourgois, 1978.

———. "La Césure du speculatif." In *L'Imitation des modernes (Typographies II)*. Paris: Editions Galilée, 1986.

———. "La Dissimulation (Nietzsche, la question de l'art et la 'littérature'")." In Maurice de Gandillac and Bernard Pautrat, eds., *Nietzsche aujourd'hui?* Vol. 2: *Passion*. Paris: Union Générale d'Editions, 1973.

———. "La Fable (littérature et philosophie)." In *Le Sujet de la philosophie (Typographies I)*. Paris: Aubier-Flammarion, 1979.

———. *La Fiction du politique*. Paris: Christian Bourgois, 1987.

———. *La Poésie comme expérience*. Paris: Christian Bourgois, 1986.

———. "La Transcendance finie/t dans la politique." In Jean-François Lyotard, Luc Ferry, Jean-Luc Nancy, Etienne Balibar, and Philippe Lacoue-Labarthe, eds., *Rejouer le politique*. Paris: Galilée, 1981.

———. "La Transcendance finie/t dans la politique." In *L'Imitation des modernes (Typographies II)*. Paris: Editions Galilée, 1986.

———. "L'Echo du sujet." In *Le Sujet de la philosophie (Typographies I)*. Paris: Aubier-Flammarion, 1979.

———. "Le Détour." *Poétique* 5 (1971): 53–76.

———. "Le Détour." In *Le Sujet de la philosophie (Typographies I)*. Paris: Aubier-Flammarion, 1979.

———. *Le Sujet de la philosophie (Typographies I)*. Paris: Aubier-Flammarion, 1979.

———. *L'Imitation des modernes (Typographies II)*. Paris: Editions Galilée, 1986.

———. "Littérature et philosophie." *Poétique* 1 (1970): 51–63.

———. "L'Oblitération." *Critique* 313 (1973): 487–513.

———. "L' Oblitération." In *Le Sujet de la philosophie (Typographies I)*. Paris: Aubier-Flammarion, 1979.

———. *Musica Ficta (Figures de Wagner)*. Paris: Christian Bourgois, 1991.

———. *Musica Ficta (Figures of Wagner)* Trans. Felicia McCarren. Stanford, CA: Stanford University Press, 1994.

———. "Neither an Accident nor a Mistake." Trans. Paula Wissing. *Critical Enquiry* 15 (1989): 481–84.

———. "Nietzsche Apocryphe." In *Le Sujet de la philosophie (Typographies I)*. Paris: Aubier-Flammarion, 1979.

———. "Obliteration." In *The Subject of Philosophy*. Trans. Thomas Tresize et al. Minneapolis: University of Minnesota Press, 1993.

———. *Poetry as Experience*. Trans. Andrea Tarnowski. Stanford, CA : Stanford University Press, 1999.

———. "The Response of Ulysses." Trans. Avital Ronell. In Eduardo Cadava, Peter Connor, and Jean-Luc Nancy, eds., *Who Comes after the Subject?* New York: Routledge, 1991.

———. "The Scene Is Primal." In *The Subject of Philosophy*. Trans. Thomas Tresize et al. Minneapolis: University of Minnesota Press, 1993.

———. *The Subject of Philosophy*. Trans. Thomas Tresize et al. Minneapolis: University of Minnesota Press, 1993.

———. "Sublime Truth," In Jean-François Courtine et al., *Of the Sublime: Presence in Question*. Trans. Jeffrey S. Librett. Albany: State University of New York Press, 1993.

———. "Transcendence Ends in Politics." In *Typography: Mimesis, Philosophy, Politics*. Ed. Christopher Fynsk. Trans. Christopher Fynsk et al. Cambridge, MA: Harvard University Press, 1989.

———. "Typographie." In Sylviane Agacinski et al., eds., *Mimésis des articulations*. Paris: Aubier-Flammarion, 1975.

———. "Typography." In *Typography: Mimesis, Philosophy, Politics*. Ed. Christopher Fynsk. Trans. Christopher Fynsk et al. Cambridge, MA: Harvard University Press, 1989.

———. *Typography: Mimesis, Philosophy, Politics*. Ed. Christopher Fynsk. Trans. Christopher Fynsk et al. Cambridge, MA: Harvard University Press, 1989.

Works Coauthored or Coedited by Philippe Lacoue-Labarthe

———. *Retreating the Political.* Ed. Simon Sparks. London: Routledge, 1997.

Lacoue-Labarthe, Philippe, and François Martin. *Retrait de l'artiste, en deux personnes/"Retrait" of the Artist, in Two Persons* (bilingual ed.). Trans. Mira Kamdar. Lyons: Editions mem/Arte Facts et Frac Rhône Alpes, 1985.

Lacoue-Labarthe, Philippe, and Jean-Luc Nancy. *L'Absolu littéraire: théorie de la littérature du romantisme allemand.* Paris: Editions du Seuil, 1978.

———, eds. *Les Fins de l'homme: à partir du travail de Jacques Derrida.* Paris: Editions Galilée, 1981.

———. *Le Mythe nazi.* La Tour d'Aigues: Editions de l'Aube, 1991.

———, eds. *Le Retrait du politique.* Paris: Editions Galilée, 1983.

———. *Le Titre de la lettre: une lecture de Lacan.* Paris: Editions Galilée, 1973.

———. *The Literary Absolute: The Theory of Literature in German Romanticism.* Trans., introd., and additional notes Philip Barnard and Cheryl Lester. Albany: State University of New York Press, 1988.

———. *The Title of the Letter: A Reading of Lacan.* Trans. David Pettigrew and François Raffoul. Albany: State University of New York Press, 1992.

Lyotard, Jean-François, Luc Ferry, Jean-Luc Nancy, Etienne Balibar, and Philippe Lacoue-Labarthe, eds. *Rejouer le politique.* Paris: Galilée, 1981.

Other Works

Agacinski, Sylviane, et al. *Mimésis des articulations.* Paris: Aubier-Flammarion, 1975.

Allison, David B., ed. and introd. *The New Nietzsche: Contemporary Styles of Interpretation.* New York: Dell, 1977.

Aquinas, St. Thomas. *Summa Theologiae,* vol. 2. Trans. Timothy McDermott, O. P. London: Eyre and Spottiswoode, 1964.

Aristotle. *The Complete Works of Aristotle,* vol. 2. Rev. Oxford translation. Ed. John Barnes. Princeton, NJ: Princeton University Press, 1984.

———. *Poetics.* Trans. James Hutton. New York: Norton, 1982.

Beitchman, Philip. *I Am a Process with No Subject.* Gainesville: University of Florida Press, 1988.

Benjamin, Walter. "The Concept of Criticism in German Romanticism." Trans. David Lachterman, Howard Eiland, and Ian Balfour. In *Selected Writings*, vol. 1: *1913–1926*. Ed. Marcus Bullock and Michael W. Jennings. Cambridge, MA: Belknap Press of Harvard University Press, 1996.

———. "Der Begriff der Kunstkritik in der deutschen Romantik," In *Gesammelte Schriften*, vol. 1. Ed. Rolf Tiedemann and Hermann Schweppenhäuser, with Theodor Adorno and Gershom Scholem. Frankfurt: Suhrkamp, 1974.

———. *Gesammelte Schriften*, vol. 1. Ed. Rolf Tiedemann and Hermann Schweppenhäuser, with Theodor Adorno and Gershom Scholem. Frankfurt: Suhrkamp, 1974.

———. "Goethes Wahlverwandtschaften." In *Gesammelte Schriften*, vol. 1. Ed. Rolf Tiedemann and Hermann Schweppenhäuser, with Theodor Adorno and Gershom Scholem. Frankfurt: Suhrkamp, 1974.

———. *The Origin of German Tragic Drama*. Trans. John Osborne. Rev. ed. London: Verso, 1998.

———. *Selected Writings*, vol. 1: *1913–1926*. Ed. Marcus Bullock and Michael W. Jennings. Cambridge, MA: Belknap Press of Harvard University Press, 1996.

Bernet, Rudolf. "The Other in Myself." In Simon Critchley and Peter Dews, eds., *Deconstructive Subjectivities*. Albany: State University of New York Press, 1996.

Blanchot, Maurice. *The Blanchot Reader*. Ed. Michael Holland. Oxford: Blackwell Publishers, 1995.

———. *The Gaze of Orpheus and Other Literary Essays*. Ed. P. Adams Sitney. Trans. Lydia Davis. Barrytown, NY: Station Hill Press, 1981.

———. "Hölderlin's Itinerary." In *The Space of Literature*. Trans. and introd. Ann Smock. Lincoln: University of Nebraska Press, 1982.

———. *The Infinite Conversation*. Trans. and foreword Susan Hanson. Minneapolis: University of Minnesota Press, 1993.

———. *L'Entretien infini*. Paris: Editions Gallimard, 1969.

———. *Le Pas au-delà*. Paris: Editions Gallimard, 1973.

———. *L'Espace littéraire*. Paris: Editions Gallimard, 1955.

———. "Literature and the Right to Death." In *The Gaze of Orpheus and Other Literary Essays*. Ed. P. Adams Sitney. Trans. Lydia Davis. Barrytown, NY: Station Hill Press, 1981.

———. "Literature and the Right to Death." In *The Work of Fire*. Trans. Charlotte Mandell. Stanford, CA: Stanford University Press, 1995.

--------. "Our Clandestine Companion." In Richard A. Cohen, ed., *Face to Face with Levinas*. Albany: State University of New York Press, 1986.

--------. *The Space of Literature*. Trans. and introd. Ann Smock. Lincoln: University of Nebraska Press, 1982.

--------. *The Step Not Beyond*. Trans. and introd. Lycette Nelson. Albany: State University of New York Press, 1992.

--------. *Thomas the Obscure*. Rev. ed. Trans. Robert Lamberton. New York: Station Hill Press, 1988.

--------. "Who?" In Eduardo Cadava, Peter Connor, and Jean-Luc Nancy, eds., *Who Comes after the Subject?* New York: Routledge, 1991.

--------. *The Work of Fire*. Trans. Charlotte Mandell. Stanford, CA: Stanford University Press, 1995.

--------. *The Writing of the Disaster*. Trans. Anne Smock. Rev. ed. Lincoln: University of Nebraska Press, 1995.

Blond, Phillip, ed. *Post-Secular Philosophy: Between Philosophy and Theology*. London: Routledge, 1998.

Bloom, Harold, ed. and introd. *Poets of Sensibility and the Sublime*. New York: Chelsea House Publishers, 1986.

Bourdieu, Pierre. *The Political Ontology of Martin Heidegger*. Trans. Peter Collier. Cambridge: Polity Press, 1991.

Bowie, Andrew. *Aesthetics and Subjectivity: From Kant to Nietzsche*. Manchester: Manchester University Press, 1990.

Cadava, Eduardo, Peter Connor, and Jean-Luc Nancy, eds. *Who Comes after the Subject?* New York: Routledge, 1991.

Cohen, Richard A., ed. *Face to Face with Levinas*. Albany: State University of New York Press, 1986.

Courtine, Jean-François, et al. *Du Sublime*. Paris: Editions Belin, 1988.

--------. *Of the Sublime: Presence in Question*. Trans. and afterword Jeffrey S. Librett. Albany: State University of New York Press, 1993.

Critchley, Simon. *The Ethics of Deconstruction: Derrida and Levinas*. Oxford: Blackwell, 1992.

--------. "Prolegomena to Any Post-Deconstructive Subjectivity." In Simon Critchley and Peter Dews, eds., *Deconstructive Subjectivities*. Albany: State University of New York Press, 1996.

--------, and Peter Dews, eds. *Deconstructive Subjectivities*. Albany: State University of New York Press, 1996.

Derrida, Jacques. *De la grammatologie*. Paris: Editions de Minuit, 1967.

————. "Désistance." In *Psyché: inventions de l'autre*. Paris: Editions Galilée, 1987.

————. *Dissemination*. Trans., introd., and additional notes Barbara Johnson. Chicago: University of Chicago Press, 1981.

————. "The Double Session." In *Dissemination*. Trans., introd., and additional notes Barbara Johnson. Chicago: University of Chicago Press, 1981.

————. "'Eating Well,' or the Calculation of the Subject: An Interview with Jacques Derrida." In Eduardo Cadava, Peter Connor, and Jean-Luc Nancy, eds., *Who Comes after the Subject?* New York: Routledge, 1991.

————. "From Restricted to General Economy: A Hegelianism without Reserve." In *Writing and Difference*. Trans., introd., and additional notes Alan Bass. London: Routledge and Kegan Paul, 1978.

————. "Introduction: Desistance." Trans. Christopher Fynsk. In Philippe Lacoue-Labarthe, *Typography: Mimesis, Philosophy, Politics*. Ed. Christopher Fynsk. Trans. Christopher Fynsk, et al. Cambridge, MA: Harvard University Press, 1989.

————. *La Carte postale de Socrate à Freud et au-delà*. Paris: Flammarion, 1980.

————. *L'Ecriture et la différence*. Paris: Editions du Seuil, 1967.

————. "Lettre à un ami japonais." In *Psyché: inventions de l'autre*. Paris: Editions Galilée, 1987.

————. *Marges de la philosophie*. Paris: Editions de Minuit, 1972.

————. *Margins of Philosophy*. Trans. with additional notes Alan Bass. Chicago: University of Chicago Press, 1992.

————. *Of Grammatology*. Trans. and preface Gayatri Chakravorty Spivak. Corrected ed. Baltimore: Johns Hopkins University Press, 1998.

————. *Of Spirit: Heidegger and the Question*. Trans. Geoffrey Bennington and Rachel Bowlby. Chicago: University of Chicago Press, 1989.

————. "Plato's Pharmacy." In *Dissemination*. Trans., introd., and additional notes Barbara Johnson. Chicago: University of Chicago Press, 1981.

————. *Positions*. Paris: Editions de Minuit, 1972.

————. "Positions." *Diacritics* 3.1 (1973): 40.

————. *Positions*. Trans. and notes Alan Bass. Chicago: University of Chicago Press, 1981.

————. *Psyché: inventions de l'autre*. Paris: Editions Galilée, 1987.

————. *Writing and Difference*. Trans., introd., and additional notes Alan Bass. London: Routledge and Kegan Paul, 1978.

Descartes, René. *The Philosophical Writings of Descartes*, vol. 2. Trans. John Cottingham, Robert Stoothoff, and Dugald Murdoch. Cambridge: Cambridge University Press, 1984.

DiCenso, James. Review of *The Title of the Letter: A Reading of Lacan*, by Philippe Lacoue-Labarthe and Jean-Luc Nancy. *Journal of the American Academy of Religion* 63 (1995): 162–64.

Diderot, Denis. "The Paradox of Acting." Trans. Walter Herries Pollock. In *"The Paradox of Acting" and "Masks or Faces?,"* ed. William Follett. New York: Hill and Wang, 1957.

————. *Paradoxe sur le comédien*. Paris: Librairie Plon, 1929.

Dreyfus, Hubert L. *Being-in-the-World: A Commentary on Heidegger's "Being and Time, Division I."* Cambridge, MA: MIT Press, 1991.

Fischer, Francis. "Jean-Luc Nancy: The Place of a Thinking." Trans. Richard Stamp. In Darren Sheppard, Simon Sparks, and Colin Thomas, eds., *On Jean-Luc Nancy: The Sense of Philosophy*. London: Routledge, 1997.

Fraser, Nancy. "The French Derrideans: Politicizing Deconstruction or Deconstructing the Political?" In Gary M. Madison, ed. and introd., *Working through Derrida*. Evanston, IL: Northwestern University Press, 1993.

Freud, Sigmund. *Character and Culture*. Ed. Philip Rieff. New York: Macmillan, 1963.

————. "Der Moses des Michaelangelo." In *Studienausgabe*, vol. 10. Ed. Alexander Mitscherlich, Angela Richards, and James Strachey. Frankfurt: Fischer, 1969.

————. *Studienausgabe*, vol. 10. Ed. Alexander Mitscherlich, Angela Richards, and James Strachey. Frankfurt: S. Fischer, 1969.

Gasché, Rodolphe. "Ideality in Fragmentation." Foreword to Friedrich Schlegel, *Philosophical Fragments*. Trans. Peter Firchow. Minneapolis: University of Minnesota Press, 1991.

Gebauer, Gunter, and Christoph Wulf. *Mimesis: Culture, Art, Society*. Trans. Don Reneau. Berkeley: University of California Press, 1995.

Girard, René. "Delirium as System." Trans. Paisley N. Livingston and Tobin Siebers. In *"To double business bound": Essays on Literature, Mimesis, and Anthropology*. Baltimore: Johns Hopkins University Press, 1978.

————. "double business." In *"To double business bound": Essays on Literature, Mimesis, and Anthropology*. Baltimore: Johns Hopkins University Press, 1978.

————. "Interview: René Girard." *Diacritics* 8 (1978): 31–54.

————. "Système du délire." *Critique* 28 (1972): 957–96.

————. *"To ∂ouble buJineJJ boun∂": EJJayJ on Literature, MimeJiJ, an∂ Anthropology*. Baltimore: Johns Hopkins University Press, 1978.

————. *Violence an∂ the Sacre∂*. Trans. Patrick Gregory. Baltimore: Johns Hopkins University Press, 1977.

Goux, Jean-Joseph. "Politics and Modern Art: Heidegger's Dilemma." Review of *La Fiction ∂u Politique*, by Philippe Lacoue-Labarthe, and *Le NaziJme et la culture*, by Lionel Richard. Trans. Michelle Sharp. *Diacritics* 19.3–4 (1989): 10–24.

Graubner, Hans. "Kant." In Horst Turk, ed., *KlaJJiker ∂er Literaturtheorie: Von Boileau biJ BartheJ*. Munich: Beck, 1979.

Harris, H. S. *Hegel'J Development: Towar∂ the Sunlight, 1770–1801*. Oxford: Clarendon Press, 1972.

Hart, Kevin. "The Blanchot Experience." Review of *Maurice Blanchot: partenaire inviJible—EJJai biographique*, by Christophe Bident; *Awaiting Oblivion*, by Maurice Blanchot, trans. John Gregg; and *The Station Hill Blanchot Rea∂er*, ed. George Quasha. *The AuJtralian'J Review of BookJ* 4. 2 (1999): 17–19.

————. "The Experience of Poetry." *Boxkite* 2 (1998): 285–304.

————. *LoJing the Power to Say "I": An EJJay Celebrating the Four Hun∂re∂th AnniverJary of the Birth of René DeJcarteJ*. Melbourne: Art School Press, 1996.

————. *The TreJpaJJ of the Sign: DeconJtruction, Theology an∂ PhiloJophy*. Cambridge: Cambridge University Press, 1989.

Hegel, Georg Wilhelm Friedrich. *AeJtheticJ: LectureJ on Fine Art*. 2 vols. Trans. T. M. Knox. Oxford: Oxford University Press, 1975.

————. *LectureJ on the PhiloJophy of Religion*, vol. 2: *Determinate Religion*. Ed. Peter C. Hodgson. Trans. R. F. Brown, P. C. Hodgson, and J. M. Stewart, with the assistance of H. S. Harris. Berkeley: University of California Press, 1987.

————. *The Phenomenology of Min∂*. Trans. and introd. J. B. Baillie. New York: Harper and Row, 1967.

————. *Science of Logic*. Trans. A. V. Miller. New York: Humanities Press, 1969.

Heidegger, Martin. *Being an∂ Time: A TranJlation of "Sein un∂ Zeit."* Trans. Joan Stambaugh. Albany: State University of New York Press, 1996.

————. "Der Ursprung des Kunstwerkes." In *Holzwege*. Frankfurt: Vittorio Klostermann, 1950.

———. *Die Selbstbehauptung der deutschen Universität.* Breslau: Korn, 1935.

———. *Essais et conférences.* Paris: Editions Gallimard, 1958.

———. *Holzwege.* Frankfurt: Vittorio Klostermann, 1950.

———. *Introduction to Metaphysics.* Trans. Ralph Mannheim. New Haven, CT: Yale University Press, 1959.

———. *Kant and the Problem of Metaphysics.* Trans. Richard Taft. 4th rev. ed. Bloomington: Indiana University Press, 1990.

———. *The Metaphysical Foundations of Logic.* Trans. Michael Heim. Bloomington: Indiana University Press, 1984.

———. *Nietzsche,* vol. 1. Pfüllingen: Gunther Neske, 1961.

———. *Nietzsche,* vol. 1: *The Will to Power as Art.* Trans., notes, and analysis David Farrell Krell. San Francisco: Harper and Row, 1979.

———. "Only a God Can Save Us: *Der Spiegel's* Interview with Martin Heidegger." Trans. Maria Alter and John D. Caputo. In Richard Wolin, ed., *The Heidegger Controversy: A Critical Reader.* Cambridge, MA: MIT Press, 1993.

———. "'Only a God Can Save Us Now': An Interview with Martin Heidegger." *Graduate Faculty Philosophy Journal* 6 (1977): 5–27.

———. "The Origin of the Work of Art." In *Poetry, Language, Thought.* Trans. Albert Hofstadter. New York: Harper and Row, 1975.

———. *Poetry, Language, Thought.* Trans. Albert Hofstadter. New York: Harper and Row, 1975.

———. "The Question Concerning Technology." In *"The Question Concerning Technology" and Other Essays.* Trans. and introd. William Lovitt. New York: Harper and Row, 1977.

———. *"The Question Concerning Technology" and Other Essays.* Trans. and introd. William Lovitt. New York: Harper and Row, 1977.

———. "Science and Reflection." In *"The Question Concerning Technology" and Other Essays.* Trans. and introd. William Lovitt. New York: Harper and Row, 1977.

———. *Sein und Zeit.* 7th ed. Tübingen: Max Verlag, 1953.

———. "The Self-Assertion of the German University." Trans. Karsten Harries. *Review of Metaphysics* 38 (1985): 470–80.

———. *Wegmarken.* 2nd ed. Frankfurt: Vittorio Klostermann, 1978.

———. *What Is Called Thinking?* Trans. J. Glenn Gray. New York: Harper and Row, 1968.

———. "What Is Metaphysics?" Trans. Walter Kaufmann. In Walter Kaufmann, ed., introd., preface, and new translations, *Existen-*

tialism from Dostoevsky to Sartre. Rev. ed. New York: New American Library, 1975.

———. "Who Is Nietzsche's Zarathustra?" Trans. Bernard Magnus. In *The New Nietzsche: Contemporary Styles of Interpretation.* Ed. and introd. David. B. Allison. New York: Dell, 1977.

———. "The Word of Nietzsche: God Is Dead." In *"The Question Concerning Technology" and Other Essays.* Trans. and introd. William Lovitt. New York: Harper and Row, 1977.

Helfer, Martha B. *The Retreat of Representation: The Concept of* Darstellung *in German Critical Discourse.* Albany: State University of New York Press, 1996.

———. Review of *Representation and Its Discontents: The Critical Legacy of German Romanticism,* by Azade Seyhan. *Journal of English and Germanic Philology* 93 (1994): 101–3.

Hill, Leslie. *Blanchot: Extreme Contemporary.* London: Routledge, 1997.

Hölderlin, Friedrich. "Anmerkungen zum Oedipus." In *Werke und Briefe.* Ed. Friedrich Beissner. Frankfurt: Insel Verlag, 1969.

———. "Der Grund zum Empedocles." In *Werke und Briefe.* Ed. Friedrich Beissner. Frankfurt: Insel Verlag, 1969.

———. *Friedrich Hölderlin: Essays and Letters on Theory.* Trans. and ed. Thomas Pfau. Albany: State University of New York Press, 1988.

———. "The Ground for Empedocles." In *Friedrich Hölderlin: Essays and Letters on Theory.* Trans. and ed. Thomas Pfau. Albany: State University of New York Press, 1988.

———. *L'Antigone de Sophocle.* Ed. and trans. Philippe Lacoue-Labarthe. Paris: Christian Bourgois, 1978.

———. "Remarks on Oedipus." In *Friedrich Hölderlin: Essays and Letters on Theory.* Trans. and ed. Thomas Pfau. Albany: State University of New York Press, 1988.

———. *Werke und Briefe.* Ed. Friedrich Beissner. Frankfurt: Insel Verlag, 1969.

Hume, David. *Essays Moral, Political, and Literary.* Ed., foreword, notes, and glossary Eugene F. Miller, with an apparatus of variant readings from the 1889 edition by T. H. Green and T. H. Grose. Rev. ed. Indianapolis: Liberty Classics, 1987.

———. *A Treatise of Human Nature.* Ed. L. A. Selby Bigge. 2nd ed. Oxford: Clarendon Press, 1978.

Kant, Immanuel. *Critique of Judgment.* Trans. and introd. J. H. Bernard. New York: Hafner Press, 1951.

―――. *Critique of Judgment.* Trans. and introd. Werner S. Pluhar. Foreword Mary J. Gregor. Indianapolis: Hackett Publishing Co., 1987.

―――. *Critique of Practical Reason.* Trans. Lewis White Beck. 3rd. ed. Upper Saddle River, NJ: Prentice-Hall, 1993.

―――. *Critique of Pure Reason.* Trans. Norman Kemp Smith. New York: St. Martin's Press, 1965.

―――. *Immanuel Kant Werkausgabe,* vols. 3, 4: *Kritik der reinen Vernunft.* Ed.Wilhelm Weischedel. Frankfurt: Suhrkamp, 1974.

―――. *Immanuel Kant Werkausgabe,* vol. 7: *Kritik der praktischen Vernunft.* Ed. Wilhelm Weischedel. Frankfurt: Suhrkamp, 1974.

―――. *Immanuel Kant Werkausgabe,* vol. 10: *Kritik der Urteilskraft.* Ed. Wilhelm Weischedel. Frankfurt: Suhrkamp, 1977.

―――. *Kants Gesammelte Schriften.* 22 vols. Berlin: Walter de Gruyter, 1900–1942.

Kaufmann, Walter, ed., introd., preface, and new translations. *Existentialism from Dostoevsky to Sartre.* Rev. ed. New York: New American Library, 1975.

Kofman, Sarah. "Descartes Entrapped." In Eduardo Cadava, Peter Connor, and Jean-Luc Nancy, eds., *Who Comes after the Subject?* New York: Routledge, 1991.

Lacan, Jacques. "The Agency of the Letter in the Unconscious or Reason Since Freud." In *Ecrits: A Selection.* Trans. Alan Sheridan. New York: London: Tavistock, 1977.

―――. *Ecrits.* Paris: Editions du Seuil, 1966.

―――. *Ecrits: A Selection.* Trans. Alan Sheridan. New York: London: Tavistock, 1977.

Librett, Jeffrey S. "Interruptions of Necessity: Being between Meaning and Power in Jean-Luc Nancy." In Darren Sheppard, Simon Sparks, and Colin Thomas, eds., *On Jean-Luc Nancy: The Sense of Philosophy.* London: Routledge, 1997.

Longinus. *Du Sublime.* Ed. and trans. Henri Lebègue. Paris: Les Belles Lettres, 1965.

―――. *On the Sublime.* Trans. and commentary James A. Arieti and John M. Crossett. New York: Mellen, 1985.

Löwith, Karl. "Les implications politiques de la philosophie de l'éxistence chez Heidegger." Trans. Joseph Rovan. *Les Temps Modernes* 2 (1946): 343–60.

Madison, Gary M., ed. and introd. *Working through Derrida.* Evanston, IL: Northwestern University Press, 1993.

Marion, Jean-Luc. "The Final Appeal of the Subject." In Simon Critchley and Peter Dews, eds., *Deconstructive Subjectivities*. Albany: State University of New York Press, 1996.

Martineau, Emmanuel. "Mimésis dans la 'Poétique': pour une solution phénoménologique." *La Revue de Métaphysique et de Morale* 81 (1976): 438–66.

May, Todd. "The Community's Absence in Lyotard, Nancy, and Lacoue-Labarthe." *Philosophy Today* 37 (1993): 275–84.

Milbank, John, et al., eds. *Radical Orthodoxy: A New Theology*. London: Routledge, 1999.

Nancy, Jean-Luc. *The Birth to Presence*. Trans. Brian Holmes, et al. Stanford, CA: Stanford University Press, 1993.

———. "De l'écriture: qu'elle ne révèle rien." *Rue Descartes* 10 (1994): 107.

———. *The Experience of Freedom*. Trans. Bridget McDonald. Foreword Peter Fenves. Stanford, CA: Stanford University Press, 1993.

———. *The Gravity of Thought*. Trans. François Raffoul and Gregory Recco. Atlantic Highlands, NJ: Humanities Press, 1997.

———. *The Inoperative Community*. Ed. Peter Connor. Trans. Peter Connor, et al. Minneapolis: University of Minnesota Press, 1991.

———. *La Communauté désoeuvrée*. Paris: Christian Bourgois, 1986.

———. *L'Expérience de la liberté*. Paris: Editions Galilée, 1988.

———. "L'Offrande Sublime." In Jean-François Courtine, et al., *Du Sublime*. Paris: Editions Belin, 1988.

———. "Logodaedalus (Kant écrivain)." *Poétique* 21 (1975): 24–52.

———. "The Sublime Offering." In Jean-François Courtine, et al., *Of the Sublime: Presence in Question*. Trans. Jeffrey S. Librett. Albany: State University of New York Press, 1993.

———. *Une Pensée finie*. Paris: Editions Galilée, 1990.

Nietzsche, Friedrich. *Beyond Good and Evil*. Trans. and commentary Walter Kaufmann. New York: Vintage Books, 1966.

———. *The Birth of Tragedy*. Ed. and introd. Michael Tanner. Trans. Shaun Whiteside. Harmondsworth: Penguin, 1993.

———. *Das Philosophenbuch*. In *Gesammelte Werke*, vol. 6. Munich: Musarion, 1922.

———. *Das Philosophenbuch / Le Livre du philosophe*. Trans. Angèle K. Marietti. Paris: Aubier-Flammarion, 1969.

———. *Friedrich Nietzsche on Rhetoric and Language*. Trans., ed., and critical introd. Sander L. Gilman, Carole Blair, and David J. Parent. New York: Oxford University Press, 1989.

————. *Gesammelte Werke.* 23 vols. Munich: Musarion, 1920–1929.

————. "How the 'True World' Finally Became a Fable (The History of an Error)." In *The Portable Nietzsche*, trans., introd., preface, and notes Walter Kaufmann. Rev. ed. London: Chatto and Windus, 1971.

————. *The Portable Nietzsche.* Trans., introd., preface, and notes Walter Kaufmann. Rev. ed. London: Chatto and Windus, 1971.

————. *The Will to Power.* Ed. and commentary Walter Kaufmann. Trans. Walter Kaufmann and R. J. Hollingdale. New York: Random House, 1967.

Novalis. *Monologue.* In *Philosophical Writings.* Trans. and ed. Margaret Mahony Stoljar. Albany: State University of New York Press, 1997.

————. *Philosophical Writings.* Trans. and ed. Margaret Mahony Stoljar. Albany: State University of New York Press, 1997.

O'Hara, Daniel T. Review of *Typography: Mimesis, Philosophy, Politics*, by Philippe Lacoue-Labarthe. *Journal of Modern Literature* 17 (1990): 298–99.

Ott, Hugo. *Martin Heidegger: A Political Life.* Trans. Allan Blunden. London: Fontana–HarperCollins, 1993.

Pickstock, Catherine. "Music: Soul, City and Cosmos after Augustine." In John Milbank, et al., eds., *Radical Orthodoxy: A New Theology.* London: Routledge, 1999.

Plato. *The Collected Dialogues of Plato, Including the Letters.* Ed. Edith Hamilton and Huntington Cairns. Princeton, NJ: Princeton University Press, 1961.

————. *The Laws of Plato.* Trans., notes, and interpretative essay Thomas L. Pangle. New York: Basic Books, 1980.

————. *The Republic.* Trans. Paul Shorey. In *The Collected Dialogues of Plato, Including the Letters.* Ed. Edith Hamilton and Huntington Cairns. Princeton, NJ: Princeton University Press, 1961.

————. *The Republic.* Trans. and introd. Desmond Lee. 2nd rev. ed. Harmondsworth: Penguin, 1987.

Reik, Theodor. *From Thirty Years with Freud.* Trans. Richard Winston. New York: Farrar and Rinehart, 1940.

————. *The Haunting Melody: Psychoanalytic Experiences in Life and Music.* New York: Grove Press, 1953.

Rimbaud, Arthur. *Oeuvres complètes.* Introd. and notes Antoine Adam. Rev. ed. Paris: Editions Gallimard, 1972.

Schelling, F. W. J. *The Unconditional in Human Knowledge: Four Early Essays, 1794–1796.* Trans. Fritz Marti. Lewisburg, PA: Bucknell University Press, 1980.

Schlegel, Friedrich. *Philosophical Fragments*. Trans. Peter Firchow. Minneapolis: University of Minnesota Press, 1991.

Schopenhauer, Arthur. *The World as Will and Representation*, vol. 1. Trans. E. J. F. Payne. London: Dover Publications, 1968.

Seyhan, Azade. *Representation and Its Discontents: The Critical Legacy of German Romanticism*. Berkeley: University of California Press, 1992.

Shelley, Mary Wollstonecraft. *Frankenstein*. Ed. and introd. Maurice Hindle. New York: Penguin, 1985.

Sheppard, Darren, Simon Sparks, and Colin Thomas, eds. *On Jean-Luc Nancy: The Sense of Philosophy*. London: Routledge, 1997.

Silverman, Hugh J., ed. *Continental Philosophy II: Derrida and Deconstruction*. New York: Routledge, 1989.

―――. "Derrida, Heidegger, and the Time of the Line." In Hugh J. Silverman, ed., *Continental Philosophy II: Derrida and Deconstruction*. New York: Routledge, 1989.

Szondi, Peter. *Versuch über das Tragische*. Frankfurt: Insel Verlag, 1964.

Taylor, Mark C. *Erring: A Postmodern A/theology*. Chicago: University of Chicago Press, 1984.

Turk, Horst, ed. *Klassiker der Literaturtheorie: Von Boileau bis Barthes*. Munich: Beck, 1979.

Warminski, Andrzej. *Readings in Interpretation: Hölderlin, Hegel, Heidegger*. Minneapolis: University of Minnesota Press, 1987.

Williams, Rowan. "Logic and Spirit in Hegel." In Phillip Blond, ed., *Post-Secular Philosophy: Between Philosophy and Theology*. London: Routledge, 1998.

Wolin, Richard, ed. *The Heidegger Controversy: A Critical Reader*. Cambridge, MA: MIT Press, 1993.

Index

Deconstructive subject, possibility of, 14–16, 193–227
Deleuze, Gilles, xiv
Demosthenes, 177
Derrida, Jacques, xi, xiii, 2, 4, 15, 17–18, 22, 35, 98, 106, 119, 160, 230n6, 232n33, 259n27; and Lacoue-Labarthe, xi, xiv, 13, 194; and representation of the subject, 11; and Heidegger's thought, 12; and *désistance* of the subject, 40–45, 193–204, 225–27; deconstructive economy, 90–92, 125–26; related to Lacoue-Labarthe and Blanchot, 193–227; and deconstitution of the subject, 198–99, 214; hyperbologic in, 250n6
Descartes, René, 6, 75–76, 23n13; Cartesian subject as "Cogito", 6–9, 54, 146, 212–13, 224, 231n13, 18
Désistance of the subject, 16, 22, 106, 109–10, 160, 233n3, 238nn6–12; origin of Derrida's use of the term, 40–45; and autobiography, 53–68; and hyperbologic subjectal loss, 193–204
Désistement of the subject, 41; as *Désistance*, 42, 196–97
Dews, 232n31
DiCenso, James, 244–45n80
Différance, 12–13, 30, 233n37
Diderot, Denis, 16, 38, 40; "The Paradox of Acting", 46–54, 57–60, 66–67, 96–98, 125, 221–22
Dionysus, 111–15
Discourse, equivocity of, 29–30
(Dis)-distancing (*Entfernung/éloignement*), 108–9, 216, 267n1
Dreyfus, Hubert, 34
Dying, 211–12

Experience, 236–37n37; as *Erfahrung* and *Erlebnis*, 34, 236n34, 262nn4, 25, 269–70n41; as writing, 122–23, 272n74; as *vécu* (real-life experience), 262nn4, 25

Fable. *See* Lacoue-Labarthe, Philippe—"The Fable"
Fischer, Francis, 159
Fynsk, Christopher, 233–34nn1, 3
Foucault, Michel, xiv
Fraser, Nancy, 255n3
Freud, Sigmund, xiv, 4, 38, 54, 56, 58, 63, 170

Gasché, Rudolphe, 88
Gebauer, Gunter, 237n42
Gide, André, 32
Girard, René, xiv, 16, 22; mimetic desire as original doubling, 35–39
Goux, Jean-Joseph, 131
Graubner, Hans, 75, 87–88
Guattari, Felix, xiv

Hart, Kevin, xv, 205–6, 211–15, 232n29; 269–70n41
Hegel, G. W. F, 7, 10, 14, 167–70, 210–11, 54, 73, 106, 109, 119–20; on art, 167–70, 173, 184, 231n15, 232n29, 252–53n35
Heidegger, Martin, xi, xiv, 2, 4, 7, 21, 23, 117–18, 120, 202, 209, 216, 224, 232n30; *Dasein* as non-subject 10–12, 232n31, 236n34, 257–58n21, 271n65; *Kehre*, 11; *Destruktion*, 11–12, 35, 232n33; Rectoral Address of 1933, 17, 128, 132, 136–41, 154–55; analysis of Plato's *Republic*, 21–28; "The Question Concerning Technology," 24–25; *Erfahrung* and *Erlebnis* in, 34; on Nietzsche, 106; *Entfernung*, 109; and National Socialism (Nazism), 128, 130–35, 265n67; "The Word of Nietzsche: God is Dead," 142–55; on the beautiful-sublime in Kant, 167–17; "The Origin of the Work of Art," 172–76; the "unthought" in, 200, 268n15
Helfer, Martha, 3, 70, 75, 77–88, 229n3
Heuer, Fritz, 4
Hill, Leslie, 205–7
Hölderlin, Friedrich, 55, 98; *Der Grund*

Literature, 70; and philosophy, xi; as
absolute, 69–80; and
dispossession of self, 194; in
Blanchot, 206–8. *See also*
Literature
Longinus, 164, 166, 176–82
Lovitt, William, 149
Löwith, Karl, 258*n*26

McMahon, Melissa, xv
Mahler, Gustav, 55–56, 58, 61–68
Marion, Jean-Luc, 232*n*31, 257–58*n*21,
271*n*65
Martin, François, 236–37*n*37
Martineau, Emile, 178
Marx, Karl, 231*n*15
Meaning, 160–63
Michaelangelo, 170
Mimesis, in Diderot, 46–51; dismissal of
in Plato's *Republic*, 21–39; as *mise-
en-abyme*, 32; Platonic compared
with Aristotelian 45, 49–51
mise-en-abyme, 32
Music, component within language,
110; and representation of the
subject, 110–13
Mussolini, Benito, 259–60*n*31

Nancy, Jean-Luc, xi, xiii–xiv, 2, 4, 10,
13–18, 34, 156–92
— *The Experience of Freedom*: 261*n*3
— exscription of presence: 160
— *The Gravity of Thought*: 158–63,
192
— *The Inoperative Community*: 261*n*3
— and Lacoue-Labarthe: xiii–xiv;
The Literary Absolute, 16, 70–77
(discussed in Helfer's *The Retreat
of* Representation: 77–81, 87–89),
93–94, 114 representations of
subjectal loss compared, 156–64;
disagreement on noneidetic in
Kant, 265–66*n*76
— philosophy as "opening": 159–61
— *Retreating the Political*: 255*n*2
— sense (*sens*): 160; as feeling,
187–89; as movement, 191–92

— signification, and its exhaustion:
162–64
— subject as sensed presentational
movement: 191–92, 227
— the sublime: as transporting art,
182–84; as "opposite" to
philosophy, 185; as presentation,
in its movement, 186–87; as (self-
)offering, 187–89
— "The Sublime Offering": 182–91
— *The Title of the Letter: A Reading of
Lacan*: 158, 244–45*n*80
Narrative, as *haple diegesis*, 28–29
Negative Darstellung, 78–94
Nietzsche, Friedrich, xiv, 2, 4, 9, 34,
129, 201, 231*n*15, 232*n*33; and
Cartesian *cogito*, 9; in Heidegger,
106–10, fragments on rhetoric,
110–15, *The Birth of Tragedy*,
110–113; *The Book of the
Philosopher*, 113–15; "How the
True World Finally Became a
Fable" 116–22; 128; nihilism and
the death of God, 130–55, 163
Nietzschean subject, 17; 110–15
Nihilism, 131–35; 143–55
Non-subject, 109–10
Novalis, 212, 215, 271*n*57

O'Hara, Daniel T., 234*n*3
Ott, Hugo, 259–60*n*31

Paradox, and mimesis in Diderot,
46–51; and speculative
interpretation of tragedy,
101–102
Pickstock, Catherine, 242–43*n*63
Plato, xiv; 7, 12, 20, 45, 50–51, 100, 201,
125, 166, 178, 203, 222; *Republic*,
and expulsion of mimesis, 21–39,
235*n*15; *Laws*, 27, *pharmakon*,
235–36*n*28
Presence, and its subversion, 11–12,
205–7
Presentation, 1; and representation,
1–19; of the subject, 1, 15; as
Selbstdarstellung, 126

Reik, Theodor, 55–68
Representation
—and the caesura, 104
—and presentation: entwinement between them, 1–6, 83, 89, 157
—as rendering present of the subject, 5
—of the subject. *See* Subject, representation of
—and subjectivity, 1–19
Rhetoric, in Nietzsche, 110–15
Rhythm. *See* Subject—presentation of: as rhythm
Rimbaud, Arthur, 221, 273*n*85
Romanticism, German, notion of *Darstellung* in 4–5, 70; treatment of Kantian negative *Darstellung* in, 77–80
Rousseau, Jean-Jacques, 6

Saussure, Ferdinand de, xiv, 12
Schelling, Friedrich von, xiv, 72, 98–101, 120
Schiller, Friedrich von, 170
Schlegel brothers, xiv
Schlegel, Friedrich, 74
Schopenhauer, Friedrich, 231*n*15
Selbstdarstellung, 75–76, 79–80
Self. *See* Subject
Sense, as *sens* in Nancy, 159
Seyhan, Azade, 4, 78
Shakespeare, William, 58
Signification, and the subject, 162–64; power of, 162; exhaustion of, 163
Silverman, Hugh, 12, 233*n*1
Socrates, 27–32, 125
Sophocles, 58
Stambaugh, Joan, 232*n*30
Subject
—Aristotelian: xiv, 6–7, 230*n*12
—between philosophy and literature: xi, xiv; 116–23
—in Blanchot: 18
—Cartesian: 7–9, 76
—*Darstellung* of: 71–94
—(de)constitution of: 109–10
—deconstructive: 14–19
—*désistant. See Désistance*

—as enunciator of paradox in Diderot: 46–51
—interplay between loss and gain: 20–22
—Kantian and post-Kantian: 7–11
—as language: 212
—loss of: in writing, 13–14; 32–34; 122–25, 205–13 (Blanchot); within mimesis, 20–33, during enunciation, 46–54, 201; as rhythm, 55–58, 61–68; within literature, 69–77; through excess of (re)presentation, 93–94, 126–27; as "originary" and "deconstitutive," 109, 209–10; between literature and philosophy, 116–23; in thinking, 159; in experience, 160; in language, 210–11. *See also* Hyperbologic loss of the subject; Subject: withdrawal of
—non-classical, possibility of: 193–95
—political: in Heidegger and Nietzsche: 128–55
—presentation of: as rhythm, 55–58, 61–68; in rhetoric, 110–12, 242–43*n*63, 243*n*68; impossibility, 246*n*10
—representation of: as autopresentation or self-presentation (see *Selbstdarstellung*); as necessary representation, 15; in musical component of language, 110–13; interplay between *muthos* and *logos*, 116–18
—return of: 20–21, 34, 39–40, 49, 54, 60–61, 68, 95, 203–4
—as sensed presentational movement: 191–92, 227
—and signification: 162–63
—substantiality of: 6–7, 245–46*n*8
—as thought: 158
—the West as absolute version of, 256*n*8
—withdrawal of: within mimesis, 45, 51–54; within autobiography,

55–68; volitional and non-volitional, 60; ceaselessness of, 123, 254–55*n*71; within acting, within writing, 205–12. *See also Désistance*; Hyperbologic loss of the subject; subject, loss of

Subjectivity, 1; and representation, 1–19; and mimesis, 20–34; post-metaphysical, 157; unsuccessful in securing itself, 194; in Blanchot, 210–15; in Rimbaud, 221, 273*n*85

Sublime, Kantian: 86–94; and presentational excess, 74; related to the Kantian beautiful, 74–83, 86–94; related to the sublime in Longinus, Heidegger, and Hegel, 164–92; in Lacoue-Labarthe's "Sublime Truth," 164–87; in Nancy's "The Sublime Offering," 187–92; and hyperbological subjectal loss in Lacoue-Labarthe

172–80; and hyperbological loss in Nancy 189–91

Szondi, Peter, 98–99

Taylor, Mark C., 4
Thinking, in Nancy, 159
Tieck, Ludwig, 246*n*17
Truth, as *aletheia*, 25–26; as fable, 116–23

Unheimlichkeit (uncanniness), of subjectal withdrawal, 61–68

Warminski, Andrzej, 252*n*33
Williams, Rowan, 252*n*35
Writing, and *différance*, 12; and loss of the subject, 13–14, 32–34, 122–25, 204–13; and experience as "sense," 159–63. *See also* Literature

Wulf, Christoph, 237*n*42

Perspectives in
Continental Philosophy Series
John D. Caputo, series editor

14. Mark C. Taylor, *Journeys to Selfhood: Hegel and Kierkegaard*. Second edition.

15. Dominique Janicaud, Jean-François Courtine, Jean-Louis Chrét-ien, Michel Henry, Jean-Luc Marion, and Paul Ricœur, *Phenomenology and the "Theological Turn": The French Debate*.

16. Karl Jaspers, *The Question of German Guilt*. Introduction by Joseph W. Koterski, S.J.

17. Jean-Luc Marion, *The Idol and Distance: Five Studies*. Translated with an introduction by Thomas A. Carlson.

18. Jeffrey Dudiak, *The Intrigue of Ethics: A Reading of the Idea of Discourse in the Thought of Emmanuel Levinas*.

19. Robyn Horner, *Rethinking God as Gift: Marion, Derrida, and the Limits of Phenomenology*.

20. Mark Dooley, *The Politics of Exodus: Søren Keirkegaard's Ethics of Responsibility*.

21. Merold Westphal, *Toward a Postmodern Christian Faith: Overcoming Onto-Theology*.

22. Edith Wyschogrod, Jean-Joseph Goux and Eric Boynton, eds., *The Enigma of Gift and Sacrifice*.

23. Stanislas Breton, *The Word and the Cross*. Translated with an introduction by Jacquelyn Porter.

24. Jean-Luc Marion, *Prolegomena to Charity*. Translated by Stephen E. Lewis.

25. Peter H. Spader, *Scheler's Ethical Personalism: Its Logic, Development, and Promise*.

26. Jean-Louis Chrétien, *The Unforgettable and the Unhoped For*. Translated by Jeffrey Bloechl.

27. Don Cupitt, *Is Nothing Sacred? The Non-Realist Philosophy of Religion: Selected Essays*.

28. Jean-Luc Marion, *In Excess: Studies of Saturated Phenomena*. Translated by Robyn Horner and Vincent Berraud.

29. Phillip Goodchild, *Rethinking Philosophy of Religion: Approaches from Continental Philosophy*.

30. William J. Richardson, S.J., *Heidegger: Through Phenomenology to Thought*.

31. Jeffrey Andrew Barash, *Martin Heidegger and the Problem of Historical Meaning*.

32. Jean-Louis Chrétien, *Hand to Hand: Listening to the Work of Art*. Translated by Stephen E. Lewis.

33. Jean-Louis Chrétien, *The Call and the Response*. Translated with an introduction by Anne Davenport.

34. D. C. Schindler, *Han Urs von Balthasar and the Dramatic Structure of Truth: A Philosophical Investigation*.

35. Julian Wolfreys, ed., *Thinking Difference: Critics in Conversation*.

36. Allen Scult, *Being Jewish/Reading Heidegger: An Ontological Encounter.*

37. Richard Kearney, *Debates in Continental Philosophy: Conversations with Contemporary Thinkers.*

38. Jennifer Anna Gosetti-Ferencei, *Heidegger, Hölderlin, and the Subject of Poetic Language: Towards a New Poetics of Dasein.*

39. Jolita Pons, *Stealing a Gift: Kirkegaard's Pseudonyms and the Bible.*

40. Jean-Yves Lacoste, *Experience and the Absolute: Disputed Questions on the Humanity of Man.* Translated by Mark Raftery-Skehan.

41. Charles P. Bigger, *Between* Chora *and the Good: Metaphor's Metaphysical Neighborhood.*

42. Dominique Janicaud, *Phenomenology "Wide Open": After the French Debate.* Translated by Charles N. Cabral.

43. Ian Leask and Eoin Cassidy, eds. *Givenness and God: Questions of Jean-Luc Marion.*

44. Jacques Derrida, *Sovereignties in Question: The Poetics of Paul Celan.* Edited by Thomas Dutoit and Outi Pasanen.

45. William Desmond, *Is There a Sabbath for Thought? Between Religion and Philosophy.*

46. Bruce Ellis Benson and Norman Wirzba, eds. *The Phenomoenology of Prayer.*

47. S. Clark Buckner and Matthew Statler, eds. *Styles of Piety: Practicing Philosophy after the Death of God.*

48. Kevin Hart and Barbara Wall, eds. *The Experience of God: A Postmodern Response.*

49. John Panteleimon Manoussakis, *After God: Richard Kearney and the Religious Turn in Continental Philosophy.*